THE TRANQUILLITY STORIES

THE
TRANQUILLITY
STORIES

—•◆•—

Col. Harold P. Sheldon

The complete texts of
Tranquillity,
Tranquillity Revisited
and Tranquillity Regained,
with a new foreword by
Ralf W. Coykendall, Jr.

WINCHESTER PRESS

Library of Congress Catalog Card Number: 74:78703

ISBN 0-87691-115-7

Published by Winchester Press
460 Park Avenue, New York 10022

PRINTED IN THE UNITED STATES OF AMERICA

This edition of the Tranquillity stories
is dedicated to the author's Dark-Haired Lady,
to the editor's Fair-Haired Lady,
and to all their offspring.

ACKNOWLEDGMENTS

Several of the stories in this volume first appeared in *Field & Stream, Outdoor Life, Outdoors, The American Rifleman, The National Sportsman,* and *The Sportsman.* The courtesy of these magazines in allowing these stories to be reprinted here is gratefully acknowledged.

The editor also wishes to express his thanks to Marjorie Sheldon, Cam Vaughn, Ev Hoyt, and the Dark-Haired Lady (Janet Sheldon), without whose help this volume would have been incomplete.

CONTENTS

TRANQUILLITY

TRANQUILLITY REVISITED

TRANQUILLITY REGAINED

THE
TRANQUILLITY
STORIES

FOREWORD

When Winchester Press asked me to help with this reissue of the Tranquillity stories by Colonel Harold P. Sheldon, I was delighted. After all, the mythical Township of Tranquillity in Vermont is where I bagged my first ruffed grouse, first woodcock, and first whitetail deer, when my father took me there to shoot with the legendary Colonel, more than thirty years ago.

In reviewing Sheldon's stories and revisiting his favorite haunts I have discovered that while Tranquillity Township and the Tranquillity stories have withstood the test of time, few people remember the man who created both. It is with this in mind that I add the following to the introduction to *Tranquillity* written by Nash Buckingham in 1936.

Harold P. Sheldon was born on Valley Farm, the Sheldon family homestead in Fair Haven, Vermont, in 1887. He studied at Georgetown and George Washington universities and was granted an honorary degree as master of science from Norwich University "in recognition of his services as soldier, author, and conservationist."

THE SOLDIER

As a soldier Sheldon worked his way from private in the Vermont National Guard to his retiring rank of lieutenant colonel on the staff of the 43rd Division. During World War I he saw combat with the 102nd Machinegun Battalion, Yankee Division, and was wounded during the Meuse-Argonne confrontation. After being invalided home, Sheldon served as post commandant at Fort Ethan Allen, retiring to civilian life in 1919.

THE CONSERVATIONIST

Colonel Sheldon was also a dedicated conservationist. Some have said that he hunted less in his later years because he loved the game he sought too much to harm it, and that he preferred writing about hunting to hunting. Be that as it may, Sheldon was a protector of wildlife, several decades before ecology became a popular crusade.

Valley Farm, the Sheldon family homestead and the hub of the Tranquillity stories in this volume.

Sgt. Harold P. Sheldon (front row center) at Camp Perry in 1913.

1st Lt. Sheldon at Fort Ethan Allen.

Capt. H. P. Sheldon at Fort Ethan Allen, Vermont, in 1914.

Miss Janet King visits Captain Sheldon at Valley Farm in 1915.
The future 'Dark-Haired Lady' (head bowed) is surrounded by the Sheldon clan
with Hal Sheldon at the far right.

The 'Dark-Haired Lady' and Capt. Sheldon right after
their marriage in May, 1917.

Sheldon's son, Noel, at five or six years of age.

Col. Sheldon (left), his son, Noel, and brother, Harmon, pluck a day's bag on the Sheldon farm in Tranquillity Township.

The Colonel and Noel, at the end of a day's shooting.

The Captain (right) visits Mr. Nash. (See the story of the same name for details regarding Col. Sheldon's visit to Nash Buckingham's domain.)

Hal Sheldon pauses for one of his familiar lunch breaks.

Col. Sheldon is shown here with another of his many sporting interests, target shooting.

Col. Sheldon (left) with the first migratory waterfowl to be flown across the United States. The mallards arrived in Washington, D. C. from San Francisco on March 8, 1940.

H. P. Sheldon (left) in the Bureau of Biological Survey's Chris Craft.

Col. Sheldon in a photograph taken by Ralf Coykendall, Sr., the editor's father.

The Colonel and his Dark-Haired Lady in Tucson, Arizona, in 1943.

Hal Sheldon in familiar garb seated on the running board of his 'famous' La Salle in the late 1940s.

From 1921 to 1926 the Colonel served as game commissioner of Vermont. Following this he was appointed, under civil service, as chief conservation officer of the U.S. Bureau of Biological Survey and was later made chief of public relations for what is now known as the Fish and Wildlife Service of the Department of the Interior. Sheldon's philosophy as a conservationist is reflected in the following excerpts from a speech he wrote for then Secretary of Agriculture, Henry A. Wallace, to deliver at the 1937 North American Wildlife Conference.

The past history of the wildlife movement is filled with evidence of lack of unity on the part of those who have been most interested in perpetuating an abundance of birds, animals and fishes. This inability to organize in order to achieve a common purpose is unquestionably the reason why the formulation of a permanent national policy has been delayed so long. It is the reason why important legislation on the subject has been retarded, sometimes for many years from the time of its original proposal, or allowed finally to die in inanition. For example, the need to establish Federal waterfowl refuges and sanctuaries and to reclaim marsh and water areas for the preservation of aquatic life was first announced by Dr. Nelson of the Biological Survey nearly 20 years ago, but it was not until 1929 that the Migratory Bird Conservation Act authorizing the program was adopted, and it was not until 1934 that adequate funds were furnished to carry out this vital work. Yet everyone interested in waterfowl restoration recognized the urgency and the essential importance of the project, and hoped for its early commencement. There have been so many instances of this sort connected with our attempts to save the renewable resources, that it may be regarded almost as a rule that the important actions to benefit these resources have always been taken ten, twenty, or even thirty years after the need for them was first realized, and therefore too late to be wholly effective.

Delays resulting from lack of organization have cost us much. If major reforms concerning the use of land, water, forests and wildlife had been adopted 50 or 100 years earlier than they were, there would have been little cause for our present anxiety concerning the grave problems of soil erosion and the uses of submarginal land; our streams and lakes would now be free of pollution; we would still have vast wilderness areas in reserve and an abundance of all the original forms of wildlife.

As a people we have been intensively engaged in developing and using machinery to subdue nature; we have turned on the power generated from other natural resources of coal, petroleum, and electricity to the soil and things which grow from the soil. Wildlife is one of these. It is necessary to readjust our perspective and devote a much larger proportion of our interest to the subject of life itself. Every form of life has value and interest of some sort; even the most insignificant creatures may be found to exercise the most profound influences upon mankind.

Sheldon served with the Fish and Wildlife Service until 1943, when he retired to devote more time to his other vocation, writing.

THE WRITER

The Tranquillity Stories represent only one element of the Colonel's literary career. During the 1930s and 1940s Sheldon's articles on hunting, fishing, and related subjects appeared in *Field & Stream, Outdoor Life, The American Rifleman,* and several other outdoor magazines. In addition, he edited columns for *Country Life, The Sportsman,* and *Outdoors.* Although he was best known for his evocative treatment of the sporting life, Sheldon was an experienced technical writer as well. His articles on guns and gun collecting reflect both a journalistic facility and an estimable knowledge of firearms.

THE GUN COLLECTOR

It is not surprising, and quite in keeping with his background and his way of life, that Colonel Sheldon had an extensive gun collection. At the time of his death in 1951, his gun room in Middlebury, Vermont, contained the following guns and accessories.

Holland & Holland 20-gauge double, two pair barrels, 25″ and 30″. Blueing worn, barrels perfect, locks perfect. Fitted leather case.
W. W. Greener Model FH50 16-gauge double, 27″ barrels. Excellent, barrels perfect.
Francotte 12-gauge trap gun, single 33″ half-octagon barrel.
Two Browning over and unders, 12-gauge, one with 26″ and one with 32″ barrels. Both in new condition.
Browning over and under, 20-gauge, 26″ barrels.
Remington 20-gauge "Sportsman" with two barrels, 26″ with raised rib.
Parker 28-gauge, 26″ double.

Springfield Sporter 30–06, barrel, action and stock by Bod Owens.
Mannlicher-Schoenhauer 6.5. Full-length stock, Zeiss-Zielklein scope.
Holland & Holland rock rifle, single barrel, break action, .295 bore, semi-smooth. Excellent outside, barrel pitted, engraving fine.
W. W. Greener. Relined for hornet, barrel pitted, but otherwise in fine condition. Weaver scope with Lee dot.
Winchester 22/3000 low sidewall, double triggers. K-6 Weaver Redfield Mount.
Mossberg .22 semi-automatic Weaver J-25 with Lee dot, excellent.

Moore cap-and-ball muzzle loader, about .38 cal, excellent condition.
Egg of London muzzle-loading 16-gauge.

Cal Price (Orange, Texas gunsmith) muzzle loader with Weaver M8 scope
and Lee dot.

Colt Woodsman, good condition.
2 Colt .45 Service Automatics.
Starr Army .44.
Colt Navy, excellent.
Pepper Box, Allen and Thurber.
French Service .44.

.222 Stevens Hornet, Weaver K-2.5 scope.
Bausch and Lomb 20× Spotting scope.
Mossberg 2M4C.
Bausch and Lomb Balvar scope.
Weaver KV scope.
Stith Bear Cub 2.
Weaver K-10 scope.
Weaver K-4 scope.
Z-B Mauser converted to K-Lovell with Stith Bear Cub 4× scope with Lee
dot.

Woodward 16-gauge over and under.
Savage Model 220, 20-gauge.
Mossberg Model 185K, 20-gauge.
Mossberg Model 151K.
Marlin Model 39 with Weaver J2.5 scope.
Winchester .32 W.C.F. with Winchester A5 scope.
Winchester high sidewall .22 with Pope barrel.
Griffin and Howe .22 Springfield Sporter.
Sharps .22, Lyman target scope.

THE HOST

If one attribute stands out in the career of soldier, sportsman, author Harold P. Sheldon, it is comradeship. Sheldon's warm and engaging manner is clearly reflected in the following letter written by my late father.

A day's grouse shooting with the Colonel is about as pleasant an undertaking as you can imagine. It does not start abruptly in the cold and ghostly dawn but rather after the sun is up and the bacon and eggs are leisurely downed—after a reasonable number of cups of coffee and cigarettes are disposed of before an open fire. Then follows an unhurried loading of the car. Guns and shells, broiler and coffee pot, sausages, bread and butter, and bourbon are tucked neatly away and, at some mid-morning hour, the wheels crunch on the gravel and a day's shooting is underweigh.

*Between flaming maples and gray stone walls you advance with talk and chuck-
ling and, finally, around the bend in the hillside road, pull into a hardly discernible
woods road where, on the left, a spring trickles out from beneath a limestone ledge
and, on the right, the green and gold Vermont countryside rolls off as far as the eye
can cover. The spring water is combined with jest a tech of bourbon, cigarettes are
smoked as you sit in the warm sun on the running board.*

*Cups are returned to their places and guns removed from theirs. Then into the
cover. Easy does it. Beyond that big pine that you just see there are a couple of old
apple trees. Keep in the clear so that you can shoot. Presently comes the sharp crack
of a fowling piece, the plump of falling bird. Appropriate ceremonies follow. Where
the sun strikes warm beside a modest brook the car pulls in for lunch.*

*The aromatic qualities of lunch 'a la Sheldon are beyond compare. Old apple
wood burns under sausage grill as coffee steams by the back of the fire, the breeze
mixes the pungency of pine with these, and the man smells of tobacco and bourbon.*

*Time seems to stand still but the Colonel allows that if we don't move it will be
dark before we get through the grapevine cover. The afternoon goes like the morning.
A mixture of sitting on old walls for talk and tobacco, pauses where particularly
blendable spring water appears beneath appropriate limestone ledges, but also up
sharp meadow land into birches and pines. Powder is burned to good effect.*

*Sundown finds you swinging back to the car parked by an old deserted farmhouse.
"It's the Lord's will that we have a drink." The colonel proceeds unerringly to a
clear, cold spring for the mixing. Conversation dies off as the dusk gathers. Lights
prick out in the sleeping valleys. That far one is over across the lake. It is supper
time. Hell—it is past supper time. We climb into the car. Sometimes when the
headlights go on there is a deer standing in the road a hundred yards away quietly
watching.*

Yes sir. A day's grouse shooting with the Colonel is fun.

There are some who remember Colonel Harold P. Sheldon for other reasons, but to me he was, first and foremost, the man who wrote the stories. He
created Tranquillity and its inhabitants, and they endure, now and forever.

As I write this there's a touch of frost in the air. The aromas of woodsmoke
and ripened apples blend, drift on the evening breeze, and my mind is elsewhere. Vermont's grouse and woodcock season opens tomorrow and I'm taking my son to Tranquillity.

Tomorrow we'll walk with ghosts in covers more filled with memories than
birds, and I'll tell Chip how it used to be. I'll tell him about Colonel Sheldon
and how it was when I first visited Tranquillity with his grandfather, and
we'll talk about this book.

At noon we'll stop beside a limestone ledge and cook lunch. When the fire
cools and Chip grows bored with my long-winded yarns we'll head for well-
remembered cover and hunt grouse and woodcock till the sun goes down.

Tomorrow night, as we drive home in the gathering dark, Chip will ask
why we wasted so much time wandering around and talking when we could

have hunted all day. I'll smile, turning back the years, and tell him that someday, when he takes his son to Tranquillity, he'll know.

In my copy of *Tranquillity* the Colonel wrote: "When you think of these things at some future time, they may delight you." Little did he know that someday I would play a small part in passing his words and his stories on to another generation that I know will delight in them.

Ralf W. Coykendall, Jr.
Weston, Vermont
September, 1973

ORIGINAL
INTRODUCTION
TO *TRANQUILLITY*

Composing myself for introduction of Colonel H. P. Sheldon and his collected outdoor sketches, I acknowledge emotions of gratitude, pride and enthusiasm for the honor. Gratitude for having shared with so fine a character many glorious days (some of them recounted here) at wildfowl and upland gunning; for happy evenings together at our hearths and tablesides, and for gatherings at camp and clubs marked by trenchering, wassail, and the spinning of yarns; the pride for his professional and official career maintained always with integrity. Enthusiasm for what I predict will be signal appreciation by critics and booklovers of these virile contributions to the world's scant supply of worth-while literature of the chase, for within these pages are blended native humor, deft characterizations, resplendent competency of detail and that haunting delicacy and beauty of theme that achieves anchorage in one's soul.

Eleven years ago, I was invited to head the first game restoration department ever installed by an arms and ammunition concern. My initial study was to analyze the objectives, programs and policies of forty-eight state game and fish departments. By long odds the most constructive, far-seeing and inspiring replies came from the then Game Commissioner of Vermont. And thus, between Colonel Sheldon and me, there developed a friendship by correspondence. Shortly thereafter he was appointed Chief Conservation Officer of the United States Bureau of Biological Survey.

We met at a convention of the International Association of Game and Fish Commissioners, in Mobile, Alabama, in September, 1927. A few months later I became Executive Secretary of the American Wildfowlers, with headquarters in Washington, D. C. Our organization's plans were allied with problems of wildfowl welfare encountered by the Biological Survey. During the next four years Colonel Sheldon and I together traversed the country's outstanding waterfowling grounds and habitats. Together we witnessed the encouraging and seamy sides of the wildlife situation.

Naturally, too, as a wearer of a United States Deputy Game Protector's badge, I particularly observed the "esprit de corps" of Colonel Sheldon's enforcement arm; and my conviction grew that in handling his slender force and dealing with multifold problems of his scantily financed division, Colonel Sheldon had the power to inspire that efficient responsiveness from those under his direction which is the reward of leadership and executive ability. Frequently called upon to listen intently but courteously to "belly-aching" by chronic selfishness seeking special gunning privileges, it can be said of him that naught save what was best for wildlife resources first, and the sportsmen's interest next, ever secured his initials to an official communiqué. Rural or urban hunters the country over and sportsmen who abide by the shooting referee's regulations who know the Colonel's gracious impartiality and keen-eyed ability with scatter-gun or rifle, realize that at Washington they have a kindred spirit who calls his shots fairly but stands to his guns always in the interest of fair play for wildlife. All said and done, however, such homespun qualifications are but throw-backs to his Vermont pioneer ancestry. I present passages from the Colonel's World War chronicler.

"Ancestors who fought the Hurons, Mohawks and Abenakis at Deerfield; the French and Indians at Crown Point. There is strong white men's medicine running down Vermont's blood lines. Back in 1887 two important things happened up there. The 'Blizzard' and Harold P. Sheldon, at Fair Haven, November 13. His childhood was spent amid rugged surroundings. A heath of heart's delight in fish and game and boyish adventure to a lad born to lead and bear arms. The sputter of percussion locks merging with black-powder and breech loaders. Play at redskins and deer slayers from which he emerged filled with determination to emulate heroic figures in the history of his old State. Forever tugging at him, call of the flag!

"He was one of the four children of Leander Harmon Sheldon and Emma Pearl Sheldon. Both parents were notable for their strength of character no less than for their genuine kindliness and toleration, their wit, and their deep love of books and friends. Both were born story tellers and there was many an evening when the crowded dining room echoed with laughter over some anecdote told by the host or his bright-eyed lovely little consort whose children and grandchildren still come home to pay her their homage under the same old maple-shaded rooftree. Sometimes there were stories of a sterner nature handed down from generation to generation of wars and Indian raids and incidents of pioneer days, of panthers, bears and the wilderness itself. Occasionally when the children begged for it there would be a ghost story accompanied by the lugubrious rattle of chains on back stairways to the shuddering delight of the youthful audience.

"In 1910, we find young Sheldon a 'buck' private at Fort Ethan Allen. Perhaps in the rear rank, too, but with determined ambition to earn a commission and with a flair for pistol and rifle shooting usually brought to full fruition at his mecca—Camp Perry. It is 1915 and 'Bloody Mike' learns the controls at one of the Army's first aviation schools. Now it is 1917 and First Lieutenant Harold P. Sheldon is 'over there' early, with the 102nd machine gunners of the Yankee Division. Don Camiers, the Belgian front with the British. Chemin des Dames, the Toul sector, Seicheprey, Apremont, Chateau Thierry, St. Mihiel, the Meuse-Argonne—all are names he helped humbly and fearlessly to glorify in American history. But during the Meuse-Argonne at untimely German .77 'unbreeched' (as he laughs it off) the by then Captain. Hospitals, more hospitals—home—and long, slow recovery. 1919 and his retirement as Post Commandant at the same old Fort Ethan Allen. The clasp of many strong hands, and tears shining through richer in honor than all the decorations within the bestowal of Mars. Brigade and Divisional citations; the Order of the Purple Heart; and an Honorary Degree as Master of Science from Norwich University "in recognition of services as soldier, conservationist and author.' Something for the buck private of Fort Ethan Allen and his Dark-Haired Lady to smile back upon."

She, before her marriage to her soldier, was Miss Janet Elizabeth King of Detroit, the daughter of Louis B. King and a descendant of Captain Robert King of General Washington's staff. There are two children, Janice Lee and Noel King.

It is a "fur piece" from sniping woodchucks on Green Mountain hillsides to camouflaged hide-outs of No-Man's land. But, as reward, the sweet peace of misty wildfowl wastes pouring winged myriads from the north to the Salton sea, 'Cajan marshes, and cypress brakes of the Mississippi Valley. The bugle is muted now to sonorous night voices of Anser canadensis. So, follow "the Captain" where ye may, voices from every region he has gunned, will be calling him friend.

In my youth a very dear old gentleman presented to me a shooting diary hand penned through many decades. Child that I was, I sensed when he put it in my hands that somehow its giving was linked mysteriously to tears that shone in his eyes. I asked, wonderingly, "for me?" And he whispered—"Yes, Boy, I give you back my years!" So because of their fineness and fitness of outdoor spirit, these pages will endure to prosper sportsmanship, seeded in the soil, ripened by the suns, winds and beneficent rains of the Red Gods and sturdied by a trigger-guarded and imperishable heritage.

NASH BUCKINGHAM

TRANQUILLITY

TRANQUILLITY

—————— ◆ • ◆ ——————

Tranquillity! Although not the name of a certain small township that lies peacefully spread over narrow valleys buttressed by the soft gray limestone ledges of the Lower Champlain country, it will serve. It is near enough the real name and is the one most likely to come to the mind of a traveler making leisurely progress from one somnolent hamlet to another over the narrow winding dirt roads that provide the only means of vehicular communication between them. These twisting highways are the "turnpikes" or main roads. The back roads are even more picturesque; an artist might consider himself well lost following their endless convolutions between hedges of sumach, clematis, and wild grapevine, grown up over stone walls and rail fences. Now and again these friendly bypaths allow him a glimpse of an ancient farmhouse snug and cool beneath its maples, and he may hear the pleasant voices of the farmer and his "help" busy in orchard or meadow. At one turn a gap in the roadside screen discloses the narrow, shimmering channel of the lower Lake with the mighty mass of the Adirondacks rising beyond the gray battlements of the old Fort. A league or two toward the east are the Green Mountains. If it is the autumn season, their lower slopes are bathed in the incredible glory of color, their crests still clad in the same somber mantle of evergreen by the which French explorers first identified them more than 300 years ago.

The region is notable for its sweet, fertile valleys lying between forested hills and the long ramparts of gray limestone. From these hills clear streams come hurrying down into these valleys, but where, prone to forget their precipitous haste, they wander thereafter lazily between their alder fringed banks, over golden bars of gravel, and under covered bridges, lending their aid occasionally in the turning of an old, moss-grown water wheel to grind up the fragrant cider apples or to operate a small sawmill. When at such common gathering places you may still hear the pungent twang of Yankee speech, as neighbors exchange current gossip or offer disparaging comment of the affairs of the nation.

Year by year the sharp savor of Yankee speech diminishes, however, and year by year a few more of its priceless idioms are lost to common usage and remain preserved in a few books, of which those of Rowland Robinson excel all others. Modern transportation and swift and ready means of communication are the agencies of deterioration; they have done much to blunt the edge of Yankee dialect, and it must be anticipated that in time the inhabitants of Tranquillity Township will be like the residents of any other American hamlet—almost.

The place was settled, so they say, by four ranger scouts who discovered it while campaigning with the British against the French and Indians. Attracted by the abundance of fish and game, they came there to live when the lilies of France had been lowered for the last time from the proud Citadel of Quebec. The region continues to vindicate the judgment of the Four Rangers. Its hardwood ridges shelter an abundance of deer and lesser game; its brooks are well supplied with trout, and the lowland lakes and rivers with bass, pike, perch and all variety of common fishes. Half of the male population of the township use the gun and rifle, and all of the men and boys are anglers of some sort.

Here in Tranquillity Township dwell in peace and harmony Judge Stovall, "the Judge," Captain Macomber, variously known to his cronies and to our readers as "the Captain" or sometimes "the Sniper," and a legion of their friends, and here occurred most of the incidents now to be related for the reader's edification.

The Judge, who is a lineal descendant of one of the Four Rangers, has never taken wife. He may be found, if court is not in session, and if there is no rise of Ephemeridae occurring on the Belden Brook nor a fall of woodcock in the Sawmill Cover, he may be found, I say, sitting at his ease in the comfortable library in his old brick mansion at the head of Washington Street where Ellen and Jason, housekeeper extraordinary and all-around man of rare talents, administer to his physical and spiritual welfare.

If in the absence of all these contingencies he shouldn't be there, Jason will probably direct the visitor to look for the tough, rotund figure two doors down the street where the Captain, a descendant of another of the Four Rangers, lives with the lovely Dark-Haired Lady and their two robust children. It is just possible that the Judge will be there, fooling around with some trout flies, or assisting his friend in making out the order for shot cartridges for the coming season, or perhaps calking the duck boat. If he's doing none of these things, he'll be chatting with the Dark-Haired Lady or the youngsters in that happy circumstance of sincere and mutual admiration.

In case he isn't to be found at the Captain's, he may be in Doctor Buck's office just past the corner of Washington and State, for he and the bluff, brusque, kindly healer are fast friends. Theirs is the sort of understanding that enables them to argue for hours over the proper cock to a dry fly and then to sit speechless in the same skiff together for an equal length of time while they fish the evening rise on the Trout Pond.

The Dark-Haired Lady regards these friendships with complete approval. It pleases her to see the trio departing on some peaceful excursion to the woods or waters. She has known what it is like to scan the headlines for news of each fresh offensive and to live in dread anticipation of a brief, crushing message from the War Department informing her that her Captain had gone the glorious way of so many of his soldier ancestors.

There *had* been a message finally after weeks of silence. She could still recall the long train journey that ensued, the confusion at the Debarkation Hospital, the endless waiting in stark corridors heavy with the smell of ether and iodoform, and, finally, the first glimpse of the familiar form on the cot, drawn and weary, but, God be thanked, alive!

There were long months that followed while wounds healed, and then at last she had him safe home learning to walk all over again. There were nights, too, when a wild shout would warn her that in his dreams he was back in some deadly, desperate struggle from which even her gentle, reassuring voice and touch recalled him but slowly.

All these things were past but they were part of the Dark-Haired Lady's gentle and understanding spirit, so that she loved his friends for loving him and for bringing him back to her from the day's adventurings safe, sound, laughing, hungry, tired and thirsty. Sometimes if the weather was particularly bad she could discern just the trace of a limp, but that was nothing to what might have been.

It may be doubted if anywhere on earth you could find friends more loyal and devoted and, being what they are and their spiritual heritage what it is, less likely to say anything about it.

NOT
WITHOUT
HONOR

The most rock-bound of all the traditions of Tranquillity Village requires each able-bodied house-holder on the morning of May 30th each year to rise early and unfurl Old Glory over his front porch. After breakfast the children of the village go to the woods to gather wildflowers with which to decorate the flag-marked headstones in the old cemetery—they bring great bunches of wild violets, of crimson and white trillium, the creamy ivory of the bloodroot, and, when the season has been fortuitous, as often happens, there are clusters of the shy pink lady's slipper and the rare marsh azaleas. While the village youngsters are thus engaged, the matrons cut sprays of lilac and syringa. All morning long, quiet groups wander among the gray headstones, leaving behind them dashes of fresh, lovely color scattered over the low mounds in that quiet place. That there were soldier graves enough to be decorated, Heaven knows! Here lay the founders of the village—the almost legendary Four Rangers—who had fought under Abercrombie at Ticonderoga and Wolfe at Abraham's Heights to win from the French the very land where they had settled when peace was won, and where now the children of their children's children's children laid bunches of blue and white hepatica on the sod above their old mouldering bones.

Only a small proportion of Tranquillity's soldier sons slept in the village cemetery. The rest of them bivouacked in alien fields, places with names like Lundys Lane, Cowpens, Saratoga, Yorktown, Chapultepec, Cerro Gordo, Plattsburg, Manassas, Antietam, Cedar Creek, Yellow Tavern, Gettysburg, and San Juan, to name a few. Others slept out in "the pleasant land of France." Long after "the Captains and the Kings" had departed, some but not all of those who had fallen on the Marne and in the Argonne came quietly home to Tranquillity in their flag-draped coffins, and for a considerable time scarcely a week went by in which the old burying ground didn't echo to the measured crash of volley firing and the poignant notes of "Taps."

It is not, however, a day of public mourning. Far from it. Here and there

6

among the graves some woman kneels and you see the flutter of her handkerchief, but in general the day is an occasion of solemn pride. There are apt to be some tight throats and wet eyes in Memorial Hall when the white-haired Post Adjutant rises and calls the roll.

"Allen!" "Ames!" "Arthur!" "Belden!" "Cummings, Edward!" "Cummings, James!" and so on down the list, with the cracked old voices answering up briskly, "Here!" "Here!" "Here!"

It's a short roster now—only eight the last time—and the throat and eye trouble comes whenever the Adjutant calls a name and there is no answer save a brief silence broken at last by the roll of the drum.

The World War came along just in the nick of time to restore to these ceremonies some of the sparkle that used to mark the exercises in the days when the boys who had followed Grant, Meade and Sheridan were still young enough to step out well in ranks and shoulder their muskets with snap and precision. For one thing the Legion Post had one of the finest bands in the whole country with a full complement of the long French trumpets which do so much for martial music. When Long Jim Forbes stepped to the front of the band with the twelve trumpeters ranked behind him—each man with his trumpet held jauntily against his hip—and when Jim raised his sword to signal for "Madelon" or "Le Regiment du Sombre et Meuse," it would make any man tingle to see those bright bugles tossed high in the salute and to hear their gay challenging notes ring out across the old village square.

No; there is much about the day that is bright and vivid and brave and not at all sad, but one May 30th was an exception.

A few days earlier an old veteran of the Civil War had heard in his dulling ears a last "Call to Quarters," and now the whole township was turned out to escort its old friend to the quiet bivouac on the hillside where his own place had been prepared for him by loving hands. There were signs of mourning in plenty—if one knew how to recognize them when he saw them.

The grocer would say to the harness maker:

"The old Major hez gone, they say. I swan, I don't know how we'll get along without him. Next to old Colonel Cushing I suppose he waz abaout the best-liked man in Tranquillity."

"No daoubt about it," the other would reply soberly. "Hain't goin' to forget haow the two of 'em took up my quarrel time that feller sued me on my title. The Major come from away, too, but he couldn't hev been no friendlier if he'd been born an' raised right here in the village."

Such humble tributes were current everywhere along the shaded streets. There casualness might have kept the stranger from realizing that he was in a community truly bowed down by grief.

Gifted with an understanding even beyond that of most of her sex, the Dark-Haired Lady had repressed a housewifely urge to brighten up the tarnished gold of the wound and service chevrons on the sleeves of her Captain's

O.D. coat. A touch of silver polish on a wad of cotton would do it easily, but they had to be left just as they were and she knew it. Nevertheless every bronze button and every battle star on the campaign ribbon shone with a burnished luster when it was time for the Captain to dress. So did the Sam Browne belt, the saber hilt and scabbard and the sleek tan boots.

In the afternoon he would march at the head of three close-ranked platoons of his comrades, trig and taut and looking to her eyes just as he had one day a few years ago when she had watched his regiment march off to the tune of "The Girl I Left Behind Me" to a destination that the orders euphemistically mentioned as "Unknown." The destination today was known and the route was shorter, yet in a way it was longer, too, since for one of them it reached out to eternity. The line of march began at Memorial Hall, then down State Street, turning left on Washington and over Prospect to where the wrought-iron gates of Cedar Hill Cemetery stood wide in welcome to the one whom they would bring with them riding along on a caisson under the vivid flag and followed by a few old men in old blue uniforms with black soft hats shading their old eyes.

From Memorial Hall to the Cemetery it is only a scant half mile, but now it seems too great a distance for legs once good enough to carry their owners on many a forced march with the Army of the Potomac. In fact it has been customary for several years to provide horse-drawn carriages for the old soldiers. This year they needed only one.

Dalrymple, who owned the livery stable, told his boys to put the pair of chestnuts on the three-seated surrey.

"That'll take care of all of 'em," he explained. "Comfortably, too, naow 'at the old Major ain't ridin' with 'em. Le's see, ain't but eight of 'em left, is they?"

Nevertheless when Dalrymple pulled up his pair in front of Memorial Hall with a decorous flourish he met with an unlooked-for rebuff.

Uncle Bill Paraday, the fox and honey hunter—Sergeant William Paraday, of Stannard's Brigade—ordered him indignantly and peremptorily to return his "danged burooch" to the stable.

"We're a marchin' today, an' I ruther guess, by Mighty, we ain't so dummed ol' and crippled up but what we c'n manage to foller the ol' Major on foot an' keep up to him, too, on his last ride! No, sir!"

So, after all, the horses and the glittering carriage were not in the slow procession that moved along the street toward sundown. Eight old men in blue followed the lumbering caisson on foot, doing their very best to compel from stiffened joints and weary muscles some semblance of youthful gait and temper.

Judge Stovall for once in his career had stooped to ask for political preference. It was a strange plum he sought, too. Through his friend, the Governor, he had solicited the loan of a field gun and men to serve it, and word had come back to say that the State was glad to honor a citizen so worthy.

The gun had arrived that morning and was placed in the Square with its slender muzzle laid level, its crew standing easy, the focal point of the eyes of all the urchins in town who had managed to escape the services in the Hall, which, no doubt, would only have bored them anyhow. The parade was formed at last, and at the first note of the slow march a cloud of white smoke burst from the gun's muzzle and the crash of its great voice echoed among the hills. As the cortege moved toward the cemetery the gun at minute intervals continued to do honor to the man on the caisson, its solemn thunder falling on the quivering air while the acrid smoke of the discharges drifted across the emptied streets.

It ceased when the open grave was reached. A hush ensued, unbroken by any sound from the multitude that had entered the environs and now stood among the headstones. A thrush, a friendly bird, chose that perfect moment of silence to sing in the maples.

Parson Drake read the service ending with the humble, beautiful supplication,

"Lord, suffer now thy servant to depart in peace!"

Then Colonel Cushing detached his tall figure from the little group of veterans in blue and came forward to the graveside.

For a long minute he gazed down upon the walnut casket that gave what shelter there remained for his old friend.

When he turned there was a look of humility on his fine old face. The Colonel was an orator, a trained, expert and polished speaker, a man who understood the courtly, gracious usages of the spoken word. A few years back, when a group of rascals in high places had conspired to commit treasons against the very nation they were pledged to serve, it had been his voice and words that denounced them in phrases that were like saber slashes and drove the money changers from the temple.

But this afternoon, the sun sinking to the crest of Mount Defiance and the grave of the old Major open before him, he felt himself not in the mood for practiced oratory. He rested a hand on the dark polished wood and spoke simply.

"Some of you may not know.how Major John Bristol happened to come to our town. I met him during the heat of battle at Gettysburg. We disagreed that day. But afterward while we lay for months in the same hospital we forgot our earlier differences. An affection developed between us that has lasted nearly sixty years. He was persuaded, when the war was over, to come to Tranquillity and join me in the practice of law. There is no single person here who has not benefited in some way from having known this kindly courteous man, myself most of all. We shall miss him—a gallant soldier, a loyal friend and a great gentleman."

The clear voice faltered for the first time, but the gray head was erect, even though tears ran down on either cheek, when he turned.

"He told me once, long ago, that if it should be not too inappropriate a request he would greatly like to have his favorite marching song played during the services that we are performing for him today."

He raised his hand in signal to Long Jim Forbes, who stood waiting for it, and who in turn faced his musicians and flashed his sword.

The long trumpets flourished, their silvery notes rang out. Then came the full band with the fifes screaming, the drums rattling and the horns perfectly launched into a gay and gallant refrain. It was both reckless and wistful—a soldier tune if ever there was one—the sort of thing that a column on route march likes to hear from its band when it is entering a village where there will be pretty girls looking out of the windows along the street. Not *just* the sort of thing you'd expect to hear at a funeral, perhaps, but then, if you listened, you seemed to hear the crying of lost, gallant things in the wail of the fifes that was enough to tear your heart out. It ran and raced and laughed and wept and rollicked among the old stones, and filled the place with strange ghosts summoned from far fields. Then the brilliant, sparkling, homesick thing swept to a close. There was a final dauntless roll from the snare drums, a skirl from the pipes—and silence.

Colonel Cushing and Sergeant Bill Paraday stepped forward and lifted the flag from the coffin.

There was nothing unusual about the rest of the ceremony. A Legion platoon fired the regulation volleys and a Legion trumpeter blew taps in the twilight gathering under the elms and maples. No one there saw anything not in harmony with the spirit and meaning of the day in the fact that the soldier tune played by the Yankee band that day at the grave of their beloved townsman was the Southland's "Dixie" and that the flag lifted so gently from the coffin lid by the two old Union veterans was the Stars and Bars.

WILD
HONEY

One morning in early September when the clusters of wild gentian and goldenrod bloom were humming with the presence of myriads of honey gatherers, Uncle Bill Paraday rose from the breakfast table and announced that it was his intention to go and find a wild bee tree.

Aunt Candace thought the proposed activity seemed infinitely more sensible than the fox hunting which her companion persistently engaged in whenever weather permitted during the winter months, and she proceeded forthwith to prepare a luncheon for the honey hunter, while he foraged in the woodshed for his bee box and a hatchet.

Equipped at last in proper fashion, he set out across the lower meadow in the direction of Belden Brook and the woods.

The art of the bee hunter is nearly lost elsewhere, perhaps because the destruction of woodlands has lessened opportunities to practice it, or more likely because domestic apiaries are now so numerous and so productive of the limpid stuff that there no longer exists the incentive to raid the wild stores for the dark, pungent treasure so greatly prized by the pioneers in the days when other forms of sweetening were scarce and expensive.

In a few New England communities the old craft persists and is practiced—mostly for the fun of the thing—but Uncle Bill enjoyed the flavor of the adventure no less than he did the wild tang of the spoils.

"This tame honey hain't wuth a tinker's cuss. Hain't no taste to it. Naow you git ye some wild honey to spread on your cakes an', by Mighty, you hev got suthin'! Tastes none the worse for a mite o' bee bread in it, nuther."

He stopped presently to observe a succession of bees working in a cluster of red clover blooms—his eye following carefully the swift departure of one burden bearer after another. After some minutes he slid back the lid of his bee box and deftly imprisoned a newcomer in a compartment where an ounce or so of extracted honey lay at the disposal of the foolish captive who lost no time in loading himself with the easily gathered plunder.

"Naow, go it, ye lettle cuss," Uncle Bill adjured him, slipping back the cover to release the laden one, "an' tell your friends what ye've faound."

The old man placed the box carefully on a shingle, filled his pipe, and patiently awaited the return of the scout. In a few minutes the bee was back, bringing with him two or three companions. All of them greedily stuffed their sacks with the free honey and again departed.

By timing their arrival the watcher calculated according to some formula of his own the distance to their hive. With this and knowledge of the flight line now clearly established, he was able to reach a conclusion—and one not altogether satisfactory.

"Your hive is suthin' like two miles off, an' that an' the line you're taking makes me believe you're Briggses bees. You be, too! Go tell your mother she wants ye!"

With that inhospitable dismissal, he shook the remaining visitors out of the box and moved on to try again with some other rover.

After a few attempts he was successful and presently had a well-defined flight of bees coming and going in a more promising direction. Convinced of this he closed the lid on a half dozen hostages and moved forward a hundred paces or so to pause again and open the box, watching closely, however, as each captive clambered out, took heavy wing, and after a short upward spiral darted away, to return again as before with fresh workers.

The process was patiently repeated again and again until at last by mid-afternoon the marvelous instinct of the bees had betrayed them and brought the old man step by step to a wooded hollow where stood a great basswood. Here was the treasure hoard. From a hole high up on the trunk a skein of living gold spun in the sunlight, constantly forming and dissolving, weaving and glinting. That the swarm was large was indicated by the density and thickness of the cord of bees flowing to and from the opening, and this in turn augured well for the weight of comb inside.

Uncle Bill had found a "bee tree."

He "claimed" it by cutting two deep notches in the trunk to identify the discoverer. Having done this he picked up his box and departed, secure in the knowledge that no one—not even the owner of the woodland—would contemplate any infringement upon his established rights in his find.

That evening the Captain had just settled himself into a comfortable chair on the porch, prepared, with a glass of something cool and pungent close at hand, to watch the miracle of the twilight flow upward into the sky from some vast pool of lambent flame hidden behind the Adirondacks. He loved the hour with its special colors and its humble, restful sounds. On fair evenings he rarely failed to be where he could view the delicately shifting spectacle of light and gloom stealing across mountain, lake and forest.

The gate creaked to admit the Judge and the Doctor. These gentlemen, as was their custom when other affairs permitted, silently joined their friend in reverent contemplation of the scene. The Dark-Haired Lady came quietly with her special smile for these two old friends and a tall refreshing glass, breathing the fragrance of Old Jamaica, for each of them.

The last fading crimson glow had been withdrawn behind Mount Defiance before anyone spoke, and then it was the Judge.

"Uncle Bill wants us to help him cut a bee tree tomorrow. It's up in Belden's Woods. I'd like to go; never saw it done. It would please the old man, too."

"Well," remarked the Captain, "I never supposed I'd get to hunting bees, but if you're going, I'll go. I expect you'll be digging ginseng and hunting skunks next. The descent to Avernus is easy, and it began when the Judge took up 'coon huntin' last fall. How long," he persisted, "do you two expect to maintain your somewhat sullied professional reputations in the County if you engage in such fiddlin' undignified pastimes?"

The Doctor ignored the jibe.

"*I* shall not turn the light of my countenance from any enterprise that will turn my thoughts from felons, summer colic, and housemaid's knee," said he, "reputation or no reputation."

So, lacking a dissenting voice, it was agreed. And on the following day the trio debarked in the Paraday dooryard where they were welcomed with gifts of axes, buckets, and swabs of cotton netting by Uncle Bill, and with doughnuts and cider by his good wife.

As these things were being disposed of according to their various uses, a tall, shambling figure straddled over the orchard fence and moved toward them.

"Oh! Gosh A'mighty!" Uncle Bill, perceiving the apparition, exclaimed under his breath, but fervently. Here's ol' Guidance Witherbee! God help me naow! The last man—ef you c'n call him so—that I wanter see—naow, or any other time! The dummed ol' mealy-mouthed dodunk! He's wuss to me than hives in hayin'! Somehow he's heard about the bee tree. He'll wanter go, too, an' he'll lectur' an' preach an' hold forth—but he won't lay a hand to an axe helve! Dum him!"

A suave and unctuous voice interrupted the old man's furious subterranean tirade.

"Mornin' Neighbor Paraday! Mornin' gentlemen! Been lookin' fer one o' my heifers 'at strayed away from the fold, so to speak, an' 'is wanderin' aout on the hills away, fur off from the gates o' gold,' as the hymn says."

His slow speech was punctuated by noisy inhalations that gave to his remarks a peculiarly mournful effect as of one who labors righteously in a world hopelessly given over to wickedness. His eyes rolled slowly from one to another of his embarrassed audience, fixing each in turn with an oxlike regard as if he would uncover the very secrets of their erring souls but missing meanwhile no single detail of the preparations afoot.

"Yis! Yis!" he continued. "We must all strive to fetch in the wanderin' ones, even though we hev to toil an' scrabble over the rocks an' brush o' sin to git 'em."

Then, appearing to notice the peculiar nature of the party's equipment for the first time, he exclaimed with every evidence of surprise and benign pleasure.

"Wal, wal! Faound a bee tree, hev ye?"

"Damn him!" grunted Uncle Bill in an aside to the Doctor. "Wants us to b'lieve he'd jest faound it out! I don't mind his tricks half as much as I do havin' him think he's foolin' me with 'em. Naow listen to him!"

The newcomer surveyed the arrangements with a bland expanding benignity, rocking slowly on his heels and stroking a beard so long and luxuriant that it half concealed the bosom of his blue gingham shirt.

"Naow, since I've jined ye so unexpected jist at this fittin' time, I've a good notion to go 'long with ye! Yis, I hev. I c'n be of considerable help on a experdition of this natur' fer I hev let daown many a bee tree in my time. There hain't no one c'n tell ye better haow to go abaout it. I jedge ye've already hardened your hearts to the act o' takin' by force o' arms honey which b'longs by rights to God's helpless insecks? I see ye hev, so I won't argue the pint. Minnie, my dear wife, will sartainly enj'y havin' ten, fifteen paounds o' wil' honey in the pantry, too. She's uncommon fond of it. Now, Miz Paraday, ef ye c'n spare me a glass o' that cider—'tain't worked none, I hope—an' a han'ful of your nut cakes, I believe we're abaout ready to start, ain't we?"

They set off presently. It must be admitted that the spirits of the original four were considerably dampened by the presence of the intruder, whose bony hands bore none of the burden of equipment and so left him to devote his whole attention to learned discourses delivered upon one subject or another.

When well within the border of the woods they halted briefly for a rest and a drink from an icy spring beside the path. The Doctor pulled our a cigar and proffered it to their uninvited guest. It was declined.

"No , Doctor," he sighed reproachfully, "I don't use the filthy weed in no shape, manner ner form: neither smoking, chewing ner snuff. Don't believe in it, in fac', an'—'ceptin' present comp'ny—hain't no use for them 'at does. 'Them who do use it air lierble to drink,' as the song hez it. Minnie, my dear wife, she don't approve of it, nuther."

The friends so far had scarcely uttered a word, so submerged were they by the calamity that had befallen their adventure. In truth there were three who found it highly amusing, but Uncle Bill muttered and fumed beneath his breath as his sense of outrage mounted, though he continued to hold his peace.

"No, sir," continued the torment, "I don't use stimerlants o' any description. I git my paower and stren'th from obedience to the laws o' the speckrum."

"The what?" asked the Doctor.

"The speckrum," the other explained kindly, turning his bovine glance upon the puzzled medical man. "Meanin' the division o' color an' light accordin' to the signs o' the zodiac an' the movements an' interpertations o' the heavenly bodies makin' up the solar system. Different seasons, ye see, call fer different colors. The way to use 'em is secret an' can't be divulged to the public 'cause they hain't eddicated up to it, ner yit prepared for its benefits, but if ye ask it I c'n recommend ye to the Master o' the Speckrum daown in Boston an' he'll doubtless take ye in an' unfold the mysteries to ye. It'll cost ye three dollars, which amaount you c'n hand to me, and it includes a year's subscription to 'Paower, Health an' Light,' our sassiety's journal. It works wonders, I tell ye—gives ye domernation over the beasts o' the fields an' the faowls o' the air."

"He'd ort to use some of it on Minnie," growled Uncle Bill to the Captain. "She's got all the domernation in that fam'ly! They tell me she stands Guidance right up on his hind laigs 'bout once a week. Ketched the ol' fool smokin' one time an' made him sleep in the cowbarn for a fortnight. But she ain't here naow when we need her, dum it!"

Behind them they heard the flat, nasal voice and the gusty interpolations and caught fragments of dissertations on the "speckrum" and on something else that Guidance referred to as the "subtile emernations of individual paower," but they gave it no further attention for Uncle Bill now pointed to the great basswood that marked their destination.

As they distributed the engines of war, Guidance sat himself down on a stump and began proffering advice, to which none of the others listened, as they made preparations under direction of Uncle Bill for sapping, siege, and the final assault.

"She's holler clean to the butt," he opined, tapping the wide trunk with the back of his axe. "I guess we'd better let her daown len'thways o' the holler—'twon't break up so much comb."

He pulled from a sack an ordinary bellows such as is a part of the equipment of any domestic hearth. This specimen, however, had a tin box attached, into which the old bee hunter stuffered a half pound of "Blue Paper" shag tobacco and ignited it. A few jerks at the handles caused a stream of thick, rank smoke to spurt from the snout.

"Naow, when we cut through to the holler, you stick the nuzzle in an' gi' her two or three dosts. It'll kinder doze 'em down a leetle an' make 'em more peaceable."

"Terbaccer," observed the stump moralist, "hez a turrible stultifyin' effect on humerns no less'n on bees."

Giving no heed to the lesson, the old bee hunter handed the device to the Judge who promptly strangled on a stray whiff of the fearful vapor.

"Any bee that gets a noseful of that," he gasped, "won't even know what stultified him!"

The four took turns at the axe with such good effect that soon there was an opening to the cavity into which the Judge promptly squirted a dose of his soporific, repeating it at intervals as the breach widened to a deep, white-edged slot. After an hour of steady chopping, the great tree began to quiver pathetically under the strokes.

Uncle Bill glanced into the top and dropped the axe hastily.

"Naow, boys, git into the nets an' gloves an' tie your sleeves daown. Don't leave nary an opening fer they'll sarch it out if ye do."

With some reluctance he held a wad of netting toward their guest who declined it condescendingly.

"Don't need it," he announced, "ner you wouldn't, nuther, if ye follored the teachin's o' the Master o' the Speckrum. Won't nary a bee harm ye, ner pizenous snakes, vines, fruits, et cetery, ner animiles. Renders ye proof agin all manner o' bodily fevers an' ailments. Tain't too late to jine the Sassiety if ye'd like to han' me the small sum asked."

His voice was drowned by the loud snapping of single fibers in the basswood trunk like the crackle of skirmishers' rifles, which at once increased to a loud rending, groaning sound as the great tree wavered, its top trembling in the upper sunlight for a last agonized moment before it swept earthward with a long thunderous roar.

The impact rent the trunk from top to bottom, disclosing dark masses of stored honey, over which the poor bees crawled confusedly dazed by the chaos and by applications of the Judge's "Blue Paper Long Cut."

As the reverberations of the fall died away, the air became resonant with the sound of tiny wings and there was a curious hot odor that carried a warning as distinct as the whir of a snake's rattles and made the raiders look well to the arrangement of their nets and gloves.

Old Guidance perched serenely on his stump and observed these benighted precautions with a trace of bland sufferance.

"Danged ef the ol' fool don't believe in his emernations," said Uncle Bill. "I thought he'd light out the minute the tree come daown."

Individual bees were now rousing to combat and obviously searching for an enemy. One crawled inside the Doctor's glove, and what it did there brought an agonized whoop from that sportsman.

"Ye see?" said Guidance kindly. "Ye hain't puttin' out the emernations, Doctor. Naow it's a fac' dem'strated by sarchin' the records o' the Scriptur' that Dan'l was a practitioner o' aour science. Yes, sir, all that kept 'em off him that time he was thrun among them ragin' Nubian lierns—no, come to think of it, 'twam't Nubian lierns, nuther, Nubians was them indecent naked slave hussies—well, whatever kind o' lierns they—"

At this moment two bees of the many now milling about in the upper air in blind search of the hive entrance which was no longer there, caught the exciting odors of bee anger and ruptured honey cells rising from their shattered citadel. Laying their lances, the pair coasted down against the rising whirl of scent. The first object that met their hostile glances—and the only thing in motion at the time—was the frond of Guidance's whiskers waggling busily against the dappled background of the forest floor.

They whirled as one bee and, like the troopers at Balaklava, charged home.

The aspiring scientist on the stump emitted an agonized yelp and began to claw frantically at his beard.

"Gracious! Gracious! he bellowed. "Bring fire quick!"

Uncle Bill took in the situation at a glance. From the nerveless hands of the Judge he snatched the bellows and pumped a deadly choking blast of rank tobacco smoke into the writhing whiskers, just as half a dozen fresh warriors arrived with bulletlike speed to drive home the charge.

Human nature—even when fortified by the precepts of the Master of the Spectrum—could stand no more. With a strangled howl, Guidance tumbled backward over the stump, gathered his long arms and legs into some semblance of organization, and departed, diverging from the direct route homeward only enough to tear through a clump of thick-growing hazel in a frantic effort to shake off his tormentors.

After he had disappeared, and while his dolorous squalls could still be heard faintly, Uncle Bill observed with wicked satisfaction that tattered fragments of gingham fluttered idly among the hazel bushes.

"Won't hev no more clo'es onto him than a jay bird time he gits home," reflected the bee hunter, his voice sounding sepulchrally through the enveloping folds of his bee net. "He'll be smellin' o' Blue Paper Long Cut, too—will for a week—an' his face swelled up. Minnie'll give him a month in the cowbarn, the poor deluded devil!"

He turned to his task of scooping methodically great slabs and sections of the fragrant dark comb from the hollow of the prostrate basswood, his friends assisting him, although somewhat more clumsily, to pack the plunder in the capacious buckets.

A little later he interrupted their labors again to say that there wan't nothing like bees in a feller's whiskers to l'arn him the vanity of the pursuit of earthly treasure, because you couldn't help scrabble for 'em or wish't ye hadn't when ye faound 'em.

"The subtile emernations kinda busted daown, didn't they?" he observed again as he clamped down the lid on a packed bucket. "I swan, when I git this honey home, if I ever do, and take this cussed bee net off, I'm agoin' to laugh an' praise God fer a week."

But when the spoils had been gathered and apportioned, the kindly old gentleman put aside a ten-quart bucket of prime dark comb.

"Guess I'll take that along to Guidance," he explained. "The dummed dodunk! Bad 'nough to hev bees wi'out hevin' a womern like Minnie in your whiskers, too!"

OL' SASSIFY DOES HER STUFF

So far as the knowledge of the writer extendeth, there have been no statues made of Jim Hooper and no bronze tablets let into the sagging log walls of the cabin where he was born by the people of a grateful republic. Measured by the standards of the New England community where he lived and drank and died, Jim failed to earn so much as an average merit mark. By trade he was a woodcutter, as much as anything, and the pictures that remain of that long figure wielding a four-pound double-bitted axe with skill, power, and grace show a man entitled to respect. It is those others of Jim returning to his cabin on "The Marsh" after a losing bout with the mixture of alcohol and water that was his favorite inspirational beverage that show reason for his low moral rating in the neighborhood. Jim loved the woods and leisure and irresponsibility and was of a spiritual kinship with Rip Van Winkle. So did the Captain, and so was the Captain, and naturally the Captain and Jim were friends.

Jim knew the woods and the waters. He knew the marshes and fields and where to find game, but when it was found he could seldom pull off a decent shot, for he was not a good marksman. He knew all the fishing waters, but he rarely caught anything remarkable. He lived on "The Marsh"—a broad fen thickly studded with muskrat houses and the favorite resort of 'coons and mink—but his catch of fur was the smallest and poorest of any taken in the neighborhood. He was poor, good-natured, and shiftless; lean, gangling, and tireless; lazy where profitable employment threatened, but seething with energy when it was ginseng digging, 'coon or rabbit hunting, or bullhead fishing, or some similar fiddling, footless project.

Jim drifted to a stop in front of the Captain's home one October afternoon and beckoned him out to the roadway—he would never go into the house if he could avoid it.

"Cap'n," said he, grinning, "I hev faound ye some woodcock. Congo Jackson sez to me, sezzee, 'They's a mess o' woodcock usin' the Ol' Fitzgerald

Place,' sezzee, 'an' I b'lieve,' sezzee, 'that ef a feller c'n shoot on the wing,' sezzee, 'that he could git him a harndsome mess.' Sezzi, 'I'll fetch a feller up,' sezzi, 'at kin comb 'em,' sezzi, 'an' I ain't so dummed poor at shootin' on the fly myself, by Judast!' Naow, Cap'n, let's git an airly start tomorrer mornin'. Kin ye go?"

"I'll be at your house at sun up," the Captain told him, for in those days before market shooting and summer shooting had been stopped by Federal authority, the woodcock was a rare bird in covers where now, by reason of proper laws, he is again abundant. Woodcock were indeed much scarcer than good deeds in a naughty world and a chance at these birds had never before come the Captain's way. He could actually have counted all the individual specimens seen up to that time on the fingers of both hands notwithstanding the fact that from spring to winter he roamed the very covers that in years gone by had yielded splendid bags.

"All right, Cap'n. Say, ye don't happen tu have no sech thing as a little paowder an' shot, du ye? I hain't got a mite o' ammernition 'n' clean fergot tu git me some tu the store."

It didn't look like a clause in a contract, but that is precisely what it was, for it was understood that the Captain was liable for "ammernition" and tobacco if Jim showed him gunning.

The next morning he set out with a half pint flask of black powder and another of shot for Jim's muzzle-loader, and a package of "yellow paper" Mechanic's Delight for his pipe. Also, his pockets carried a lunch and a couple of dozen loaded brass shells for his own little double sixteen.

Jim's cabin lay just across the old stone bridge. He was already abroad when the Captain came up, but there was some delay while he fed himself, his pigs, his dogs, and finally his "game roosters"—of these warrior birds, he had a dozen or two. Then he got his gun down from the pegs, found a handful of paper for wadding, and they set out along a dim path into the woods. A child, naked save for one brief garment and certain rich smears of molasses, followed them, but not far.

"Naow, Pud," remonstrated Jim, turning and bending above his progeny, "du ye want I sh'ld warm yore sed daown? You hyper fer the haouse!"

The youngster appeared to be acutely aware of the peculiar vulnerability of the locality selected for "warming" and vanished like a cub bear without a word.

Wet sprays of the dogwood branches touched their faces, and their nostrils were filled with the sweet pungency of the hazels and the queer pleasant odor of the ripe toadstools that everywhere displayed their treacherous appetizing colors. Their shoes thumped against stones as they crossed the ridges and splashed in the black mud as they strode through the intervening hollows. Grouse whirred up before their approach, but they did not attempt a shot. For one reason, they were after woodcock; for another, they were moving at far too fast a clip to indulge in any business with their shotguns. Jim traveled like an Indian, and though the Captain had trailed with many a terrible walker, he had yet to meet one who could make his boot heels fly as could Jim who at his regular, ordinary pace always kept him at that distressing gait that is more than the fastest walk, and just uncomfortably less than a trot. The good-natured chap never knew how close to "quits" he often had his companion.

"Congo" Jackson was, in his way, as rare a bird as the woodcock in that community, for his skin was like black ivory. He was, in fact, a runaway slave brought North on "the underground railroad" just before the Civil War. He had settled there in a clearing in the great woods, where he built a cabin, cleared an acre or two of land, and lived the hard life of a free man. He was a good old soul and an object of intense interest to the youngsters by reason of his strange history, his ebony skin, and the hermit life he led. He was digging his crop of potatoes when they came up, and he straightened his bent back and bobbed his gray poll cheerily in answer to their hail.

Jim immediately stopped, rested the butt of his gun on the ground, his forearms across the muzzle, and braced his right heel flatwise against the inner side of his left knee. This was a characteristic pose, and indicated that he was ready for a sociable chat. Completely winded from the six-mile "go-as-you-please," the Captain chose to perch on the top rail of Congo's garden fence.

"Naow, Jackson, this here is the feller I told ye abaout. He's a wingshot, an' an almighty good one, tu! I guess me an' Ol' Sassify c'n sing 'em a song, tu, though I hain't in no wise as cute at it as the Cap'n, here, bein' as I hain't much o' a han' to practise. We come up to git them woodcock you was tellin' abaout. Ef ye'll say where they are we'll cut along naow an' thank ye kindly."

"Yas, indeedy!" agreed the old darky, hobbling a few steps in the direction of the gate. As he shuffled along he gave the Captain a swift and comprehensive scrutiny, which was returned with interest, whereupon he bobbed his gray head again and tugged at his forelock with thumb and black forefinger—a curious kind of salute that the Captain had seen before, and the meaning of which he comprehended.

The old fellow pointed down a narrow valley where a brook ran about the tangled roots of black alders, and where scraggly old apple trees stood forlornly and dropped their many-colored fruit as if they themselves were indifferent to a treasure that no one but deer, partridges, woodchucks, and squirrels ever came to reap.

"'Spect you all fin' dem big haid snipe 'long side de run in de alder brush," said Congo, in a voice that was soft and uncouth to northern ears. "Done scahed out heaps o' 'em 'mongst de trees in de ol' orchard, too. Y'all gwine git some right smaht shootin'! Plenty pheasants up de run." The Captain gathered that by "pheasant" he referred to ruffed grouse. "Um humph!" Congo continued reminiscently, "Ol' Marse useter shoot de woodcock down in Lacr-anny in de ol' days. De boy dat didn't move spry in de canes en keep de buhds jumpin' jest ez likely git some er de buhd shot, too! He! He! Yas, *suh!* Right servigerous ol' man wuz de Ol' Marse where he cotch a boy prankin' on him!"

The Captain wanted to stay and hear more about this terrible man who plastered his slaves with bird shot if they lagged in beating out woodcock, for the whole picture was romantically strange to him, the planter with his white hat and his slave whip—so he pictured him—his long swallow-tail coat, his fierce goatee whiskers, and the scared black boys prancing in the cane brakes, among the moccasin snakes, alligators, and other tropical slimy horrors; but Jim had no interest in these things and was ready for action.

They descended the slope to the valley. It could be seen from the occasional cellar hole with its clump of ragged rose bushes that on this spot had once been a farm. Jim said that there had been a half dozen farms in the valley.

"What became of 'em, Jim?"

"Dunno ez I ever heard. Ain't been no one lived here since I c'n remember. Moved aout, er died, er suthin', I guess. Mebbe the Injuns got 'em. Ain't no haouses standin' ner hain't been in my time. Nothin' but ol' orchards 'n' suller holes. Naow, I'll load my gun an' gwup one side o' the brook 'n' you gwup t'other, 'n' we'll git us some woodcock."

The loading was done, carefully as befitted so redoubtable a weapon as Ol' Sassify—the Captain never learned the origin of the gun's nickname nor its meaning—and they moved forward.

Beside a huge limestone boulder, where the ground was strewn with decaying apples from an ancient tree, Jim nearly stepped on the first woodcock. The Captain heard the bird's quaint whistle and the subdued whip of his wings as he went aloft, and turned in time to see the 'cock twisting away upstream. Jim stared a moment, threw up his gun, and began a long, fumbling, inept attempt to sight down on the elusive target. It was agony to the Captain, acquainted with the swift, smart performance of the wingshot, and this fatal bungling wrung him. A dozen times he mentally pulled the trigger for Jim, only to see him catch himself on the verge of firing, recover, and begin all over again the hopeless process. Then when all was lost there came the "pip!" of the exploding gun cap and the "kerboom!" of the charge. Smoke and fragments of the newspaper wadding drifted through the alders.

For some seconds Jim stood poised and expectant, as if he still conceived that the vanished bird might desist from this nonsense and come back and drop dead at the shooter's feet. Then he slowly relaxed and began fumbling for powder flask, wadding, shot, and caps.

"I declar', Cap'n," he drawled, as he set about recharging the smoking tube, "it's turrible hard tu draw a bead on 'em with a consarned ol' gun like I got! Naow, that'n o' yourn handles cute—I p'sume t' say the gun hez a gret deal tu do with shootin'!"

"You've got to shoot quick, Jim," the Captain explained, giving him in one brief dose about all that he knew of the technique of bird shooting—or has learned since, for that matter.

"But it won't du tu shoot onless ye kin sight on 'em, an' wi'aout the cussed birds quit bobbin' an' flurrupin, ye can't git nary a bead on 'em—leastways not wi' a dummed cantankerous ol' gun."

The next 'cock was the Captain's. It sprang from a tiny clearing in a clump of "steeple top" bushes, and he saw the long bill, the black eye, shiny as a shoebutton, and the strange jetty markings on the plumage. Partridge, he was familiar with, and they no longer "scared the liver out of him"; but this fellow was something else.

"Bang!" went the first barrel, the lusty black powder blazing before the gun was halfway up or the bird ten paces distant. The white smoke hung exasperatingly, and finally the Captain plunged forward through it and caught sight of his bird hovering like a big bat above the alders. In haste he switched the gun and fired again and saw the bird pitch downward. Running forward into the tangle, he found and gathered his game and cared little that his tearing passage had flushed another 'cock that went away unshot at.

The retrived bird went into one pocket of his shooting coat, and the empty brass cartridge case, moist and reeking, went into another, to be carried home and recharged for the next excursion. Jim, meanwhile, was moving silently up his side of the brook. A partridge feeding in an old apple tree perceived the gaunt, furtive figure and began twittering excitedly while it cocked its silly head and stared. Jim's eye was instantly on the bird and the long gun came up, but the game was off and whirring away under the orchard boughs before the gunner could bring himself to press the trigger.

"Gosh dum it!" he exclaimed, as he lowered his weapon, "I can't seem tu du nothin' wi' the cussed ol' gun!"

At his feet there was a sudden apparition of brown and black and the shrill twitter of a rising woodcock. Jim and Ol' Sassify followed the bird's flight with the same terrific hesitant intensity, but again the game was far out of danger before the heavy voice of the old fowling piece proclaimed a decision arrived at too late.

They came next upon the mouldy foundation stones of an old mill, and where the pond had been was now a swamp too wet and soft and cold for the comfort of either bird or man. The gently sloping banks gave splendid ground, however, and Jim went around one edge while the Captain proceeded around the other. Jim was soon out of sight in a tract of alders and thorn-apple bushes, but from time to time his companion heard the thunder of his gun and had mental pictures of Jim "dumming" and "consarning" the poor old weapon.

The Captain has flushed the brown, long-billed rascal in many a cover since that day, and with increasing frequency as the years have passed; he has sought him in company with the finest sportsmen of this or any other country, but he never knew any day with the woodcock that was a better one than that. Every bird that rose was a mystery on the wing, and a miracle was wrought every time that his gun brought one down. Now and then a grouse would roar aloft, and once he saw a red fox slip away through the alder stems. Squirrels barked and squalled in the hickories on the warm hillsides, and crows gossiped, not unmusically, and shook their sable feathers in the sunshine. A day like that, with the rich odors of fruitful autumn mingled with the sharper tang of powder smoke in his nostrils and with the knowledge that in the next thirty paces a woodcock or partridge would spring from underfoot, was reason enough for living.

At noon, they met and "boiled the pot" and ate their lunch beside an ancient spring. Jim was downcast and disconsolate and eyed his grim and veteran weapon glumly.

"By Mighty!" he decided, between bites of a tremendous pork sandwich, "I shall sell the dummed ol' fusee to Rawl nex' time he comes by an' git me a britch-loader, so I shall! It don't no more'n roll the shot out'n the berril! I do b'lieve she's britch-burnt!" And he gave the gun a scornful cuff, as if it were a disobedient dog.

They set out homeward, following a dim forest road at a pace moderate enough to permit them to take a shot now and then at a grouse. They saw no more woodcock after leaving that remote cover.

"Used to be slews on 'em," Jim observed. "Sody Walker an' Marve Goodfellow used tu kill lots on 'em an' send 'em off tu some furrin place tu sell 'em. They got ez high ez a dollar a pair! They wuz slick ones, I tell ye! Why, Cap'n, it wan't nothing six, seven year ago tu git a baker's dozen o' woodcock any day in them alders ri' daown by the Ol' Sawmill Haouse! So wuz they faount in Grady's Swamp an' in your Pa's Rock Pastur'. Nobody went no gret distance tu git 'em—they didn't haf tu. But they all died aout er went sumwhere's else. I snummy, I hain't seen a dozen woodcock in four years—not until today, leastways."

The truth of the matter was that those old gunners, who began shooting about the fourth of July and kept steadily at it until November, put too great a strain on a species that seldom lays more than four eggs to a clutch. Now twenty years later one may enjoy the peculiarly satisfying experience of finding those ancient covers, once exhausted, again populated with a modest number of these quaint birds.

"Whup!" exclaimed Jim in a low ejaculation that halted the Captain instantly. Ahead of them a trim gray bird stepped across the leaf-strewn road and, hopping upon a log, eyed them attentively.

The lock of Ol' Sassify clicked meanacingly as her long tube rose to a level and the Captain set his nerves against the shock of the explosion. Jim bent his neck and squinted down the barrel while the partridge moved its head jerkily from side to side and seemed about to vanish. Finally Jim pulled the trigger and Ol' Sassify responded with a vengeful roar. Through the smoke the bird could be seen beating the earth in a dying flurry of wings as Jim ran forward.

"Thar, sir! By Judast Priest! I spottered him, didn't I?" he crowed, holding the game triumphantly aloft for the Captain's admiration. "I combed that feller! By John Scott, boy, it takes a good gun tu git one o' them critters! I daoubt if a britch-loader could hev kerried that far! No, sir, jest gi' me Ol' Sassify an' I'll talk turkey tu these pa'tridges every time!"

IN SEARCH
OF EXCITEMENT

The thing that for a time threatened to disturb a friendship of years' duration began with an incident that occurred on one of the thousands of this nation's Washington Streets one October afternoon. For two weeks previously the Judge had been something less than his usual frank, genial self. The Captain had detected signs of preoccupation, of worry, and of an absorption in problems apparently too deep or delicate for sharing with his old friend.

That very morning, upon the Captain's suggestion that the two of them journey up the North Branch of the Winooski to gun the Sawdust Cover for grouse and woodcock, the older gunner had been oddly hesitant. He wouldn't—or, more likely, couldn't—look his friend squarely in the face; he shuffled his feet and frowned portentously, and spoke of voluminous records to be read and considered and of meeting a friend who would be arriving on the afternoon train.

The other was suspicious.

"What's come over you?" he inquired. "If you weren't so fat and lazy I'd suspect you'd found a bee tree, and if you weren't so old and homely I'd think it was a female. Come on now! What is it?"

The Judge fidgeted, and finally gave hoarse reply.

"Work," he croaked desperately.

Thus denied, his friend gave up all thoughts of shooting and spent a dull day at his own office separating the accumulated correspondence of the bird-shooting season into two piles. Into one he sorted inquiries already so ancient that further delay would matter little, while into the other went inquiries so recently dated that they could well await further attention for at least another week or two.

Then, at four o'clock in the golden light of a prime October afternoon, on his way to the post office he encountered the Judge, with the friend who came by train, face to face on Washington Street.

The "friend" was a huge dog, tawny gray as to coat, with some of the family insignia of the Airedale and a bit that the astonished Captain identified as borzoi.

25

"So that's it, is it!" he exclaimed bitterly. " 'Coon huntin'! I knew darned well there was something furtive and unnatural about this! Well, I am shocked! I am, indeed! A man of your standing planning to go racing and yelling through the midnight silences, swinging lanterns and pulling porcupine quills and getting plastered by skunks! Dear me! I supposed you were for woodcock and trout!"

The Judge flinched visibly under these harsh accusations and thereafter for some weeks the two friends conducted their affairs under truce. No mention was made of Bozo, the 'coon dog, but the Captain knew from the ghostly bellowings in the hills, where the cornfields were, no less than from the unwonted rheumatic twinges of which the other occasionally complained, that the Judge, while honorably pursuing legitimate game by day, was off nightly with the big dog in the clandestine chase of 'coon. Moreover there was about him at times a faint effluvia, the vaguest suggestion of a fragrance not of racoons or roses.

The Judge finally collapsed.

"Listen," said he desperately, one day while the two of them were at lunch in the Grapevine Cover. His old Scott, its figured Damascus barrels and dark wood gleaming dully, lay at his feet. "Listen, and don't be so darned intolerant. I've got the grandest 'coon dog in the county—I guess perhaps in the world! In a week's time we've bagged twenty-one 'coons!"

"How many porcupines and skunks?" inquired his companion coldly.

"Oh, not very many," said the other hastily. "The quills come out easy, and as for skunks if you wear overalls all you have to do is hang 'em over a bush for a few days. It's practically nothing. And believe me 'coon hunting is exciting! Grouse shooting," he considered, "has gone a little stale for me—I can't seem to get the old time thrill from it."

"How many days for the overalls?" asked the Captain rigidly.

"Three—or four at the very most—if there's a good frost every night," declared the Judge eagerly.

"You're fooling yourself," his companion assured him. "But your best friend will tell you! There you are, the Presiding Justice in gown and wig and, like enough, a flannel shirt and corduroys underneath, seated with the other dignified justices. The case is called: 'The State vs. Pecontic Power Company.' And there you are, I say, stinkin' of wild onions!"

"But, once a friend, always a friend, is my motto. I'll try it once, dull though it will be."

"You'll find you're wrong! It's exciting!" the other asserted. "You'll see! I'll pick you up at eight-thirty tonight . Got any overalls?"

"Yes," his friend replied, "but I'm not going to charge in on any skunks that your Hound of the Baskervilles picks a quarrel with! That 'coon dog! Phooey!"

The Captain found more cause for amazement when his friend pulled up in the driveway at the hour appointed. On the scuffed rear cushion of the ancient car sat Bozo enveloped in such an engaging atmosphere of dignity, eagerness, friendliness, and skunk as to almost send the Dark-Haired Lady into a mild hysteria. She got a grip on herself, however, when she noted the solemn, pathetic expression in the pleading eyes of both the Judge and his big dog.

"Why! He's a beauty! What a lovely head!" she exclaimed—and made another friend for life.

"And what's all this junk?" exclaimed her mate, surveying the contents of the car.

There were an automobile battery, presumably to be wired to a bulb and reflector tucked in beside it, and an old repeating shotgun which he had never seen before and which had long ago abandoned the last faint pretense to youth, together with any embellishments of varnish and blueing. There was, too, a bundle of Roman candles, gay in blue, white, and red paper coverings, that stimulated a justifiable curiosity, a jug of water, and a lunch basket.

"Goodby, darlin'," he addressed the lady, having finished the inspection, "if you ever see me again I'll be a changed man—I probably won't smell the same, anyway. Friendship! Hah! Excitement! Bah! *I'm* the bird who'll have to carry that fourteen-pound battery all over the Horn o' the Moon country! *That's* why I was invited!"

Their course led along the dirt road that followed the alder-fringed waters of the North Branch. A softly luminous moon hung low in the sky, encircled by a faint band of pale light which presaged rain even as did the doleful gusty hootings of the great owls calling their melancholy comments on the decayed state of worldly affairs one to another. Each solemn "Whoo-hoo-hoo-hoo-hoo-whoo!" was followed by several seconds of silence as if the recipient of these grave remarks required due time to digest their solemn import and to determine upon an appropriately grave reply. Rabbits bobbed their white scuts across the headlight beams, and occasionally the two friends perceived the vague color and motion of wings against the brilliance, but whether of owl or woodcock they rarely could determine.

At last they arrived at a spot where a cornfield set back into an angle of the creek, where elms draped with festoons of wild grape bent gracefully above the dark amber waters.

Bozo began rocking uneasily to and fro on his enormous front pads, his yellow eyes gleaming with restrained eagerness.

The Judge stopped the car and opened the door.

"Go find 'em!" he directed simply.

The big dog vanished instantly and silently into the luminous darkness.

"What do we do now?" asked the Captain.

"Nothing. If he gets a 'coon treed he'll holler. If he doesn't strike a trail he'll come back. Also if he finds a porcupine or skunk—God help us! But he won't bay for anything but 'coon, and then only when he's treed."

"Why don't you break him of skunk and porcupine?"

"Can't," was the reply. "Did you ever know a bird dog, even a field trial champion, that wouldn't go full throttle on a rabbit if he thought you weren't looking? 'Coon dogs are no different."

He filled his pipe and lighted it, his rugged, kindly, intelligent face showing briefly in the flare of the match.

The Captain sought the solution of another mystery.

"What are the fireworks for?" he wanted to know.

"To move 'em," explained the other. " 'Coons will hide in a tree so you can't shine 'em with a spotlight, but a Roman candle stirs 'em up so you can see 'em."

"What a fine, dignified sport," observed the Captain. But he listened nevertheless for some indication coming through the wall of darkness that the big dog had treed game.

None came, and after a while Bozo himself trotted across the ridged field, climbed to the rear seat and licked his chops impatiently.

The Judge started the car.

"Try it farther along," he remarked.

Twice more the same procedure was repeated, and still Bozo had not broken his sphinx-like silence. After each dark mute adventure, he returned and with the same air of knowledgeableness climbed to his perch, spun a red tongue around his broad chops, and waited impatiently to be transported to new fields of opportunity.

Finally they arrived at the edge of The Horn of the Moon, a mountainous, almost mythical wilderness seldom penetrated by any but the most adventurous deer hunters—and by them for only brief periods each season. Here again Bozo vanished on silent pads. The Judge had an air of tension about him.

"Excitement?" the Captain complained querulously. "Here it is darned near to midnight and not a thing yet! Not even a skunk! I'd be glad even of a skunk if he didn't stink. . . ."

The Judge stopped the objection with an upraised hand.

"Listen!" he commanded. "Hear that? Hear him! Hark to him! Bozo's got him! Grab that battery! Come on! Yi! Boy! Sic him, feller!"

Across the moonlit silences rolled a brave, majestic organ note—a glorious, exultant sound. To save his soul the Captain could not have checked the sudden prickle of his skin or the cool and airy feeling at the base of his skull. The snap of a hostile rifle bullet could engender that same light, strange, transient feeling of adventure. Responding to it, he went over the side of the car in a bound with a bundle of Roman candles in one hand and the heavy battery in the other, striving to follow a pudgy will o' the wisp who carried only a flashlight and a shotgun and displayed a tremendous deerlike agility in fleeing over frosty meadows and vaulting stump fences.

Hampered and confounded by the heavy battery, the Captain became aware that the distance between himself and the Master of the 'Coon Hound—who now himself seemed to be running free on breast-high scent—was increasing. Gradually the tiny splashes of radiance from the other's flashlight weakened and faded. Presently they disappeared entirely. In the ensuing gloom the Captain ran full tilt into a wire fence and was thrown heavily for a loss of a yard or two. Thoroughly roused now, he rose to his feet. Grunting with rage he heaved his fourteen-pound incubus furiously over the fence in a manner to test its maker's most optimistic claims for its durability, and clambered over after it. He was filled with an almost intolerable bitterness.

"Wish the whole Supreme Court could see him!" he muttered. " 'Coon huntin'! Hell! He ought to be impeached for this night's work!"

Above the sounds of his own panting, painful progress he heard the voice of Bozo, and in spite of his impotent rage he thrilled to that compelling resonance. And now there were other sounds from the direction whence the flashlight had last been sighted—wild, shrill and eerie plaints which he finally identified as being the view halloo of his stately friend, the Judge.

"Gone completely wild," he thought disgustedly, as he trotted down a frosty declivity that somehow seemed familiar. He knew why an instant later when he stepped abruptly off a grassy edge into four feet of icy water.

"Belden's Brook, by the Black Bull o' Bashan! And the very hole where I took that three-pounder in May!" he gasped as he doggedly hauled the battery out on the opposite shore and resumed the pursuit with his wet breeches slapping wretchedly about his thighs.

But yet another thrill awaited him before he was to reach the spot where by now the 'coon dog and the Judge had joined voices in the most unearthly duet ever listened to by the affrighted denizens of The Horn of the Moon. It came when, encountering a seven-rail fence, he painfully hoisted the battery to the top rail and as painfully climbed up after it. Swinging his long legs across, he seized the hateful burden and leaped.

He landed upon something warm, slippery, and vigorous that leaped at the contact and let out a tremendous "Baw!" It scared the poor burden bearer into a cold shudder and kept him there until he had time to realize that he had probably landed full upon a specimen of someone's "young cattle" which at this season of the year roamed the hills like deer.

Guided now and greatly encouraged by the nearer yelpings and bayings of the Mister Justice and his dog, he staggered forward a few yards to where a strip of mingled hardwood and evergreen came down a hillside. At a little distance within the nearer edge, a great hemlock raised its shaggy column to the darkness overhead. The feeble stabs of light from the Judge's torch did absolutely nothing to relieve the quiet, brooding mystery of the upper branches.

To one side Bozo, gaunt and strange in the dim reflection, sat on his haunches. His mouth was open, his eyes ablaze, and he sang his serenade well and truly.

"Where the devil have you been?" inquired the Judge impatiently.

"Don't tempt me to speak! You false rogue!" the victim grated. "Git your 'coon! Go ahead an' git him! And then, when you've got your ringtailed squaller, I'll tell you something about yourself and about where I've been with your confounded battery! Right now I wish't you had it hung on your neck like a millstone to be cast into outer darkness!"

"No sense in gettin' excited," the other reproved him. "Your citations are confused and misquoted anyhow! Get it connected up now and turn the spot up into that tree! Looks like a den tree. Bozo's about crazy—probably half a dozen of 'em up there. Hurry it up! Never saw you so awkward! Not tired, are you?"

"No, sir! Not a bit, sir! It really wasn't any trouble, sir! Swimmin' the creek yonder with that cute little dingus was fun—and falling on top of one of Proctor's yearlings. It was awfully amusing! Ready now, sir!"

"Thought I heard something blat," said the Judge absently. "Thought it was you, however. All right! Snap it on!"

A narrow beam of intense white brilliance shot upward into the gloom of the hemlock's branches and began slowing searching every lofty green cavern.

"Not a shine," the Judge remarked finally. "Move it around to the other side and try it."

This maneuver brought no better success.

"Set the spot down and try a candle up in there," directed the pudgy sportsman. "The dog knows. He's got 'em. The candle will move 'em."

The Captain obediently picked up a candle, found a match and stuck the damp fuse into the flame. It responded with a smoky hiss, a sudden shower of golden sparks, and a whizzing ball of red fire that missed the Judge's intent upturned face by inches, and brought from him an instant expostulatory roar. Then the Captain began sending the hissing wads of flame methodically up among the branches.

"Just like an old time Democratic caucus," he observed caustically. "Spotlights, torches, fireworks, and a dumb, silver-tongued orator. Hold on! There's something moving up there! See that limb shake?"

"That'll be one of 'em! Douse the candle and put the spot on that limb. That's the way, right next the trunk!"

The glare picked up two blood-red pin points about thirty feet up, sparks of angry ruby against the solid green of the hemlock fronds. A low, menacing mutter of sound came to their ears, whereat Bozo's harmony rose to a new and tragic note.

The Judge looked at his friend.

"That's no 'coon," said he solemnly.

"Darned right, it ain't!" was the reply. "It's a bear, and an almighty big, mad one, too! I can see him now! And here we are with a mess of Roman candles and a handful of birdshot loads! Well, if he takes a notion to come down and join us in our jolly rambles I'm going to let him carry the damned battery!"

"Listen!" exclaimed his friend, fumbling among his pockets. "I've got a round ball cartridge somewhere—and here it is!" He held out a frayed pink case with a dull glint of rounded lead showing through the wad.

"Get it into the gun then," the Captain directed without any enthusiasm. "And," he added grimly, "don't you *miss* him! Hanging out your overalls over a bush won't help us any if that feller gets amongst us. Guess probably the shoulder is the safest place with one of those slugs. Wait, and I'll set the spot on him."

He did so and came back to the Judge, who was preparing for the shot while Bozo's voice, now that the game was sighted, rose to fearful ecstasies.

The Judge raised the gun and brought the front sight against the dark, menacing mass in the tree.

There was a brief spurt of bluish flame and the whang of the gun. The bear roared and lurched, and then pitched downward out of the single beam of the spotlight into the darkness. The startled hunters heard the crash of branches, a heavy thump, a roar of rage, mingled with the courageous growl of the dog. A ferocious bedlam burst up and lasted for a space of seconds. The spotlight meanwhile squirted its useless beam among the branches, leaving the actual battlefield in a blackness made only blacker by the contrast.

Then there was a yelp of pain and something thudded against the Judge's sturdy legs. Under the shock he reeled, and seemed to hover in midair for an instant before he collapsed into a thicket. His gun flew from his hand and its barrel landed across the Captain's skull with a crack plainly audible above the vicious sounds of flight and combat. The gentleman promptly recovered his wits and snatched the weapon, instinctively jerking a fresh load into the barrel with a single lightning-fast motion. And barely in time, for a vague, dark thing shot toward him and ran full against the gun's lowered muzzle. At the impact he pulled the trigger. He had a feeling as if he had been brushed by a comet's tail or some equally irresistible cosmic force; his feet left the ground, and then he was tangled up with the Judge in a hardhack thicket in a breathless, nightmarish sort of struggle. When he tried to get up the Judge tripped him, and when the Judge struggled to rise they both went down together. Meanwhile the sound of deadly combat continued to make the place hideous. The spotlight steadfastly played its pure and peaceful beam into the hemlock.

Momentarily expecting to have a raging bear upon him, the Captain with a final frantic effort tore himself free of his trammels and rose to his feet. He groped for the gun, found it and reloaded hastily, wishing fleetingly for something more potent than a bird load in this crisis. Then he found the spotlight reflector and turned the beam of light upon the spot whence came the bitter, muffled snarling sounds. It disclosed the bear, dead as a door nail, with Bozo, gashed and bloody, valiantly endeavoring to shake the pelt off his recent adversary.

Reassured, the lean sportsman next turned his attention to the Judge who still lay where he had fallen. He, too, had ceased to struggle, but stifled moans came from his compressed lips. A chill fear smote the Captain.

"Are you hurt, Judge? Are you hurt?" he asked. It seemed an age before he could get the light where he needed it, and before he heard the voice of his old friend, curiously hushed and strange.

"I believe I am, Boy. It's my back. I can't get up or move my legs. They feel sort of cold and numb. I guess, old friend, I've gone 'coon hunting once too many times."

"My God!" implored the Captain. "Don't say that! Let me look!"

On the stricken fields of France he had never stooped to a wounded man with the dread that now assailed him as he bent above the Judge and began a careful examination, to which the older man submitted quietly and with calm courage.

He completed the examination.

"Steady now!" he admonished as his competent hands sought for a purchase. "It's got to be done but I'll try not to hurt!"

There was a swift twist, a tug, and the victim felt the dreadful constriction relax. Then, to his amazement, his friend let out a whoop that was anything but lugubrious, and rolled over in an unseemly spasm of shouting mirth.

"That's no way to behave in the awful presence of Death," protested the Judge in shocked, vigorous indignation. "What's the matter with you?"

"Nothing's the matter with me—nor with you, either! Get up if you want to—you can—your back ain't broken! You just had a hardhack sapling twisted through your belt! Oh! Dear! Dear! And no wonder you felt cold—you haven't any more pants on you than that cherubim in the window of the Congregational Church! You're bare as a bullfrog! That bear must have slapped 'em off in one swipe! There ain't a scratch on you, but from the waist down you look like an orangutan in a zoo."

"I suppose that's what I ought to expect from going 'coon hunting with a fool," snapped the Judge as he rose slowly to his feet.

Sometime later, in the small hours of morning, when the Judge was once again decently clad and the big bear had been hung safely in the woodshed in readinesss to receive the admiring inspection of the inhabitants of Tranquillity Village in the morning, the Captain sat with his friend over a cup of hot coffee in the latter's library. His left hand rested on Bozo's tawny head while the big dog worshiped him with his yellow eyes.

"It's more fun than I thought," said he addressing the Judge. "I apologize for everything I said about 'coon hunting. You said it was exciting, and, by Criminy, you proved it!"

His fingers stroked the wide, high arch of Bozo's skull.

"You've got a grand dog, Judge."

"Do you want him?" asked his friend.

"What!"

"I said, do you want him! Are you deaf? He seems to have taken up with you—and I doubt if I go in much for 'coon hunting hereafter. I want to live out my days in peace and quiet with woodcock and trout. Take him, Boy, he's your dog. I feel that I'm lucky to get out of this dangerous business!"

THE CAPTAIN
VISITS
MR. NASH

There is within the boundaries of the hospitable State of Arkansas a vast region the title to which is clouded. The land itself, partially protected from inundation by a series of levees built many years ago by the patient labor of those humble collaborators, the Negro and the mule, is but little higher than the level of the yellow Mississippi that sweeps majestically between its low shores. Behind these earthworks there is an infinitude of cotton field and cypress swamp, cane-brake and willow-fringed slough. There are able advocates who urge that the title to this rich realm, with its miles of ragweed and sedge, briar-choked gullies and old corn and cotton fields, rests with Bob White, with reservations in the deed in favor of the wild turkey, the woodcock, the squirrel, and the rabbit. Other eminent authorities, armed with proper credentials furnished by the State Game Department, have spent long, pleasant hours upon the sloughs and willow pockets, or about the rice fields, securing evidence to show that the domain is actually under perpetual grant to the webfeet, with all other resident game birds, beasts, or fish, in the role of squatters.

Our friend the Captain wandering far from his Vermont hills had no intention of offering himself in any partisan attitude when, in company with "Mister Nash," he invaded the debatable ground for the first time on a certain crisp November evening. The car boomed over the thick planking of a long causeway which carried them above the levee and the borrow-pits and then with an agreeable low song took to a wide cement highway. No veteran gunner would need to consult the calendar to know that it was the shooting season. The air that poured in through the window beside the driver's seat was cool and sweet with a fragrance that one associated only with ripened autumn. It smelled of purple fox-grapes, of frost-stricken marshes, of resting earth. The lights of the car flowed swiftly across long ridged fields, where the dark stalks clung forlornly to a few bedraggled dabs of cotton, overlooked when the dusky skirmish lines of pickers had passed; it glanced superficially along the oaks and gumtrees fringing the dank swamps, but its shallow bravery could not penetrate the gloomy depths where pools gleamed black among the roots, and 'coon and 'possum went about their vague affairs. Not so many years ago, so Nash informed his friend, the only means of ingress to this vast region was by horse or mule over narrow mucky roads, winding half-submerged beneath a high canopy of unbroken forest. The yell of the wolf-pack might then be heard at night, and bear, deer, and turkey could be taken within a few miles of the mighty river by any gunner sufficiently persistent to penetrate the region. Even now, for all that it is spanned with broad ribbons of cement and gravel, the region still keeps unimpaired its ancient atmos-phere of isolation and mystery—the subtle spirit (not wholly friendly) of a do-main so essentially wild that it ignores all evidences of a blatant and insecure domestication. These great southern lowlands have this ancient patience in common and an infinite brooding philosophy that awes a sentient person and impresses him with the disquieting thought that man may be, after all, but a vexatious interloper, a transient plague, doomed to ultimate banishment when a quiet and orderly Nature grows tired of his noisy confusion.

After a time, the car turned into a gravel road and finally, having crossed over a star-sprinkled lagoon on a narrow wooden bridge, came to a full stop. With guns and shell bags looped over their shoulders, the two companions set out to finish the journey on foot, slipping and stumbling and splashing into puddles and gathering great clots of the plastic clay on their boots. There was a good half mile of this.

"Why not have a few loads of gravel dumped on your road?" inquired the Captain.

" 'Sweet are the uses of adversity!' " Nash explained. "If shooting is too easy to get, it's not likely to be appreciated, or else it's apt to be overshot. We find we enjoy our shooting more if we have to wade through a little real mud to get to it."

But the clubhouse offered an ample reward of comfort to every persevering Christian who crossed this Slough of Despond. In the big room a fire blazed and filled the place with the aromatic fragrance of resinous pine. Jennie, the cook, curtsied a welcome to them from her post near the stove and turned hastily again to her bubbling pots and sizzling pans. Big Jim, who was little and very black, and Little Jim, who was very big and very black, lifted their burdens from the two gunners and discoursed about the ducks.

"De pockets in back o' Numbah Ten blin' is jes' bilin' wid mallets," they reported. "Lots o' teal an' gray ducks, too. Spec' you gen'lemen gwine ter have a sho nuff duckshoot come mawnin'."

The clubhouse stood under the shelter of the live oaks, within a few yards of the worn landing where the light ducking skiffs were tied. From the porch the Captain could hear the soft murmur of the negro voices within the cabin and the occasional screech of a hot skillet as Jennie assisted a plump teal to-ward a crackling biscuit-brown and entirely glorious destiny, but above these homely sounds came the thrilling swish and whicker of wild wings, as flock after flock of fowl swept in from the river and cut down aslant the looming cypresses. Presently from out the murk would come the unmistakable throaty gabble of welcome, followed by the long, sustained splash of the flocks alighting and the confused pattering roll of thousands of feeding birds.

Long before daylight next morning, Big Jim tiptoed into the room with an armful of pine splinters. These he arranged against the backlog so expertly that it was but a matter of minutes until flames were roaring up the black throat of the fireplace and beating back the frosty air that flooded the room from the open windows. Nor did this conclude his kindly ministrations. He went out and returned immediately with a pot of steaming coffee, which the gunners drank sitting up among the blankets. This commendable custom, the guest reflected, as he sipped the hot and fragrant brew and felt the rising tide of courage in his veins, is probably traditional in a land where dueling had flourished, and where etiquette still requires coffee to be served to gentlemen before gunpowder.

The light was gathering as Little Jim paddled the skiff across the narrow strip of open water. Coots skittered from the course, to splash back into the water and resume feeding almost within reach of Jim's pushpole. A gang of geese rose from the water and filled the quiet environs with their strangely thrilling clangor. Anhingas, or water turkeys—by no means the least picturesque of our water birds—passed overhead. Then the skiff entered the gloom of the cypresses—great trees with spreading boles ten or twelve feet in diameter at the water line. And now the mallards and bluebills began getting up in front of the gunner and his paddler and vanishing down the dim and misty aisles of the swamp. A great fat greenhead and his sober mate sat cozily on a log and calmly observed the approach and passage of the boat.

"Deecoys," explained Little Jim. "Dem birds done got loose from de stools an' jes' hang 'round. Dey ain't ezackly wil'—an' yit you jes' cain't *quite* cotch 'em, nuther!"

A little farther, and they came upon three more of these noncombatants, and these also sat quite unperturbed, though the skiff passed within ten feet of them and though their wild kin were everywhere leaping to noisy flight before the invasion.

"Deecoys," said Jim laconically again.

Beyond the heavy belt of cypress they came then to a wide fen covered to the depth of a foot or two with murky water, in which grew irregular patches of cane, and here and there, towering above the lesser tangle, a clump of lofty willow trees. The place was threaded with an intricate weaving of narrow canals, twisting in every direction, and the water was thick with a loose, submerged mat of coontail moss.

Number Ten blind was a comfortable stake and platform blind built into the cane at a bend in one of these canals. Across the pool a clump of great willows fronted the stand.

Little Jim began placing the stool and had been thus engaged for five minutes when the Captain observed a great goose walk quietly out from beneath the blind ten yards distant and eye him with a polite curiosity that was certainly equal to his own. Just so would you exchange perfectly courteous glances with some distinguished-appearing stranger whom you have encountered in your club—his easy assurance, his every indication of good breeding and poise, convince you of his right to be where you have found him, in your own familiar, exclusive haunts. This goose, a noble bird, looked the Captain fairly in the eye with just that precise degree of friendly reserve that is the visual signal of respectability. The Captain had the impression that the goose was rather pleased to see them than otherwise, and that if he spoke he might say:

"Good morning, sir. Have I your chair? By the way, your man doesn't happen to have a spare handful of corn about him?"

The Captain said:

"Jim, shove that sack of corn over here. This decoy looks hungry."

"Yas, suh," replied Jim, busy with a snarled tether. Without looking up, he obediently gave the sack a shove with his foot. "Us'll feed 'em all jest so soon I git 'em staked out."

At this, the great goose turned quietly to right face, took three long, easy, nonchalant strides, and went aloft in a crashing tumult of beating wings, shredded moss, and flying water. It seemed to the astonished sportsman that the sturdy canes bent before the mighty momentum of that passage. Certainly he had never seen a bigger goose—nor a wilder one.

The uproar galvanized Little Jim.

"Shoot! Shoot!"

But the twenty-bore lay empty in the rack under the narrow decking of the skiff, and Wild Bill Hickock himself could never have handled the gun fast enough to load and catch the departing bird. After the first three seconds of dismay and confusion were over the Captain felt more relieved than otherwise over the bird's escape, for he thought such gallant bluffing deserved success. Undoubtedly the goose had been surprised while feeding on corn scattered for the decoys underneath the blind. Without room sufficient for a take-off, the bird had studied the situation, accepted the hazards, and walked boldly out to where he could get distance to spread his mighty pinions.

The tumult died. The Captain looked at Little Jim.

"Thought he was another decoy."

"Gettin' right in de blin'," said Jim wonderingly. "Dat goose cert'nly gittin' amiable. My! My!"

Nash joined them, and climbing into the blind the two friends set up their guns and arranged the cartridge bags. Nash specialized on extreme range, and his weapon was a double twelve-bore, long and heavy, chambered and regulated for the big three-inch cartridges loaded with progressive powder and the new copper-plated shot. And well he could handle it!

Little Jim had scarcely backed his skiff into the cane beside the blind when a pair of mallards came into view high above the willows.

"Heah dey come!" warned the Negro.

"I'm going to take 'em!" Nash whispered, eyeing the birds carefully as they swung to a line that would bring them over the blind. They looked to be a hundred yards high, but they were nearer sixty yards up.

Nash slowly raised the big gun, and Jim, distressed, began pleading for delay.

"Don't shoot, Mistuh Nash! Dem birds gwine ter come right in! Cain't hit 'em way up so high! Don't—"

"Whoomp! Whoomp!" the big gun interrupted positively.

Even at that distance the Captain saw distinctly the puffs of flying feathers—practically sure evidence, where ducks are concerned, of a clean kill—and down and down, whirring like a pair of bombs dropped from an airplane, came the two mallards, as dead as any two ducks that ever were fairly centered at thirty paces.

"Oh! Mistuh Nash! Oh! My gosh A'mighty!" exclaimed the astonished paddler, staring incredulously at the dead birds tossing on the waves set up by their impact.

Later the Captain overheard him telling Big Jim about it in the cook-shack.

"De No'the'n gent'man handle dat little gun right brief, but Mistuh Buck he gone an' got himself one o' dem Andy aircraf' guns lak us boys had in de war. He don' require to know nothin' 'bout a duck 'cept dat it's in Arkansaw. Um hum! Jes' so dey's on dis side ob Mississippi Ribber, he sho' is able to carry 'em down!"

Except for certain flocks of wary mallards or widgeon reconnoitering the slough from high in the air, the two gunners could rarely see the ducks until they were almost upon them. The walls of cypress, the thick clumps of willows, and the masses of cane effectually limited the vision, and low-flying fowl carried out their preliminary maneuverings in complete concealment behind these natural masks. At one instant not a bird would be in sight, save, perhaps, the indifferent coots squattering and bickering across the pool, and then, wings whistling with speed, a flock of teal would press like a flight of arrows—almost too swiftly for the eye to follow. Or the watchers would be twitched out of a lazy, gossiping interlude by a sudden roar of wings and a belated volley of quackings and hissings from the unready decoys, and here would be a dozen big mallards rushing down upon them over the ramage of willows, their wings already cupped and bodies rocking expertly as they slowed to landing speed. Nine times out of ten, the gunner who had been trained on canvasback, redheads, and scaup on coastal waters would level on one of these poised birds with a feeling of utter, careless competency—and drive his load of shot some three feet over and behind the deceptive target, for the trick of leading an accelerating target is easy compared to that of synchronizing with a target that is losing speed as abruptly as a mallard can manage it. With the crack of the right barrel for his cue, the mallard instantly reverses the problem for the gunner, and one must then deal as best he may with a duck that almost between flash and recoil seems to have leaped upward a sheer fifteen feet. Between overshooting the unsuspecting incomers and undershooting the highly informed and physically able outgoers, full many an ounce load of chilled sixes accomplished nothing more sanguinary than shredding the willow foliage or raising a brief white welt on the surface of the pool.

Nash, exhibiting a perfect knowledge of his weapon, as well as a sporting and entirely commendable sense of proportion, limited his shooting to an artistic performance on long-range ducks, where the combination of specially bored gun and heavy shot load and a highly developed shooting skill found problems equal to these extended abilities. The Captain endeavored to deal humanely with such "brief acting" fowl as came to closer ranges over the decoys. And if in trying to apply Currituck principles of gun pointing to Arkansas problems he missed about as many as he hit, he at least found consolation in the reflection that a greenhead alive and on the wing is a joy to the sportsman and to the artist as well, while dead and in the bag he is nothing more or less than a feat accomplished—something now to be plucked, broiled, and eaten.

The sun poured warmly into the sheltered pocket in the cane, and for once the Captain questioned the regal supremacy of the canvasback and thought without regret of ice-coated blinds on the Potomac where, quilted like a Tartar against the furious cold wind that scalds an exposed cheek like hot steam, he had watched great squadrons of the big birds winnowing across a wintry sky and found cause also to wonder at the stubborn fortitude of the ducks and of those who gun for ducks in such weather when the latter might, were it not for this perversity of character, sit before an open fire and read a book.

Club regulations—and they take their edicts quite as seriously, if not as flamboyantly, as Mr. Mussolini takes his own—require all shooting to stop at noon. Though you visit this club with letters of introduction from the greatest and the best, and though you lack one bird when the whistle blows—and he just trimming his sails to cut across the decoys—you will be well advised to open your gun, extract the charges, and prepare to depart with cheerful grace. And one should not mistake the purport of the mild statement prohibiting the sending of a pusher into the club's refuge areas to drive ducks out to the blinds, or the request that each gunner make every effort to prevent the escape of cripples, for beyond indicating the sovereign wishes of generous and hospitable hosts, these simple rules are effective in maintaining a sort of earthly paradise for ducks. Very probably if a guest exceeded his limit, or shot that last bird, or violated any of the other rules, nothing would ever be said about it to him, but he would never, never, never again be invited to sit in Number Ten while the teal swished down the canal.

It lacked a scant two minutes of quitting time when Nash tilted the long barrels of the Swamp Angel and centered a single greenhead a good twenty yards above the top of the tallest cypress. It was a most spectacular shot. The heavy bird whistled earthward, and landed in an explosion of empty buckets, slats, paddles, and decoy crates in the bottom of Jim's skiff. An Austrian whiz-bang might have done more damage, but it could scarcely have made more of a racket.

"Mistuh Nash! Please, suh, don' send dis boy no mo' manna f'm on high! Reques' dat big gun please to cast de bread on de water. Eff'n dat duck lan' in my lap I ain't gwine ter have a thing on but a coat and vest, an' dat's de truth!"

"I never saw a duck placed better," Nash remarked with a grin, "except once down on Horseshoe Lake when Hamp Long landed a big duck bang into a cooking fire where Uncle Horace was broiling bacon. Horace was shooting a muzzle-loader that trip, and he thought his powder flask had let go. It rained coals and sowbelly for three minutes. Pick 'em up, Jim, for it's quitting time, and I'm hungry enough to eat the knobs off a four-poster!"

OLD MAN RIVER'S GEESE

"Jesse! Oh! Jesse!"

"Yassuh!"

"Jesse!"

"Yassuh!"

"Jesse!"

"Yassuh, Cap'n!"

"Jesse! Don't you—don't you—" began Mr. Bill Wickens in stern portentous tones, but having by that time forgotten his original purpose was forced to pause a moment to reflect. "Don't you stand oveh there an' holler 'yassuh' at me! You come oveh here and build this fire!"

"Yassuh, Cap'n!"

The chief goose-hunter from his cot beside the door said "Damn!" and then muttered in somber tones, "He'll take his own sweet time about it, too! If I yell again he'll just say 'Yassuh!' "

In the darkness of the bunkhouse someone sniggered.

Silence then, except for the low slumberous bass of the mighty river's voice as its ceaseless current swepty past the landing, and the confused eerie gabble of wild fowl on the sandbar opposite the island. The more experienced wildfowlers dropped off again into light, exquisite "cat-naps," well knowing that this premonitory uproar was nothing in itself and that the true awakening of the camp would not follow for a good fifteen or twenty minutes. Jesse, over in the cook-house under the live oak, knew it, too, and "took his own sweet time" about whatever it was that he was doing. He had the Negro's sure understanding of his own particular white folks; he was certain that nothing serious was going to happen for quite some time yet.

But a stone had been dropped into the still pool of sleep. The Judge awakened, stretched luxuriously beneath the warm blankets, and decided that this cozy, sleepy comfort was worth all the cold sand-pits and wild geese in the great valley. He weakly decided that he would not go out today. But instantly into his brain came a vision of the pit he had dug so cunningly the

41

evening before, his decoys set so artfully around it. He imagined a swishing of
wings, a confusion of great gray, black and white bodies as a flock of wild
birds swept over the ambush. His half-closed eyes flew open as the full power
of the hunter's heritage—more potent influence than Romany blood—worked
within him to wean him effectually from all backsliding.

Someone lighted a cigarette—the smoke mingling with the cold sweet air
had a curiously appetizing fragrance—and the host, roused by the flare of the
match from his brief doze to a sense of his neglected responsibilities and the
passage of precious time, shouted frantically again.

"Jesse!!"

"Yassuh!" replied Jesse, softly, meekly, and entering on the instant with an
armful of wood.

"Where in the devil have you been?"

"Bless Gawd, Cap'n, jes' gittin' dis heah kin'lings." Not a tremor of a
muscle or the flash of a white eyeball to indicate that the good-natured negro
had carefully arranged this daily mischievous little comedy and was enjoying
it thoroughly. "Brekfus' 'll be ready in 'bout ten minutes," he added blandly.
"Gent'men wants de coffee brung oveh heah?"

The gent'men did.

An ancient houseboat pulled from the waters of "Ole Miss' " and wedged
firmly among the trees of Rabbit Island made the comfortable headquarters
from which they debouched before dawn each day to make their campaign
against the wild geese along the Mississippi sandbars. There were eight of
them—their host, the Judge, the Captain, Mister Nash, two friends who lived
in the neighborhood, the negro cook and psychologist Jesse, and Alex, the en-
gineer and boatman.

Other than this and similar obscure references, history will probably have
little to say about gasoline-boat motors and the lonely, desperate battles between man and his invention that are fought before daylight at thousands of
landings on the lakes and waterways of the country each morning of the open
season on wildfowl. In the bitter darkness, and while Jesse was frizzling bacon
in the cookhouse, Alex rose and went grimly down the clay path to the landing, where he snatched the canvas from the engine. This act constituted the
challenge—it was the formal hurling of the spear into the enemy's territory.
The engine suffered the provocation coldly. Alex, with a far-away, preoccupied expression in his eyes, gazed off across the black water. But his
hands meanwhile were treacherously busy looping the starting cord like a
hangman's noose around the motor's neck. Suddenly Alex dropped his air of
indifference and leaped backward in the silent, ferocious gesture of the gar-
rotter. The engine, however, threw the loop deftly aside, belched a wreath of
evil vapor into Alex's face, and settled scornfully back against the stern. Its
motto seemed to be, "Let the starter beware!" and its expression beneath a
hirsute fringe of wires indicated that it believed Alex to be a poor, ineffectual,
deminition ass. Alex's introductory statements, low and passionate, were lost

in the turgid monotone of "Ole Miss'." At the sixteenth attempt the engine feinted Alex out of posiion by emitting a dozen promising coughs, and when that duelist lunged in to close the choke the motor pinched his hand in two places and burned it in three and retired into a wicked, gloating, supercilious silence. Up in the mysterious darkness at the head of the Island a "squinch owl" laughed—a sudden, sardonic, shivery sound—and Jesse, his eyeballs gleaming fearfully in the glow from the cook-stove, remarked piously:

"Mistuh Alex oughtn't talk so long an' so loud an' so sacramental. De 'Big 'Coon' walks jes' befo' de day pu'pos to fasten down on folks dat's bellerin' in sin. Um *hum!*" With an ear cocked for the final resounding periods of Alex's wild, distempered declamation, the darky summoned all able goose-hunters to breakfast.

A faint, unearthly glow like fox-fire washed the edge of the eastern sky when they finally gathered at the landing with shotguns and cartridge bags. The two live geese—the decoys—had their heads sticking alertly from holes in the sacks in which they were being carried to the scene of their histrionic triumphs. Now and then one of these birds pinched a button or a gunner's ear. In the latter case the owner of the ear released a thin, high scream and pranced about in the mud until the sting abated.

If one is interested in a minor agony that is shrewd and brief, let him leave a frosty ear on a frosty morning where a lusty goose can tweak it!

The host, unmindful of the pranks of his mischievous decoys, gazed at the dark murmuring flood that swept at their feet, as it once had swept at the feet of De Soto, and listened to its voice.

"It's a good river," said he, finally.

A "good river" meant that they would cross the narrow chute of water on the upstream side of a sunken willow tree—a "bad river," that they would cross below it. A small difference, apparently, but not to the trained rivermen who know the feline moods of "Ole Miss'." When such as they speak of the mighty stream they refer to it as *a* river, and not *the* river, for it is not today as it was yesterday. Daily, and almost hourly, "Ole Miss' " has a fresh and baffling identity. The natives study the delicate swirls, the broad, smooth eddies; they look twice at the choppy, brisk little waves that alone show where a mighty cross-current—powerful enough to drown a stout skiff—hides like a monster at the foot of a bar; they gauge the height of the flood and listen sometimes to the moist, smacking gluttonous sounds where the giant feeds on a mile of woodland or a fat field of cotton or cane. Any error in the reading of the lines and whorls of that great palm means to a certainty much wasted laborious effort—and it may mean death. To the stranger it is not conceivable that malignancy can hide beneath a skin so warm and brown and smooth. But there is the "Big 'Coon" who walks when the night is old—the fantastic thing, half real and half imaginary, half mischievous and half sinister, that plays tricks with bars, reefs, channels, chutes, eddies, and currents until at times the wariest old river-rat is utterly confounded and the careless one is drowned. Where yesterday the fat, sun-drinking mallards sat in a contented row and the sandpipers ran and bobbed and bowed on a white mile of solid sand, there is, perhaps, today a deep and sullen pool. Where the traveler crossed at sunset in safety the stealthy river ghost has hidden, in the night, a jagged cypress root and armed it with a still force to strangle a swimmer within arm's length of shore. The stranger cannot know the "Big 'Coon"—the cunning, pagan spirit of the ancient flood that plays now with a bit of drift-wood, like a yellow kitten in the sun, and in six hours may be leveling levee and forest, farm and town, in a thunderous, watery tumult of destruction—the "Big 'Coon" paddling on furtive feet over bar and bank from dusk until dawn—the "Big 'Coon"—the river ghost unseen by mortal eye, whose presence is felt only by Jesse and his kindred and by a few other simple, primitive folk who seek for wild geese at dawn upon the river bars.

Wherever the "working" river cuts a new channel across a bend—an incessant idle industry—it forms a fresh sandbar, and to those bars the wild geese come daily in the winter months to gather gravel, bask in the sun, and pluck at the scattered grasses that sprout in swift luxuriance wherever a clot of rich mud has lodged. The wise fowl bivouac in companies or battalions with pickets formally at their posts, while the veterans in the main camp doze, feed, or gossip, as do the soliders of marching regiments the wide world over. How these careful matters are arranged no man knows, but it is a fact that the birds rest precisely at the spot where any keen military strategist would have located a bivouac to insure it from surprise attack by land or from the water. Look long and clearly, and you will find that there is seldom a gully, ditch, or depression ending within long shotgun range of the flock that would afford cover to hide a creeping enemy. To get within shooting distance of these birds, so smart in the black, white, and gray of their regimentals, the gunner must truly rise from the earth itself. This fact actually defines the purpose of the goose-pit, the ordinary stragegy of the Mississippi goose-hunter.

The goose-pits had been dug the day before, trim holes five feet deep and two feet wide, the edges made flush with the surface of the broad sandbar. Mister Nash would share one noble grave with the Captain from Vermont. A set of profile decoys cut from heavy waxed cardboard and painted to resemble the wild bird were grouped sociably around the pit. One tethered live bird squatted comfortably on the sand ready to orate mightily whenever a wild flock should appear in the sky. She, with the inanimate decoys, gave the spot a salubrious appearance that was quite fictitious.

Once in the pit—and he endeavors to be there before daylight—the veteran gunner remains underground until sunset practicing the Indian art of patience. Yet this waiting is not monotonous. There are the geese moving about all day long, and every flock that comes in sight may be possible "customers." Ducks pass and repass on whickering wings—mallards, teal, widgeon, and bluebills—and some settle in the adjacent shallows. The river talks continuously, and the pit wall under one's shoulder transmits the vibrant, soft, rushing tread of the mighty marcher. Upon some men who hide the spark of profitless imagination in their souls, the river weaves a "conjur"; it coaxes such philosophical victims into a somewhat wistful contemplation of the stream's romantic history. Strange and grotesque the craft that have slipped downstream past that ancient headland. Strange have been their cargoes and stranger their crews. We know only that the mound-builders, and after them the Indians, passed here. The Spaniards, too, with their courtly graces and their bitter cruelties, their blades of Toledo and their horses shod with red copper, French soldiers and the stubborn English fighters, hardy American pioneers, rivermen, planters, gamblers in velvet waistcoats and cuffs of lace, armed with bowie and deringer, slave dealers, slaves, log rafts from far up the Ohio and Missouri, gun-boats—all these have passed where today you sit and watch the birds and the brown fluid tapestry of history slide past your ambuscade.

For some time after the two climbed down into the pit there was nothing to do but watch the rising colors of the dawn come pulsing up out of the east. Layer upon layer of mist lifted from the water and rolled back into a fleecy wall towering high over the island.

Jesse was singing as he washed the breakfast dishes and his fine baritone came across the water in an improvised relic of minstrelsy. The words were entirely unintelligible, but the air which accompanied the gibberish had a strength and dignity not unlike "Old Hundred."

"What's he singing, Nash?"

"He's singing about how 'he ain't gwine ter work no mo' fo' Mistuh Younce, c'ase he's so mean to me,' " translated the Captain's companion after listening a moment. "He's just singing what he happens to be thinking about—these country Negroes do that. They sing when crops are good," he added. "That kind of impromptu melody is a sure sign of a fat year."

A mallard drake came through the thinning fog with the deceptive velocity of an old-fashioned iron cannon ball—he appeared to be moving at a deliberate pace, but actually the bird was flying like an arrow from a hunting-bow—the calm air parting for his passage with a sharp hissing sound. In an instant he was but a diminishing speck upstream, and then he was gone.

An otter—a rare sight in this day—crossed the slough and slipped like a knife into a landlocked pool.

An unearthly shape now rose awkwardly from the shallow water near the foot of the bar, and with much grotesque difficulty gained balance and a slow level speed. As it passed up river by the pit it loosed a series of dolorous, distressful croakings—the inarticulate sounds, apparently, of a vast intolerable misery. If the Master of Purgatory includes in his awful domains a dismal, reeking bog beset with bottomless mire pits and steaming with dark noisome vapors lighted fitfully and fearfully with witch-fire where poor souls must flit eternally, then it was in such a spot and from such lost beings that this bird learned its dolorous note. The harsh discords spoiled the soft harmony of Jesse's song.

"Heron," remarked Nash, watching the bird. "He'll go upstream somewhere and stand in a slough all day long and spear fish. At sundown, back he'll come with a gizzard full and complaining like an old *bon vivant* with the colic."

But the heron in his unhappiness took nothing away from the splendid beauty and majesty of the river dawn as he, too, went his way with his javelin held straightly at rest and the broad blue vanes moving in slow suspended rhythm with the glow of the coming sun upon him. Behind the willows the morning mounted aloft in wider, deeper sweeps of glorious color. It seemed to the Captain that an invisible orchestra was massed behind the horizon, guided in this tremendous silent prelude by a perfect master of harmonies whose baton brought forth spurts and dashes and soaring tumultuous crescendos of color instead of sound.

And now at the proper moment from some "forlorn world" beyond the long wall of crimson vapor came a clear rally of trumpets, a wild motif introduced into the ecstatic scheme of the morning as one hears sometimes beneath the rich full tones of the instruments of the orchestra the warning voices of the violins carrying the first traces of a portentous theme that will presently overwhelm the pastoral music in an intensity of emotion. Of all natural sounds ever heard upon this earth the swelling clangor of a wild goose flock has more of that gypsy power to swell the heart and wing man's imagination than any other. It is music as old and sad as autumn, and as young and light and martial as spring—this crying from the sky of far forgotten things—this diminishing voice of a fading world once keen and salty with the sharp flavor of adventure. It is wistful and bold. Perhaps this sound has a deeper significance than we remember; perhaps it was this same high free trumpeting across the sky that first stirred man's imagination and led him out upon the dim, bitter, bloody path to immortality.

How, one wonders, can a man feel these things and still shoot wild geese? The Captain wondered, but he did not know. His companion felt it, too, for crouching there, gun in hand, he drew a deep shivering breath of ecstasy that came more from the beauty and mystery of the thing that surrounded them than from the fact that this wild flock might sweep over the pit in decent shotgun range.

Over the wreathing fog-banks appeared a line of dark objects. The stately waving movement of the birds is a surer means of identification than the traditional wedge formation of the flock, for many commoner species of wildfowl find the flying U as useful as does the goose.

The live decoy strode to the end of her tether and shouted a resonant greeting to the travelers. Her bold vociferations invited the strangers to còme down to the bar, but they were also a traitorous warning to the gunners to be ready with the guns. Standing erect, eager welcome expressed in every line of her body, the bland old sinner sent up a perfect gabble of unrestrained welcome to the wild birds, though she knew well what would happen if they came in range. In a bird that affords so many evidences of loyalty and family and flock affection as does the Canada goose, this duplicity is incredible. The rascally crow, a mischievous trouble-maker if there ever was one, will devote a happy half day to the baiting of a blind old owl—whom he hates with mortal hatred—but he will stop his malicious sport and undergo considerable trouble and risk to himself to warn of the approach of a man with a gun and to hustle his quondam foe out of danger. But the wild goose caught and partially tamed will cheerfully assist in the betrayal of his fellows and show unmistakable signs of pleasure and satisfaction when a victim comes plunging down upon the bar at the crash of the gun. The tethered one will then strut, gloat, and chuckle—a shameless feathered cynicist—over the culmination of a ruse that has been successful. Perhaps this demoralization of character—which is observable in live duck decoys also—is a result of association with mankind.

The clamor of the geese increased. With their eyes just at the level of the pit edge, the Captain and Mister Nash watched the flock and saw it slant downward on a long incline toward the sandbar.

"They're going to come in," Nash whispered, and the two sank to the very bottom of the pit to avoid any chance that the wary ones might see their white faces through the interstices between the clustered cardboard decoys. From then on they would have to follow the birds by sound alone, and it would need good judgment and cool nerve control to stay motionless in the bottom of the hole while that clangorous charge swept up the bar and over the decoys. The tethered goose was in a frenzy of hospitable shoutings, and the wild birds responded in a thrilling babble of sound. They swung down over the foot of the bar sweeping toward the pit up wind, like airplanes gliding down to a landing field. In five seconds the gunners were visited with enough breath-taking excitement to repay them for all the cold, dreary, dismal, and fruitless vigils that they had endured in seasons past. Even Nash, who had hunted geese for thirty years or so, was breathing hard, and the Captain was shivering like a spaniel and trying grimly to concentrate on the fact that a wild goose is always moving much faster than he apears to be, and one must therefore guard against this illusion when he leaps up to shoot.

The gabble was suddenly silenced, but the air was stirred by the "whiff—whiff—whiff" of mighty pinions.

"Now!"

As the Captain rose behind the slender barrels of his twenty-bore he seemed to emerge into the very crest of a wave of charging hussars who were on the point of overwhelming him and burying him in his pit as Napoleon's cavalry smothered in the sunken road at Waterloo. Out of the hurtling mass of birds he hastily selected one. "Spat!" The lethal sound was feeble, inadequate, and nearly lost in all the renewed shouting and tumult. But the stinging lead had bitten hard, and the victim staggered. "Spat!" and, majestic as a stricken ship, the great bird shuddered and plunged down upon the sand. Dimly the Captain was aware that Nash's great goose-gun had bellowed twice, and then the remainder of the squadron divided, flared off from the fatal spot, and swept away over the willows to safety.

"No man ought to shoot many geese," Nash observed as they crawled out to retrieve, "no matter how generous his opportunities. But every American ought to have one experience like this. It's the very exquisite, ultimate, clotted cream of river-shooting."

Other flocks, more wary, however, than the first, passed the gunners by or sometimes swung back and forth for long indecisive minutes across the bar. The men could tell from the maneuverings, as well as from the voices of the geese, that they were more than half persuaded. All of these finally decided against the venture and headed off to some lost pond in the willows, where at intervals throughout the day they raised a great babble over some incident of a nature unknown to the men in the goose pit. There was no more shooting, but at noon Jesse came out to the bar with hot coffee and sandwiches and while the two friends ate told them of his own gunning experiences, and in particular of the time when, awaking from a doze in the bottom of a similar pit, he found a goose standing on the rim and surveying him curiously.

"Did you get him, Jesse?"

"No, suh, 'deed I didn'! I thort dat goose wuz one o' Marse Wicken's decoys an' I talk to him confidential fo' a good five minutes on de strenth o' dat opinion. He ain't signify he wuzn't a decoy, an' yit he ain't declar' he wuz, an' I ain't suspicion nothin' ontwell he says 'Wauk!' an' sweep a mess o' sand down on me. When I is fin'ly organdized he's halfway to de point yander."

After a time the western sky behind the gum-trees and sycamores on Rabbit Island blazed in a fading crimson glory. Great flocks of waterfowl trailed like smoke across the glowing firmament on their way to their feeding grounds for the night. The heron, croaking and clanking like a wretched ghost, but flying like a slow-flung lance, came back to his perch on the shore. On the Island, Jesse rattled the stove lids and stoked the fire until the comforting gleams danced under the darkling leaves, and Alex, with his tamed motor purring like a rocket, cut his boat in a swirling arc across the "good river" and beached it at the waiting gunners' feet. The "squinch-owl" released his weird sardonic commentary on the dying day. And Jesse the cook, settling the coffee-pot with one hand, felt with the other for his "jack ball" to conjure up a foil against the malignancies of the "Big 'Coon" that walks jes' befo' day.

And that is goose-hunting. Something of the wild excitement of battle; something, also, of the fine, poised skill of the fly fisherman; much of expectancy, surprise, and disappointment; a flavor of fun; and the epic beauty and peace of a great brown river.

THE
SECOND BATTLE
OF GETTYSBURG

Aunt 'Tildy's latest delectation, consisting of batter-dipped partridge—each one a lump of fragrant succulence fried to the same pale bronze of the sedge fields where they had been found and slain the day before—had been gone for two hours. Aided by a heaping platterful of crisp potatoes, slices of cracklin' bread, muscadine preserves and a great pot of coffee fresh from the kitchen hearth, a full dozen of the delicious birds were now encouraging a drowsy contentment among the sportsmen as they sprawled before the fire in the "big room" at Red Knoll. It still lacked an hour of bedtime, even for men abroad all day following as keen a quartet of setters as ever were braced and tossed down anywhere in the lower valley of the Old Mississippi. The dogs had been fed, and their pads searched for thorns, the guns cleaned and tackle repaired, and now the gunners sat in a blissful and wordless contemplation of the joys that were theirs.

The door creaked softly to admit Uncle Horace bringing fresh firewood. Black as a boot was Uncle Horace, with a benign fringe of white wool encircling his wrinkled poll, and bent with the gentle burdens of four score happy, useful years. No more for him the duck blind when at dawn the chill fog sweeps across the rice-fields and the mallards are on the wing, no more for him the long days astride his mule, following his white folks and his dogs. But behind the old rascal's eyes, bright as a wren's, was stowed a treasury of wisdom, of recollection and philosophy so unique that its like was not to be found elsewhere in the world.

His advent, gentle though it had been, had roused them—perhaps this had been the old man's purpose to do. Having mended the fire, he withdrew, to reappear presently with a tray filled with illicit paraphernalia. With this he wrought deftly, measuring brown sugar and wringing lemon peel, and afterward presenting in a courtly flourish the results of his intricate labors.

Meanwhile, not a word had been spoken, but now, sipping the amber liquid, Mister Nash said:

"Uncle Horace, better fill another tumbler for yourself, pull up a chair, and tell us straightly the truth about that great dove shoot at Turkey Bend, to the best of your knowledge and belief."

"Thankee kindly, Mistah Nash, an' dat I will," replied the old Negro. Listening, it occurred to the Captain that Nash and Uncle Horace, guided by rare sympathy and understanding, had been subtly arranging events since suppertime to provide this moment and, moreover, to prepare the rest of them for it. There had been some casual remarks at the table about dove-shooting—insignificant bits of flotsam dropped here and there into the broad stream of the conversation—apparently without any more purpose than can be ascribed to the detached and seemingly unimportant stuff that floats by on the brown current of "Ole Miss'." But the Captain realized now that these bits, bobbing and eddying here and there, were somehow controlled by a deeper scheme; that there was, after all, a kinship among them like that of the flotsam of the river, a definite attraction drawing them all together to form at last an incident worthy of profound consideration.

During supper, Horace, serving Aunt 'Tildy's partridge, had joined in the discussion of the subject, spacing his comments respectfully between ladlings of gravy. The relative value of wheat, hemp or millet plantings as attractions for the birds, the best size of shot, and general lay of the field, and whether the gentlemen's breakfast should precede or immediately follow the morning shoot—Horace thought it should be served first—all these details received some judicious attention. It was obvious that neither Mister Nash nor Uncle Horace held much with modern practice—their memories turned fondly back to the traditional dove shoots of the deep South, when gentlemen came a-riding across misty fords before daybreak, each accompanied to the rendezvous by a servant mounted on a mule, carrying a Manton or a Purdey or a Greener or a Scott in its mahogany case slung across the saddle. The Turkey Bend shoot had been mentioned again with a customary absence of detail. For the Captain had heard of it before—a legendary affair occurring apparently about 1880, at which some extraordinary shooting had transpired. But all inquiries as to particular circumstances had always led nowhere; either they were lost on the mists of tradition, or else the inquirer had been led deftly away, like a whippet by a stuffed rabbit. The Captain had come finally to the conclusion that whatever the tale, it was not one to be unfolded for the ear of every passing stranger, and so with proper delicacy refrained from further inquiries. But Horace, it seemed, had witnessed the affair, and at last having satisfied apparently some initiatory requirements, the guests were now to be permitted to hear the story of the mysterious episode.

Uncle Horace sipped and sighed. The light from the hearth played across the old man's faded cotton shirt and raised dark, saintly gleams from his face.

"Um *hum!*" he began judgmatically, referring to the beady amber-colored mixture in his glass, "a mite more er lemon wouldn' weaken hit none. An' yit hit don' do t' monkey wid dese 'scriptions atta dey been 'stablished. Dat wuz

de kin' o' monkey-business whut caused de whol' o' de Turkey Ben' trouble—
a smart fat yaller N'Yawleans nigger defyin' de Scripture and foolin' wid de
ingrediments o' milk punch. 'Poly Jackson wuz dat boy's name, an' poly did
he do." A chuckle shook the old man's frame. "Marse Dave Fayston fotch
him up de ribber t' Red Knoll 'count o' he kin cook right good. I'se 'bleeged
to admit, suh, dat 'Poly boy, while he don' know nuthin' 'bout sho' nuff good
liquah, wuz right cunnin' wid er skillet. In p'tickler ef yo' gin him a han'ful o'
aigs, a couple o' t'maters an' some onions an' bacon an' all kin' o' no' count
odds an' ends, I boun' he'd shake out sometin' whut'd fotch a scairt 'possum
right outen a gum tree an' down amongst de dawgs. De smell o' dat dish
cookin' des' kind o' paralyzed a man—an' when yo' come to th'ow yo'self
upon hit wid a ladle in one han' an' a slab er hoecake in d'uther—well, suh,
dar yo' wuz! In all my days I ain't nevah met up wid no person, black er
white, male er female, dat kin transmorgrify hen aigs de way dat boy kin do.
Ner dey ain't nuthin' I evah comed across yit dat smell quite so appetizin' ez
onions an' aigs an' bacon an' N'Yawleans coffee early in de mawnin' er a
shootin' day."

Uncle Horace paused. It was obvious that to him who had sniffed these fragrances and fed on these viands, 'Poly's skill in Creole cookery was of a sort
deserving the tribute of a minute of respectful silence, like that by which the
Armistice and other great events of national importance are honored.

"Dove shoots wuz big doin's in de ol' days," he resumed, "an' all de folks
'ould rally roun' one fiel' er 'nuther whar dey had invites, long befo' daybreak
on de fus' day. Some yeahs de fus' shoot would be h'yar, sometimes us would
meet at Marse Priestly's at Bellevue, sometimes at de Breckenridge plantation, but wharevah hit wuz, us boys would be ridin' h'yar an' d'ah fo' days
carryin' 'pissles an' makin' 'rrangements fo' de big jubilee. Dove shootin', yo'
see, suh, sigmafied de comin' o' de season o' guns an' horses an' dawgs.
Pa'tridge shootin' and turkey shootin' an' deer an' fox huntin'—not t' mention squir'l an' 'possum hunts—an' de holidays, wid feasten' an' dancin', sho'
to be comin' 'fo' long!"

The old fellow indulged in another moment of meditation.

"Dat yeah," he resumed, "Marse Dave wuz holdin' de fus' shoot right
h'yar at Red Knoll. De ten-acre fiel' yant de bayou wuz standin' thick wid
late wheat, an' de full haids wuz jes' er bustin' down de stalks, an' de doves
wuz a usin' so thick look like you coulden' fi' inter 'em wid a one-ball gun
widout killin' a basketful.

"So Marse Dave, he tol' me t' git on a mule an' kerry invites to Marse
Priestly at Bellevue, an' t' Colonel Steve Breckenridge, likewise t' Colonel Bill
Sumner, an' t' young Bob Quinn—Marse Bob wuz er debbil fo' mischief—an'
likewise t' Major Jones an' ez many mo'. In de meantime, he had dis 'Poly
nigger and d'uther boys buildin' a fireplace in de live oaks next t' de fiel' an'
fixin' benches an' tables fo' de bobbycue.

"Den come up de question o' whut an' whar de eatin' an' liquidatin' wuz to occur.

" 'Poly,' Marse Dave sez, 'I b'lieve de bes' scheme is t' give de gent'men hot coffee an' milk punch so soon as dey 'rives, waitin' de reg'lar brekfus' 'til de buhds stop flyin' good, long erbout eight o'clock er dar' 'bouts.'

" 'Poly say, 'Yaas, suh!'

" 'An', 'Poly, git up a cask o' dat 1812 brandy—one o' dem kaigs whut wuz buried in de bayou bank endurin' de wah,' sezzee, 'when de confounded Yankees'—'scuse me suh—'when de confounded No'the'ners wuz a rampin' th'u dese parts a-seekin' whut dey kin devour, an' have it at de fiel',' sezzee. 'Let it be de prop an' mainstay uv de punch,' sezzee. 'Fo' de brekfus' dish, le's have dem aigs Creole, puhpa'ed wid onions, peppers, t'maters an' bacon—jes' dat an' nothin' mo'—un'nerstan'—but co'nbread an' hot coffee served in 'bunance an' pipin' hot. I aim to show de gent'mens a trick er two 'bout punch an dove shootin' an' aigs.'

"Well, suh, long fo' daybreak we wuz at de 'pointed place. 'Poly he had de fiah goin' brisk, an' ez fas' as de gent'men come ridin' in , dey would light down an' come to de blaze—fo' de air wuz middlin' sharp 'long de bottoms—an' we'd ladle 'em out de punch an' de coffee. Atta' while Marse Dave cut his eye to'des de East an' 'low hit time to take stan's. So de shootin' mens dey went on off th'u de woods to de aidge o' de fiel' whar dey places an' pickups wuz.

" 'Poly he watched 'em all go, standin' dar wid a drippin' punch ladle in his han', an' he say to me, sezzee, 'Ho'ace, dat pale lookin' liquah sholy mussa' done los' hits stren'th wid age. De folks done drunk up two buckets o' milk punch a'ready,' sezzee.

" 'Mebbe yo' right,' I tol' him, not payin' no p'tickler mind, 'but she allus done had plenty animosity up t' now. Boy, yo' better mix up 'nuther bucket, 'case when de gent'mens gits t' shootin' good dey gwine start hollerin' fo' reinfo'cements.'

" 'Dat I will,' say 'Poly."

A less knowing one might have thought Horace's sigh was for the tragedy of the spoilt brandy. But Nash, having more intuition, instructed the old sinner to replenish his glass. Having accomplished this, and having tested the fluid for reassurance as to the perfection of its proportions, the narrator resumed his tale.

"Well, suh, dat wuz de bigges' dove shoot evah in dis county. If'n de gent'mens hadn't got deyse'fs sidetracked, I b'lieve we'd ha' busted all de records fo' dove shootin' anywhar. I wuz pickin' up buhds fo' Marse Dave, an' I couldn' in no way keep up wid him. D'uthers wuz doin' 'bout ez well, an' fo' an hour de firin' wuz fas' an' straight. 'Poly kept plyin' the fiel' wid de punch bucket an' de ladle, an' 'twixt de shoutin' fo' 'Poly an' de shoutin' fo' boys to fotch shells an' de bangin o' de guns de 'casion wuz ez merry ez er camp meetin'.

"De fus' I notice anythin' wrong wuz when Marse Dave miss two single buhds, one right aftah d'uther. 'Bam—Bam!' an' 'bam!—bam!' agin, soon ez he could load—nice easy shots, too, dey wuz—an' Marse Dave ain't miss a dove befo' in ten yeah!

" 'Whut de debbil, Ho'ace,' sezzee, rubbin' his haid. 'I had dem buhds straight down de rib,' sezzee, 'de hull flock of 'em,' sezzee, 'bofe times.'

"I say, 'Yas, suh,' kinda wonderin' lak.

"De sun wuz up by dis time an' wa'm. De buhds jes' erbout ez thick ez bees, but dey ain't so many fallin', spite er de fact de shootin' des ez loud an' fas' ez befo'.

" 'Bout dat time I heah ole Colonel Sumner 'dressin' som' stray'nyus remarks t' Colonel Breckenridge. Dem two ain't quite so 'greeable ez mout be, 'count o' some diff'unce in 'pinion ez to who wuz h'yar an' who wuz dar at de Gettysburg fightin'. Ol' Colonel Sumner argify dat ef'n Colonel Breckenridge had suppohted him wid his big brass cannons on dat 'casion, he'd tukken de hull damn Yankee—'scuse me, suh—he'd tukken de hull damn No'the'n Army. Colonel Breckenridge nachully contend dat dis ain' so. Dey bin 'sputin' de point fo' twenty yeahs widout 'rrivin' nowhar.

"Well, Colonel Sumner he holler at Colonel Breckenridge, an' say, 'Hav' a care, suh, ef yo' please, whar at yo' is discha'gin yo' piece,' he say. 'Yo' done put a load widin two paces o' my stan', suh!'

" 'Suh,' 'sponds Colonel Sumner, 'ef'n yo' stay behine yo' tree, ez yo' did at de Gettysburg trouble, suh, yo' will be in no danger f'om my weapons,' sezzee.

"Marse Dave pacify 'em, fo' dey wuz bofe red an' bristlin' like a couple o' gobblers. An' we fin'lly gets 'em back to dey stan's widout neither challenges ner bloodshed. But bofe o' dem wuz pretty mad yit.

" 'Ho'ace,' Marse Dave say to me, 'dem two ol' gladiators ac' like dey is tight as bees; I b'lieves us'll do well t' watch 'em er us'll have de whole war over agin right h'yar in dis fiel',' say. 'Hit sho' look like dey is full ez ticks, but I don' see how come such—dey ain't took nuthin' but er few sips o' dat milk punch, an' hit cain't be dat a few ladles o' punch kin disturb gent'men ez dram-proof ez whut dem two is,' sezzee.

"So he kin' o' keep an eye on 'em fo' a spell.

"Presently he say, 'Ho'ace, looka h'yar, who is d'uther gent'man behine dat tree wid Colonel Breckenridge?'

" 'Nobudy, suh,' I say, 'nobudy but de Colonel.'

" 'Look agin, Ho'ace.'

" 'Not nobuddy, suh,' I tol' him again.

"Marse Dave say, sorter 'sprised, 'Zat so? Den, Ho'ace, I 'bleeged t' confess dey is sumpin' pow'ful odd 'bout dis h'yar business. Us bettah blow de brekfus' call an' cl'ar de fiel' fo' sumpin' happens,' he say.

"But jes' ez he say dat, ol' Colonel Sumner give a whoop an' slap his coat-tails like a bee stung 'im, an' th'owed down on Colonel Breckenridge's tree.—

'Ker bam!' say, 'take dat, you onpricipled ol' scounnel! Firin' into yo' own troops! or my name ain' Sumner!'

"Colonel Breckenridge mek haste an' retu'n de compliment wid his lef' barrel, an' in no time at all dey wuz yellin' an' cussin' an 'shootin' at one 'nother, p'int blank. Den somebody—I 'spect dat Quinn boy did it fo' pure debblement—put a load o' dove shot inter Marse Watson's tree, an' befo' yo' could spit dey's all at it. Bless Gawd de stan's is a good sebenty paces apaht, an' numbah eights ain't gwine t' do much damage at dat range—less'n o' co'se yo' gits one in de eye—but dey sho' do sting like de debbil, an' de mo' dey sting, de hotter de gent'mens gits.

"So fur, Marse Dave ain't engaged, an' he observe de proceedin's wid amazement, an' yit hit make him laugh, too, fo' it wuz sho' ridic'lous t' see dem white folks leapin' an' prancin' and cussin' an' shootin' wid de doves circlin' overhaid like dey wuz 'stonished at sech conduct. Hit am a fac' dat dey ain't no dignity 'bout a charge o' buhd-shot. Gent'men who kin be proud an' stately when pistol balls is flyin' des' boun' t' dodge an' squirm when folks gits t' slingin' dem little hot stingin' fellers.

"Marse Dave say, 'Us got t' stop dis, somehow,' sezzee. 'Those damned idjits gwine ruin dis shoot. Dar go Cap'n Bulwer openin' on young Quinn! How in de worl' did all dis git goin'? Look dar,' he say, p'inting, 'look at ol' man Priestly wid his ol' fo'teen-gauge muzzle-loader! He ain't shootin' so often ez de yuthers, but I d'clar he fetches a whoop an' a cuss ev'y time he do let go.'

"Soon he gits a new worriment. 'Ho'ace,' he say, over de roar o' de skirmish, 'some idjit gwine ter lose his haid in a minute an' start cuttin' ca'tridges like us do fo' deer shootin', an' den us gwine t' have a sho' nuff battle!'

" 'Marse Dave,' I say, 'listen t' me, suh, please. I knows whut'll stop dis massacree—brekfus'—dat fool 'Poly's Creole aigs, suh! De gent'mens is hongry, but dey so 'vigorated right at de present time dat dey don't know dey is hongry. Ef'n we kin git 'em a whiff o' dem aigs an' onions, dey'll come outer dey trance ez meek ez a 'coon kotched in er chicken roost.'

"De Cap'n say, 'By Judas, Ho'ace, I b'lieve yo' right! Do yo' reckon yo' kin make hit to de cookin' place wid'out drawin' fire? So fur,' he say, 'de 'sponsibilities of courtesy has 'strained dese gent'men from shootin' at dey host, but in dey present fix I dunno whether I kin confidently rely on my sacred neutrality er not,' he say. 'Ol' Man Priestly ain't puticulully kin'ly tow'ds me since Bluebell won over Sweet Dreams at de Steeplechase las' season, any how, an' I don' like to risk temptin' him wid a fair running target in de open. Howevah, dey kin be 'pended 'pon not t' shoot a boy—'thout some provocation,' he say, 'so you slip out er h'yar an' git to dat damn fool 'Poly an' tell him, fo' me, t' git his aigs an' onions an' fixin's t'gedder an' de bigges' skillet he kin fin'. Tell 'im t' fotch de coffee pot an' de charcoal burner an' assemble his fo'ces on de windward side o' de fiel'—yander live oak is 'bout right,' he say, feelin' fo' de breeze—'an' den to git at dem aigs Creole wid de utmos' dispatch er I gwine tek de seat off'n his pants!'

"So I done ez Marse Dave direct an' hot foot it over to whar 'Poly wuz at, an' gib him de 'structions.

" 'Poly say, 'Whut de debbil got inter dem gent'men. Dey went outer h'yar walkin' strict an' friendly ez er flock o' turkeys!'

" 'Well, de hull caboodle o' 'em got dey hackles riz now an' hit ain' no time t' relax,' I say. 'Yo' git dem aigs out dar an' de onions an' bacon an' coffee an' begin yo' fumigations.'

"Well, suh, we got de fixtures out to de fiel', an' dar under de live oaks 'Poly went to shakin' de big skillet an' soon de immortal fragrumce o' de Creole aigs wuz driftin' across de fiel' an' blendin' wid de smoke o' de gunpowder. De firin' had slacked, mostly 'case de gent'mens wuz runnin' sho't er ammunition an' dassent run out to git no mo'.

"When I wuz sure dat de fragrumce had got clear 'n down to Marse Priestly in stand Numbah Ten, we sounded 'Cease firin',' an' den blow de ol' Confed'rit brekfus' call.

"One by one de gent'mens come out, an' some ob 'em wuz limpin' a mite an' d'uthers wuz rubbin' deyse'fs, an' all ob 'em wuz lookin' mighty puzzled an' sheepish."

At this point, Uncle Horace paused to sup additional vigor. Flames purred about the logs, and outside in the frosty moonlight lonely "squinch" owls whimpered.

Reluctantly Uncle Horace put down his glass and resumed.

"Marse Dave say, 'Serve de aigs, 'Poly,' an' hit wuz done. Likewise de co'nbread an' de coffee. In all my bo'n days I never did see mo' vengeance done t' vittles, an' de mo' o' dem Creole aigs dey flung 'emselves eroun', de ca'mer dem gent'mens gits, an' de ca'mer dey gits de mo' sheepish dey 'comes.

"Finally Colonel Sumner riz himself up an' say: 'I am completely at a loss,' he say, 't' 'count fo' my ext'odinahy conduc' this mawnin', an' I desiah heah an' now to offer my humble apologies to our host, and likewise t' any gent'men who were present an' who may have sustained injuries, either f'om my langwidge er my fiah,' he say. 'Colonel Breckenridge, I 'pologize to yo', suh, in p'tickler fo' my unwarranted heat an' violence, an' I furthuh desiah t' say dat on de Gettysburg 'casion yo' conduc' wuz exemplary, suh. De position an' strength o' de counfounded Yankees'—'scuse me, suh—'o' de confounded No'the'ners wuz such dat all de fo'ces o' Hell couldn't a' budged 'em.'

"Colonel Breckenridge done ekally han'some an' 'lowed he couldn't in nowise 'count fo' his unseemly conduc', an' d' uthers jined in, 'splainin' an' 'pologizin' an' takin' mo' helpin's o' aigs an' coffee.

"Marse Dave inquire ef'en anybody got hurt in de ruckus, an' hit develop dat all de gent'men got some shot inter 'em som'whar, an' dey helps one 'nother dig 'em out an' put raw brandy on de places. Colonel Breckenridge done stan' aloof while dis goin' on, an' Colonel Sumner inquiah, 'Colonel, has yo' got any dove shot in yo', suh? If so, kin I assist yo' to remove 'em?'

"Colonel Breckenridge say, 'I am 'bleeged to yo', suh, fo' yo' consideration, an' I do b'lieve I got de best paht o' three loads under my hide, but dey is in a po'tion o' my anatomy where de attention o' lovin' an' sympathetic friends would be highly embarrassin',' he say. 'I b'lieve de character o' my wounds requiahs de ca'm, impussonal services of a physician.'

"An' wid dat dey all start whoopin' an' laughin' fit ter split.

"Us boys done all bin pretty nervous up t' now an' walkin' soft an' brief an' sober, 'case hit ain't advisable t' fo'm positive opinions when white folks ain't know dey own minds, but now us jines in de laughin'.

"Marse Dave say, 'Us best keep close concernin' dese ondignified pro-ceedin's, fo' we'll be de ridicule er de county ef'n dis mawnin's wuk evah gits out. But how in de worl',' he say, 'did it happen? Well, thank de Lawd, it's ovah an' no great damage done. 'Poly! Draw off some o' dat brandy an' serve de gent'men!'

" 'Poly say, 'Marse Dave, ef yo' please suh, yo' bes' had de Bourbon.—Yo' is boun' t' be disapp'inted in de brandy,' sezzee.

" 'What yo' mean, boy!'

" 'Well, suh , seems dat ol' liquah done got antiquated wid age. Hit ain't got no mo' coluh, er smell, er taste, er powah to it dan whut col' tea done got. When I open de kaig fo' t' fix de punch dis mawnin' I reelize dat brandy done los' hits animosity, suh.'

" 'Hum,' sez Marse Dave, moughty int'rested, 'an' whut did yo' do 'bout hit?'

" 'Well, suh, on 'count of de enfeebled nature o' de liquah, I done double de cha'ge in de punch,' say 'Poly, 'an' when dat don't seem to git nobody nowhar I gib her a little suppoht wid a jemmy john o' dat Bourbon.'

"Marse Dave say, 'Great Scott! No wonder dis all come t' pass,' sezzee, put-tin' fo'th his han' an' shakin' de brandy kaig. 'Gent'men, by de Lawd Harry, we've invertently consumed, by rough estimate, near two gallons o' de bes' brandy dis side er N'Yawleans! Hit ain't su'prisin' dat we has expe'ienced some 'zileration dis mawnin'. 'Poly, yo' idjit, f'om now on yo' is to confine yo' activities to cookin', an' yo' is fo'tunate to git outen dis mess wid yo' hide onstriped. Yo' don' onderstan' fluids ez yo' do aigs.'

"Den he call me up an' say, 'Ho'ace, yo' is de s'preme custodian o' de wicked flagon f'om now on,' he say, 'de ruler o' de kaig, an' de trusted gover-nor er de bin an' bottle.—Give ovah de keys, 'Poly! An' Ho'ace—'

" 'Yassuh.'

" 'Yo' may begin yo' duties by solicitin' de wishes o' de gent'men!'

"An' so," concluded the ancient black one, rising to discharge these respon-sibilities, "hit has been up'n to dis good day."

BY ADVICE
OF COUNSEL

In all other matters a man may be as frank and friendly as the sunlight on a trout stream, but he will, if he is an upland gunner, become as deceitful as Satan himself if you question him concerning woodcock cover. At your artless inquiry, "Where are you finding your birds?" your friend will give you a swift, evasive, sidelong look and go under like a submarine. His ensuing tactics are calculated to keep you from learning anything of value, while he himself, the dissembling rascal, is on the alert in the hope that you may be so incredibly careless as to let fall some hints as to where *you* are finding *yours*. Fortunately for the peace of the nation, there are always one or two strips of woodcock cover well known to every local gunner—public property where no one can find a bird except when a flight is falling, or on the first day of the season—but these old standbys do furnish the material for a creditable lie when you are asked where you found those four plump woodcock you have just displayed.

There must be many lovely bits of woodcock cover that these birds frequent, and which are known to none but the original discoverer. Doubtless there are many more that are never found at all. It would seem, however, that two active men shooting grouse and woodcock in the same district season upon season for twenty years would have located every yard of woodcock cover thereabouts, but the Judge entertained, as lawyers do, a reasonable doubt in these premises—a doubt that was not shared by the lean Captain, who was confident that his empty cartridge cases mouldered in every patch of wet woodland in the township.

In addition to a half dozen strictly concealed assets, the pair of them knew of as many more covers not so utterly exclusive. There were two grand covers—areas so rich and extensive that it was more than a full day's work to comb either of them—and there were a score of petty covers—fence corners, a yard or two of moist earth under a neglected apple tree, or a certain patch of brambles where one could always spring a single bird, or perhaps two. Shooting days are short, and with such wealth already located and available, the two friends had small incentive to explore. There was nothing to be gained by spending a day in a region that might be worthless. But the wise action of the State authorities in closing the season on grouse placed a new factor in the shooting vacation of the two gunners.

"Not that I have to kill a bird every quarter hour to really enjoy myself," remarked the Judge, "but I do appreciate an excuse to stay out the whole blessed day at this particularly glorious season of the year. All too soon cometh Winter and foul weather. You know, with the woodcock coming back as they have these past few years, it's no trick at all to bag four of 'em in a few hours. The partridge was the bird that kept us busy and wore out our shooting-boots. Now that he's off the list, we'll have a lot of time on our hands if we aren't careful."

"We can make the woodcock bag last longer if we take only a bird or two in a place," suggested his companion.

"We can do that, and we'll also have time to prospect for more cover. I've always wanted to locate the place Lance Briggs has told us about—it must be somewhere on the northern slope of Wolf Hill."

"It *can't* be there. I know every rock and gooseberry bush on that hill! There *is* a thin strip of birch in the little valley on top of the ridge that holds a few birds, but the northern slope is barren. Nothing there but old fields, and the soil is harsh and stony—no woodcock there, my boy."

The Judge was mildly insistent, however.

"Lance has been telling me about birds up there for years. He never sees me in town without mentioning it, and the best location I can make of his description is Wolf Hill. I thought he might be talking about woodpeckers, but I questioned him very tactfully one day. He gave a good description of a timberdoodle and, what's more, he insisted that he'd never seen one in a tree. No; he knows woodcock. He says there are lots of partridge in there, too."

And so the matter rested for two weeks with the splendid October days slipping by so rapidly that the time from dawn, with the white vapors rising slowly from every stream and fen, until sunset, when the last crimson colors of day faded behind the Adirondacks, seemed but the briefest space, and the men needed the proof afforded by weary muscles and briar-scratched skin to help them to realize that ten hours is ten hours by the clock, whatever the season. The two invaded every woodcock cover they knew and by dint of much high-minded self-denial kept within the legal limits on the birds. They made excursions, too, after black duck and teal and snipe and gathered squirrels for an occasional pie. The grouse, most seriously reduced in wide areas of its range, seemed to have been touched by the fatal influences but lightly in this remote section, and the big birds were constantly roaring up in front of the setter. It was the proper thing when a grouse took wing thus to follow him out of sight with eye to rib and then remark as the unfired gun was lowered:

"Wasn't that a pretty chance? You don't see 'em fly that way in open season! I could have nailed *him*!"

The flight was at its mysterious height now, and woodcock came in nightly. Covers where no birds had been found for years had moderate numbers of this unique variety of American feathered game. For a few days the flight held, and then the birds began moving farther southward under the urge of nightly frosts that grew gradually sharper. Finally the two gunners could find birds only here and there in warm secluded pockets, and they needed really to extend themselves to make a modest bag. The time was ripe for exploration.

"Let's drive over that old road in back of Wolf Hill tomorrow morning and for once give that side a thorough combing," suggested the Judge. "If we can't find anything, or if it looks too unpromising, we can keep on through to the Grape Vine Cover and find a few birds there."

Wolf Hill, probably so named for some forgotten incident of pioneer days, was a long limestone ramp rising from the levels of the Champlain Valley. Its broken, rugged crest carried a veritable wilderness of neglected woodland where grouse went about their affairs almost undisturbed by man from one twelve months to the next, and deer and bobcats and lesser creatures enjoyed an immunity scarcely less qualified. The mighty flank of the hill, somewhat more accessible to the Valley farms, was broken up into pasture lots and orchards of sugar maples and hickories, where the squirrels found splendid sanctuary and an inexhaustible supply of food. But except for a shallow depression at the northern slope where a slow trickle of water seeped downward among the roots of chimney-top and gray birch, Wolf Hill, so hospitable to other wild creatures, appeared to offer no comfort or harbor to the woodcock. This one spot, however, always held from one to four good birds, and rare shooting they gave when found there, for the pines grew thickly on both flanks of the stream, and the birds would dart into the shadows like grouse and could not be flushed again.

On the morning of the expedition, the Captain drove past this spot without pausing and went on down the narrow dirt road between thickets of birch and thorn-apple. The Judge, his leather gun-case between his knees, scanned the autumn hillside for any of the signs that indicate moist upland ground. Sport, the setter, took no less an interest in the scenery and whined and gasped his delight in the ecstasy of scents that tickled his sensitive nose.

A few old apple trees grew among the pine thickets and grapevine, and gorgeous sumachs spread their tangles over the old crumbling stone walls.

"It's perfect partridge cover, but far too dry and hard for woodcock," said one.

"Let's keep down into the valley anyway," the Judge persisted.

At the foot of the long hill, a clear, deep stream flowed beneath a wooden bridge, and the thorn-apple hedges gave place to dense banks of snowball bushes, with its tiny globular white fruit shining among the crimson stems. Some growths—the birch, alder and chimney-top, among others—are telltales of ground that is suitable for woodcock. The snowball is another shrub that flourishes best where the soil is moist and fine and rich enough to provide a natural abundance of earthworms, snails, and similar tidbits sweet to the woodcock's particular palate. Many a bird has been sprung from the edges of such thickets. The Captain turned the car into a side road that was hardly more than a grassy race between the rampant hedges of the snowball. Beyond the hedge they saw a smooth strip of grassy meadow, empty of life except for a flock of crows stalking about in the brilliant sunshine. The two sportsmen surveyed this scene with less enthusiasm, perhaps, than its natural charm would warrant.

"Wait a minute! What's that yellow stuff?"

The Judge pointed to a strip of light greenish yellow foliage vivid against the darker hues of the hillside beyond.

"Poplar, isn't it? Well, poplar grows on woodcock ground, too. Let's get out and go over there."

It was well that they did, for as they approached there came into view a strip of stuff lying closely along the banks of the brook and entirely hidden from sight from the road by abruptly rising ground. It was principally a mixture of alders, thorn, white birches, and, farther back, the slash of young poplars that had first attracted attention. Moreover, there was a mile of it in sight before it vanished behind the shoulders of a hill.

"Um! Hum!" remarked the Judge softly, slipping a pair of cartridges into his sixteen-gauge.

"Just look at that now! Right here all these years and we never knew it! Oh, blessed poplars!"

They had scarcely entered the strip when the lean gunner called out: "They're here all right! Here's chalkings! Oh! A mess of 'em! Great Scott—" and continued with a semitechnical, somewhat indelicate description of the generous digestive activities of woodcock that is of no particular importance to this narrative.

He was right. The earth under the alders and thorns looked as if a dozen drunken paperhangers had engaged in a friendly battle with their whitewash brushes. The sign was unmistakably fresh, and Sport, his brown and white muzzle a foot above the ground, was whipping his lean and glossy flanks in and out of the thickets. By the light in his brown eyes and the slant of his stern, he indicated his expectancy of coming immediately upon game. The gunners separated to good skirmishing distance and moved forward behind the eager, careful setter. Pace by pace the ground was covered, but there was no brisk whirr of wings, no twittering whistle, and no sight of brown bird whisking away through the alders.

"You don't suppose they went out last night, do you?" the Judge inquired doubtfully.

"Why should they? It wasn't any colder last night than it was the night before. No; they're here somewhere, if we can find 'em."

They went on beating acre after acre of alder and birch, the saplings crowding thickly from the soft sweet soil, and other acres where wild berry vines and thornbush levied painful toll upon the gunners, even through the heavy canvas of shooting-jackets and breeches. Sport made one solid stand and seemed relieved to have located something tangible at last. When his master stepped past the dog, there came a most unexpected uproar, and a ring-necked pheasant went out of a bunch of willows and soared away across the brook.

"By George! A pheasant away up here!" the Captain exclaimed, and Sport glanced around apologetically, as if he would have said, "Really, now, I hadn't an idea that it was one of those things!"

Shortly before lunch-time, as the Captain entered a small patch of alders fairly high on the hillside, something moved suddenly at his feet, and the first woodcock—a big hen—got up before him and went away through the tops. Watching its flight, the gunner had the illusion that splinters and sparkles of sunlight glanced from the twigs as the bird passed—and, except for a baffled sensation and a whiff of burnt powder in the air, that was all he had from the encounter. In the next clump a second bird sprang up, and this one was caught by the twenty-bore at the top of its initial leap.

"I've found 'em!" he called to his companion. But the opinion was optimistic and premature. Not another bird could they find on that hillside. The two retired for lunch chagrined and puzzled, for never before had either found so much evidence of woodcock and so few birds.

"They've gone. Must have moved last night," declared the Judge, and his friend nodded in reluctant agreement.

There remained, however, a thick stand of alder and birch growing over a knoll covering some three to four acres of ground that seemed a bit too high to hold birds. An old rail fence angled along one edge of the place—a grand corner for native "partridge" and a sweet spot to entice a gunner to pause and smoke a contemplative pipe in the warm October sunshine. But there was nothing there to promise woodcock after the failure of the perfect ground of the morning. The Judge and his friend responded to the invitation of a broad, lichen-cushioned top rail and smoked and dangled their heels and gossiped for a time. Then, by common indifferent consent, they clambered down and followed the setter into the thicket.

"Point!" exclaimed the Judge softly.

There was Sport, a rigid, high-headed creature, standing magnificently against the dull tints of the thicket. One brown eye he rolled beseechingly in the Captain's direction, a partisan appeal to hurry and secure stock in the enterprise before dividends were declared. But before that gentleman could move, three woodcock went up at once, whistling and twittering as they took their different ways over the alder tops. One came down amid a shower of shattered twigs as the Judge fired.

That was the beginning of the hottest corner on woodcock ever recorded in those parts, and that it was not more carefully recorded is due to the prevailing general excitement and stress. The Judge, follower of a careful and conservative habit of thought, concluded that the place harbored forty woodcock. The Captain, whose report possibly was influenced by the astounding fact that he had seen four birds in the air at once, thought there were half a hundred. They sprang at every step, and when a shot was fired the alders seethed with nervous, twittering timberdoodles. There were birds that one could see, and there were others only vaguely recorded in the dim and outer cedges of vision.

Sport, whose excellent reputation had been earned by years of meritorious conduct in quail country, forgot the righteous habits of his days and put in an hour of the sort of behavior that is best forgotten. To him, woodcock were odd and unusual little beggars, confused and confusing, of dubious legitimacy as gamebirds. They had, he thought, a miserable hair-trigger habit of jumping when you thought they'd lie tight, and lying tight when they ought to jump. Look at that one now! Springing way over there by that thornapple—no one within twenty yards of him! And—whoa!—this one whistling like a fool and getting up right in a man's whiskers! The ground is simply dredged with scent—you can't be sure of anything. Maybe *I am* getting a little nervous! Whoa! There goes another! And another! My! My! What *will* the Cap'n say to me?

At this point a sympathetic authority stepped in, and Sport was retired to the fence for a recess to enable him to recover his equanimity and to profit by advice of his counsel. Thus fortified, he again took to the alders and with restored composure behaved from then on with accustomed dignity and distinction.

The Judge and the Captain, governed alike by law and conscience, quit with the legal limit of four birds each, honestly including the single that they had taken in the morning.

"That," remarked the Judge, glancing back to where the alders were making a patch of misty purple against the dun hillside, "is the finest bit of woodcock cover between the Adirondacks and the Atlantic! The birds feed all over the valley and come into the corner to rest during the day. What wouldn't Bill Holsapple give to know of this place!"

"What'll we tell him if he asks us?" inquired his friend.

"Lie. Lie to him. Lie with all the bland, ingenuous dexterity at your command. Tell him we got 'em all in the Sawmill Cover—that there was a late flight in. And, listen! Keep your ears open, too, while you're doing it. I've always suspected that Bill has a piece of cover somewhere up around Clark Pond where he gets a lot of prime shooting. If he gets off his guard talking about birds, he may drop an unintentional clue about it!"

The Judge slipped his gun barrels into the case and put the case in the car. Then he paused for a contemplative moment, the lines of his broad, good-natured face reflecting a passing melancholy conclusion—a charitable, gently regretful acceptance of the fact of human frailty. The Judge was an honorable man.

"That scoundrel," said he, continuing his thought aloud, "is so *damnably* deceitful about these things that you can't depend upon him to give you an honest answer to a straight question!"

SQUIRREL SHOOTING WITH JIM

It was a fortunate thing for the Captain that Jim Hooper was a charitable man, and therefore not inclined to allow a passel of women, however neat and terrifying they might be, to interfere with a genuine friendship; and fortunate again that hard, unremitting manual labor was not to him, as it was to many others, reared on harsh Puritan precepts, a form of worship. He could always be persuaded to give his long, lean frame a holiday from toil. Had he been sensitive on these points the Captain must have missed many a splendid expedition after pa'tridges or woodcock and such other game as was then and may still be found along the alder runs or on the wooded slopes of the Valley. It must be confessed that there was a certain shiftlessness about Jim—a mild moral obliquity—that certainly did not earn for him the admiration of the feminine portion of the Captain's family. He was a charming fellow really, and an ideal comrade upon any venture into the realm of the woods and waters.

The moon was still filling the valley with white radiance, and there was no trace of coming dawn above the wooded crest of the Munger Hill when Jim came striding across the frosty earth of the Captain's dooryard with his long rifle across his arm and his tattered trouser legs flapping against his lean and sinewy shanks. Corn-hoeing or wood-chopping could very well await later rising hours, but squirrel-shooting—the purpose for the day—or duck, deer, or pa'tridge shooting, like duelling, are affairs that require participants to be on their ground at dawn.

Jim entered the warm kitchen at the Captain's invitation and, standing his rifle in one corner, accepted a handful of doughnuts from the crock. In daylight hours no power on earth could persuade him to come into the house—so intensely did he suffer from the spiritual discomfort engendered by that silent, fatally effective feminine disapproval—but he now felt reasonably secure to perch before the fire while the Captain finished his coffee and bacon, for it would be hours before these dreaded women-folk appeared. By that time the two riflemen would be over the hills and far away, and even the rank acrid tang of Jim's shag tobacco vanished from the low-ceilinged kitchen.

But he watched the paling stars in the eastern sky with anxious eyes.

"Gittin' light, Cap'n. We'd better hyper."

"Where'll we go, Jim?" the other asked as he wriggled into his jacket and picked up his own rifle.

"Why, naow, I b'lieve we'd better go over to Bigelow's Woods. There's a great lot o' pig walnuts back in there an' the squir'ls air jest throwin' the mast daown like hail-stuns."

The outer air had a keen touch that made them grateful for jackets and gloves. In a few hours this frost would dissolve and the sun flood the Valley with a golden warmth like June, but more subtly invigorating than the yellow mead of old Britain. The rime crisped under their moccasined feet as they crossed the pasture lot and breasted the western slope; it limned every twig, and its weight was too much for many of the sugar maple's gold and scarlet leaves; one by one, with little pathetic sounds of parting, they lost their delicate holds and came whispering down to earth.

Jim's long legs, already limbered by a two-mile walk from his cabin, were formidable engines of propulsion. He set a fearful pace across the hill, and the Captain suffered all the cramping, constricted agonies that precede the arrival of the "second wind" and in his distress missed half the glories of the frost-rimmed valley below him. The pleasant, homely sounds of cock and dog and kine came only faintly to his humming ears. But presently his stark physical crisis was passed, his stride more nearly matched that of his comrade, and the dry, sharp pains in legs and lungs dissolved in a warm mounting glow of well-being. The eight-pound rifle was an eight-pound weapon after all, and not a section of a battery of mountain howitzers—clearly the worst was over. A stony hill road led them downward into another valley where the mists from the Powder Mill Pond rose sluggishly and drifted along a slow current of upper air.

Bigelow's Woods—a lovely strip of hardwoods five miles long and half as wide—has for generations echoed to the crack of squirrel rifles. In earlier days it heard also the twang of bow, the hiss of arrows, and the sudden shrilling of the war whoop. Abnaki and Iroquois, French and English, Colonial Rangers and soldiers of the Black Watch, all knew this lovely valley as a primitive battleground. The loftier patriarchs—that towering maple and that weathered beech—have watched the passing of the King's men in scarlet and buff on their way to the bloody fields of Hubbardton and Bennington. The old military way is still traceable here and there, but the red-capped woodpeckers now sound the long roll in the solitudes where once echoed the brisk drumtapping of His British Majesty's marching regiments.

The two hunters crossed a barnyard. The glow of a lantern shining through the chinks of the stable and the musical thrumming sound of milk spurting against the bottom of a pail indicated that the farmer was astir at his morning tasks. Perhaps in the presence of this normal, thrifty industry the hunters, contemplating their own profitless project, felt a twinge of self-reproach, but if so, it was only enough to give spice to their freedom. They climbed a rail fence, passed through a dripping fringe of purple aster and bright goldenrod and immediately entered the woods. There a pause was made while Jim loaded his rifle—an interesting operation in this day of the breech-loader.

The weapon had a heavy, three-foot barrel, brown as a coffee bean, with the well-cared-for bore as perfect as when it left the Remington benches so many years ago. The stock of curly maple was handsome enough, thought the Captain, in its natural grain, set off by the bright brass of trigger-guard and patch-box, and scarcely needed the inlaid figures of grouse, bear, and deer, done in coin silver by some patient hand. Into a horn charger Jim poured a good thimbleful of black rifle powder and emptied it into the long barrel. Next, he produced a disc of tallowed linen from the patch-box and a leaden ball from the buckskin bullet-pouch. The patch was placed over the muzzle, the ball carefully centered, and the whole sent home with a single smooth thrust of the brass-tipped rod. The rod was returned to the guides, the nipple capped, and Jim was ready for the first squirrel. The whole operation had delayed them much less than a minute—so smooth and practiced was the performance.

It was now perceptibly lighter than it was ten minutes before. Dawn was at hand, announced by the brisk *chirr-rr* of red squirrels, as well as by the squealing of two bluejays gathering their breakfasts in the top of a great beech. Though he has a reputation for sly rascality, and is supposed by some to devote his Fridays to the wicked task of carrying sand to Hades to be used in keeping the clinkers from forming in the everlasting furnaces, in accordance with an unholy contract he has with Lucifer, it is difficult to cherish a dislike for the bluejay. His sins, real or imaginary, are atoned for by his bold, bright presence in the autumn woods, by his strange assortment of notes, and by his alert, prankish curiosity concerning everything that moves. A villain he may be, but he will harry a marauding cat until that humorless animal gives up its fell purpose and flees squalling and with flattened ears for the protection of the home buildings. He has a trick—and very disconcerting it is to the squirrel shooter—of getting himself unseen into the leafy top of a beech and setting up a spasmodic commotion in the foliage, at the same time tossing down bits of mast wrenched off by his powerful bill. The most experienced sniper will be fooled by the performance into the belief that a fat gray is "working" up there, and it may be that many minutes will elapse before a flash of vivid blue and a derisive whistle identify the creature. The bluejay's impudent squall when he discovers you soft-footing it across the forest floor is meant to humiliate and make you realize how awkward and obvious and futile you really are. This note resembles the screech of an ungreased wooden pulleyblock and undoubtedly, from the instant silence that falls upon the woodland whenever it is uttered, is recognized by other wild creatures as an alarm note. Having mocked you and betrayed you, the audacious bird flies off whistling and cat-calling, a sparkle of pale vivid blue and gleaming jet among the treetops. You may as well stand motionless where you are, for it will be some minutes before you hear the vague rustlings, the sudden swish of released boughs which indicate that the squirrels have forgotten the jay's *alerte* call and have resumed feeding.

Jim, stepping silently on the balls of his feet, had wasted a strained ten minutes stalking a perfidious pair of these birds. To the Captain's ears, his progress has been perfectly noiseless, but the jays have seen or heard him and set up their mischievous clamor. In no wise disconcerted, Jim rested his rifle-butt on his boot and ejected a tremendous squirt of tobacco juice. Presently, he was moving again, as quietly as a drift of smoke toward a hickory whence for some minutes there had come a light patter of gnawed shell. After some time, during which Jim edged carefully around the tree, the long rifle came up and hung for an instant. There was a spurt of white smoke, a sharp, ringing crack, and down from the treetop tumbled a plump gray to lie among the dappled leaves while Jim, not moving from his tracks, measured and poured the powder and thrust a fresh ball home upon the charge.

A sudden rattle of claws on bark startled the Captain as a second squirrel, emerging from a hole in a maple, leaped agilely to a branch and, curving his magnificent plume over his back, sent out the gasping squall of his kind. It is a sound not readily associated with a squirrel by the inexperienced who hear it for the first time, and may easily be mistaken for the bark of the red fox. This fellow was no idle performer, for at every squall a veritable convulsion shook his whole fat fervid carcass from head to tail. Whether it was a challenge, or a love-song, or merely a vocal exercise, was uncertain, probably the latter, for the squirrel seemed to be interested in the mere production of the sound, rather than in scanning the woodland for the arrival of a mate or a rival champion. In any event, it was this chap's swan-song, terminated swiftly by the light, sharp report of the Captain's rifle.

A telescopic sight is desirable equipment on any squirrel rifle. It is not only a great aid to accuracy, but it gives one the power to see clearly many things and matters too indistinct or distant to be defined by the naked eye. It will tell instantly whether that is a butternut or a squirrel's head yonder in the crotch of the basswood, and one can closely investigate, without moving from where he sits, the origins of all those small sounds and furtive stirrings that tantalize one. With a good glass a rifleman can read the complacent expression in the eye of an unsuspecting crow just alighted on a dead stub sixty paces distant and imagine his shocked dismay if he knew of this hateful surveillance. Or, perhaps one watches a fox chasing its own black-tipped tail in a moment of indulgent playfulness. And really, to the squirrel shooter who is armed as the Captain was, with a .22-caliber rifle, the telescopic sight is a necessity if, humanely, he wishes to kill his game cleanly and not have his holiday clouded with reproachful reminders of wounded squirrels dying slowly in their inaccessible holes. The gray squirrel has a vitality disproportionate to the size of the animal, and the .22 Long Rifle bullet will not kill the game instantly and certainly unless it strikes the head, neck, or shoulder. Hit anywhere else with the tiny projectile, it is more than probable that the squirrel will escape to perish slowly in its hiding place. The telescopic sight makes one certain of a clean kill or, what is next best, a clean miss. Jim's percussion rifle, loaded with a relatively heavy powder charge and a round ball, was infinitely more deadly, though it would ruin a squirrel for frying-pan purposes if hit anywhere but in the head.

While the Captain sat there a goshawk darted past him, silent and swift and deadly, and he felt that inconsistent enmity which man feels toward any game-killer but himself. A pair of chipmunks celebrating holiday after harvest played fox and geese among the leaves, making much noise about it. Then, and this is one of the rewards of still hunting with a rifle, a brown shape came sailing quietly and low, to alight on the ground not thirty paces from him. To one familiar only with the thunderous tumult that the ruffed grouse makes in getting up before a man or a dog, it is inconceivable that the same bird can fly as silently as the owl. This bird stood poised for an instant alert for danger, and at the first slight movement of the rifle stepped briskly behind a tree trunk and did not reappear. The Captain knew that he was being neatly whipsawed, but was helpless to overcome this superior strategy. The bird was walking rapidly away, keeping the tree trunk exactly between them. When finally the Captain leaned outward to see past the obstruction, the canny bird instantly took wing in a whirl of flying leaves and thunderous sound.

With three squirrels in his pocket, the Captain moved in the direction where he had last heard the crack of Jim's rifle and soon saw him moving slowly about under a big maple and gazing intently upward. Jim seemed relieved to see the Captain.

"There's a big one somewhere's up here," he whispered gustily. "I seen him gwup an' I know durned well he ain't come daown. I b'lieve he's circlin' on me. Damn it! I been 'raound and 'raound this tree 'til I feel ju' like a Plymouth Rock rooster wi' his neck wrung! If you'll go 'raound t'other side, I b'lieve one or t'other on us'll git a crack at him."

The Captain did as requested, but could descry no sign of the betraying gray plume, nor of the slender body pressed compactly against the gray bark.

"He's layin' on a limb somewhere," opined the veteran. He picked up a stick and drew it roughly to and fro across the tree trunk, cautioning his companion meanwhile to keep his eye "peeled."

Sure enough, the Captain thought he detected a vague motion far out toward the end of a high branch and with the aid of the telescope made out the form of the squirrel lying there so snug and close that he seemed a part of the tree itself.

"Why did he move when you rubbed the tree, Jim?" he inquired.

Jim chuckled.

"Sounds to him like one o' us wuz climbin' up to git him," he explained. " 'T'won't allus work, but sometimes an ol' squir'l will git worried if he thinks you're shinning his tree an' he'll climb aout on a limb sos't he kin jump if he hez to do so.

"Oh! I tell ye what," he continued, "there ain't no critter in the woods—no; not even the fox—that's cuter than a squir'l that's larned his business!"

They followed an old wood road that led them through a mile or two of ancient woodland. Moving very quietly and slowly, they saw numbers of squirrels and picked up a few more. They came to an old clearing, with its log cabin long since a mere heap of brown mould under a wild tangle of raspberry vines, but with a neglected plot of flowers growing beside the worn stone slab that had been the doorstep of this primitive home—a vernal monument to some pioneer mistress long since forgotten and lost from the dusty records of mankind, but still remembered for her love of beauty by her lilies in this quiet, remote place.

At the edge of the old orchard, the Captain caught an instant glimpse of a trig form among the yellow fallen fruit under a scraggly apple tree. The crack of his rifle precipitated a nerve-shaking uproar as grouse after grouse darted from the tree and went thundering away. On the ground the single victim beat an expiring tattoo, and the rifleman gathered a noble bird to add to the string of squirrels and rouse Jim's envious admiration.

Their road led them out to a small woodland pond, where Jim, after a careful stalk, shot a black mallard sunning himself in the sedgy shallows and was inclined to regard his companion's "pa'tridge" with condescension afterward. Partridges were seen every day, but ducks were rare fowl in these parts and prized accordingly.

"Fer all that I c'n see," said Jim in response to an inquiry while they sat on a log beside the pond and ate their lunch, "squir'ls air jest as many naow as when I wuz a yunker an' hunted 'em with Pap's ol' shotgun. Pa'tridges hev good seasons an' bad seasons, an' so do rabbits. Ther' wuz a long time when no one hereabouts ever seen so much as a track of a deer, but the squir'ls keep jest about the same, an' I b'lieve from my p'int of view squir'ls air the best game for a feller 'at loves to shoot a rifle. Pa'tridge an' woodcock shootin' air fun, bet ye hev to go slammin' an' bangin' away through the bresh an' ye don't see half the things that ye may if ye go along quiet an' still and watchful. No, sir. Ye gi' me my day with a good rifle an' plenty o' paowder an' ball an' terbacker, an' it's my idee o' somethin' better'n 'tater diggin'!"

ODD
OR
EVEN

The Captain shuffled the thin packet of envelopes which the postmaster passed to him and promptly tossed half of them into the wastebasket. Simultaneously he emitted a snort of exasperation.

"Sucker list stuff," he explained in answer to a glance of inquiry from his friend. "There ought to be a law against it, Judge. Half my mail these days is from people who ask the most intimate and personal questions about the state of my health. Some of 'em, confound their effrontery, display the liveliest interest in functions that oughtn't to be discussed outside a hospital—and the lower end of the ward at that!"

"You must sometime have subscribed for some hair restorer, or to learn how to speak fluent French in two lessons," remarked the Judge suavely. "I never get that sort of mail. Nobody seems to be concerned about my duodenum."

"If you've got one whatever it is it probably hasn't worked for years!" his friend retorted. His face lightened suddenly, and he ran a quick finger under the tab of an envelope stamped with a Mississippi postmark. The address was in a bold, clear script, and the fine heavy parchment bore a crest well known to those savants of the College of Heralds.

"Here's a letter from old Johnny Reb," he exclaimed. "You don't suppose he's—by golly, he is, though! Judge, the Old Rebel is coming up to shoot with us at last! He says—but here, read it yourself!" He completed a swift perusal and handed the letter to his friend.

"You dear old Abolitionist," the letter ran, "I have decided to invade the North. The confounded tales that you and that legal scalawag told me when you were down here last season concerning the astonishing sporting characteristics of the Yankee grouse and woodcock are responsible for my decision. I am starting Tuesday with eight good cylinders, a charitable determination to let bygones be bygones, and my two old hammer Parkers. I should arrive on

Thursday evening"—"that means any time after twelve o'clock noon to a Mississippian," the Judge interjected—"and," the letter continued, "if you and the Judge—my compliments to him, please—fail to show me grouse and timberdoodles in overflowing abundance, not the highest peak in your Green Mountains will afford your refuge from my wrath, nor the depths of Champlain extend sanctuary.

"Faithfully yours

"John Armistead Bristol.

"P.S. Tell His Honor that this will be the first visit from any member of my family to your State since the St. Albans Raid.   J.A.B."

"They didn't stay long then, and I'll tell him so when I see him, the impudent rascal!" the Judge retorted patriotically to this quip. " 'Legal scalawag,' eh? We'll show him a Yankee trick with these Yankee grouse that'll make him think his cartridges are loaded with sand! Boy! I'm glad he's coming! I never expect to encounter a more likeable cuss—nor one with a sweeter disposition. What fun he gave us with the quail and the ducks last year!"

"He can shoot, too," the other reminded him. "He came along and picked up a Springfield up in Jaulgonne Wood one time an' stood off a platoon of the Prussian Guard for twenty minutes—those birds hadn't just come out for the air, either!—until my crowd could straighten a bent stripping finger in a jammed Hotchkiss. You've seen him shoot quail just like two ticks of a clock. Well, it was just like that. I was busy at the time, but whenever I looked up to see if they could heave a grenade that far, Johnny was shoving in a fresh clip. 'No hurry, Yank,' he'd tell me, 'I've got the elevation to an inch.'

"Thursday—let's see—if he stays on the road and doesn't get shot for a rebel spy somewhere in Massachusetts, he'll get here day after tomorrow."

" 'In the evening,' " the Judge quoted.

And so it was. The frosty twilight of an October day had settled in the long Valley. From the somber panel of pines that edged the farther bank of the Marsh as the dusk thickened an owl regularly launched a series of gusty whoops that brought a shiver of apprehension to the frivolous cottontails mustering for a moonlight frolic in the clearing where the old Benson cabin sank slowly earthward in mouldering vine covered ruin. A flock of black ducks dropping in out of the twilight on swishing wings quacked throaty inquiries to friends already riding at anchor in the dense shadows underneath the cranberry bushes out among the bogs.

It was at this fitting hour that a gray car, long and slim of muzzle, swept into the Captain's dooryard and came to a stop in the soft yellow radiance from the kitchen windows. John Armistead Bristol slid his slender person from behind the wheel, but before he could descend further of his own volition, he was violently set upon and yanked out upon his feet by two vociferous maniacs. One of these was as lean as himself; the other inclined to a certain deceitful appearance of pudginess—deceitful, because the Judge actually was as fit and as tireless as a black bear. These two immediately began yelling for Jason to store the car and carry the luggage to the corner room, and for Ellen to set off a jug of hot water and to slice lemons. Interspersed with these directions to the domestic staff, there was a perfect hullabaloo of back-slapping and hand-shaking and cries of "Johnny Reb! You're really here!" And, this from the Judge, " 'Legal scalawag,' eh? I've a good mind to wallop you for that, sir!"

John Armistead shook the cramps from his arms and legs, worked his chilled fingers, and grinned from ear to ear.

"So this is *Veh*mont!" said he. "Ain't nobody fiahed on me yet! Have you any birds?"

"Listen," said the Captain, holding up a hand for silence.

From somewhere out of the mystery of the azure vault above the maples came down a continuous flow of small sounds—sounds so faint as never to register on any but the alert and sensitive ears of those who know how and when to listen for the pulse of the seasons. They heard tiny whistles, the whispering of invisible wings, elfin murmurings, squeaks and ghostly rustlings—the route sounds of a host of minor feathered migrants on the march. Through this lesser threnody a flock of wild geese sent down their lonely strident clangor, "Ee—yonk—ee—yonk—ee—yonk—yonk—yonk."

The ancient wonder, never to be wholly solved by man, gripped the three. Even old Jason, with the battered case of Parkers beneath his arm, halted on the doorstep and cocked an ear to the sky, his practical soul enthralled by this high and ghostly gossip.

The Judge broke the spell.

"The covers will be full of woodcock by mornin'," he prophesied.

John Armistead awoke at seven o'clock to discover the rosy light from the rising day filtering into the room through the branches of a maple just outside the window. The leaves formed a screen of color more gorgeous than anything he had imagined to be possible. In fifteen minutes he was dressed and out on the lawn to have his first view of this old corner of the New World to which his love of the gun and good fellowship had at last brought him.

The old brown house where the Captain lived stood on a sloping sward. A clear little brook from the hills flowed across the foot of the velvety lawn. Gigantic maples—an even half dozen of them—stood closely about the place and held their huge arms protectively over this ancient Yankee roof-tree, and the glory of their autumn garb was such that the surrounding atmosphere seemed to be stained with an impalpable tincture of gold and scarlet. Above the close hills to the west, Johnny discerned still loftier shadows faintly seen through the drifting mists of the morning. These dim bulks, he concluded, were looming giants of the Adirondacks, but the Green Mountains were hidden from view at this place by a rocky ridge that closed the eastern side of the valley. The first chipmunk he had ever seen whisked abruptly around the trunk of a maple and began a friendly flippant conversation with the stranger. A screen door slapped somewhere, and a golden cocker spaniel came out, ignoring the chipmunk, and sat solemnly down at Johnny's feet. After him came the Captain, summoning his friend to breakfast.

"The Judge will be here in twenty minutes," he announced. "What do you think of my country, Johnny?"

"It's a right pretty country," was the sober reply. "I swear I nevah saw such color! I could look at these maples all day long! How old do you reckon they are? Standin' close to the house this way, ain't you concerned about falling limbs or blow-downs? Looks like they might smash your house like an egg shell."

"Let's see—a hundred—mor'n that—they must be a hundred an' thirty years old anyway," replied his host. "There were eight of 'em once. Two have fallen. But when they fall they don't fall on the house. They manage to fall away from it somehow, no matter what the direction of the wind that destroys 'em";—he laid his hand on the rough gray bark of one—"they care as much for the old house as we do," he explained simply.

Before the meal was finished, the Judge drove into the yard, came in to pay his compliments to the Dark-Haired Lady, and then sat down to discuss the day's prospects while the others finished their coffee.

"The Old Township is the place to take him today. With a flight in last night, those covers along the Belden Brook will be fairly twittering with woodcock. Ever shoot woodcock, Johnny?"

"No," said Johnny, "I've seen a few of 'em down along the bayou headings, but I nevah fiahed at one. Wood snipe, we call 'em."

"Grouse?"

"Nevah even saw one outside a glass case," the Southerner admitted.

There followed a consultation of experts over Johnny's arms and equipment. He was advised to take his quail gun, the companion weapon being designed for the heavier responsibilities of duck and goose shooting along Mississippi sandbars. His friends, however, promised him later work for the fowling-piece among the black ducks and bluebills of Champlain.

"Throw in a couple of boxes of chilled 8's. They're heavy enough for grouse and small enough for timberdoodles."

"*Two* boxes? And your bag limits fo' grouse an' fo' woodcock? Eight birds altogether?"

"You won't use 'em all," he was advised, "but you may need a few from the second box."

Privately Johnny concluded that if he couldn't secure a limit of eight birds with less than 25 cartridges, he'd be—but then he noticed the Captain dumping one box of 20's into his shooting jacket and storing another in the car along with the lunch basket. Being too wise to scorch his tongue on another man's porridge, he held his peace—and was later glad that he had.

"How about my clothing?" he next wanted to know. "I brought a pair of canvas trousers to pull oveh my corduroys where the briahs are bad."

"You won't need 'em. In fact, if you're a little careful, you might almost hunt all day long in low shoes and golf hose. We have briars up here, of course, but they're not the murderous cat-clawed beauties that ravaged the coat off my suffering back when we were 'down South' last year. No snakes, either, if you will please excuse a few timber rattlers in midsummer. Nothing like that cottonmouthed 'Congo' that crawled into my blind with me that morning you took us out to shoot turkeys."

The Judge shuddered, recalling the thick-bodied, blunt-tailed horror of the Southern swamps, cold and loathsomely slow in every movement but its deadly thrust.

"Shucks," said Johnny, "moccasins ain't bad—just so they don't hit you."

"No; I suppose not," his friend acceded thoughtfully. "Well, let's see how you stand up now for a grouse hunter. Flannel shirt, corduroy breeches, wool stockings, and medium high hunting-boots, a light shooting-jacket, and if, to top it off with, you've got a close-fitting cap of some sort I believe you're all correct."

"Now, then," advised the lean Yankee solicitously when they were out on the road, "we shall undoubtedly meet some of the inhabitants of this region in our travels to and fro. As your host, I take the deepest interest in your personal welfare. I s'pose you can't help talking as if you had a little dab o' cotton on your tongue, but if you *will* endeavor not to call a doughnut a 'cruller,' and a door a 'do' ' and a field a 'fiel' '—"

Johnny's fist promptly thudded on the speaker's ribs and in an instant the rear of the car was full of flying arms and legs.

The Judge stopped the vehicle.

"Quit that!" he ordered sternly, "I don't care a cent about either one of you, but I ain't going to have my lunch tramped on by a pair of idiots. Get up out of there now! What are you fighting about, anyway?"

Panting and giggling, the two resumed their seats.

"The danged scoundrel accused me of callin' a do' a *do*'," explained Johnny.

The Judge had for some time past been coaxing the car along a gradually rising road. Its rain-washed surface gave no evidence of frequent traffic. Steep forest-clad cliffs and hills rose abruptly on either side of the track, and the giant beeches looming seventy feet above laced their bronze foliage above them in a lofty flying arch. The beeches, Johnny knew, the oaks and hickories and pines also, but other varieties of tree, shrub and roadside plant were unfamiliar to his alien eyes, and he asked many questions concerning them. After a time they ceased climbing and emerged upon a narrow valley, where a brook

flowed in and out among the pines and alders and birches. The jurist tooled
the car a few yards up a dim wood road and stopped.

"Here we are," he announced.

It was then that Johnny discovered an important omission.

"Where's the dogs?" he asked. "Danged if we ain't fo'got 'em completely!"

The Captain reassured him.

"Sometimes we use 'em and sometimes we don't. These grouse nowadays
are hard game for a dog to handle. Woodcock will lie pretty well, but the
grouse mostly are too smart to let a dog come up on 'em unless it happens to
be a wet, misty sort of a day. When it's like this—bright and clear—and when
the leaves are falling, these birds will lie for a man more often than they will
for his dog. When you shoot, mark your down bird and don't lose any time
getting to him."

He continued his instruction.

"You'll find an old cow path following along the brook. Keep right along
that and cock both barrels and peel your eyes. The Judge will be fifty yards
on the further side, and I'll be an equal distance on this side. Whistle if you
lose us, so we'll know where everyone is and no one'll get shot."

They left him and Johnny, pulling both hammers to the oily snick of full
cock, advanced down a black dirt path, where the yellow leaves of the hazel
lay. The pungent smell of its golden blossoms was sharp in his nostrils. It was
bird country, his instincts warned him, even if it was vastly different from the
ragweed and sedge fields of Mississippi. Frequently enough to enable him to
judge their positions, he heard the scrape of branches against a jacket sleeve,
the sound of a bootheel on a stone or the low whistled calls of his friends on
either side. The air was like a thin dry wine, the brook gurgled and whispered
beside him.

Turning a corner, he came suddenly upon a long-billed, beady-eyed,
gnomelike creature crouching on the moist black earth in the middle of the
path, within six feet of him. The preposterous bill and the black eye set almost at the top of the head identified the bird as a woodcock, no less than did
the russet and black of its plumage. Johnny stopped instantly, intent on observing what to him was a rare specimen. The woodcock obligingly strutted a
few steps, spreading its short tail nervously, before it sprang aloft on whistling
wings. A single impulse appeared to take the bird to the tops of the hazel
brush, but having arrived at this elevation, it seemed then to be uncertain as
to the best course to pursue and hovered and floated, dropping and turning
aimlessly above the path. Johnny caught a hasty aim and fired. At the shot,
the bird convulsively snapped its wings tight shut and dropped like a stone.

"Got him," announced the gunner with satisfaction, in answer to an inquiry from one of his companions.

Reloading the right barrel, he advanced to gather his game, which he presently located lying among the leaves in a curious posture. Its head was

pressed flat to the earth and one bright eye was turned aloft. The gunner tucked his weapon under his arm and extended his hand to pick up his game. His fingers all but touched the glossy feathers, when the woodcock exploded into another swift and lofty spiral, rising so close that the startled man actually felt the flick of feathers against his face. This time there was none of the previous hesitancy of flight, but instead, a swift purposeful dart such as a frightened pigeon makes. Johnny recovered and fired a hasty shot, but the bird was already far out of range. He watched it in swift flight far down the valley, where it disappeared finally high on the slope of a hillside a full half mile distant.

"Two woodcock for you, Johnny?" inquired the Captain, who had heard the whistle and rustle of rising wings.

"No—don't start countin' on me now! That was all the same bird—and I ain't got him yet. But I declare I believe these woodcock are surely easy to hit! Why this here one flapped around my head for ten seconds before he finally took himself off."

A few yards farther the brook sank from view behind high banks densely screened with hemlock. An old field once tilled by pioneers, but long since abandoned to thickets of alder and birch, sloped gently upward from the stream. While Johnny surveyed this prospect, the Judge joined him.

"There's where we'll find the woodcock," his companion assured him, pointing to the alder copses, "and probably a few grouse feeding on the buds."

"Look here, Johnny," he called presently from the edge of the first thicket. "They're here all right."

He stopped over a patch of moist earth at the edge of a clump of chimney-top and pointed to half a dozen broad chalky smears. The soil was pierced with an odd pattern of tiny holes, as if someone had thrust repeatedly with a small dagger.

"There's his sign and his seal," said the Judge, while the other examined the marks curiously. "And now I'll tell you something." His voice sank to a confidential murmur. "Keep out along the edges of these thickets and you'll get the best shooting. You see, woodcock, unlike quail, usually fly toward an opening. There are just five of these runs in this little valley. The last one, up at the farther end, is undoubtedly the best bit of bird cover in the County."

Then he did a strange little thing for one of his years and dignity. He held out the fingers of one hand and waggled them, after the fashion of a school-boy counting the days until Saturday, and Johnny was amazed to hear his friend recite in undertones the old familiar playground rhyme:

> "Eeny—meeny—miny—mo,
> Catch a nigger by the toe;
> When he hollers, let him go.
> Eeny—meeny—miny—mo."

"What are you saying?" asked Johnny.

"Nothing—nothing at all. Just a little childish nonsense that keeps running in my head," the Judge explained. Then in louder voice he hailed the Captain. "Here, my boy, I'll get into this thicket and hustle the birds out to you chaps. Then you can take the next one and drive 'em out to Johnny and me, and so on."

The Captain offered a courteous demurrer.

"No! No! I'd like to see you get the first chance at the birds, Judge. I'll go in here and you stay outside and shoot."

"Why, I won't hear of such a thing!" protested the Judge graciously. And without waiting for further denials he plunged in among the alders. At this the Captain favored Johnny with a wink but offered no explanation for his roguish gesture.

"These No'the'ners are certainly strong on field courtesy," thought Johnny. "I'll have to mind my own manners."

The pleasant little incident was temporarily forgotten at once, for the Judge nearly stepped on a grouse within ten paces of the thicket edge. Johnny was astounded at the ensuing uproar. He couldn't believe that no more than a single bird was making such a thunder of sound, and fully expected to see at least a dozen of them bustle out from among the purple stems of the alders. He heard the sharp clap of the Judge's gun, and following it his wholly unnecessary shout of warning. Then, cutting over on one wing, like an airplane turning a racing field pylon, came the fastest thing in the way of a game bird that he had ever seen. He noticed the tufted head, the jetty ruffs of the collar and the lighter markings of the bird's breast, and beyond these sharply defined details and serving as a perfect background was the sparkle of the sunlight on the alder twigs. He knew that this was the composition of a picture that he would never forget as long as he lived. He knew also his utter inability to hit this thundering streak but that he must make the attempt nevertheless.

In spite of his best effort to snap the gun ahead he felt sure as he pressed the trigger that the load would go a full yard behind his target, but to his intense surprise there was a sudden whirl of feathers, an instantaneous check to that splendid flight, and the grouse went down, bouncing a dozen yards across the grass before it stopped and lay still.

Johnny wondered which of his friends had accomplished the miracle.

"Good shot, Johnny!" exclaimed the Captain. Evidently he had not fired.

"Did the Judge shoot?" Johnny asked.

"Once, but he missed him. He's your bird, you know," was the reply. "And how do you like our grouse? Did you ever see a grander fellow on the wing?"

"Never," conceded Johnny, "but, Great Day in the Mawnin', I'll never live long enough to learn to hit one of those aerial torpedoes!"

His friend chuckled.

"But you just did," he pointed out.

The thicket yielded two more woodcock, one of which fell to the Captain's 20-bore. The other, Johnny missed as it crossed tantalizingly before him and dropped into the next run.

They progressed to the next thicket.

"My turn now," remarked the lean sportsman, buttoning his jacket preparatory to breasting the tangled mass of alders, birches, and chimney-top.

"Yes, yes—so it is," concurred the Judge.

Here Johnny gathered another grouse—a high, fast, and beautiful shot at a bird that rose with four others from a matted fence-row and attempted to cross back over the gunner to reach the higher woods. This success seemed only to intensify his previous conviction that he could never learn to shoot grouse. As they progressed it became apparent that there were woodcock in every thicket, as the Judge had prophesied. Once Johnny had the experience, unusual even with woodcock gunners of long service, of seeing three of these birds on the ground at one time—all of them squatting sedately underneath a clump of stiff and thorny locust saplings. Nor would they budge for all his treats, and he finally was forced to wriggle in among the thorny branches. Then all three rose at once as if tossed aloft by a single spring and took devious flights, while the stiff twigs of the locusts, with casual impertinence, blocked every effort that the gunner made to raise his weapon. As he backed painfully out of the locusts after this defeat, it occurred to him that he had yet to gather his first woodcock, though he had been given a half dozen fair opportunities.

"It's the way they have of drifting and side-slipping," one explained. "You're accustomed to fast level-flying birds. That's why you can hit these grouse even when you think you can't. The woodcock deceive you, just as a slow curve fools a batter who can time a fast ball. Take more time—let 'em get away a bit—and hold low."

His guest applied the prescription and let the next bird gain more distance before he shot, when he was rewarded at last by the tiny drift of cut feathers in the air and a long-billed fellow to go in his pocket with the grouse.

Noon found the trio abreast of the last and grandest cover of all, and there they halted for refreshment. The blackened coffee-pot, veteran of many a similar campaign, bubbled and hummed over a tiny fire in a sunny hollow and finally poured from its smoky snout a brown and fragrant beverage to go with the sandwiches from the lunch basket.

This was a novel feature to a gunner's lunch for Johnny, but it had his unqualified approval.

"Judge," he announced, "in common with many others of similar tastes and proclivities, I have been accustomed for many years to believe that a dram of good brandy was a necessary part of a shooter's lunch. You have shown me a better one—hot coffee certainly is the only proper beverage for such occasions. I aim to get me a coffee-bucket for quail-shootin' when I go home."

He slipped back one sleeve of his jacket to disclose a dozen pitted white scars and bluish welts on a sinewy forearm.

"Duck shot," he informed his friends significantly, "and very good reasons for supportin' the cause of hot coffee in the field."

The Judge, who was always ready to lay a fly in front of the Captain's nose, gravely endorsed these views. "I have always entertained," said he, "the most profound doubts as to the propriety of consuming liquor on occasions where firearms are being handled. I am aware that my conclusions are in disagreement with many respected authorities—Frank Forester, for one, and before him, Edward Markland, the first English commentator on wingshooting, who, as you no doubt know, cordially recommended now and then a sup of vigor to pursue the game! not to mention certain contemporary opinions. But I would point out that both these gentlemen were congenital tea drinkers and knew nothing of the recuperative powers resident in a cup of well-made coffee."

The Captain had listened to the momentous discussion with evident restraint and a sardonic gleam in his eye.

"What a fine moral lot you are!" he exclaimed. "What confounded hypocrisy, I'd say! By the Lord Harry, I'm glad I haven't a flask along! I'd hate to risk it to test the quality of your convictions—either one of you!"

Having thus, as he thought, cleared the air of any trace of pedantry and intolerance, he rose to rinse the grounds from the coffee-bucket and pack away the simple utensils.

"Time to start," he declared, watching the Judge from the corner of his eye. "We've the last big strip of cover still to do. The one we finished before lunch was the next to the last in this valley. I beat that one, you remember, Johnny? Now this last piece is undoubtedly the best bit of mixed grouse and woodcock ground in New England, but thicker inside than feathers in a pillow. It's your turn, isn't it Judge, to beat the brush?" he concluded innocently.

That gentleman, who had been complacently smoking his briar, his shoulders settled against a stump, came suddenly alert at these words, and doubt and sharp dismay were expressed in his every feature.

"Eeny—meeny," he muttered, waggling his fingers incredulously, while the Captain watched him with wicked delight and Johnny watched both his friends in bewilderment. "Oh, you danged rascal!" roared the Judge after a moment. "Whipsawed me again, didn't you! Taking turns to make it come out that I'd have to beat the brush in the Last Cover, so you can stay outside and shoot! And that the best piece we'll find today!" he moaned. "Now, lookee here,"—his tones became less peremptory—"now lookee here—you've fixed it so I've had to beat this strip the last three times we've hunted it. You know you have! Now, is that fair? Now, is that honorable? Now, purely on sentimental grounds, is that any way to treat a friend?"

"Don't you try to wheedle me, you old shyster! Don't you think I didn't see you counting your fingers down there this morning and muttering and then generously offering to beat the first piece! You thought you'd figured me into the last one, didn't you? Been gloating over it all the morning, haven't you? Now, doggone you, take your medicine! Oh, dear, dear! Johnny, see the hangdog look on him!" He went off into a gale of derisive merriment.

Far from feeling any resentment the Judge possibly was enjoying the situation quite as much as either of his friends. But he had his part to play.

"All right—all right. Stop that infernal cackling, will you? I'll do it." He picked up his gun, buttoned his old shooting-jacket snugly over his rotund form, and moved toward the valley where the famous Last Cover lay along the hillside like a drift of purple smoke. The victorious Captain dropped a pair of cartridges into his gun, closed the breech, and went to a point in the open pasture from which he could command the eastern flank of the thicket. Silently he motioned Johnny to the opposite side.

The Judge, looking the perfect picture of injured innocence patiently enduring tyrannical persecution, trudged down the slope, splashed through the clear water of the stream, and set himself at the first thick screen of brush. There the author of "Legal Systems of Accounting," a gay little mathematical treatise of some four hundred pages that had earned for him an unassailable reputation as an authority on mathematics—there he halted and faced his tormentor.

"The world," said he bitterly, "is a cruel place for the aged and the helpless. But I'll have you in here sometime, my lad, clear up to your ears and putting out the birds to me! For one of these days I'm bound to figure it out whether that first cover down there is odd or even!"

A
NOVEMBER
TALE

—◆—

Jimmie "took to" gunning with the avidity of a Canuck baby to a maple sugar egg. From the day when his father had hung his old black hat on a fence post and given the ten-year-old his first shooting lesson with the fine Ballard, the boy had progressed so that now at fourteen there were few mature squirrel hunters in the township who cared to match their skill against his in public competition. Young eyes, young nerves and muscles, and a disposition that led him to listen much and talk little in the presence of older riflemen had given him a control over the heavy rifle that was considered more than ordinary, even in a neighborhood where every man was a good rifleman and a dozen more were experts. He was a careful boy—his father had seen to that—and the fact that the old rifle had once in an accident killed a man was a grim reminder that served to keep Jimmie alert to the fatal possibilities of the weapon. The older men no longer said with nervous apprehension:

"Keerful where you p'int that gun, youngster!"

In fact, he was an accepted member of the clan of squirrel hunters and entitled to sit at the nightly conclaves at Narramore's store, though he understood that he ran the lively risk of being ostracized from the agreeable fellowship if he talked too much. Youngsters of whatever attainments were not expected to proffer information upon such mature and serious problems as concerned squirrel and pa'tridge shooting.

In one other respect he had surpassed the older sportsmen of the village. He was known to possess the magic touch that made him a wing shot. In a community where the rifle was still the standard hunting arm for all game, furred or feathered, the art of the shotgun was little known, and understood not at all. Two men who came each year from Albany to shoot grouse and woodcock, and who boarded at Narramore's, were thus gifted with the ability to hit their birds flying, and their doings were marveled at and puzzled over by the native gunners. It was conceded that wing shooting was a "gift"— something granted one at birth by Providence and not possibly to be acquired in the manner in which one gained skill with a rifle. Jimmie had this strange knack, too. Henry Benson had seen the boy "knock a pillerful o' feathers outen a pa'tridge goin' full tilt" over in Stannard's pasture one day! Another, tending a line of muskrat traps on the marsh early one September morning, had seen him shoot a black duck "arter it hed ackterally riz outen the water! Kilt it deader'n a nit, by thunder!"

So Jimmie was regarded as a "nacheral shot"—one marked by nature for splendid accomplishments. As a matter of fact, the boy had hung around Narramore's a good deal, and the good-natured, careless sportsmen from the city, little dreaming that they were as gods who showed miracles and wonders, had taught him something of shotgun shooting. When his father had picked up at a bargain a fine little sixteen gauge double shotgun and a box of brass cartridge cases for two cords of body beech and ten silver dollars, Jimmie's practice at chips and sardine cans was limited only by his ability to purchase powder, shot, caps, and wads, and he rapidly became a very passable wing shot.

In spite of these matters, he knew that the doors of the inner lodge were still closed against him—he had never killed a fox ahead of his own hound. The fox hunters formed a small group of their own, magnificent in their dignity and awful in their reticence. Not for them the footless gabble of pa'tridges and gray squirrels; not even those who had slain the white-tailed deer were qualified to join in their deliberations. They were men of wisdom and sagacity—deep thinkers, strategists, and sure performers, whose counsel was sought by the selectmen in times of trouble.

These fox hunters knew every hound in the county, and in some mysterious way maintained an unwritten pedigree of each qualified dog. Their low-voiced comments concerned "Walkers," "Red Bones," and "Blue Ticks," and they supervised, with the collusion of others of their caste in neighboring townships, the birth, rearing, training, and mating of every foxhound in the long valley. They also knew every vixen's den on the Ledge and the Riverbank, and they guarded these founts of sport well from the attacks of farmers armed with spades and picks. To a fertile vixen they rendered knightly homage and would no more have smitten her with a load of "double B's" than they would have slaughtered their own good wives.

When autumn came with frosty mornings that encouraged the growth of prime fur and distilled a heavy dew that held the hot musky fox scent for hours, the clan hunted. Not for them the wild clamor of the pack, or the thrill of the horn or the thunder of running horses, but rather the solitary vigil on some remote hillside runway—a serious, careful game, very like chess, requiring an involved strategy, in which the guides were the wind, the weather and the solemn, bell-like music of the single hound. Sometimes two dogs were used, especially when a puppy was being initiated into the serious ritual of his profession. Sometimes the play was ended by the heavy boom of the black powder growling behind the charge of double B's in the long barrel of the ten bore. Sometimes, as frequently, perhaps, the sagacious fox triumphed over dog and man. In any event, it was a sport that held its devotees and made them somewhat indifferent to other amusements.

Jimmie had tried it often enough. With the patient persistence of an Indian he had perched under the tree that gave the famous Old Beech Runway its name, while Rove bayed and chanted like a Moslem priest in the depths of Yount's Woods. But while he froze under the beech, the chase went over Grady's Hill. If he selected Grady's Hill, the fox, with the slow, intent hound following at an impersonal interval, slipped like a coppery, shining shadow past the beech. The boy had no secondary position to fall back to when these first stands failed. An older hunter, missing his game at one point, would make a hasty calculation and hasten to another remote spot to wait again for fox and dog. So long as the dog could trail and keep the fox moving, an experienced hunter might continue his sport indefinitely, moving from runway to runway according to the mysterious rules he knew, and at each stand await a shot with a lively anticipation that fed on previous disappointments. Sam Yount or Dick Hassett or any of the coterie could have helped the boy learn the runways, but, though they were kindly men, none of them would do so. That matter was forbidden, and every candidate for honors was required to learn his rote unaided.

On a November evening, Jimmie finished milking, shook down a few forkfuls of hay for the cattle, and emerged from the barn to find a soft luminosity resting on the landscape. A steady fall of white flakes glistened in the yellow rays of the lantern and hissed softly past his face when he bent to pour the foaming bucket of milk into the mouth of the copper strainer. Old Rove, enlivened by some anticipatory message from the weather sprites, came from his bed in the woodshed to meet the boy, and after glancing up once with his sad, amber eyes turned and led the way to the house, the snowflakes sparkling with a brief brilliancy in the dancing light of the lantern before they winked out on his tan and sable coat.

"What's up tomorrow, Sonny? Foxes or pa'tridges?" inquired his father good-naturedly, and the mother looked up from the glowing stove long enough to smile at the boy. "I shall hev to show you the proper way to shoot a fox, I guess," he continued, and Jimmie grinned sheepishly at the mild joke.

"Foxes, I guess," he mumbled. "It's snowin'."

"Pshaw! Boy! Wasting your time on foxes when you c'n just as well as not get a good mess o' pa'tridges!"

The twinkle in his father's gray eye robbed the banter of any sting, but Jimmie was sensitive on this subject of foxes, and when after supper he got out a handful of empty cartridge cases and busied himself measuring and ramming down the charges, he was careful to sit so that his father could not see that the shot selected were the big, blue pellets, the redoubtable "double

B's" of the New England fox hunter, and not the tiny grains used for squirrel, partridge, and other lesser game.

The still darkness of early morning filled the Valley when Jimmie emerged from the kitchen door with Rove slatting against his legs in his eagerness to be abroad. The snow had ceased, and a damp white blanket a couple of inches in depth creaked under the boy's "Pontiacs" as he crossed the yard and struck out for the Hassett Swamp. Rove galloped ahead, stopping again and again to bury his long snout in the snow, first to sniff softly and then to puff the white stuff into the air with a prodigious snort when the scent he detected turned out to be that of field mouse or cottontail, instead of nobler game. Owls whooped vastly from the swamp, and were answered by other disembodied voices from the hill. Over the ragged crest of the Ledge the East reflected a faint illumination hardly brighter than the unearthly radiance of the stars. Other hunters were abroad, or soon would be, for he heard the creak and slam of a door over at Yount's and a single musical note as Sam's famous Red Bone hound welcomed his master and the dawn of a hunting day with one deep, joyful bellow.

Jimmie hastened his steps, and soon the stark ragged clumps of the black alders and the stunted swamp cedars were discernible in the strengthening light. The swamp was a favorite hunting spot for the Valley foxes. Here they came for field mice or an occasional partridge, or even a woodcock in season. The boy had often observed the flattened, rumpled snow with a few crimson stains marking the end of a rabbit trail and the apparent beginning of a line of dainty fox prints. These signs might well have puzzled a city-bred youngster, for the story written in the snow told a plain tale of a rabbit hopping leisurely homeward after an hour or two of nocturnal frolicking with a congenial score of gay bucks and bunnies suddenly and mysteriously metamorphosed into a red fox at the cost of a few drops of blood and a brief struggle in the snow. But Jimmie, familiar with the tragic riddle, would search to the side of the trail until he found at the base of a cedar or in the dun fern stems on some hummock the flat depression where the agile brigand had awaited the moment for the leap and the fatal snap of the pointed jaws.

At this early hour, the foxes would still be abroad, full fed perhaps, and with the wind-like fleetness somewhat clogged by a paunch full of warm rabbit flesh. In another half hour every red vixen's son would be high on the hill, snugly curled in the dry leaves of a favorite lookout to snatch the forty comfortable winks that every hardworking fox is entitled to. But now the scent would be hot and high and the fox near. Rove knew all this and disappeared in the dusky thickets with his marvelous nose to the ground. For some time the boy could follow his progress by the battens of snow dislodged from the bushes as the dog brushed against the stems, but soon the last movement ceased and a thick, motionless mood claimed the swamp. Ten minutes passed, and a northern hare, invisible but for his eyes and the jetty tips of his ears, hopped soundlessly into a little clearing and regarded the intruder with a blank and silly stare. Presently, it flipped out a great hind foot and expertly scratched an ear without interrupting its shallow, pointless observation of this new, dark stump. Then, as a single singing bugle note broke from the depths of the swamp, it came to the alert and fled in a soundless panic. Jimmie jumped inside his skin, for it is startling to man, whose muscles do not have the gift of instantaneous velocity, to witness this hair-trigger shifting from immobility to flickering action—the common possession of any wild creature alarmed to fight or flight.

"Umph! Umph!" cried Rove, lacking but a confirmatory sniff or two to enable him to warrant to the still Valley the true, golden metal of his find. Then as the warm, rank musk of his quarry struck full into his nostrils, he cast away all uncertainty and opened his deep throat to the full rolling song of the hunt.

"Ow! Ow! Ow! Oo—oo—oooh! Ow! Ow! Ow! Oo—oo—oooh!"

Clear as a bugle, but with the added depth and richness of the 'cello, the wild music rolled across the Valley and was thrown back from the lofty Ledge to be tossed again from hill to hill, until its diminishing reiteration was drowned in a fresh volume of song that rolled from the hound's throat in a cadence regular and sustained. Rove was a foxhound bred to the line, and to those lean New Englanders the "bugle" was as indispensable as the "nose." Let rabbit hounds betray their mean and careless ancestry by the shrill, squealing discords that they could not restrain when the scent was hot! Rove, chanting the glory of his race, would sing truly every note from invocation to benediction, whether the run continued for an hour or for ten, yes, or thrice the larger number.

The boy, standing in the soft snow listened for a moment.

"He's started!" he breathed. "Fresh! Mebbe jumped him! Oh! My Golly!"

A hot pride flushed his cheeks. So, years later, he would wordlessly exult with a swelling breast while he stood in the trenches with his waiting men and heard the rushing thunder of an American artillery barrage roaring across the arc of a gray morning sky. There is a close and subtle kinship between war and hunting. Jimmie only knew that something heady and strong was in his blood while the Ledge changed "Oo! Oo! Oooh!" and Grady's Hill boomed a fainter "Ow! Ow! Ow!" and Rove, in full stride, threw a ceaseless stream of fresh music into the antiphonal jargon that roused every farm dog in the Valley.

The chase immediately left the swamp. The fox crossed the Martin Meadow and headed straight down the Valley. For a time the boy's heart sank, for in that direction lay the river with its bluff, sandy banks honeycombed with fox holes. Not usually did a fox run straight to earth, but sometimes a full-fed yearling would decline the hound's challenge and seek ignominious safety in the home den, regardless of the damage he might bring to the vulpine community by such betrayal.

But this fox was no craven. Just as the hound's clangor faded to the very edge of silence, the chase turned in a slow arc, and as the boy's straining ears caught the increasing volume, he snatched his gun off his forearm and legged it for the Nutting pasture. Ahead of him lay the gentle slope of a hill partially overgrown with young pines and paper birches. He had flushed many a woodcock from those congenial tangles, but his thought was not on the queer, long-billed toothsome bird as he clambered over the rail fence and set himself at the hill. Just at the crest, a huge butternut reared its mighty trunk, and where it stood a low, collapsed stone wall came up from an orchard of sugar maples to meet the final angle of a rail fence that at this point emerged from the woods. It was a favorite crossing for foxes, and Jimmie had often seen their pad marks running along under the shelter of the old wall. While he was still some three hundred long strides from the angle, he heard Rove heading up the brook toward the sugar grove. He broke into a run, but the damp snow balled under his thumping heels until he felt as if he were stumbling on insecure stilts that broke and crumbled always at the most awkward moment and sent him slipping and sliding helplessly until he could grasp a sapling and correct his direction. So it was that puffing, stumbling, and chagrined, he heard Rove burst in among the maples and saw a coppery thing as light as thistledown float past the butternut and with leisurely and scornful gait disappear into the woods.

He reached the fence in time to intercept the dog, determined to call Rove off and try, before it was too late, to start another fox. He knew that, pitted against an "ol' stager" such as this fox had proved to be, his own scant knowledge of runways and the strategy of the chase made it most unlikely that he would have so much as a second tantalizing glimpse of that fleet figure. But calling Rove off a warm trail was not a matter so easily accomplished, Jimmie discovered. The dog, completely isolated by the solemn ritual of his priesthood, came steadily up the wall and passed, chanting melodiously, within ten feet of his master, and all Jimmie's shouts and whistles and coaxings did not serve to penetrate the animal's hypnotic devotion to his task. He passed like a preoccupied stranger, and in turn vanished into the white silence of the woods.

"The old fool!" mourned Jimmie disconsolately. "As far as that fox is concerned, I might jest as well go home or go pa'tridge huntin' or somethin'. I wisht I knew where to turn that fox! Gosh! Wan't he a beauty, though!"

Compelled by the curb of circumstance to consider the desirability of the prize he might have, rather than the prize he desired, he reached a philosophical conclusion and presently set off cheerfully for the Grady pasture, where endless tangles of hazel bushes, wild grapevines, poplars, and pines gave food and concealment to the coveys of ruffed grouse. After all, pa'tridge shooting was good sport—none better. Barring only the glowing pelt of a fine fox for which Narramore would pay ten dollars in cash or eleven "in trade," there was no spoil of the hills more welcome than a brace of plump pa'tridge.

So, fortified by his reflections, he nearly persuaded himself that he had never entertained any designs against foxes anyhow—a thought, however, that did not reconcile easily with the presence of a half dozen heavily charged fox loads in his jacket pocket. He trudged through the Grady Woods, in whose tall hickories he had, earlier in the season, shot many a nimble squirrel, and paused for a moment to gaze at the decaying stump of the big oak that the Hessian soldiers had cut a century and more ago in some forgotten Revolutionary foraging or raid. From time to time he heard the faint, far-off baying of the hound, now so distant with his hopeless chase that the clangor of his great voice seemed no louder than the piping of the tiny nuthatch clinging to a tree trunk just over his head. Once there was a sudden burst of wild music from the direction of the river, and the boy recognized the pure, resonant voice of Sam Yount's hound, and knew that the veteran hunter was abroad.

On Grady's Hill he brushed the melting snow from a stump and sat down to rest and watch the energetic scamperings of a red squirrel getting up nuts for breakfast from one of his many storage cellars. He wondered how the little scamp could remember all these hiding places, or if he didn't really remember them; but smelled them out instead.

A half hour passed, and his thoughts were interrupted by a glimpse of an apparition that slipped through the hazel bushes like a shadow and vanished behind a knoll. So swift and fleeting was the impression, just caught in the edge of his vision, that he wasn't sure what had moved, or whether anything really had moved at all. But he shifted his gun on his knees and watched the crest and flanks of the knoll carefully. The squirrel suddenly left off his untidy burrowing in the snow and fled up a hickory, where he set up a violent resentful squalling. Away off, Jimmie heard the faint babble of hounds' voices.

So quickly that he did not see it come, a splendid creature appeared on the knoll. It was like magic. The boy's gaze had never left the spot, and yet there stood the fox, a beautiful, wary thing, with its forefeet on a boulder and its black sharp nose pointed back over its shoulders as it listened to the distant chanting of the dogs. Standing so, the creature never knew whence came its death blow. With pulses thundering, by a mighty wilful effort forcing his hands to slow caution, the boy brought up the gun until the stock touched his cheek and his eyes stared straight down the barrels. It took an age to accomplish this, for it had to be done in a fashion as imperceptible as the movement of mist rising from a stream. The least twitch of a hand or eye, he knew, would send that poised figure from view like a flash. Finally the brass sight at the muzzle hovered just behind the victim's foreshoulders, and then the gun roared and belched a thick cloud of white smoke.

When Jimmie emerged from the pungent powder wreaths at a run, the knoll was bare and the fox gone—vanished as abruptly as it had appeared.

Bitter disappointment filled the boy's heart and brought a suspicious moisture to his eyes. In the snow were the pad marks where the fox had stood, and
a half dozen long furrows where the double B's had raked. More than this he
perceived—there were tiny tufts of bronze and black fur scattered over the
white surface.

"Anyways, it was a fox an' I rasped him!" Jimmie muttered. "I helt right!"

Twenty feet down the slope he spied the close group of prints made by a
running fox and here, too, were more wisps of fur and a crimson sprinkle. Just
in the hazels lay the fox, stone dead, with one black forefoot between his fast-
clenched jaws.

Too exultant to feel remorse for the tragic end he had put to a life, the boy
dragged his prize to the knoll, where he knelt in order to admire every fascinating detail of the lustrous coat, the jetty ears, the dainty pads that would
never again carry their owner like a puff of thistledown, the sharp muzzle
keen to sniff out the hiding place of a family of field mice or a partridge under the snow, the teeth, sharp as needles, that had clipped so many little lives.
No other fox would ever be so wonderful. So intent was the boy that the
voices of the hounds down at the foot of the hill failed to reach his con-
sciousness. The slow, methodical baying was close at hand when Jimmie finally realized it and looked up to see, not Rove, his companion of the morning, but the gaunt, long-legged hound that belonged to the veteran Sam
Yount. There could be no mistake about it, he was trailing Jimmie's fox, and
Jimmie, the victim of a heartless Fate, had shot his first fox ahead of another
man's dog!

The realization brought him in one sickening swoop from exultation to utter debasement, and when Music, the Yount hound, came up to give his victim a formal shake, the boy could have wept at witnessing this dumb patent
of ownership. For the fox belonged to Yount under the rules by which all decent fox hunters conducted their sport. It was the rule,—if the dog was hunting "free" the game was Jimmie's, but if Yount was out with his gun, the
prize belonged to Music's master. Even this faint color of hope soon faded,
for there was a crunching of snow-covered boots, and the boy saw the long
figure of his neighbor approaching, a heavy double gun over one shoulder.

"Mornin', Jimmie! Got him, did ye? My! Ain't he a nice one?" He brought
his grave, good-humored face nearer to the dead fox as a sharper interest stirred him. He turned the limp carcass and examined it long and critically. "I
sw'ar, youngster, I b'lieve you've kilt the Moscow Medder Fox! Yis, sir! I
b'lieve you've come it on the ol' daddy of 'em all! Your Pa an' all of the rest
on us, too, hev been chasin' that critter f'r six, seven years now. I vummy!
Ain't he a cute one?"

"He—he's yourn, Mr. Yount!" declared the boy sturdily. "I thought Rove
had him, but 'twan't Rove—'twuz Music. I—I guess if ye don't mind I'll leave
ye naow an' go 'long."

The lean hunter turned a pair of keen gray eyes on the boyish face in a look that noted the tightly held lips and the eyes that blinked in the brilliant sunlight.

"Sho!" said he, "I'll go 'long with ye if you'll wait two shakes 'til I git this old feller's pelt off."

Thus held to the rack, Jimmie stood by and watched the deft operation with an admiration that persisted in spite of his sudden dislike for a man who would thus cold-bloodedly accept his dues without so much as a "thank ye, kindly." The veteran worked with a sure skill. Not an unnecessary knife cut, not a single drop of moisture to mat the beautiful fur; nothing, in fact, but a series of motions so deft and swift that the pelt appeared to come off by its own volition.

"There, sir!" grunted Sam, as he held the fur aloft and shook it out, while Music rose on his hind legs for one dignified sniff of his vanquished adversary's shining mantle. "Narramore'll pay twelve dollars for that pelt, I'll bet ye!"

"I—I guess so!" Jimmie admitted painfully, miserably unaware of the quizzical twinkle in the gray eyes. "Yis," he added, striving for the proper impersonal tone, "yis—I guess he's wuth all o' that."

Yount suddenly turned and tucked the fur into the boy's jacket pocket—tucked it in according to the foxhunter's custom, so that the great brush hung down outside where all who looked might see that here walked a proven one of the fraternity.

"Sho! Jimmie!" he chuckled, "I wuz jest foolin! You kilt him an' he's yourn!"

Then, seeing a prideful protest in the young face, he did a second knightly deed.

"He wuz Rove's fox, anyhow—Music kinder cut in on him over back o' Grady's!"

"Well, if so, I thank ye kindly, Mr. Yount!" stammered Jimmie in a voice that quivered with happiness. "I hope ye git one, too."

"Sartain to! Come on, Music! The day's young yit! Le's go start another!" cried Sam cheerfully. "Say Jimmie! You tell your father that I said you're a reg'lar buster! Will ye?"

He turned and strode away, a homely figure enough; and Music, after one solemn, faintly puzzled look at the magnificent brush of the Lord of the Moscow Meadows hanging gracefully from Jimmie's pocket, turned and trotted after him.

THE CLIMAX CAPPED

Inky darkness wrapped the Valley and shut from the vision all details of the familiar landscape, but the Narramore brook, roaring and gurgling as its rain-swollen torrent swept under the wooden bridge, gave the Captain his course and bearings as he made his way toward the Judge's house on this wild November night. All day long the storm had lashed the countryside with sweeping volleys of chill gray rain. It flattened the frost-stricken weeds in the fence corners, swept the sodden wreckage of summer into the roadside ditches, and brought the stubborn last of the leaves down from tossing branches of the maples. The weather had been so forbidding even as to discourage our two hardy sportsmen from venturing forth, and when the elements succeeded in daunting the amiable Judge and his lean friend, it was certain that few of the wild creatures would stir abroad. The foxes curled in their burrows on the river bank had slept fitfully, waking and blinking their yellow eyes and harking to the sound of the slashing tempest outside. The rabbits stuck to their forms or hunched snugly in their warrens; the partridges—the ruffed grouse of New England—found lofty shelter among the thick branches of pine or hemlock, crowding close against the swaying trunks of the trees; the squirrels stayed in their holes in the hollow boles of butternut and maple; and only the "hell divers," cutting their wakes here and there on the beaten surface of the Marsh, seemed to find any enjoyment in the gray tempest of wind and autumn rain.

But at the Judge's house, all was warmth and cozy comfort. The little spaniel, informed of the Captain's approach by some sense not included in humanity's five, met the guest at the door and, with wagging stub-tail, escorted him to the room that served the Court House Gentleman both as library and den. A fire of old apple wood blazed on the hearth, distilling a smoky fragrance into the wide room, and before it sat the pudgy Judge with, as might be expected, a burnished weapon lying across his sturdy knees, while its mate reposed in a flat mahogany case on a low table at his elbow.

"And so here you are!" chided the caller. "You procrastinatin' old coot!

Crying all the week because I wouldn't 'give you time to read up a little law,' and now, with a whole day to yourself, do you spend it reading law? You do not! I'll bet you've been tinkering with firearms all day! Never turned a page now, did you?"

"Order! Order!" bellowed the Judge, delighted at this prospect of a better finish to a lonely day. "Of course, I've been studying—a demnition important case, too. 'Twelve-bores versus Twenty-bores,' by an eminent British authority who knows what he's talking about!"

"Judgment rendered in favor of the Twelve-bore, of course," remarked the other. "You wouldn't be so darned perky if it weren't. What are you fiddling with there? The old Captain Narramore guns?"

He took one of the weapons from the Judge, while his friend lifted its counterpart from the case and began furbishing it with a bit of oily flannel.

The guns, muzzle-loaders, and as alike as two peas in their mahogany and green velvet pod, had been the property of a sportsman ancestor of the Judge's who one day cleaned them carefully, packed them securely in their case, and went away to die across a gun trail at Chancellorsville. The Captain had handled them a hundred times, admiring their perfect workmanship and the superb balance imparted by the genius of Joe Manton nearly a century ago.

"I believe I could hit a partridge with this one," he now declared, dropping into a chair.

"You'll have a chance to prove it tommorow," said his friend, "for I've decided we'll use these guns again. I've got plenty of powder, shot, wads and caps. That high wind means it'll clear in the night, with a fine day to come. You don't need to go home—sleep here and have breakfast, I'll 'phone the Dark-Haired Lady that you're here and sober. I'll find a nicked razor and a worn-out toothbrush for you, and I'll fix the breakfast eggs 'cording to that Louisiana recipe. We'll hunt those ridges over in York State," he urged. "What do you say? Will you come?"

"All right—if you'll get up a jug of cider right now—'tain't worked none, I hope. But hadn't we better use our own guns? I'm dubious about these old jewels. We aren't used to 'em, Judge. We'll be likely to get two doses down one barrel and bust a collar bone, and the caps will fall off the nipples, and—"

"They can't!" the Judge interrupted triumphantly. "Look here, Joe Manton thought of that long before you did, young feller! See these threads that run around each nipple? Push a cap down over those, and you can hardly pull it off, 'less you fire it. Have you got to have ejectors and single triggers in order to make a bag of birds?" he demanded scornfully. "I want to know!"

"All right, I can do it if you can, I guess. But let's get that cider up!"

Fifty years in the Valley had made the Judge weatherwise, and when the two arose sometime before sunrise the next morning, they found a clear and rosy sky overhead. The wind had fallen with the dawn.

The Judge produced a better razor than he had promised, and while the Captain labored to enhance his personal appearance his friend—who, in the matter of cooking, could have given Antoine a race any day—fixed out a generous platter of kidneys, eggs, and sausages.

"Now, then," said the Judge, when these good things had been freely dealt with, "come into the library and I'll issue you your ammunition. Here's your powder flask filled with a pound of good black powder, with the charger set to throw three drams to a load, and your shot pouch—two pounds of chilled sevens in it. Dump these caps in your watch pocket and your wads into your jacket pocket—right-hand side—and we're ready. Ellen has fixed the lunch."

He paused a moment, and then from a pouch in the gun case extracted a half dozen round lead balls. Three of these he handed to his companion.

"The deer season is open in York State," he reminded him, "and we might run onto a buck. It's good deer country, that limestone region, with all those hickories and oaks and beeches."

The Captain, while accepting the remote possibility of encountering a buck, was not so sanguine on the prospect of hitting anything with this type of projectile.

"Never saw a shotgun yet that would put a round ball into a meeting-house window at thirty paces," said he, "and by the time you've got the shot *up* and the ball *down*, your buck will be gone—and the season closed probably."

"*These* guns will shoot 'em straight," asserted his friend. "I know, because I tried 'em one day up in Paraday's pasture. At fifty paces you can knock the neck off a bottle with 'em. You needn't squirm—you're going gunning the way your granddaddy did, and if you don't get some game you can't blame it on the gun!"

The Judge's car took them comfortably to the State Line, where they left the highway to follow henceforth a narrow dirt road that wound in and out of creek bottoms and over hills, where the fading fringe of roadside goldenrod and wild asters brushed their fronds against the sides of the laboring vehicle. Now and then from some nameless summit they caught glimpses of the distant Lake, its waters gleaming through the bordering woodlands now nearly stripped of summer foliage. Chipmunks and an occasional gray squirrel scampered across the road, and once a partridge whirred out of a grapevine at a fence corner. Once, too, a gorgeous ringneck stalked from a hedge and stared at them until the Captain dismounted and made an attempt to charge his unfamiliar weapon, when the pheasant, cackling derisively, took noisy wing and flew far down into the middle of a swamp.

"Load her up if you want to," said the Judge. "We're nearly there anyway, and she's safe enough if you don't cap those nipples. If you get a cap on you can't get it off again because of those threads I showed you."

"I'll wait and load when you load," the other decided.

They were now in the limestone region, a country formed by the patient forces of Nature upon a buttress of broad ribs of gray stone. These ridges lay side by side, separated with considerable regularity by narrow valleys down which idled slow streams of clear water. Open spaces of pasture land occurred here and there, the grass showing green and vigorous despite the punishing frosts that elsewhere at this season had pinched the sap from other herbage. Clumps of pine and juniper grew there, too, and the ubiquitous thornapple and wild grape indicated why the region found favor with the grouse. Sheep paths led upwards from the valleys, winding in and out among the broken boulders to the ridge tops. On this higher ground grew oaks and hickories, pines and sumach clumps, and great beeches, their trunks as gray as the limestone in which their ancient roots were bedded. Woodcock rarely, if ever, came into these ridges—neither the soil nor the growth was suited to the birds' requirements—but the grouse found the environment wholly to their liking. The two friends seldom went to the region in search of game until late in the season when heavy frosts and cold rains had moved the woodcock southward from the swamps and alder runs nearer home. After that, for the few remaining days of the legal season, they sought the bold gray native bird in these remote haunts, and occasionally bagged a cock pheasant there, for these aliens had in recent years come northward from Hudson Valley in numbers and successfully established their colonies.

No council of war was necessary with the two friends—they knew the game too well—and while the Captain followed one edge of the valley, keeping close to the base of the ridge, the Judge took the other edge. When a valley had been searched in this fashion, they climbed to the top of the next ridge, turned about face, and keeping a good interval between them worked back like a pair of hawks beating a field for mice. Arriving opposite the original starting point, they scrambled down to the broad floor of the next ravine and began all over again.

The simple system afforded the greatest number of opportunities, for the wily grouse, in escaping one gunner, often crossed the ravine into range of the other. An opportunity of this sort was soon offered. The Judge, following a sheep path into a thicket of juniper, heard the rising thunder of a bird that he could not see, and his shout of "Mark!" rang across the valley. His companion a hundred yards away looked up to see the grouse dip to the slope of the valley. On through the sunlight it came, its wings blurred with speed as it gained pace to scale the crest above the watching gunner, who pulled both hammers of his gun to full cock and set himself to take the shot. The bird was upon him in an instant, zooming upward like a 'plane coming up from a nose dive, the air pressing down the penciled plumage so firmly as to give to the bird the appearance of polished metal. The old gun came up, quick as a stroke from a cat's paw, the smoke spurted, the grouse whirled down against the bank with a thud plainly audible to the Judge across the valley.

"That was a pretty shot!" the older man remarked when they met at the end of the ravine. "The old gun didn't fail you, did it? The cap was there when you wanted it, wasn't it? A good part of the pleasure of game-bird shooting is in the stirring pictures it furnishes of scenes like that one, and, no doubt about it, the use of smokeless powder takes something spectacular out of bird-shooting. I like to observe a spout of smoke once in a while as you see it in old sporting engravings."

The Captain harbored a mild superstition.

"I'd almost rather miss the first bird of the day than to bag it," said he. "Some of the worst days' shooting I've ever been guilty of began in just this too-perfect way. Something will go wrong yet," he concluded dubiously as they emerged on the crest and separated for the next beat.

Some distance ahead, the Judge's questing eye picked up a broad gleam of scarlet in the edge of a clump of small pines. He knew that the splash of vigorous color came from the laden twigs of a thorn-apple tree in full fruit. Such a sight is full of significance to the grouse shooter, and the sportsman accordingly prepared his weapon and advanced on quiet feet.

Presently there was a flick of motion, too lightning-quick for the eye to absorb any of its detail, and a big grouse shot out from the cover of a pine and pitched over the brink into the valley. The load of sevens arrived a handbreadth too late, but the shot ripped a swath across the brown carpet of the pine needles and knocked a sulphurous dust from the gray stones over which the bird had dropped.

The crash of the gun did even more than this, for it galvanized a half dozen other birds which had been breakfasting on the fruit, and sent them dashing for safety. Some pitched over the edge after their leader, but two of them whirred out across the plateau and gave the Judge a fair chance for his second barrel, and he had the thrill of seeing through the smoke of the discharge the downright plunge of the stricken bird.

When the Judge had retrieved his game and recharged his weapon from flask and pouch, the two sportsmen decided that it was worth while to interrupt the beat long enough to scramble down into the hollow whence most of the flock had vanished, and try to locate some of these stragglers. They spent some time in the effort, struggling through thickets and over boulders, and were rewarded only by such benefits as normally attend sharp exercise and, once or twice, by the faint thunder of wings as one or another of their intended victims flushed far ahead of them.

So, after a time they climbed back to the ridge and resumed their original course. Here they had better success. The Judge bagged a grouse almost immediately, and his friend, observing some furtive movement in a clump of sumach, came within an ace of cutting down a hen pheasant, when this forbidden bird took wing instead of the grouse he had so confidently expected.

"I had the gun three inches off his beak," he told the Judge with some confusion of gender when they stopped for lunch, "and the trigger half pulled, when I saw her tail. I'd 'a' been in a nice fix if I'd killed it, wouldn't I? Have you seen any deer sign?"

"Just some old tracks," replied the Judge, "while we were down in the bottom there."

"Well," the other informed him, "you may have a chance to use a couple of those big slugs yet—that beech grove over there looks as if all the deer in the Adirondacks had been feeding in it—fresh, too."

They had not proceeded a hundred paces from the spot where they had lunched when, with a thump of tiny hooves, a doe and two fawns sprang out of a thicket and stood watching the gunners for a minute before trotting off to the thicker woods.

"There are the sign-makers," said the Judge, and the other agreed that the three dainty animals had probably wrought the disturbance he had noted underneath the beeches. For a time, however, he watched the thickets more closely, half expecting a glimpse of an antlered head, but he soon lost interest in the prospect when the Judge routed out another flock of grouse. These birds, disdaining to seek the safety in the valley, scattered out far down the ridge, where they hid behind brush-grown boulders and fallen logs. One came bursting from a brush-heap almost into the Judge's face, and then hung before him "like a rag on a stick," as the exasperated jurist described it, for as long as it took him to fire one load a foot too high and the other a foot too low. Another impudent rascal stepped off a log into the Captain's path, and, clucking tantalizingly while the sportsman stood tense with gun ready for the rise he instantly anticipated, walked calmly behind a juniper not six feet high and vanished utterly. The gunner, guessing the trick, for it was an old one, dashed upon the juniper without a second's delay, but the bird had disappeared as mysteriously as if it had stepped into a fairy ring. And although he knew that the quarry had promptly sailed away on quiet wings, keeping the shrub between them, still that did not explain how the bird could have reached the nearest cover a hundred yards away in the second or two allowed it. That, however, was the only possible solution—a common enough ruse, too, with these clever birds. As he turned away, meditating on the marvelous ingenuity of the grouse, the bird roared up behind him from beneath the juniper, where it had lain all during the time the Captain had stood over the innocent shrub! The strategist deserved a better reward than the load of shot which smote him in full flight, and which brought him bouncing along the close-cropped pasture sward with a trail of feathers floating after him.

"If you'd kept still, you'd have won," the gunner admonished, as he smoothed the rumpled feathers and pocketed the bird, "but I suppose the joke was too good to keep, and you just had to let me know you'd fooled me."

He paused to charge his gun, and enjoyed a certain satisfaction in the complicated process so different from the simple act of dropping a cartridge into an open breech. Being of reflective disposition, he then fell to speculating upon the man who originally had owned this weapon. What delight he must have taken in the possession and use of his two superb bird guns, and what feelings of doubt and regret he must have known when the stern obligations of patriotism compelled him to put these splendid playthings away and to arm himself in grimmer fashion! Had he suspected perhaps that he would never use them again? And had he in that last brief moment, slipping into darkness beneath the smoke and roar of his battery, had he then a lost and wistful vision of these autumn-clad hills and valleys glowing in the sunlight and the gray grouse waiting for him in the well-remembered coverts?

The sound of his friend's gun dismissed the reverie. A partridge, evidently flushed and missed by the jurist, was cutting across the ridge, and while he watched it, the bird tilted on set wings and disappeared along the bank in front of him. The Captain marked the spot and went forward, stepping softly and with eyes and ears on guard to catch the first warning movement. He was suddenly aware that he was staring straight into the eyes of a splendid buck. The creature had been lying among the leaves in a thicket of hazel brush, and had risen to its feet as the gunner approached, but the Captain had seen no motion—the buck seemed absolutely to materialize out of nothing more solid than the golden lights and the tan shadows of the thicket.

"Too far for bird-shot," thought the man, "they'd hurt him, but wouldn't kill him. If I move to get one of those balls down, he'll run."

The two stood motionless for a half minute. Then, since it was all that he could do, the man moved a hand cautiously toward his pocket. Instantly the deer turned, and, swift as light, slipped into the thicket like a weasel and was gone as silently as he had appeared.

After a breathless minute, the Captain backed quietly away from the spot, careful lest sound or scent alarm the animal, for he was sure the buck had halted again at no great distance among the thickets that covered the flank of the ridge. A plan already was shaped in his mind. When he was clear of the thickets, he ran out until he could get the Judge's attention, beckoned him over, and in low tones described what had transpired.

"Listen, now! He's still in that ravine, and if I work slowly up it from below him, he's sure to skulk along ahead of me until he can get into the big woods. He won't try to cross the open unless he's scared—he thinks I didn't see him, or he'd have run when I moved, instead of slinking away.

"Don't stop to pull the shot charges—drop the balls down on top of 'em—it'll kick, but that buck is worth it! Now, cut wide around and get two or three hundred yards up the bank and be ready. I'll bring him right past your nose!"

"You go, and I'll drive him," the Judge offered generously, as he slipped the deadly missiles down the barrels of his gun.

"No—I've shot more deer than you have. Don't argue about it! Besides, I know where he is. Hurry!"

The Judge trotted off as directed, moving at a faster pace than one would have believed his short legs were capable of, and the other watched him until he reached the ravine and settled himself where he evidently had a satisfactory view of the hillside below him.

Then the Captain began his part of the maneuver. Keeping well out, as the Judge had done, he moved in the opposite direction until he knew that he was well below the buck. There he entered the ravine and began a careful stalk. After a long interval, he heard distinctly a faint thump, the fretful protest of a deer disturbed, but not panic-stricken, and knew from this that the game was ahead of him and that, so far at least, the plot was developing satisfactorily. Presently, in proof of this, he came upon tracks, large and unmistakable, printed in the loose dirt of a sheep path and pointing in the direction desired. After a further cautious advance, he thought that the buck must now be nearing the Judge's ambush, and he listened for the inevitable shot.

Slowly now—and the buck would walk right out to the Judge, presenting a shot that couldn't be missed. Still no crash from the waiting gun. Could the deer have detected the trap and slipped quietly out of it? The trail still led in the right direction. A little farther then, but carefully—

The Judge's voice sounding almost in his ear made the stalker jump.

"You may as well quit playing Daniel Boone and come up out of there!" it said bitterly.

"Where's the buck?" gasped his friend.

"Gone," said the other laconically.

He sat at the foot of a beech, his gun across his knees, and his eyes fixed on some far, dreary horizon.

"Well, what happened? Can't you talk? Did you see him? Didn't he come out in range? Did you have buck fever?"

"Right there he came," said the Judge solemnly, "right along that path—and may my tongue cleave to the roof of my mouth if I ever saw a bigger one!"

"Why didn't you shoot?"

"Right on his shoulder I held the bead," the Judge continued, but it was apparent that the statement was not meant as an answer to the other's question. Indeed, the speaker seemed not to have heard the query at all. His tones and manner were those of a person in a state of hypnosis, whose speech and expression is compelled. "And then I pulled the trigger," he added.

"Did it misfire then?"

"It didn't go," said the Judge; "it didn't go, because—because the cap had fallen off the nipple."

"Hah!" ejaculated the Captain explosively. "But you still had your left barrel—"

The Judge lifted his stricken countenance. He visioned the long years yet to come when he must still associate with this man and endure his loathsome and persistent conception of humor. In that instant, temptation assailed him—a quick, deft little lie right now would save him untold humiliation. But he put the unworthy thought aside in a heroic gesture of self-abnegation.

"Oh! Death, where is thy sting?" he demanded. "The damned cap fell off that one, too!"

ACCORDING
TO THE
CONSTITUTION

The Dark-Haired Lady had packed a wardrobe trunk as big as a voting booth and departed down the Hudson Valley to attend a class reunion.

"Sun Dance," the Captain called it when speaking of the matter to his friend, the Judge. "Those girls will be parading around the Campus and sitting up on top of Sunset Hill, gazing at the moon and yelping the songs of Alma Mater, for a week or more. In a way, these female college orgies are worse than Legion conventions—they last longer. Meanwhile," he added complacently, "I'm supposed to come over and board with you."

"That puts us both on the town," said the Judge, shaking his head, "I'm supposed to board with *you* while old Ellen visits her brother's folks down at Pawlet. Darn poor staff work, if you ask *me*. But what of it! Hassett's Restaurant can still scramble eggs and broil good tenderloins. *And* we won't have to leave the brook right in the middle of the evening rise in order to get home for dinner. But for female tyranny, I'd have had that old blue-backed trout up in the Kettle Hole long before this. He doesn't start feeding until all the other fish have quit."

The Captain grinned as he measured the possibilities of a week at the peak of the season without any domestic responsibilities.

"We'll fish!" he declared.

On an evening a few days later the two friends stumbled along the old road that makes such a futile attempt to follow the twisting course of the Alder Brook. When the moist soil of the worn cart tracks muffled their footfalls, they could hear through the limpid May twilight the rush and gurgle of the stream, the melancholy plaint of the whippoorwills, and the whir of a diving nighthawk like a long roll on muffled drums. The air was heavy with the scent of newly burst leaf buds, and of moist earth, and with the fragrance of thorn-apple blossoms.

Their creels were heavy, and as they trudged along companionably in the gathering darkness they were nearly content.

The Judge broke the silence.

"Great fishin'," said he. "Old Blue Back came up and rolled to a Number 10 Stone, and I missed him, darn it! So help me, the swirl he made was three feet across—and he never broached. But I've got eight of the prettiest fish you ever saw—good, dark, fat fish, just right for eating."

"Nine for me," his friend replied. "And I'm hungry enough to eat 'em raw. Seems as if I'd rather, almost, than to have Hassett's cook ruin 'em the way he does. Slick with grease, half done, and garnished with some damn thing! Phaugh! To fulfill his manifest destiny a brook trout has to be split and broiled over open coals or broiled with a slice of salt pork or bacon in an iron skillet over a middling brisk fire. I've even had good results frying smallish ones in deep olive oil. In any case they oughtn't to be garnished or sauced. Just lay 'em brown and smoking on a hot, clean blue and white platter, or a fresh ash chip if you're in the woods, and make your grace short and fervent. I swear the very thought of it's got me to cryin'!"

"Then let's take 'em home and cook 'em ourselves," the Judge proposed, swallowing hard. "I'm of the old school that used to believe that it was as much a part of a sportsman's qualifications to know how to cook his game as to know how to take it."

But their car had been left in Uncle Bill Paraday's dooryard, and as the two anglers emerged from the lane a pair of great, gaunt foxhounds came out to give them dignified welcome, and the old gentleman himself hailed them hospitably from the porch.

"Got ye a nice mess, didn't ye? Knew ye would. Knew from the way the nighthawks have been skivin' around that the fish would be up. Le's see 'em."

The baskets were opened to Uncle Bill's critical inspection.

"My, but they air a harndsome mess!" said he approvingly. "Now, I'll tell ye what le's do. Your womern folks ain't to home, be they? Thought not. You wouldn't be fishing so late ef they was. Le's take them trout down to the spring an' clean 'em good an' let Candace cook 'em—she won't spile 'em, I'll warrant ye—an' we'll hev a time. Why don't ye? Candace's got a pan of corn-bread and a kettleful of cowslip greens cookin.' Haow about it? You fellers ain't been up for a long time."

"How about it, Mrs. Paraday?" echoed the Judge, sorely tempted, address-ing the plump, white-haired mistress of the house.

"Why, surely," she cried, "I'd love to have a bite of trout. *He* don't go fishin' much. Wastes his time shoolin' around after foxes—which if you git 'em you can't eat 'em." Her gentle, humorous glance rested for a moment upon her mate.

Against such sincere invitations the two, tempted alike by the prospect of properly cooked brook trout and interesting converse, offered but the feeblest protest.

Half an hour later the four of them sat down to a heaping platterful of golden brown fish, delicate, crisp slices of salt pork, heaps of fragrant "greens," and cornbread, all supported by a huge, red, porcelain pot of hot coffee.

To the Judge and the ravenous Captain their host's briefest grace seemed all too long and dilatory.

When they finally left the table and adjourned to the porch, nothing remained save a tall heap of fishy skeletons.

"That old Blue Back fish," remarked the Judge, breaking the pleasant thoughtful silence. Across the pasture where the Brook ran sounded the 'cellos of the great bullfrogs.

"If you had a night crawler," he speculated, "and got above him and then let it drift down with the current, you'd take him."

"Why don't ye?" inquired the old man quietly.

"Wouldn't be fair," responded the Judge.

"Why not?"

After some reflection the Judge said, "Night crawlers and worms and grubs and snails and underwater bugs are a trout's regular fare. They're his to enjoy in peace and tranquillity according to the Constitution—unless you need a fish mighty bad. But the moths and gnats and flies he takes from the air—I suspect he does it as much for the sport of the thing as for food. So, if you can flick him something that looks like a fly and land it so he thinks it is a fly, you're entitled to your fish—if you can take him. At least that's the way I feel about it."

There followed a long silence. The two foxhounds came up, stretched themselves at their master's feet, emitted gusty sighs, and dropped off into fitful, whimpering slumber.

"I guess you're right," said their host after a time. "Anyway, you seem to git closer to the true religion than most of 'em."

The frogs had tuned up, by now, for their nightly symphony. The trifling disharmonies and those awkward moments when perfect synchronization seems unattainable, which trouble all orchestras during the opening number, were being straightened out satisfactorily under the austere direction of the old bullfrog who lived in a spring-fed puddle in the maple orchard. He was a tyrannical concert-master, that old fellow, and satisfied with nothing less than perfection.

"Oom!" he sounded a single note.

It gave the true pitch and cadence for the first number on the evening program.

The impetuous young frog playing second 'cello down by the Nutting house, who had to take the cue, came in too precipitately with his "Oom! Oom! Oom!" half a beat ahead of time. At this all the other frogs kept silent, and spread their toes and gently dilated their broad throats while they waited for Old Maple Orchard to bring this youngster to time.

"Oom!" sounded Maple Orchard again, and unhurriedly.

Nutting House, feeling the reproof, counted four slow beats and bellowed musically, "Ooom! Ooom! Ooom!"

"Gurp! Gurp! Gurp!" intoned the Kettle Hole frog.

"Gudung—gudung—gudung!" thundered Maple Orchard, and so swept every frog and tree toad from one end of Alder Brook to the other into a perfect May night symphony in which the soft tenors of the tree toads declared the glory of God above the mounting tumult, the Nutting House frog, with a dozen baritones supporting him, extolled the splendor and magnificence of His handiwork, and Maple Orchard, in the ensuing hush, with deep, slow, somber cadence, marked the solemn tread of His Destiny.

"Frogs air noisy tonight, ain't they?" remarked Uncle Bill. He meant that he liked it.

Aunt Candace, her last skillet scoured and put away, now came out to join the company.

Uncle Bill had a proposal to make.

"If ye ain't changed mightily since I last seen you, you boys ain't agoing to spleen aginst a horn or two of twelve-year-ol' cider brandy. An' mebbe I'll tell you a story the Judge put me in mind of awhile ago."

He rose and started cellarwards without waiting for a highly improbable demurrer, presently returning with glasses and a stone jug which, when unstoppered, flooded the soft air with a fragrance of old honey and October orchards.

The Judge passed his glass under his nose, and sniffed, and sighed, and sipped.

"Now let's have that story," he suggested.

"Well, sir," began the old man, "what you said about your idea of trout fishin' made me think of a danged scurvy trick I tried one time and got learned a lesson for it. Candace an' me ain't always had things just as comfortable as we have 'em naow. I coaxed her right out of District Number Three Schoolhouse where she was teaching, and married her. I had sixty-some-odd dollars in the bank. 'Twan't much to start on, but I well knew that if I didn't ask her Lance Burpee would—"

"Why, William! What *are* you saying! Lance Burpee! Land o' goodness! Why, I never thought a mite about him!"

Uncle Bill silenced her coquettish disclaimers with a gesture.

"As I was saying, it wan't much to start on. But I took the old Belden Farm on the Lake an' we moved out there with what furniture we could muster between us, two cows, a horse, and, Judge, two of the grandest foxhounds any man ever listened to. Bred 'em myself out of my female "Wanderer" by a rawboned, tuneful English hound that Dick Maynard owned. I wouldn't decieve you, Judge, when those two started a fox it was jest like the Doxology after a long sermon. Talk about music! 'Hull's Victory' warn't in it! Many a time I've stood at a crossin' with my old ten gauge, just wishin' I didn't have to shoot the fox and so stop the music. Yes, sir. A man from daown in Albany offered me five hundred dollars for the pair, or three hundred for either one of 'em. That was a lot o' money for those days, let me tell you. He'd heard 'em sing. But, of course, I wouldn't. Wouldn't naow, neither, if I had it to do over again."

He paused and sipped, and the Captain observed that Aunt Candace's left hand had somehow got over on Uncle Bill's arm and was resting there.

"She knows what's coming," he thought, and wondered what the Dark-Haired Lady was doing just then.

The old gentleman resumed.

"A nobler pair o' dogs I've never seen," said he simply.

"There was about sixty acres of good muskrat marsh on the farm, and I figured if we could git through 'til the ice went out in March me an' Candace would be secure. Well, sir, you wouldn't believe it! One o' our cows swallered a fence staple an' died, an' Candace took sick with the everlastin' grip right after Christmas. Doc Wakefield, he wouldn't take a cent—nine miles each way, twice a week—but what with medicine an' one thing an' another there wan't a dollar left by Candlemas Day. I was clearly desperate."

The Judge, like Jacob grappling with the Angel, seized the stone jug and served another potion all around. From the defiant way in which he settled himself into his seat, he might as well have said, "Damn the luck, anyhow!"

"If I could have run the dogs an' killed a fox naow an' then, I could have made out 'til muskrat time," resumed Uncle Bill, "but there come on a three-day blizzard followed by a sleet storm. For a fortnight the Devil himself couldn't have kept right side up, for all his redhot claws. The whole region 'raound abaout was jus' like a chiny aig. Travelin' on that ice, a hull tribe o' Penobscot Injuns wouldn't have left no more scent than a cricket. Can't no one say more."

The old gentleman paused to savor the applejack and to regard the two dogs now running some dream fox on breast-high scent. Their big pads twitched, and low, excited yelpings occasionally broke from their quivering, sleep-bound muzzles.

"Wish I could git as much fun out of having nightmares as dogs do," their master remarked enviously, "but I s'pose they won't ketch him no more'n do humans when they dream of huntin' and fishin'!

"Well," he resumed, turning his attention again to his narrative, "it was one of those times when fifteen dollars in cash would ha' been worth more than a thaousand a week afterward.

"And didn't the Devil provoke that feller from Albany to write me another letter just then, still wantin' to buy one or both dogs? I'd sit an' look at Bill and think of the time he got into the chickens. 'You old cus,' I'd say, 'I'm agoin' to sell you to Albany!' Bill would git up an' come over an' shove his nose into my hand.

"So the upshot was that since I couldn't shoot a fox or catch a muskrat, an' hadn't spunk enough to sell a dog, I tried a mean trick, an all fired mean one, too, for a man claimed to be a fox hunter—I made up my mind to put out pizen on a runway. I'm ashamed to say so, even naow, an' that was forty year ago!"

Uncle Bill's distress was evident—and so was Aunt Candace's, whose hand stroked gently the old man's coat sleeve while her attention seemed to be given wholly to the night and the frogs.

"I had some pizen to make crow bait with an' I fixed a half dozen tallow balls with it and put 'em out around an old butt'nut stub down at the end of the Slough. Every fox in the Intervale stopped at that old stub. It was just after sundown an' colder than charity when I did it. The wind was comin' down the Lake an' howling crueler than the Iroquois ever did.

"I went back to the house but I didn't sleep a wink that night. Half a dozen times I come near putting on my clothes an' going down to pick up them damn pizenous, sneakin' things. But I didn't.

"Next mornin' they were gone."

"Did you get any foxes, Uncle Bill?" asked the Captain, observing too late that Aunt Candace had been dreading the question.

"Nary a one," said the old man. "Nary a one. But I hadn't no more than got back to the house when Bill an' Bugle come crawlin' into the dooryard— an' died."

TRANQUILLITY REVISITED

TRANQUILLITY
REVISITED

Not long ago I sojourned for a time in Tranquillity Township. The woodcock and grouse offered a powerful incentive for the visit, as did the black ducks and teal which come into the watery environs of the Slough in the autumn season, but my principal purpose was to discover how matters had fared with the Judge, the bluff Doctor, the Captain and the Dark-Haired Lady, who richly deserves the affectionate admiration of all who know her. Her lot is a trying one, for her domestic affairs do not follow the customary sensible pattern of most households but must be arranged according to a calendar that divides the year into shooting and fishing seasons. Her feckless mate can seldom be persuaded to put aside a gun or a rifle except to pick up a fishing rod. There are some who think that if he were left to his own devices the Captain might manage his conduct better and achieve some sort of respectability, but it always happens that just as he has decided that Belden's Brook is probably a little too low for good fishing and that he'll stay at home and occupy himself with gainful pursuits, one or the other of his two cronies, the Judge or the Doctor, or both of them together, are sure to arrive with information indicating that while Belden's Brook is a bit low, the North Branch is at exactly the proper level for a dry fly. Away he goes then, and the Dark-Haired Lady picks up the pad and pencil and patiently puts them away with many a rueful shake of her neat little head. The Judge and the Doctor have separately complained to me that they are hampered and hindered in their professional labors by the Captain's importunings. The one must leave the felon unhanged to go and attend to a fresh fall of woodcock; the other abandon his designs on Mrs. Orslow's appendix because the Captain has a new crow call to try out. At least, such are their stories. Having heard them all, I reflect that it is well indeed that there are some months of the year when the call of the woods and fields and waters is less insistent than at others, and that at such intervals the three of them may find leisure to attend to business.

During my stay I managed to get from these persons, bit by bit, and fragment by fragment, a fair account of their late adventurings with rod, gun and rifle, and some of these are described in this volume for the doubtful benefit of anyone who may care to read them. It would be far better if the reader could hear these tales in places where I heard them, watching an autumn twilight from the crest of Hessian Bowl Hill, or perched in the noon sunlight on the old rail fence in Stannard's pasture with the smell of wood smoke, coffee and broiling sausages in our nostrils, or at night before the fire when the old farmhouse creaks and groans as the frost penetrates the ancient timbers and the drowsy company awaits the moment when the need for sound sleep will outweigh the appeal of the firelight and good gossip.

Time, I observed, had dealt gently with the countryside round about Tranquillity. The Adirondacks still stood serene against the western sky.

Fort Ticonderoga at their base frowns like an old and decrepit lion upon all that trafficks along the waters of the lake. There was a time when that place with its walls, bastions, demilunes, outworks and batteries was the potent instrument of Destiny shaping the course of two old powerful nations and guarding the cradle of one that was young and new. The Green Mountains, to the east, lack the austere and rugged character of the Adirondacks, but they have instead an aspect of power and enduring strength that is protective and never threatening to the folk who live in the valleys and hamlets. Vermont men and women journey to far places on affairs of their State and Nation. I daresay that no one of them, not the Admiral at Manila Bay when the Spaniards came out, not the laconic, shrewd man who sat in the White House, nor any of the others who have gone out from the State, but had in his mind a vision of Ascutney, or Mansfield, or Camel's Hump, or Sugar Loaf, or Bird's Eye, and knew that he would never really be at home again at any spot that lies beyond the morning or the sunset shadow of his own familiar mountain. When, returning, his eyes find against the sky the well remembered outlines of that particular dome or peak or soaring buttress, the traveler finds, also, that there is an almighty big lump in his throat. For a few minutes he dares not speak lest someone wonder at the tears on his cheeks.

The old winding narrow dirt road that connected the Turnpike with the old farmhouse home and the others beyond it was, I found, a dirt road no longer. The old road had been rough and all but impassable during March and April, but the Captain, who knew it well, tells me that he has never in this country nor in any other found a path made for the feet of man so beautiful and friendly as that one. In May its roadside fences and banks foamed with blossoms of wild plum, chokecherry, thimbleberry and shad, filling the air with spicy perfume that made boys and bumblebees a little drunk as they passed. In the autumn, to walk along the road was like walking through the vapor drifting down from the fount of all color. Pa'tridges came up from the Pine Woods to dust in the cart tracks and feed on the ebony fruit of the black cherry trees.

District No. 3 Schoolhouse, I saw, was closed but kept in perfect repair against the time when the mysterious power that governs the ebb and flow of populations should turn in its trace and the old roads would hear again the laughter and chatter of children on their way to this rustic font of knowledge. In the schoolhouse the Captain's initials are deeply carved into the old hickory desk beneath those of his ancestors. They attest his determination to make his mark before the failures and disappointments of life should deprive him of the privilege of claiming any sort or sign of distinction.

After passing the schoolhouse the first object of the Captain's boyish interest along the road had been the Red Barn—still standing, I noticed. Every passing gunner tried his gun upon the fair expanse of its planking so that it was an easy matter for a boy with a jackknife to dig out from the soft wood a fascinating variety of lethal projectiles. A handful of bullets, slugs and round balls afforded a splendid imaginative diversion to a youngster who believed—and has found nothing since to disprove it—that the Great Day in all history was the one on which someone gave him his first gun.

After the Red Barn there had been the Big Hill and beyond that the Old Johanna Martin House crumbling in ruin beneath its weathered shingles. Then there was the Big Rock, traditional scene of Indian ambuscades, and the Old Nutting House dreaming away in the warm sunshine beneath the great butternut tree in the dooryard.

But the old road is dirt no more. Its mud and its dust have been hermetically and forever sealed beneath a thick adamantine layer of crushed stone and cement; its angles—always tempting the traveler to another vista—have been relaid and corrected; the Big Rock has been removed from its age-old bed by the violent impulse of dynamite. The town is not a wealthy community. It pays its debts, supports its schools, takes care of its poor, but has little left to be spent on mere conveniences. When I inquired of the Judge the source and reason of this notable and particular impovement, he gave me that long, calm, inscrutable look that a Yankee employs at times, and said:

"The Great White Father."

The new road and the airport over on the Munger Meadow were the only points observable where modern notions have successfully invaded the ancient peace and harmony of the town. An airport is only an area of level ground, and inasmuch as the Munger Meadow was from the first the only bit of level ground in the region, its conversion has altered the original scene but little. But the removal of the Big Rock is a serious matter I conclude.

Time has dealt gently, too, with the inhabitants of the township. Jim Hooper, that shiftless comrade of the Captain's youth, long ago fired his last shot at some species of game bird or animal that was so unwise as to "set still" until the ragged gunner could "draw bead on it;" years ago he yanked his last bullhead from the amber water beneath the Stone Bridge. He has gone, I hope, to some pleasant realm where less store is set upon the virtues of toil and a man can enjoy himself lounging in the eternal sunshine with a blue paper sack of Mechanics' Delight Tobacco, and a "snort" now and then from a stone jug of Old Pepper.

There was joy when Mike, the beloved Irishman who was both soldier and poet, came to Tranquillity for a season with the grouse, ducks and woodcock, and deep sorrow when scarcely a year later word came to his friends that never again would Mike set foot on the road from the Turnpike to the old house under the maples.

The others are there, thank Heaven, only a trifle older than when the reader met them first in an earlier chronicle of the village; they are there—the Doctor, the Judge, the Dark-Haired Lady and the Captain and all their friends, kindly, humorous, tolerant, loyal and brave.

UNCLE BILL
TAKES HIS
EXERCISE

The Belden Brook which takes its musical course down the long valley behind the Paraday homestead is as good a stretch of trout water as a careful fisherman could wish for, and in October the birch and alder thickets covering the slopes on either side of the stream are populous with woodcock and grouse. It would not be fair, however, to the Judge and his friend, the Captain, to assert that the fish and the birds were the only attractions the region possessed for them. There was Uncle Bill Paraday himself, a wiry, grizzled Yankee in whose gray eyes dwelt the reflection of a worthy quizzical philosophy and whose heart was as big and sound and sweet as one of his own apples. He had been a sergeant in Stannard's famous brigade and knew well the smell of battle. He knew, too, every rod of earth in Tranquillity Township and his mind was a compendium of lore, historical and legendary, concerning the countryside and its inhabitants. The mere prospect of an opportunity to coax Uncle Bill into a reminiscent strain was enough to draw the two sportsmen if there hadn't been a fish or a game bird on the place or the possibility of a pot of Aunt Candace's baked beans.

"Now, I expect you boys to come right back here for supper," she remarked one morning. "I'm baking a pot o' beans just the way you like 'em. You c'n sit afterwards an' visit with William—he's sorter cravin' to talk with someone else besides me an' the two hounds."

Aunt Candace's beans were the glorious result of mysterious processes. No housewife in the neighborhood could match them even with Dame Paraday's original recipe all written out fair and fine on a leaf from the back of the Almanac to guide her. It, the recipe, called for the beans to be baked and simmered and blended with a "piece" of salt pork, a "smidgin" of mustard, a "mite" of onion, "some" tomato pickle, a "little" pepper and a "good lot" of best brown sugar. It was all perfectly clear to Aunt Candace, but other ladies found the quantitative analysis of the fragrant juicy product of the brown earthen beanpot confusing. A "smidgin" for example was slightly more than a "dab" but something less than a "mite," and the other units of culinary measurement were equally terms for individual interpretation.

On this particular evening when the slim silver paring of a new moon rose from behind the Adirondacks it found the feast finished and the three friends lounging comfortably in their cane-bottomed hickory chairs before the kitchen fire. They were, as usual, engaged in discourse on the subject of game. A decent string of 'cock and grouse hung on the porch outside to cool, and both the Judge and the Captain were enjoying that profound satisfaction that belongs to a gunner who has shot well and in moderation.

"Naow," remarked their host as he got his pipe alight, "I dunno as you fellers ever give much thought to all the different kinds o' wild creeturs there be in this taown, nor the reason for it. But jest consider: there's naow an' agin bear in the woods; there's slews o' deer, there's pa'tridges an' woodcock, an' squ'rls an' snipe an' rabbits an' 'coons, an' I don't know what all, includin' ducks an' geese. Naow the reason for this is that we've got all kinds o' hills and valleys and woods and past'res an' brooks an' ma'shes. We got a good big piece o' the Lake, too, an' most any kind o' a creetur c'n find jest the place it likes best, an' jest what it likes to eat." He looked at the Captain. "You come by your woods-traipsin' natural. Your great, great Gran'ther—or mebbe one more'n that—was one of 'em who settled this taown. One o' your kin was in on the dicker, too, Jedge—and them scalawags picked this place because they loved to shoot an' fish an' didn't enj'y crowdin'. They wa'n't much on farmin' I 'spect. They'd all been up the Lake together fightin' Injuns an' Frenchmen an' when at last they had 'em licked they wa'n't in no mind to settle daown to real hard unexcitin' work like farmin'. So they come here an' cleared enough land to raise corn an' beans an' p'taters an' sech. They made maple sugar an' they hunted bee trees for honey. They trapped an' they had their fill o' huntin' an' fishin'—an' sech huntin' an' fishin' it must ha' been." Uncle Bill sighed enviously.

"I do s'pose they had trouble sometimes persuadin' their wiminfolks that it was dreadful necessary to do the huntin' an' fishin' first an' the farmin' afterwards," he reflected.

Aunt Candace, bland as a buttercup, put a clean plate in the cupboard.

"It beats all," she observed, "haow curious a man reasons. There's a garden full o' p'taters that he c'n git jest by diggin', but come a frosty mornin' an' he'll let the p'taters go an' be off runnin' the hills wi' a gun an' two worthless, hungry hounds all day after a fox that maybe he won't git, and he'll come home tireder'n if he'd pulled p'tater vines all the way from here to Benson Landin'."

"That's jest the p'int," her mate said calmly, looking at his worn and calloused hands, "a feller's got to git some exercise. Let me do nothin' but dig p'taters an' split firewood an' look arter the stock fer two or three weeks an' I'd git all softened up an' flabby. Prob'bly I might in time git as fat as old Huck Norton."

Aunt Candace was unable to fit her tongue immediately to a proper response to such outrageous perversity and the old man winked slyly at his friends and went on.

"Naow, then, I feel the conviction that I ain't been gettin' my fair share o' exercise lately. Cuttin' corn an' pickin' apples has weakened me. I'm goin' to make a mighty struggle agin the temptation o' ease an' see if I c'n work up a good lather agoin' duck shootin' wi' you fellers, if you c'n make it."

His friends readily agreed to the proposal, for a day afield with Uncle Bill, who seldom hunted anything nowadays but foxes and bee trees, was sure to be filled with pleasant experiences. "Where'll we go, Uncle Bill?" asked the Judge.

"Naow, I b'lieve I'll take ye to a place that don't neither one o' ye know abaout fer all yer rammin' an' traipsin'. 'Tain't ten mile from where we're settin', neither. You fellers come past an' git me abaout six o'clock an' I'll show ye."

On their way home under the declining moon the Judge and his companion speculated vainly on the location of the promised adventure.

"I'm ready to swear that we know every duck slough in the country," said the Judge, shaking his head, "but I know better'n to doubt Uncle Bill."

Their guide was ready with his famous double hammer gun of ten bore and his lunch neatly packed in a paper sack when the Judge's old car wheezed into the Paraday dooryard a little before dawn.

Aunt Candace, her ample figure swathed in a voluminous wrap against the frosty air, came out to see them off and to claim a woman's privilege. "Naow, William, don't ye overdo!" said she. "I hope ye get some good fat ducks. My! I don't know haow long it's been since William fetched home somethin' we could eat."

"Git back inter that house!" roared Uncle Bill in tones more jovial than he ever used to address a platoon of blue-clad infantrymen, but quite as loud. "Naow," he continued in milder manner to the Judge, "you drive down to the turnpike an' turn off so'st to git on the Intervale Road. Foller along Cosman's Crik until I tell ye when to stop."

Cosman's Creek was well known to his companions, a clear, shallow stream that finally entered the lower lake; but no ducks ever visited it except the mergansers to fish in the pools and a few wood ducks that came to gather wild grapes from the vines that covered the banks and festooned the elms overhanging the limpid water.

"Cosman's!" exclaimed the Captain. "Why, there ain't any ducks in that stream!"

"I know there ain't," was the reply, "but there's some within pistol shot of it, I'll warrant ye, if the hull dummed country ain't turned bottom side up since I last seen it!"

The Intervale was a narrow flat expanse of rich loam lying between the steep limestone ridges. The creek wound along the bottom land between irregular fields of heavy corn. Each spring flood waters brought an inch or two of rich silt to deposit in these fields and add to the fertility of the soil. 'Coon hunters and squirrel shooters found the region productive of the game they sought, but wildfowlers passed it by on their way to the marshes of the lower lake.

The party crossed a worn plank bridge and at Uncle Bill's direction left the car under an elm. Then with guns, shells and lunch, the three entered a cornfield at the base of a great rugged wall of gray limestone. There had been a light frost during the night, and icy drops from the pendent blades of the corn soaked their knees and spattered in their faces.

In one spot Uncle Bill pointed silently to a half dozen ears of corn from which the husks had been stripped and the yellow kernels chiseled away.

" 'Coons," said he, and found the animals' tracks in the soft soil between the rows. They looked almost exactly like the imprints made by a baby's feet.

A hundred paces farther and the old man turned across the rows toward the foot of the ledge to a spot where the crests of a clump of willows rose above the corn. As they drew nearer there was a sudden turmoil of splashing, squealing and quacking as a hundred or more ducks rose up apparently from the ground and went wheeling away over the treetops. There was time to identify a few bunches of greenwing teal, dusky squadrons of black duck and several pairs of gorgeous wood duck, these latter fowl twisting in intricate maneuvers among the other birds and whistling their plaintive warning to all honest sportsmen to hold their fire.

"Let 'em go," said Uncle Bill. "They'll all come back by 'n' by jest in the way we want 'em to."

At the edge of the corn he pointed silently, and his companions saw the ruffled gleam of water. It was a small pool, evidently fed by a spring at the base of the ledge and so narrow that as Uncle Bill said, "You could heave a stun acrost it."

The muddy margin was covered with tracks of raccoon, muskrat, ducks and squirrels, and in one place the Captain saw the wide double-wedged signs of a buck deer.

"Well, I'll be darned, Uncle Bill," he exclaimed, "I'd never have found this place!"

"I wouldn't have, nuther," Uncle Bill replied with a chuckle, "if I hadn't fell kersmack inter the middle of it off'n that lettle ledge up there one night when I was arter 'coon. Scairt the gizzards outen a raft o' ducks that was in there, but they wa'n't no worse off'n I was, by Judas Priest!"

"Naow," he continued, "you boys kinder scatter out a leetle an' git in the aidge o' the corn an' le's see what happens."

For some time there was no sound but the tap and trickle of water dripping from the corn and a light splashing from the pool where some small creatures came to drink or play. The sun drove long golden shafts through the rising vapors of the morning, and a great blue heron came sliding down on motionless vanes to drop to a landing in the pool with a brief sound of wings. The Captain could see the big bird erect on its long legs alert for any sign that its arrival had been observed by hostile eyes and then, reassured, relaxing from its taut pose, to look about for breakfast.

A cock pheasant came parading down the corn row where the Judge sat waiting, but at some slight movement from the pudgy sportsman it cast away its vainglory and vanished ignominiously into the corn.

"Maybe I'll get to you later," the gunner thought.

Then a pair of black ducks came back and began flying a wary series of figure eights overhead. Lower and lower they came, and then the silence was shattered by the forthright roar of Uncle Bill's black powder, which in distrust of modern ammunition he loaded into old-fashioned brass cases that were battered and blackened with use and age. One bird came plunging down. The other, veering from the flash and smoke, came over the Captain. The report of his long-barreled 20-bore sounding like that of a small-caliber rifle in the thunderous rolling echoes of the big gun, but the duck's long neck snapped back and it came whistling down to strike solidly in the corn rows.

The heron rose squawking in alarm, and as he left a flight of greenwing swept along the edge of the corn, scornful of any precaution save that of flashing speed. Three of them fell out end over end at the Judge's stand and one more to the Captain.

"Rather have 'em than any duck that flies," remarked the jurist as he gathered his game, "either to shoot or to eat."

In singles, pairs and small flocks, birds appeared over the corn, coming from nowhere and vanishing again as quickly. The smoke from the bellowing discharges of Uncle Bill's weapon mixed with the mist and drifted along the corn considerably lowering the visibility. Out of the sulphurous clouds rushed a small flock of black ducks unseen by the Judge until they had passed. A smaller bird, which he identified as a teal, came past in the wake of the blacks and was caught in the load of chilled 7's. It struck almost at the Captain's feet, and he retrieved it.

"I've got your bird," he announced without enthusiasm.

"It's a teal, ain't it?" inquired the Judge, suddenly anxious. "I swear it looked like one! Now, don't tell me I've gone and killed a hen wood duck!"

"Well," demanded his friend, "what'll I do with it? Hide it in the corn, or what?"

"Not by a jugful," declared his friend valiantly. "If I killed it, I'll be responsible. I'll hand it over to Jackson myself. Darn the luck!"

"Then you're honest after all! You can keep your duck. It's a big greenwing all right."

"Now ain't you a perfect damn fool?" inquired the Judge disgustedly. "I wonder your folks didn't drown you when you were a pup!"

After an hour or two the fowl stopped flying except for an occasional single intent on finding company of its own kind with which to bask and play in the seclusion of some quiet resort.

"That's about all fer naow," said Uncle Bill after a while as they assembled a dozen and a half black ducks and teal and laid them in a row in the shade. "If we want more we c'n git 'em toward evenin'. This is a dreadful purty place an' I b'lieve I'll sit right here for a while an' smoke my pipe an' git some more exercise jest as I promised Candy I'd do. Arter we've et, I got a good notion to take the ol' gun an' see if I c'n git a mess o' squ'rl."

So they loafed and smoked and listened to Uncle Bill's anecdotes. Occasionally single vagrant duck coming high overhead gave someone a shot. If the gunner failed to score, the incident was promptly forgotten, for a miss brings its own anodyne, blotting out the stigma of defeat, whereas, when the load strikes fairly, the incident is ineradicably etched on the memory. This psychological phenomenon is responsible for the curious fact that no wildfowler can honestly recall having missed more than a dozen ducks in all his life. It is also responsible for the opinion secretly held by every wildfowler that every gunner, except himself, is an audacious, unmitigated liar.

After a leisurely lunch Uncle Bill picked up his gun and repaired to a hickory ridge beyond the bridge whence from time to time came the sullen voice of five drams of black powder as the old man methodically added another plump squirrel to his bag.

His two friends set out to find the Judge's pheasant and were so successful that they gathered that bird and two other bold Mongols before the lengthening shadows warned them to get back to the hidden pool to anticipate the evening flight of ducks. There the Judge added two greenwings to the bag and the Captain, to his great contentment, made a beautiful high double on a stray pair of gray mallards, rare birds in that region.

Uncle Bill surveyed the bag and remarked: "Got 'baout enough, ain't we?"

As he spoke a single black duck came steadily over. With its dusky plumage glistening in the rays of the declining sun and its strong pinions flashing, the bird was the living emblem of all the wild remote sloughs and potholes where wildfowl gather and men come on frosty mornings to find them. It was a sight to stir a gunner's heart and to turn his thoughts wistfully back to richer seasons or doubtfully into the future to contemplate others that might prove to be lacking in such splendid scenes and adventures.

"Enj'yin' yourself, ain't ye?" said Uncle Bill, addressing the lofty, confident traveler. He cocked the gun and raised it. Then he lowered the mighty weapon. "Well," he continued, "go 'long an' enj'y yourself some more, Mister Duck, an' good luck to ye! I'll be dummed if ye ain't purtier the way ye be than the way ye'd be, or the way *I b'lieve* ye'd be, if I had pulled the tricker."

HIGH
COVER

As was his frequent practice the Judge had come to the Captain's house to have breakfast with his friends. It was the best way he could think of to begin a gunning trip. Then, too, there was a profound affection existing between the pudgy sportsman, who must have had his lonely moments, and the Dark-Haired Lady. He enjoyed nothing better than to sit in the bright dining room, comfortable in his shooting clothes, while she poured the coffee and his host served out scrambled eggs and brown, spicy sausages. At this table the conversations were generally gay and always unpredictable, a state of affairs that delighted the Judge, who by reason of his profession had to give ear to so much dry, sober, dull wisdom that, though it may have informed the mind, certainly did not refresh the spirit.

On this occasion the Dark-Haired Lady had delivered a sort of lecture to the pair for bringing back so many "little woodcock" and so few partridges which she, at least, esteemed as nobler game. And it was true that with the season half gone the two of them together had not bagged a dozen grouse between them. Despite a great abundance of wild fruits, of thorn apples, fox grapes and the white berries of the native dogwood, the grouse were not abundant in the lower covers where they gunned for 'cock.

"It's his fault, Ma'am," the Judge explained. "He won't take me to 'em. He *knows* where they are, too. He's some kin to pa'tridge and he thinks like 'em—what little thinking he does, anyhow. But he's gone and got him a little bit of a twenty-eight-bore gun and dassent try it on a big bird like a pa'tridge. So he keeps snaking me back and forth in places where the woodcock are."

"I know where the pa'tridges are, all right," retorted his friend calmly. "They are 'way up on the big hills and ridges—places where an old, fat lazy cuss wouldn't want to go."

The Judge put down his empty cup and discouraged the Dark-Haired Lady's hospitable gesture toward the big red coffee pot. Then he glared at his friend.

"So that's it, is it?" he demanded. "I'm too old and fat to do a little climbing, am I? Go get your toy gun and let's be going! If there's a hill with pa'tridges on it too steep for me to climb, I want to see it. Thanks for the breakfast Ma'am, and you shall have a pair of birds tonight or my broken body will be found at the foot of Biddy's Knob."

Where the Old Military Road traverses the eastern part of the township it turns toward the south after crossing a number of lesser hills and follows along the course of a small stream. At the point of the angle a desperate battle had been fought during Revolutionary days. The spot is marked by a single simple shaft of stone. To the east of the stream there rises a high ridge. Its steep flanks, too abrupt for cultivation, have been given over to pastures and these are interspersed with strips of pine and hardwood. Here and there an old orchard remains to indicate the attempt of some pioneer farmer to make more profitable use of his remote and angular acres. It is a stiff climb to the crest of the ridge and even the few sheep and wild young cattle, those unerring discoverers of the easiest gradients, that share the lofty domain with the deer have been unable to find a gradual way of ascent up the final rampart.

When our two friends had struggled up the last buttress that morning they were streaming with perspiration in spite of the keen air, and by mutual consent they put down their weapons and paused for breath. Below them lay the battlefield and the valley with the stream sparkling beneath the willows. Behind them spread the shooting ground, mile after mile of rough plateau broken by outcroppings of native rock. Here, too, the hopeful settlers of the region had planted orchards. The scraggy trees still bore an abundance of knotty fruit and gallantly maintained their forsaken lines amid the overwhelming encroachment of the birches and hardhacks.

The Judge puffed and groaned and mumbled his discontent at such violent exercise.

"Well, confound you, you asked for it," his companion declared, "and now that you're up here, if you're careful not to lose any elevation during the day, it won't be bad. Let me tell you what the field uniform and equipment of the Hessian dragoon was in the year 1777. 'He wore high and heavy jackboots, with large, long spurs, stout and stiff leather breeches, gauntlets reaching high up on his arms, and a hat with a high tuft of ornamental feathers. On his side he trailed a tremendous broadsword; a short but clumsy carbine was slung over his shoulders, and down his back, like a Chinese mandarin's, dangled a long queue.' "

"What's all that to me?" the Judge wanted to know.

"Thought it might make you stop bawling," was the retort. "On July 7, 1777, a lot of those dragoons climbed up where you've just been, jackboots and all. It was hotter than hell, too. To make it worse, there was a line of Yankee riflemen lying behind trees and logs right along here pouring buck and ball into 'em as they came up to where you sit today and whimper. Ain't you ashamed?"

His friend gazed reflectively down the slope and the Captain thought that the older sportsman was imagining the smoky bloody scene—the deadly rifle-men in buckskin and homespun and the King's mercenaries stepping over the bodies of their fallen, and coming resolutely on, to the tap of their brass drums and the skirl of the British pipes.

Then the Judge picked up his old double hammer gun.

"Come on," he ordered, "and show me a pa'tridge. You can't eat a Hes-sian."

Throughout the years, while the Judge clung stubbornly to his fine old twelve-bore his friend had changed first from the twelve to the sixteen, and then with some misgivings to the twenty. The little twenty-eight-bore double was his most recent acquisition. It had proved to be a grand gun for wood-cock, but the owner knew very well that a woodcock twisting over the alder tops at twenty yards' distance was an easy test compared to a wary late season grouse. As the leaves fell the birds always became wilder and more alert, harder to hit and harder to stop when they were hit. The cartridges seemed too small to be effective in spite of their length and the printed assurance on the box that each was loaded with three-quarters of an ounce of chilled 7's.

The region which they now entered was a maze of old woodroads and paths winding about among the rocks and thickets. Since the Captain's little cocker had died the two sportsmen had not found the heart to replace that small friend and companion, so they went without a dog, trusting to their in-timate knowledge of the game and of the country itself to find their birds and to retrieve them themselves. Without direction now the Captain followed an old trail while the Judge went forward keeping out twenty paces or so on the flank.

A grouse roared away in a swirl of leaves, and the Judge with his custom-ary precision tumbled him back among the hardhacks and acknowledged his friend's congratulatory salute. As he gathered the bird a half dozen more went thundering out of the far edge of the thicket, out of range before they took wing.

"They went away down that ravine," his companion reported, "and whether any of 'em stopped there I couldn't say, but I s'pose we'd better go and see."

As they progressed the younger sportsman found himself within a few yards of a precipitous place where the foundation rock, split by some ancient violence, presented a sheer wall descending abruptly a hundred feet to a small ravine in which a clump of cedars grew in a damp depression. He knew the spot. Old Dick Wyman, the fox hunter, used to wait here hour after hour for his hound to bring a fox along the runway at the bottom of the ravine. He remembered one November morning long ago when from the turnpike be-low, his father had pointed out to him the solitary figure of Old Dick, mo-tionless atop his lofty perch with his ten-bore gun. Even at that distance the old man had appeared wrapped in the aloof dignity common to fox hunters. The small boy had marveled that a sensible grown-up man should presume to sit in one particular place in broad daylight and expect to see a fox! There were lots of foxes but no one actually saw any of them. Then he had heard the faint, mournful, musical cry of Old Dick's solitary hound, and when a few minutes later the heavy report of a black powder gun came rolling and tumbling down from the cliffs, his father had said: "The old feller got him, I guess." That had been a long time ago, and another Old Feller had gotten a many of them since then, including Old Dick himself.

His musings were interrupted by a sudden movement at the base of a small pine at the very edge of the cliff. A grouse that had been observing the gunner's approach flipped a yard off the ground and dove headlong over the escarpment. But the new gun was nearly as alert as the bird, and a load of shot raked a narrow furrow in the leaves at the brink. Not a feather floated above the chasm to indicate a hit, yet the Captain had the odd conviction often felt by gunners that he had scored. Accordingly, he crawled to the edge and peering over scanned the rubble at the base for his bird. There was no sign of it, however, and he was on the point of giving up when from somewhere in the cedars far below came an unmistakable "Thump—thump—thump— thump"—the failing, convulsive wingbeats of a dying grouse.

The Judge came up and watched while the other made his way to the bottom of the ravine and into the cedars where almost at once he came upon his bird lying flat on its breast and stone dead. When he climbed back to the Judge the latter remarked:

"That was a lucky pick up. If Pepper's ghost is along with us, as I sometimes believe he is, he's probably thinking, 'If I were a real dog instead of just the shadow of one I'd have saved you all that climb, Mister.' "

"S'pose we ought to get us another pup, pretty soon. There isn't much sense, I guess, in feeling that way about a dog," confessed the other.

"Well," said the Judge tersely, "I wouldn't have you feel differently!"

Then a curious thing happened. A tiny whirlwind, one of the sort of phenomena often described as "dust devils," sprang up from nowhere and for just a moment twisted and spiraled and tumbled about their feet before it went scurrying away beneath the hazel bushes drawing a flutter of fallen leaves after it. There was something about the lively air currents so startlingly suggestive of the actions of a small dog leaping and twisting in a demonstration of joyful affection that the Judge exclaimed: "By George!" and the other said: "Why, the little rascal!" Then they looked at one another and grinned.

But nevertheless, the older gunner remarked later to the Dark-Haired Lady that he "thought there wasn't much sense in keeping a bird dog in view of the shortness of the shooting seasons."

And she, with something in her brown eyes that was midway between a tear and a twinkle, said that she thought so, too. She had been pretty fond of Pepper herself.

A bird came off a steep hillside and swept across a ravine above the lofty tops of a grove of sugar maples and the Judge downed him. Another did the same thing, and the Captain swinging too fast with his little gun overled his target, realized his mistake, slowed down and shot yards behind. But he saw a puff of bark and dusty decayed wood fly from the side of a dead limb beyond the path of the bird and the sight gave him a sense of confidence in the power of the little double gun that he had been unable to gain from much counting of shot holes in paper patterns.

"By thunder," he muttered, addressing the weapon, as he reloaded, "it's a good thirty-five yards to that old stub, and from the way the bark flew, I guess you're big enough for pa'tridges if I can learn how to point you at 'em!"

At noon, when they stopped to eat their sandwiches under an old apple tree, the Judge had three birds to lay out on the grass. The other had only the one that he had recovered from the cedars. The older man had ceased ragging his friend about the little gun, a circumstance indicating that the Judge was actually convinced of the inadequacy of his companion's equipment and was not wishful to add to the other's disappointment in his new possession.

It was a lordly spot where they sat. Away below them spread the great valley, flooded with the mild autumnal sunshine. Wooded hills gave way to lesser hills, and far beyond, under the blue shadows of the Adirondacks, the Captain caught the gleam of water and fancied that in that still and ambient atmosphere, he could almost hear the hiss of wings as teal flashed down the channel bound for the Slough. Thin columns of blue smoke rising to the upper air betrayed the location of the scattered homesteads. "Must have been the way the Indians spotted 'em," he reflected. But today no sound of strife and terror disturbed the ancient scene. Somewhere a belated farmer hustled to get his corn into the silo and they could hear the engine and the cutter clanking emptily, the sound dropping again to a deep satisfied roar as fresh bundles of fodder were pitched into the iron maw.

"Well," remarked one finally, "I'd almost rather sit here and enjoy the scenery than to resume our career of bloodshed and carnage, but we've got to get a few more birds or take a lickin' when we get home."

They climbed a low ridge an came out upon a long shallow valley. There were clumps of pine and gray birch growing from the thin soil and solitary pyramids of thorn apple with the gray of bark and twig almost hidden by the loads of scarlet fruit. A tiny spring-fed brook trickled leisurely back and forth across the floor of the depression seizing upon every incident of rock or root to delay its departure from the pleasant place of its birth.

The Judge viewed the scene with approval.

"The last pa'tridge on earth will be found down yonder," said he, "if that disaster ever comes, which the Lord forbid!"

With the lazy stream between them they started up the valley. It would have done an old Ranger good to see how easily, alertly and almost silently these two men walked through the rough and broken cover. How many thousands of miles of such travel had been required to teach them the knack of avoiding obstacles without actually seeing them, of weaving, twisting and turning under boughs and past the reaching tangles of lower growth, never off balance and with eyes and ears constantly alert for sound or movement— that was something they could never have told you, and they probably would have been surprised if anyone had asked. They moved swiftly, yet a buck deer in his bed in a hardhack thicket never suspected their presence until the Judge was within ten paces of him. Neither did the Judge suspect the presence of the deer, for that matter, and the surprise was mutual.

Some white splashings caught the Judge's eye and he whistled to his friend and held up a warning hand. The latter paused and waited while his companion made short exploratory casts in the vicinity of the telltale chalkings. Then right at his feet, so close that he wondered why he hadn't seen the bird on the ground, a fat woodcock materialized and went darting away on whistling wings over the spires of the chimnety-top bush in an erratic flight that ended abruptly when the old hammer gun spoke once and sharply.

It looked like the Judge's day, but the god of circumstance had something in store for the man with the new gun. Four grouse had been feeding on the fruit of a thorn apple tree growing at the edge of a cluster of small pines, and as the Captain came up they took off with a great roar of wings. Two of the birds the gunner never saw, but one swerving to the left crossed an opening. This time there was no mistake, and as he fired the sportsman knew that the bird was centered even as he saw from the corner of his eye a second grouse following the same course. The two shots were as quick as two blinks of an eye and, as ordinarily interpreted by an experienced listener, would mean a miss with the right and a quick follow-up with the left barrel. At least that was what the Judge thought had happened.

"You got him, boy!" he called and then, as his friend pressed into the thicket, he called again. "He ain't in there! He's lying out on this side, deader'n a door nail!"

"That's the *first* one of 'em," explained his friend with pardonable satisfaction in his tones. "For the twelfth time in a long and active career I have unscrewed the inscrutable, measured the immeasurable, accomplished the unaccomplishable. In short, I have made a double on grouse in fair cover without a dog. Both of 'em dead in the air and not over ten yards apart!"

"Well, now, sir!" exclaimed the Judge in warm congratulatory tones, "That is certainly a major episode, especially when done with a weapon that you wouldn't even think was dangerous! It calls for something, and it's something we ain't got here. But I know where it is. And I move you, sir, that whereas it now draws toward sundown, and whereas we've enough birds anyhow, that therefore we do now descend from these heights and eminences and repair to that certain place. Besides," he added somewhat wistfully, "the Lady will want to hear about it."

THE GROUNDHOG'S REVENGE

In Vermont toward the latter part of February there begins a period that is woefully trying to gentlemen who have tired of skiing and bobsledding and who yearn for trout fishing, crow shooting and woodchuck sniping. The snow lies deep and dazzling over the wintry fields and in long, ridged drifts at the roadsides. To the uninitiated, winter appears to rule unchallenged, but the sky, first to signal the advance of a gentler, more comely season, has changed from a pale and faded color to a deep, crystalline blue, and on the hillsides the bare tracery of the hardwoods, gray throughout the preceding months, takes on a softer, warmer, mellower tone. It can scarcely be called color, for it is nothing so definite—this subtle change that occurs when the trees feel again the faint stirrings of life beneath the rough, dead texture of their skins. It is a time of alternate freezing and thawing; of slush one day and hard ice and bitter cold the next.

In this particular year of our Lord it had been an especially bad time for the Captain and the bluff Doctor. There had been a week of very promising weather—days when the snow sank visibly under the strengthening sun even though sub-zero temperatures coming down from the mountains at twilight clamped the world tightly again in a crackling, frosty grip. A few crows, the first to return, had appeared along the river, gathering their sustenance from the frozen fish, the dark red carcasses of skinned muskrats, and similar casualties and debris of the winter. The two sportsmen had found encouragement in these signs until one afternoon when a gray, cold bank of cloud drew up from the west. It had a greasy, tallowy look about it that the Captain knew and didn't like. By the time the lights in the houses were put on that evening a wind from the north was slipping like a wolf through the empty streets, snuffling at the doors and windows as it passed.

"Another cussed blizzard!" the Captain complained to the Dark-Haired Lady as he brought more wood to the fireplace.

Midnight brought proof of his prognostication with hard volleys of driven snow that rattled against window-panes like small shot.

The storm was still raging in the morning. By the next nightfall there was more snow than they had seen all winter, and the Captain, who had been feeding on hope, was made so low and disconsolate by this shattering counterattack of Boreas that when the Doctor came plunging through the drifts with a long canvas case under his arm he found his friend by the fire mournfully reading a book of adventurings in the Arctic wilderness.

"Gives me some comfort," the Captain explained, "to read about people in places that are colder and more generally damned desolate even than here; where folks eat rotten, frozen fish and frozen, rotten little auks an' things, guts and all."

"Beautiful thought, beautifully expressed," said the Doctor, putting down the gun case—for such it was—and getting out of his coat, "and if you happen to have another noggin of that hot buttered rum you're quaffing I could do with it. Good for chilb'ains, bellyache and hives."

Such is the goodly influence of hospitality, which blesses alike the giver and the recipient, that the host felt considerably better and certainly was of lighter spirit when the flagon, hot water, sugar, lemon, cinnamon and a sizable lump of butter, he had fixed a cheering potion for his friend and saw him sip at it and sniff the fragrant steam appreciatively.

With revived interest he inquired what in a blizzard was the Doctor lugging a gun for?

"Woodchucks," said the Doctor. "Not tonight, but in five or six weeks from now when the grass is up, the Indian pinks and lady slippers are blossoming, and you've forgotten what snow looks like."

"I'll never forget that. Besides it ain't ever goin' to stop snowing," remarked his friend gloomily.

"Yes, it is. And when it does you and I are going to have some fun. We may even make considerable sums of money. Look!" He stripped the canvas case away from a long, thick-barreled weapon and offered it for examination. "Just came this afternoon," he explained. "It's a woodchuck rifle in case you never saw one. I bought it. You're to shoot it and we'll split profits even. Don't know so much about rifles myself, but Colonel Trigger, the firearms authority, ordered it for me. It's what they call a 'bull gun,' a .267 Zee Zipper Zee or something like that. Weighs fourteen pounds—puts 'em all on a dime at a hundred yards. Got a telescope sight for it, too."

"Well, by Judas Priest!" his friend exclaimed as the true worthiness of the big rifle began to be understood. "You and Colonel Trigger have really bought us a rifle this time, an' no mistake!" With appreciative hand and eye he was busy testing the gun at every point.

"Intended to do so," the Doctor commented. "Always knew you could shoot better than any rifle you ever had. Thought I'd see if I could get one that can shoot better'n you can."

He sipped again at his hot drink.

"Did you ever hear of that feller over at Victory who has the fox and mink farm? They tell me he'll pay you twenty-five cents apiece for woodchucks. He uses them for feed. If you haven't lost the knack of rifle shooting, I don't see why we can't pick up a nice little profit shooting woodchucks when the snow goes off."

The snow finally did go off, though to the Captain the process seemed interminable and unnecessarily retarded by fresh storms that came like tax collectors, unwanted and unloved. There were days, however, when the weather was clear and warm and he could get out for a few hours with the new rifle and test it at the target. The first group that he shot taught him that he hadn't previously understood what was meant by the term "gilt-edged accuracy." When the air was still and he was holding well, a little three-quarter-inch tab stuck on the black of the bull's-eye would, at an even hundred yards, be hit with from five to seven of ten bullets fired at it. He spent a good deal of time, too, working down the trigger pull and easing it up with an oilstone slip, and he fiddled with the big telescope sight until he was able to string a line of bullets up or down across the face of the target at fairly evenly spaced intervals.

At last the day came when nowhere along the greening hillsides could the eye discern even a lingering stubborn patch of snow. The Doctor came in the morning to suggest an expedition in the afternoon.

"We'll go up the back road toward Wellsville. It's a ridge road and ought to be fairly dry by this time. Better take along our trout rods, too. We'll quit shooting in time to catch some fish and have supper at the shack. I'll pick you up in my car, boy."

When he came the Captain was ready with the big rifle and a pouchful of cartridges for it. He also had his beautiful four-ounce Chubb trout rod and a creel. As he stowed these things away he saw in the back of the car a big, slatted pine crate, one of the sort used by berry growers to transport a bushel of fruit.

"That's for the woodchucks," his friend explained, "and I got to thinking last night that if that fox farmer pays a quarter for a 'chuck, he'll probably pay at least a dime apiece for crows, so we'll take 'em, too—if you can hit 'em."

It was a perfect day for the venture. Their ears were filled with the sound of running brooks and the air was fragrant with the smell of new grass and of fresh earth and springing, luxuriant foliage. It seemed to the Captain that every post of the sagging rail fence at the roadside had a bluebird perched atop it ready to burst in an ecstatic puff of blue and buff feathers from sheer elation. The long muffled roll of cock grouse came frequently from the hillsides to remind them both of other days yet to come, when the same leaves that were now emerging from the bud would be stained with the glorious farewell colors of autumn and there would be stern work for the bird guns in these environs.

The first woodchuck of the day was spied two hundred yards away, near a rock in a hill pasture. When the car stopped the 'chuck legged it for a hole under the boulder and disappeared.

"Cagey one," remarked the Doctor and was about to drive on when the other stopped him. He had been examining the burrow with the telescope sight.

"He ain't all the way down," he reported. "He's got one ear and an eye over the edge and is watching us."

He slipped an arm into the gun sling, got out and sat down on the running board.

"Gosh! You can't *hit* him!" exclaimed his friend, and was answered by the crash of the rifle. A cloud of dust flew from the boulder and the rifleman rose, climbed the fence and went toward the target. The Doctor saw him stoop and lift the dead woodchuck, which presently reposed quietly in the crate with a bullet hole through his grizzled head.

It appeared that every old field and pasture held a woodchuck or two, and those that didn't have 'chucks had crows stalking about at distances from the road that these sophisticated birds considered to be safe. A dozen times the Captain with the big rifle and its tiny bullet was able to prove that the crows were wrong, and each time one of these mistaken birds joined the wood-chucks in the Doctor's crate.

About this time a light, warning shadow of suspicion crossed the Captain's mind. He knew the Doctor pretty well, and it struck him all at once that the old boy's satisfaction over the number of victims in the crate was rather more than would seem warranted by the modest financial benefits in prospect. The eminent surgeon had strange notions of humor, at times. The Captain considered all the possibilities and then inquired:

"Who's going to deliver all this fox food and get the money for it?"

The Doctor was disarmingly casual in his reply.

"Oh, let's decide that later, my boy. Why do you ask? You don't wish me to think that you'd consider it an undignified business, do you?"

"No-o, maybe not, but it's kinda warm for the time o' year and those crit-ters ain't very fragrant even so soon."

"Don't give it another thought, my boy," his friend reassured him. "Why, we must have close to four dollars in that crate already. What more can you ask—fun and money! There's another—a hellish big black one! See him! Right at the edge of that patch of alders!"

The Captain made an inspection with the 'scope.

"It's one of those soft-finished woodchucks," said he enigmatically, and fired.

When he came back to the car he was dragging with a gloved hand a huge tomcat by the tail.

"Can't bear to touch 'em barehanded, alive or dead," he explained. "He was hunting woodcock nests up in those alders. How I despise 'em! An' worse yet, I despise the folks that turn 'em loose in the name of mercy to prey on everything, rather than to drown 'em, or shoot 'em, or feed 'em. I suppose after all, you can't blame the critters so much—killing's their nature—ours, too, come to think of it," he added, reflectively surveying the heap of woodchucks and crows that he had slain, before dropping the cat into the crate. Then he laughed a little ruefully. "Maybe some day there'll be a lot of superior creatures driving around the back roads and shooting at us humans. When they get one of us they'll say, 'Good shot! That damned scoundrel was after our woodcock, wasn't he?' "

"Serve us right, too," said his companion, "but I can't get tearful over a cussed tomcat. He had a good end. What more could you ask than to wind up in a patch of alder cover hunting woodcock and never knowing what hit you? Come on and we'll find some more 'chucks."

But the other, for some reason, had little ardor left for woodchuck shooting.

"Shucks!" said he, "I've plugged enough of 'em for one day. This rifle—I never shot one like it. Can't seem to miss 'em. I guess it makes me feel a little bit too much the way the Almighty must feel when He has to go around on a nice spring day like this cracking down on people who ain't thinking of doing anything meaner than minding their own business and planting a row of radishes in the garden." He gave an apologetic chuckle. "Let's call it a day and go along down to the Brazier Brook and get some trout for supper."

The suggestion had his friend's instant approval.

It was late when the two returned to the village, for they had caught their fish, cooked them and eaten them at the weatherbeaten cabin that served them as a shelter on every occasion when their expeditions took them into this remote region. After supper they had sat for long on the cabin steps, smoking and conversing at intervals in low tones while they listened to the many-voiced brook and to the whippoorwills' plaintive music.

Nothing more had been said concerning the business of transporting an odorous crateful of woodchucks, crows and tomcat to the fox farmer in Victory and exchanging it for cold cash, but if the Captain had any suspicions, and he probably did have, they were justified. The next morning when he went to the garage to get his car he found the laden strawberry crate reposing suggestively on the back seat. He grinned appreciatively.

"I *thought* he was up to something! So the danged scoundrel came back later and sneaked 'em into my car, did he? Well, we'll fix that!"

He knew the Doctor's routine fairly well, but he hunted for some time before he found his friend's car parked on Elm Street in front of old Mrs. Peabody's place.

Later they had lunch together, and anyone who understands Yankee humor would know that neither of the pair mentioned the crate and its ill-smelling contents. They never did, either.

On the following morning the Captain found the thing back again in his own car, and this time, because the weather had been warm, he knew that it was there even before he opened the garage door.

The Doctor's car, when the Captain finally located it at the home of a patient, had the windows rolled shut and the doors locked, a circumstance that betrayed a purpose, but which forced the plotter to wait until the Doctor went for his daily visit to the hospital and where, apparently fearing no molestation in that stronghold of sanitation, he had imprudently left the vehicle unlocked.

There ensued two more days and nights during which time the crate surreptitiously changed cars four times. The Dark-Haired Lady began to complain about the horrid smell that occasionally enveloped the neighborhood, and to wonder where on earth it came from. Her mate said he hadn't noticed it lately, and that was the truth, too. His intermittent association with the crate had paralyzed his olfactory nerves to such an extent that he couldn't smell anything at all.

But other people could, and it was a curious thing to observe the actions of citizens on the sidewalk when the Captain drove past at those times when he was carrying the fox and mink provender and searching for the Doctor's car.

"By Judas Priest!" said he to himself—"those 'chucks and crows and that danged tomcat have more'n got even for anything we did to 'em! About one more day of this and they'll be able to change cars themselves without any help from anybody!"

Meantime the friends continued to meet, and Yankee fashion, spoke no word concerning cats, woodchucks or crows, though they often did comment casually on the prevalence of the warm weather. No one, seeing them together, would have suspected that they were locked in combat as intense—and, in a sense, as deadly—as any in history.

It couldn't go on forever, and on the fifth day, at the 131st hour of the siege, the Doctor broke.

He was tired of the way people looked at him, and tired of dropping casual explanatory remarks about some experimental bacteriological work he was doing. That was almost as bad as to ignore their curious startled glances and to say nothing. He hadn't given his antagonist credit for so much stubbornness, but nevertheless the situation looked most promising only a few hours before he capitulated. The preceding night, very late, he had managed to work the lock on the Captain's garage door with a piece of bent wire and so the Thing—it had well earned its capital letter by that time—was in his friend's reluctant custody. Afterward he had hidden his own car in an old stone shed a half-mile up the North Branch where no one would ever think to look for it, and during the day had made his rounds on foot. When he set out, also on foot, for the evening visit to the hospital he felt good. He felt that he had the Captain at last, and, besides that, the fresh, clean air certainly smelled nice.

But when he came back at about half-past nine o'clock to his office in the Town Hall he had a whiff of foreboding. It was more than warranted. He unlocked the office door, opened it and shuddered. There on his desk sat the crate—and what was wafted from it or expelled from it was certainly not the fresh fragrance of the strawberries it had once contained. The door and windows of the office were locked, and if he never learned how entrance had been effected, it was because the intruder, after he had made his visit, removed a small wad of chewing gum that had so conveniently held back the latch on the spring lock.

The Doctor did the thing that was equivalent to running up the white flag.

Late that night, when the streets were deserted, the defeated surgeon carried the crate gingerly to his car and drove to the center of the low arch that spans the North Branch where that stream passes under Main Street. No one was in sight when he lifted the Thing to the railing, and he thought no one was in sight when, gasping and choking, he tipped the horrid compost off the rail and heard it strike the current with a splash and a foul, loathsome gurgle.

"Good evenin' to you, Docther," said a voice, and there at his startled elbow stood Officer Minogue of the Municipal Force. In fact, Officer Minogue was the Municipal Force.

"Ye're abroad late, Docther," he remarked in friendly phrase and was about to continue with some further pleasantary when the last frightful breath from the departing woodchucks, crows and tomcat rose dankly from the stream and crossed his broad Celtic nostrils.

"Holy Mackerel! Docther! What is ut, then, that ye just heaved into the strame below? Ah, sorrow, sorrow! I niver smelt the loikes of it!"

Then another thought came into his honest policeman's skull.

"Docther, 'twas garbage! An' well ye know the ordinance agin heavin' garbage into the strame within the town limits."

The gaze he speared the Doctor with was anxious and reproachful, for they were friends, but it was also stern and accusatory for he was a conscientious public servant.

The Doctor thought fast.

"Listen, Patrick. You are a man of discretion." His voice sank to the level of one about to impart an awful confidence. "You must know that in the public interest we surgeons must sometimes do things up at the laboratory which are better not talked about. You understand, of course?"

Words leaped into the mind of Officer Minogue—awful words, ghastly words and hints but half believed when he had heard them.

"'Tis true, then!" he thought. "The black stories you do be hearin' about what they do with the poor bodies!"

"Of course," the Doctor went on, in a matter-of-fact tones, "we have to dispose of 'em somehow. I'll hold you to silence, but as an officer of the law I think you're entitled to know that what I just dumped was—"

There was no lack of physical courage in the Minogue line, with its traditions of the Boyne Wather and Clare's Brigade at Fontenoy, not to mention some hundreds of other peoples' quarrels happily participated in the world over, but all his fighting ancestors couldn't prepare the Irishman for this sort of thing.

"Tell me no more, Docther, dear!" he cried in a panic. "I want no part in this ghastly business!"

He fled the scene forthwith, muttering to himself as he did so: "Ah, to think of it now! A poor felly can't be sure of dacent Christian burial—cut into bits and thrun into the strame—God save us all!"

And that's the tale, except that once, a long time afterward, the Captain, walking with his friend, the Doctor, met the Municipal Force on the street one evening and thought he noticed something odd and furtive.

"By Judas Priest, Doc! When you spoke to Minogue just then it seemed to me that he crossed himself!"

"Did he?" said the Doctor, in a preoccupied way. "Did he now, indeed? That's extremely curious. But then the Irish are a very superstitious race."

DUSKING DUCKS IN THE MONEY HOLE

If sometime a shaft is raised to commemorate the lost privileges of Americans, there should be placed at its base, among the heaps of other somber souvenirs, a single wreath for that unique and picturesque method of wildfowling known among its devotees of former days as "dusking." "Dusking" described the twilight or early evening shooting of ducks flighting in to their nighttime feeding grounds. A New England bog, a western slough or an abandoned rice field among the live oaks beside some slow southern river—these places have power enough to engross any wildfowler; but when to their daylight charms is added the atmosphere of that mysterious hour between sundown and dark, when the hosts of wary waterfowl hiss past within yards of one's own head, the darkling pools resound with the rush and bickering and sputter of feeding birds, and the nostrils are filled with the strong, pungent, pleasant odor of the marsh, then we can understand why sportsmen of another generation often preferred an hour of such shooting to an entire day in a reasonably comfortable blind—even though they bagged fewer birds. An open marsh is the wildest place in all Christendom, and in such an environment Nature has a way of showing a man how fragile are his devices and how weak are his noisy efforts opposed to her indomitable, everlasting powers. As evening falls, something that is old and primitive moves in the shadows, the visible evidences of human industry and domesticity are engulfed in the gloom, and a furtive life, as purposeful and as important as his own, stirs about the man. The far and feeble lights on the mainland only emphasize the insecurity of his civilization, and even the gun in his hands is a weapon for his defense and preservation, and not merely a delicately powerful and complicated plaything. It is good for a man to have such experiences, for they make him humble and teach him true and proper reverence; and, while I acknowledge the force and authenticity of the conditions that have outlawed "dusking," I must bewail the passing of a sport that had so much more than sport to commend it.

Reason and experience have convinced most of us now that for the good of the game the shooting of wildfowl must stop at sundown. Each passing year sees a disconcerting decrease in the area of marshes and sloughs in this country, and the observant sportsman cannot escape the conclusion that the nightly truce permitting the harried birds opportunities to feed and rest on these increasingly limited and vital precincts is a measure properly required by law and emphatically ordered by necessity. Once, in some regions, if a farmer carelessly dropped a potato it was fairly sure to roll into a duck marsh somewhere, and in those times men who were accustomed to see more game in a few hours than we can observe in as many weeks still found the flights of wildfowl of such tremendous, spectacular magnitude as to fill even their sophisticated souls with awe and astonishment. But even then the ducks were trying to show us that night shooting was not entirely a fair method of pursuit. If we sat in the buttonbrush beside some darkling slough, we generally enjoyed one evening of splendid shooting, but the next evening in the same spot would find the flight of reckless, hungry birds considerably less. Thereafter, and until we stopped and gave the place a long rest from further persecution, there would be no sustained flight but only a few ignorant stragglers coming hopefully in where other hundreds feared to venture. The slough had been "burned out." Today, such is the relative scarcity of succulent marsh areas that "burned out" ducks may have to go many miles to find another spot where they can feed and rest. Engineers assure us that our reckless abuse of original water levels by drainage and deforestation will have ultimate serious consequences for mankind; the blight is already falling upon the web-footed tribes whose need for watery environment is more direct than our own. The gunner who, in defiance of the law, posts himself on a feeding ground to hammer away at the ducks after sundown undoubtedly does a greater harm than can be measured by the number of birds he kills, for he drives away and disturbs wildfowl, which need every ounce of food they can find and every minute of rest that the pressure of modern conditions will permit.

Very likely we should have known all this long ago, but there were few who could interpret the signs, and fewer still who would listen to such prophets. In any event, the Captain went about his preparations for an evening's shooting at the "Money Hole" with Jim Hooper with an eagerness unmarred by any cold gusts blowing down from the chill heights of conscience.

Jim, who has been described on previous occasions, was the reprobate associate of many of the Captain's earlier sporting experiences. He had an ingrained horror of any contact with a social order less shiftless than his own. So far as is known, none of the Captain's relatives on the distaff side of the family had ever upbraided Jim, but the lank, slovenly, lazy, good-natured woodsman had a shy and sensitive nature that yet suffered under their instinctive disapproval, even though it remained unspoken. On this September afernoon, at a time when the automobile was still an exciting novelty in rural districts, Jim's discretion led him to wait for his friend a quarter of a mile down the road.

He was roosting on the ancient stone wall munching an apple, but he slid easily to his feet, picked up a rickety double gun of very questionable foreign origin that had lately replaced the redoubtable muzzle-loader and stepped into the buckboard. One instant he had been on the wall, and the next he was beside the Captain on the leather cushion, yet he had not hurried. His grace, a muscular but not a spiritual quality, was as natural as that of an indolent blacksnake or of a marsh hawk loafing on the wing. The two proceeded companionably down a brown dirt road, where the soft fronds of the crimson sumach brushed their faces and the clumps of chokecherry bushes growing in every fence corner offered close-set bunches of the rich astringent fruit to them as they passed. Great flocks of robins, garbed in waistcoats hued in more sober tints than they had displayed in the sprightly month of April, abandoned their busy feeding in the wild grape tangles and fled down the road, only to repeat the same performance a few paces farther along, until at last, immune to further alarms, they allowed the equipage to pass. At one spot, two great swamp woodpeckers were molded to the side of a black cherry tree, where they fixed their claws and rested at ease on their stiff tail feathers. They gave up their probing and turned their scarlet caps inquisitively to study the travelers. When these were safely past, and danger over, the rare birds cast off the aerial anchorage and in awkward, pitching flight, precisely as though they skimmed the slopes in invisible billows, went off across the pasture to quieter realms, uttering the curious call that is timed to the spasmodic measures of their flight.

"Curious cusses, ain't they?" said Jim, watching them. "I us'ter think they wuz somethin' like a pa'tridge, an' I kilt a couple of 'em wi' a Flobert rifle one day, an' took 'em home an' tried to eat 'em. By gol', sir, they tasted suthin' like a hame strap to a harness; I'd as soon hev crow!"

The roadside hedges swarmed with birds more than they ever did in springtime. In the fields, sociable gypsy communities of meadowlarks probed for grubs or whirred away in flight so like that of the quail as later to deceive many a gunner encountering the bird in southern stubble fields. Yet, in a world that was filled with sunshine, burdened with wasting ripened fruit and crammed like a Nile granary with a harvest of seeds, only the partridges, squirrels and chickadees seemed wholly to appreciate and to revel in these many blessings. Among the other creatures there was an evident spirit of restlessness and furtive haste. The ear heard none of the gay melodies of spring and summer; the bird notes now were brief whistles and chirps, indicative of practical discussions and comment rather than the bubbling over of high spirits and gallantry. Somewhere hidden in the golden haze or in the glorious autumn foliage they saw what mankind might not discern—a warning presence that cautioned them of the swift approach of cruel moods.

"Got their leetle trunks all packed," said Jim, watching a flock of robins fluttering in the branches of an elm. "By gol'! I wish't I could go with 'em, I do." He sighed as he contemplated his own earth-bound condition and the frigid months that intervened between this present season and the return of the birds in the spring.

"Don't happen to hev no sech thing as smokin' tobaccer, du ye?" he inquired. And presently, with his corncob stuffed with "Sweet Lotus" and drawing luxuriously, he regaled the Captain—prompted, no doubt, by thoughts of the robins' travel—with an account of his first and only ride on a "steam train." He had been "consid'able scairt," it seemed, and finally, convinced that he was being carried *nolens volens* "cl'ar outen the country," had stepped off between stations.

"By Judast Prue! If I'd 'a' had a wire nail in my maouth, I b'lieve I'd 'a' bit it in two! I must hev turned all o' thutty somersaults an' busted as nice a pint o' 'Old Pepper' as ye ever see! Ye hain't no idee, less'n you've stepped off one of 'em like I did, haow fast them steam-trains air reely goin'!"

And while thus agreeably the pair chatted or were silent, the sorrel beat out a tireless pace, and before they knew it they had reached the Lake, approaching the narrow, marshy lower stretches through a winding gap in the wooded limestone ledges that lifted above the eastern margin. The Lake at this point and for miles to the south was scarcely more than a winding channel of open water bounded on either side by broad fens and irregular bays and sloughs. Waving masses of wildrice everywhere met the eye, with an occasional water maple, flushing crimson at the first bold touch of the wooing frost, holding a brush of ruddy color against the tawny background, or a tangle of buttonbrush growing greenly where the shallows sloped upward and exposed a bed of muddy ooze. The Money Hole was a recess extending away from the sluggish main channel, the only visible connection with the parent flood being a narrow creek, its surface coated with a green mat of duckweed checkered and traversed with watery trails left by muskrat or wildfowl. A currentless pool scarcely thirty paces across, near the center of the Hole, was their present objective. A light, flat-bottomed skiff was lying in an oozy berth at a muddy landing place, and they pushed the craft out through the rice to the edge of the pool, where a low-crowned straggling clump of buttonbrush afforded a natural blind. Little concealment was necessary, for the ducks, once their flight was under way, would show a determination to alight not lessened by the presence of two active gunners on the spot. The fading light, deceptive alike to ducks and duck-shooters, also helped to render a more elaborate ambuscade unnecessary.

Jim professed himself satisfied with the arrangements and prophesied plenty of ducks, though the advance through the marsh had aroused nothing but a single rail and a pair of pert grebe.

"How do you know there'll be a flight?" the Captain inquired.

His companion seemed at a loss for any tangible reason to warrant his conviction.

"Wal, naow, I dunno's I c'n say p'tic'larly. Jest that it's time for 'em to be here, an' when it's time for wildfaowl to be here, here they'll be." His remark fairly expresed the assurance of a generation accustomed to the simple tradition of plenty.

He levied a second unconstitutional tobacco tax upon his friend, "borried" a double handful of cartridges and prepared himself to await with calm enjoyment the arrival of the scouting squadrons that would precede the main array of ducks.

The marsh, belying its lonely, deserted aspect, which might have deceived the casual visitor, began to stir about them; and its swarming life, representing over and over again every province in the kingdom of animal life, began to move and go about its affairs. Small whispers of sound, the chirp of unseen bird or insect, the faint, furtive splashings under the reeds and rice, were of unknown origins, but that sudden plunging surge sending the waves scurrying through the stems could only be made by a great pickerel rushing out of a weedy robber's roost upon a cavalcade of minnows. Another splash, somehow less vicious, but equally startling, made them think of muskrat, and presently, to attest the accuracy of the guess, the little busy brown fellow swam out across the pool, trailing a mass of weeds and roots from his jaws to add to the weatherproof walls of the new hut he was building by the bank. The clear, fairy whistle of a flock of yellowlegs came to the ear and, from the opposite shore, the hoarse, discordant croak of a heron disturbed by some prowler of the marshes.

"There ain't many that'll allow that the crow can sing," Jim remarked unexpectedly, "but twicet a year he ain't so dummed poor at it—when you first hear him in the spring, just when the snow begins to melt, an' agin in the fall when he's jest gettin' ready to pull stakes. Listen to 'em!"

The voices of a flock perched in the branches of a butternut tree on a distant hillside were indeed not unmusical now, but they seemed to have a gentle, pensive quality quite different from the usual rough, jeering tones of this habitual roisterer. Whether the witsful melancholy of autumn touched their wild, mischievous spirits, as it did their own, or whether distance and the mellow haze produced these unwonted harmonies, neither Jim nor the Captain could determine.

The sun by now had touched the glowing rampart of the Adirondacks, and long bands of soft shadow lay along each ravine and valley. Jim rapped the ash from his pipe and fixed his attention on the mass of shadow creeping out from the mountain's foot and spreading over the marsh. He was so engaged when six bluewing teal, sweeping up without warning from behind, dipped over the heads of the gunners, flashed across the pool and were out of range before either could raise a hammer.

"There they be, and there they go!" exclaimed Jim. "I swan, I never see such critters to fly! Wal, here comes another one that ain't in no sech hurry."

A drake wood duck, squealing plaintively for companionship, sailed down and alighted after the unsuspecting manner of his kind and was laid low by a bellowing discharge of Jim's rickety gun that thereby had hastened by one wood duck the day when this bird, the most strikingly beautiful of American ducks, was to be placed under the protection of the Governments of Great Britain and the United States in order to save it from threatened extermination.

"There, sir! That's the way to do it!"

If anything, Jim took more pride in a sitting shot than in killing his bird on the wing—a feat he rarely accomplished. No doubt he enjoyed gunning quite as much as does the most appreciative sportsman, but game to him, as to the Indian, was food, and the surest and easiest way to secure it was always the best.

And now from out the dusky reaches of the open lake came flock after flock of ducks—black ducks, teal and wood ducks—flying low and swiftly along the channel. Many of these turned aside and swept over the pool, and many more went on to other favored feeding grounds. The gunners could not extract the empty cartridge cases fast enough to reload and salute each of the arriving squadrons. As the twilight gathered, a second flight began, endless waving lines and shifting wedges of wildfowl going down to the South Bay, perhaps, or the canals and waterways of the Hudson Valley. These hosts moved along air lanes a thousand feet above the marshes—so high, in fact, that their breasts caught the faint glow of a sunset that had vanished in the lower reaches. In the rare moments when they were not noisily engaged with the stream of ducks sweeping just above the rice tops the two men could hear the ceaseless humming whisper of the uncountable wings of these travelers hurrying, rank upon rank, along a loftier route. No bird came down from these high legions to join the lower flight, and none of those from the flocks about rose to fly with those grandly sweeping squadrons. Long after it was wholly dark, that steady sound as of distant mysterious wings still came down out of the infinite vaulted sky.

"Pooty, ain't they?" said Jim, with Yankee laconicism.

The nearer birds were invisible now, except for an instant when those that passed directly over were briefly seen against the glowing west. The wildfowlers' ears were continually filled with the hiss and whicker of wings as ducks swept in from all sides out of the dusk and passed, sometimes no more than the length of a push pole away, but without being visible to either of the watchers. Others, also unseen, alighted in the pool, and at once set up a bickering and splashing so loud and so near that it seemed as if one might reach out in the darkness and seize a wild black drake by the neck. Some of these visitors swam into the glimmering reflection of the afterglow on the water and were faintly discernible as dark, shadowy blots against which Jim's old gun blazed its fury of flame and thunder, but without accomplishing the wholesale destruction that the devastating roar and spatter seemed to portend.

The Captain's method consisted of keeping his eyes straining steadily on the space of faintly glowing sky above the mountains, while he held the gun cocked and ready, halfway to his shoulder. There was no time for the calculations incident to daytime duck shooting. A duck or two, or a flock of them, would pop out of the murk, whisk across the luminous area and instantly vanish again. A quick swing of the gun, then a touch of the trigger and a blinding burst of flame as the honest black powder thundered. If the shot was successful, a solid splash in the marsh behind announced the fact and another bird was tallied for recovery later. Once, a falling bird just missed Jim's head and struck so close that water spattered over the skiff.

"Let 'em git well over," Jim cautioned with some fervor. "Ef one of them ducks hits ye, he'll knock ye silly!"

It seemed a most remote hazard, but it is a fact that a dead duck pitching down at a fifty-mile speed has a serious projectile force, sufficient to knock a man off his feet even if it does him no worse damage.

"Got enough, hain't we?" Jim inquired presently. "We'll hev a time of it pickin' 'em up as it is."

Poking and pushing and floundering about in the darkness, the two did, indeed, have a time of it before they had gathered the last of their game. Blobs of mud, trailing wads of soaked rice stalks, a flaccid lily pad—all these things were hailed in the gloom and grabbed in the search for dead birds. Jim had his hand within three inches of an unmistakable dusky blot bobbing in a clump of rice, when, to his intense dismay and alarm, a sound and able black duck let out a vociferous bray and took wing, dashing a quart of water into Jim's face and so startling him that he gasped and strangled and nearly fell out of the skiff.

"Gosh! Haow he scar't me! Ef he'd 'a' bit me, he couldn't ha' scar't me no worse! The dummed deceivin' critter!

"That duck 'minds me of the time John White ketched a bobcat in a trap over in Proctor Holler. Arter he kilt the critter wi' a club he slung him over his shoulder an' fetched him aout. Wal, sir, he hadn't gone fur when the dummed wil'cat come to an' clawed the seat out o' John's pants before John could git him loose an' club him agin. 'Fore he got to the village the wil'cat come to agin an' they had another ruckus. John finally got him home an' sold him to Rawl Hassett fer five dollars.

" 'An' here's the club,' sez he to Rawl.

" 'What's the club fer?' sez Rawl.

" 'Sos't you can continner to kill that air indestructible resurrectin' critter,'
sez John. 'I hev hed to kill him three times a'ready an' I hain't no daoubt he
only feels the better fer the mellerin',' sez he."

Jim cautiously boated another duck, unmistakably dead, and according to
the tally, the last of the lot.

The valley was now deep in velvety blackness, only intensified by the pin
points of light in the windows of a farmhouse on the shore. The owls
whooped their challenges from the scarred and crumbling battlements of Ticonderoga, and Jim, guided by nothing that could be seen, ran the skiff
unerringly to the plank landing, where they unloaded and tied their birds
into bunches convenient for carrying.

"That duck back thar," said Jim, "the one that got up an' flew—I declare, I
kinder wish sometimes when I've kilt a deer, or a pa'tridge, or a duck, or anything else that's wil' an' harndsome an' good to eat, that another one jest like
him could git up an' run away or fly away. Er else that a man didn't git so
dummed sick o' choppin' wood an' eatin' salt pork."

AN
EXPERT
OPINION
— • ◆ • —

"I say it in sorrow," said Colonel Cushing, "but I believe the society of fishermen sustains more bubble reputations, more plausible quackery and a greater number of didactical know-it-alls than any other sport—with the possible exception of amateur horse racing. Eighteen years ago this same month of June, a fishing acquaintance whom I met at the Cast and Creel on the Battenkill gave me a dozen flies." He paused and from a pocket of his short-skirted fishing jacket produced a gigantic fly-book.

This fly-book, as such intimate articles are apt to be, was a measure of the man who used it. Someone—some ancient, patient craftsman, bespectacled and aproned—had selected the leather for it, a rich, tough piece, fine-fibered and not too flexible. He had then cut with skill and stitched with patience, waxing his whips well so that now, after nearly twenty years of service, the sides gleamed with a dull polish undimmed by time or immersion; no stitch was frayed, no seam gaped open under the strain of encompassing some ten or twelve dozen assorted flies, as well as several hundred feet of leaders. In short, the material of this magnificent fly-book, the fine, strong stitching and molding of the indomitable leather and most of all, perhaps, the tremendous size of the object all indicated that the old craftsman had a specially qualified patron in mind when he worked. Clearly, it was no book for the careless amateur trout fisherman; obviously, it was no book for the pleasant dabbler who fishes in order to be fashionable; and certainly, it was no book for the cautious person who fears to shove his shins into a deep riffle of cold water or who stays at home on a quiet gray day when the streams are running free and clear, because of the perils of black flies and mosquitoes. It was definitely and most particularly a book for a youngster of eighteen or so—as was the Colonel, in fact, when he bought it—who already anticipates that trout fishing is to be the major serious pastime of a long life and who enters upon the sport with diligence and a proper respect for its traditions and its obligations, wisely desiring his equipment to be in keeping. Two flies the Judge extracted from the book and laid in his palm for better inspection.

"Only these remain of the original dozen," he resumed. "The gentleman didn't know the name, or possibly I neglected to ask. For all that I know, it may be something as common elsewhere as a gray hackle and unfamiliar only on these local streams, or it may be the creation of a specialist, never listed anywhere and only tied in a few dozens. I might have looked it up myself, of course, but after embarrassing a few experts, I became interested to see if any of these nomenclature purists could put a name to it. In eighteen years none has done so." He fixed the Captain with a quizzical eye. "And now, my boy, it's your turn to try it. Your reputation has spread to every stream in New England. Let me see if you've earned it."

The third member of the party, the Doctor, set the butt of his rod on the sod and watched the Colonel and the Captain. Behind them in the Pond a trout took down a floating insect with a brief sucking noise and a wide, silent roll of water.

The Captain gave the flies a sharp inspection.

"Soldier Palmer," said he, in tones of secure authority, his gaze meeting the other's glance fairly. "It's funny no one has named it for you long before this."

The tableau held for a moment, and then on the green bank of the Trout Pond, with the declining sun sprinkling the participants with reflections of its own passing glory, the Colonel bent his long back in a quaintly deferential bow to the expert.

"The only man in eighteen years who really knew," he murmured.

"Well, gentlemen, the trout are rising," said the Doctor, an observation that was repeatedly confirmed by the countless splashes on the water where the six- and eight-inch fish were feeding with more vigor than finesse and by the occasional deep, slow roll where some venerable trout picked off an insect with the lazy, easy, dignified form that marks the veteran whose perfect timing, as well as whose knowledge of his own supremacy, makes rude haste unnecessary and spattering drops the sign of vulgar competition.

"Colonel, as the honored guest of the Squaretail Club, you are to choose the water you like most to fish. There's the Pond and nearly four miles of good stream, so you need feel no hesitancy in making your selection."

"Well, now, that's right nice of you boys. If it's agreeable to all, I believe I'll just take the left shore of the Pond and cast from the bank. I observe certain matters and things that seem to indicate that some notable fish are feeding just off shore. I shall fish well ahead and keep my shadow off the water."

"When you reach the point, sir, lay your cast just inside an old stake you'll see in the cove—there's a black behemoth who feeds there, and he'll run close to four pounds, I reckon," the Captain advised, as the guest moved up the bank, working out his line with smooth, slow flicks of his wrist. "Where'll we go, Doctor?"

"Why, on an evening like this we could take fish in the middle of the meadow! Look at that one roll! Let's take the skiff and drift up the channel."

They had been quietly at work for perhaps a quarter of an hour when a whoop from the Colonel—a person not normally inclined to emotional vociferation—drew their quick attention. That worthy fisherman was surging about in water nearly to his waist, grunting, gasping and occasionally letting go a frantic bawl of pure excitement. His rod was weaving and whipping like a rush in a gale, and farther out, just where the edge of the alder shadows fell on the darkling water, the erstwhile placid surface heaved and boiled and was cut athwart by slashing passages of the line. No fin showed; the struggle was deep, strong and furious.

"He's fast to one of the Old Masters!" exclaimed the Captain. Now and again on the Squaretail waters someone struck a fish of such extraordinary weight and of such unusual coloring that it was supposed to be an original denizen of the stream or a direct descendant of such. The ordinary run of fish were dark enough, in all conscience, but these ancients were a glossy black, in certain lights, showing the barely perceptible greenish tint of jade. Against their somber sides, the crimson spots glowed like sparks. Truly, they were fish to make one weep for the olden days, were these Old Masters; and their strength, prudence and utter, unrelenting courage were such that, while thousands of their lesser kind went from fly to creel and from creel to the pan on the hot griddle of the battered stove in the cabin, these superior fish were seldom struck and much more rarely taken.

The two in the skiff watched the struggle with bated breath, and a black duck with her brood swam to the edge of the rushes and watched too. The angler was fully alive to his tremendous opportunity, and for all his thrashing and whooping, he fought a neat, tight battle, keeping the opponent's flanking rushes well under control and holding a perilous reserve of line under his hand. A raft of waterlilies floated near the farther fringe of the conflict.

"If he ever makes the pads, he's gone!" said the Doctor, but time and time again the rod whipped up in a straining arc just in the instant to turn the fish from the haven. At times, his jetty snout and gaping jaws must have missed the swaying stems by inches only. But as direct rushes failed to carry him through against the supple resistance of rod and wrist, the Old Master attempted his goal by a series of tacking rushes, opposing cunningly the broad width of his side against the rod; but this maneuver, which might have won for him had he adopted it while his strength was fresh, failed him now, and though he strained every sinew and fought until the pads bobbed and quivered in the currents created, he just missed getting his nose into the saving tangle. Three minutes later, the Colonel lifted the expiring warrior in his net and prudently lugged his fish some twenty yards into the meadow before lifting the prize for the inspection of the Doctor and the Captain in the skiff.

"What did he take?" called one of the two, after admiring and congratulatory messages had been shouted back and forth.

"Soldier Palmer!" was the reply, "and he ruined it—stripped it to the bare shank!"

The Doctor gazed searchingly at his friend.

"That reminds me," said he in lower tones, "what was that fly?"

"Hanged if I know," was the bland response. "Never saw one of 'em before in my life."

"Aha! I thought so! You charlatan! You shyster! Why, the cold-blooded effrontery of it! And to the Colonel, too, who ranks you a mile and who can spot a liar just by looking at him. I can't but admire such bold, uncompromising duplicity!"

"Well, you see," the other began mildly, "he challenged me, didn't he, to name that fly? Why the devil didn't he name it himself if he's so good at it? Was he risking his reputation? Not so you could notice it, but he compelled me to risk mine, and I took him at his own game. You ought to be proud of me!"

"I am," admitted his crony, "but I'm also worried over what he'll think of you if ever finds out what that fly really is!"

"Well, that's a chance I had to take, of course. But he hasn't found out in eighteen years, has he? Besides, he's only got one of 'em left now—that Old Master has just ruined one. If he only loses the other, I'll be safe, for you can't hold a man to a description of a trout fly from memory. We've got all the fish we need, haven't we? Let's go on."

An hour later, with the twilight fading, the Colonel far up the shore regretfully reeled in his line and untied his cast. Groping about in the gloom of the alders, he got hold of his heavy creel and set out toward the cabin, following the drift of a fragrance that seemed to be an agreeable blend of frying trout, boiling coffee and browning corn bread.

"What luck?" chorused the two from the kitchen as the late fisherman stumbled up the steps into the light.

"I only saved two," was the reply, given in tones of quiet restraint, as the speaker laid, not one, but two genuine and authentic Old Masters on the dining-room table. For the space of a minute no one spoke and the great dark fish reposed there on the dark walnut with the yellow light gleaming on their ebony magnificence, their crimson spots glowing like coals.

"Great Scott!" said the Doctor and the Captain, and it was inadequate.

"I saved but the two," repeated the Colonel in low, dramatic tones, "and they cost me the last of my Soldier Palmers given me so long ago at the Cast and Creel on the Battenkill. But they are worth it."

Still later, when their old friend had feasted and departed with his two fish, the Doctor laid aside his pipe, rose and from a shelf over the lounge took down a massive tome devoted, from cover to cover, to matters pertaining solely to the noble art of fly-fishing for trout. It was a big, authentic-looking book. Turning the pages, he came to a section filled with carefully executed, exquisitely colored illustrations of trout flies. After examining some scores of these reproductions, he paused with a finger on the page to indicate a certain specimen but held it so that the name could not be read.

"What is it?" he demanded, as the other leaned forward to look. There it was—the perfect picture of the lost flies of the Battenkill.

"I swear I don't know," faltered the guilty rascal as the Doctor fixed him with an unwavering eye.

Whereupon the inquisitor moved his finger a half inch down the page, so that the delicately etched wording could be read.

(Author's Note.) Being cognizant of the ancient, cruel suspicion with which the public regards the strange coincidences of the fisherman's life, I find myself reluctant to write the conclusion of this wholly veracious narrative. As between anglers, will you, yourself, then have one guess as to the name of the particular trout fly that our friend the Doctor found in the big, authentic-looking book?

A PRIVATE AFFAIR

As it sank behind the gentle Virginia hills the sun threw a final suffusion of amber light across the Campus. It was the quiet hour before supper. Undergraduates coming from the tennis courts and the athletic field strolled along the winding brick walks swinging racquets and clubs and chattering of the important affairs and matters that engage the interests of the young. Someone at the Old Dormitory stuck a few soft precise chords from a guitar, and voices took up the merry wistful melody of "Oh! Susannah."

The Dean shoved a sleek pair of brown riding boots under his desk and thought that probably "Hooter" Gordon's gang had gotten hold of a bottle of sherry. Well, it wouldn't hurt them. He hummed a bar or two of the old familiar song:

> "I'll be comin' back from Oregon
> With my gold dust on my knee."

"Marse Robert" looked gravely down at him from a panel over the fireplace where hung a long Remington Dragoon revolver in a black leather holster with the letters C.S.A. embossed on the worn flap, and beside it a heavy cavalry saber with more than a full yard of steel projecting beyond the dented guard. The weapons were there because a man in a dusty, disheveled blue uniform had said: "Officers may retain their side arms."

At last the sunlight lifted reluctantly from the crimson crown of the gum tree outside the Dean's window, and then someone knocked gently upon a panel of the old door.

"Come in, Esau."

A fat old Negro in a white mess coat eased himself into the room.

"Cunnel, suh! He done come," he announced. Then he closed the door and advanced to the desk for a confidential report on the matter.

"Cunnel, suh! He is dest de spit an' image ob de Ol' Cap'n! I declar', suh,

144

he sholy is! An' he got his dawg too. Lawd A'mighty! Big long-haided ol' set-ter wid egg-zackly de same sassy patch on de right eye!"

"All right, Esau. Show 'em in. And then find my grandson, Mister John, and ask him to come here, please. Tell him that Mister William has arrived."

A lean stripling of eighteen or thereabouts entered, paused for a moment and then came forward as the Dean rose and put out his hand.

"Colonel Bristol, sir," said the boy with diffidence, "I'm William Stovall. I hope I find you well, sir."

"Of co'se, of co'se! William, I'm glad to see you, and if I didn't know for a certainty that your Grandad is as old and as gray and generally decrepit as I am this minute, I'd swear you were that man! Ten or fifteen pounds lighter, possibly, than I remember him, but that's all. And this must be Soldier."

At the sound of his name the big setter came up, his great plume waving, sniffed gently with a broad muzzle at the brown boots and lifted approving hazel eyes to the gray ones above him.

The Dean chuckled: "I declare, son, I never saw a man and *his* dog look more like another man and his dog." His hand dropped to the broad arch of the dog's skull. "I hope you'll let me shoot over him sometimes."

"Why, sir, Soldier and I would be completely paralyzed—I mean we'd be awfully glad if you would, sir! Grandad said he thought you might. Soldier hasn't had much experience with quail, but I 'spect he'll learn 'em."

"I expect he will," said the Dean. "His grandsire did."

"Yes, sir," said the boy with a quick, shy smile. "Grandad told me about that time."

Another youngster came in then, and the Dean made introductions.

"Son, this is William and this other gentleman is Soldier. Will you take them home, please? Tell Miss Annie that I'll be there in time for supper."

He turned again to William: "And we'll talk about your studies tomorrow, if you please. Right now you'll want a bath and some of Rachel's fried chicken—and I want to do a little thinking."

The two went out, and the Dean watching them thought how alike they were with their lean, loose-limbed bodies, straight backs and gentle manners. He sat down and lighted a cigarette.

In a weather-beaten tent in a wood on the north bank of a narrow river, young Captain William Stovall awoke, yawned and shoved his long legs over the edge of his cot. The morning rays of the sun were in the feathery tops of the pin oaks outside and there was frost in. A golden reflection illumined the rough fabric over his head. A big setter with a dissolute bluish patch over his right eye rose from a blue blanket in a corner, came over to inquire formally as to the state of the young officer's health and then turned his gaze hopefully on the entrance.

The Captain reached for boots and breeches. He spoke to the setter.

"Hi, Soldier. Think you can find 'em today? Let's try 'em, eh?"

At the sound of the voice a fat soldier with a disordered mop of red hair scratched perfunctorily at the tent flap, then stepped inside and came to a rigid "Attention!"

"Mornin', Chauncey. Stand easy. Fetch me a bucket of fresh water and bring up my breakfast."

"I already got the Cap'n's washin' water an' his breakfast, too."

"And see if you can snake out six raw eggs for Soldier."

"Got the aigs, too," remarked Chauncey stolidly.

"All right, perfect! Now let's see you convey my compliments to Lieutenant Hines and tell him he's in command today—that I'm goin' out on a reconnaissance. Tell the cook to put up three lunches—two big ones for me and Soldier and a little teeny-weeny one for you. You're gettin' too fat. You're ridin' with us, too."

"Yes, sir, Cap'n, I got the grub already. But does the Cap'n reelize this ain't no time to go shoolin' 'round after them leetle insignificant birds? Take about four of 'em to make one reel pa'tridge, anyhow! And what's to prevent us gittin' picked up by a Secesh patrol, I wanter know? Nothin'! The Cap'n may like the idee o' Andersonville Prison, but, by Judas Priest, the Cap'n's orderly don't!"

"Shut up—you'll go where I say to go! Get out my shotgun and look to the ammunition pouches, understand? Get started, and don't let me hear anything more from you but silence—an' damned little o' that!"

"I already 'tended to that," said Chauncey reproachfully.

A half-hour later they splashed through the shallows of a ford and climbed the red earth bank to the uneven and weed-smothered fields on the opposite side. Chauncey wore an air of badly concealed trepidation, and a service revolver, fresh caps glinting on the nipples, was strapped to his plump unsoldierly waist. His apprehensive gaze scrutinized every inequality of terrain and sought to penetrate the thickets of cat brier and wild plum. It was so quiet that the sudden raucous yelping of a swamp woodpecker made Chauncey flinch visibly.

The Captain laughed:

"Don't be so damned jumpy! There ain't a gray jacket within ten miles according to our patrols."

"Yessir. I guess that's right—only our patrols ain't never yit seemed to be able to git their permanent address, Cap'n. Those jaspers jest don't seem to want to cooperate with our patrols."

"Well, they ain't going to bother us today," said the officer. With a wave of his hand he sent the setter forward.

The dog moved out eagerly, plume flying, nose straight, but from the restrained manner in which he covered his ground a "shooting-dog man" would have known that he had learned his trade in the grouse and woodcock thickets of New England rather than among the sedge levels, gullies and pea fields of Dixie. His action was sure and bold, but the racing, distance-covering swoop of the quail dog was not his. It mattered not at all, for the bottom land was full of birds and Soldier could scarcely move a hundred yards without freezing fast on a fresh covey. This land was part of a great plantation, but its wide fields were empty now of workers; no mules plodded behind the untrimmed hedges, and no sound either of human joy or woe came to the ears. A blackened chimney stood in an irregular rectangle of live oaks on a hill, a mournful witness of the pointless waste and useless destruction of war.

Whenever Soldier stood, the young officer dismounted, drew a burnished double-barreled gun from the saddle scabbard and walked up to the immobile dog. He shot well, and by midmorning Chauncey had counted a score of birds into a gunny sack and was thinking longingly of the generous lunch in the saddlebags. His earlier apprehensions had not diminished—on the contrary they had mounted steadily as their course led imperceptibly toward the wooded hilly ground south of the stream. Somewhere, he knew, beyond that sunny barrier lay the Army of Northern Virginia, and from past experience with that crowd he wasn't anxious for further contact.

"Either you got to fight like Hell or run like Hell, an' I fer one ain't partial to neither," muttered the fat trooper.

Soldier crossed a weed-grown field and disappeared in a gully where bare red earth showed through the yellow sedge.

"He's probably on point," said the Captain. "I'll take this one, and then we'll find water and unsaddle for lunch."

The dog was standing rigid when they saw him, but the find, they perceived, was not his own. He was honoring another dog, a lean, hard-muscled pointer, posed in rigid style with his snakelike head turned to catch the scent that drifted to him from a tangle of frost-killed vines.

The Captain spoke in wonder. "Where'd that dog come from? Look at him! He's no tramp! That feller is a bird dog, and somebody takes good care of that animal!"

They rode nearer, and the Captain had already dismounted when an exclamation from his soldier servant directed his attention toward the top of the draw. There a man in faded gray with a shotgun across the saddle came riding on a big bay hunter. He was followed by a slender Negro swathed in a wondrous assortment of garments and mounted on a gaunt mule.

The newcomer hesitated for the briefest instant when he saw the strange setter honoring his dog's point and caught sight of the two blue-shirted men standing by. Then he came quietly on.

Suddenly Chauncey swore and clawed at his holster flap.

"Let that pistol be!" his officer told him sharply. "Don't be a damned fool! That Johnny ain't going to hurt you. He's birdin', too."

"He's probably got him a hull troop hid out in them pines," muttered

Chauncey, who snuffed in his nostrils the stench of Andersonville and felt in his belly the gripe of its starvation rations.

"If so, they'll not feel any more friendly to us if we murder the Troop Commander," advised the Captain.

The stranger was a man of his own age, lean and brown. The insignia on his jacket gave him the rank of Captain, and there was an indefinable suggestion of alert and easy confidence about him that marked him as a veteran, an active man and a cool man, one likely to be quick and violent in a fuss. As he pulled up his horse, his gray eyes glanced carelessly at the unbuttoned flap of the orderly's pistol holster. Then he dismounted easily, and there was a perfunctory exchange of salutes.

"Looks like they got 'em," he remarked, and his teeth shone in a brief smile.

Stovall grinned, too, and there was a perceptible relaxation of tension.

The Confederate looked at the dogs and appeared to cogitate.

"Cap'n, suh," said he, "may I inquire if yo' carry yo' views opposin' the rights of the States to secede from the Union into the spo'tin' field?"

"No," replied Stovall, "and even if I did I'd lay 'em aside on a day like this with two dogs fast on a covey and more of 'em in the fields. Since your dog has found this lot, I may even go so far as to say that I'd accept an invitation to shoot with you, sir."

"You have it, and right cordially, suh," was the response. "Shall we flush 'em?"

So they did, and the dogs went forward and retrieved four birds neatly picked from the opposite flanks of the bursting covey.

"My name is Bristol, suh, commanding C Troop, 1st Virginia Cavalry."

"I'm Stovall, commanding A Troop, 1st Vermont Cavalry," responded the other, and they shook hands. It was on Stovall's tongue to say that they had met before in the yard of a certain tavern in northern Virginia, but he checked the impulse. "I was about to knock off for a couple of hours, find some water and have lunch. Would you join me, Captain? We can rest the dogs and go on later."

The Southerner agreed, and presently the two officers were seated companionably on a log on the shady bank of the creek. Bristol's Negro, whose name was Esau, brought out a paper package containing a flat cake of corn bread and a few scraps of bacon, which meager fare Stovall sought unostentatiously to supplement from his own ample rations. There was no concealing the eagerness with which the newcomer's teeth bit into the slab of white bread and beef.

"Yo' General Grant has been keepin' us shuckin' 'round so fast lately that we don't seem to find time to gather up a good bait of grub," he explained. "Yo' people ain't so careless with yo' supply trains as you used to be, either, an' I want you to know that some of our ridin's boys are right peeved about yo' attitude on that subject."

"Well," said Stovall, defensively, "it's mostly their own fault. They've got a kind of boisterous way about 'em when they come to draw their rations."

They ate and chatted companionably, each feeling the pull of an instinctive liking for the other that was unhindered by wartime animosities.

Stovall found himself thinking how difficult it was to support a high fine rage against a good man who wore another sort of uniform but who liked the same things that he liked. Three years of fighting had somewhat dulled the indignation he had earlier felt against these people. Of course, they oughtn't for their own good try to split themselves off from the rest of the family and they ought also to have sense enough to see that they couldn't keep to their old romantic way of living in the face of what was happening to the rest of the country. The principle of slavery was wrong, too, but as these people managed it it wasn't so bad, after all. Not the least bit like they did things in that show he'd gone to see in Rutland City once. "Uncle Tom's Cabin or Life Among the Lowly" was the name of the play, he recalled. The bonds upon the black folk, he personally observed, were the opposite of harsh—just firm enough to keep them in ways that were good for them. Deprived of their white folks he knew that these poor souls were at once lost and pitifully demoralized. Lots of them had come into the lines, men, women and children, pathetic in their helplessness and asking only that someone feed them, give them clothes to wear and tell them what to do.

Thinking wasn't a soldier's business, that was for others to do, but nevertheless he had for some time suspected that these Southerners, the good ones, at least, had ideas fundamentally not so very different from his own.

Reflections of somewhat similar nature must have been in the Southerner's mind.

"I don't see any horns on you, suh," he remarked after a bit, "an' I conclude that my kinsman, Uncle Wally Beaufort, was maybe right about the matter. He spent much time in Boston befo' the war an' he always claimed there were *some* nice folks up No'th. But if you'll kindly allow me to observe you don't look yo' best when you come a-shootin' an' whoopin' an' raisin' Hell."

"And neither do you," said Stovall with conviction, and both knew that some sort of a pledge had been passed between them.

Once during the afternoon the Yankee unostentatiously steered the shooting party away from a wooded promontory that overlooked the wide expanse of fields. If the Confederate noticed the maneuver or attached any significance to it he said nothing. Once, a little later, he, too, mildly suggested a slight change of direction to bear away from another distant woodland.

"There might be some folks oveh in that way this evenin' who wouldn't rightly undehstan' the nature of our expedition," he remarked casually.

Never again did either of the two experience such shooting as they enjoyed that afternoon between the lines of the Army of the Potomac and the Army of Northern Virginia, as these lay licking their fresh wounds and alert for the next opportunity to grapple in a continuation of the bloody struggle that was to bring them to the gates of Richmond and from there even unto the Confederacy's Garden of Gethsemane at Appomattox. In those sunlit fields where the delicate haze of Autumn hung there was nothing to indicate that it was a stage upon which a long and bitter tragedy was moving toward the final curtain. The birds, long unmolested in the abandoned fields grown up to sedge and pea vines, had multiplied beyond description. Rabbits bounced from underfoot, and once a flock of wild turkeys rose from an old orchard in grand turmoil before the two dogs and at such close range that even the light quail charges brought down two to appease Chauncey's yearning for game "that had more'n two mouthfuls of meat on it."

He even forgot, momentarily, his perturbation as he fastened a big bronze gobbler to his saddle.

When Bristol's powder flask ran empty he called up Esau, who fished a double handful of paper rifle cartridges from the pockets of his numerous jackets, broke them open one by one and spilled the black powder into the brass spout of the canister. The packages were marked with the label of the United States Government.

"Not very good powder, either," the Southerner complained slyly.

"Judas Priest," Chauncey muttered, "ain't these boys got *nothin'* that they ain't stole?"

Before they knew it the sun was down behind the rim of the woods and it was time to part.

"Captain, suh, it has been a great day and I have enjoyed shootin' with you an' over yo' dog. He's a grand animal. I would surely love to see him work on grouse." He touched his game bag. "You'll be pleased to know that a portion of these pa'tridges will grace the General's breakfast table. He's powerful fond of fried pa'tridge."

A gleam came into Stovall's eye, and he began hauling birds out of Chauncey's sack.

"I was going to send a dozen of mine up to General Grant's mess," said he. "Let's trade. You take *my* birds to Marse Robert and I'll take yours to our General. Maybe we'll do well not to say who sent 'em."

The exchange was made, and the two rode away.

"Hope to see you again, Yank," said Bristol. "Keep yo' head down and yo' shirt tail tucked in."

"The same to you, Reb," replied Stovall.

It was a hot day in early Spring some months later, and at a ford on another quiet creek a little way to the west of Richmond men were assembling to take part in one of those small, violent and bloody affairs that were so common that they have been generally ignored by the historians of the great conflict between the North and the South. References to them are mostly buried in faded casualty lists and in field messages hastily scrawled and stained with the sweat of horse and man. The rear of a weary, desperate column of Confederate troops moved painfully along a road that paralleled the stream. A small detachment of their cavalry rode down to the ford and dismounted, and while some of the men led the animals into the concealment of the woods the others flung themselves down behind trees and stumps with drawn carbines and pistols, intent to cover the crossing until the dragging column of the infantry and guns had cleared the defile. They had not long to wait. There was presently a muffled trampling sound of horses and men beyond the creek, and blue uniforms showed briefly amid the soft green of the Spring foliage.

"Fire at will! Commence firing!" said a quiet voice.

It was followed instantly by the sharp crackle of the carbines. There was momentary confusion across the ford, and then the white puffs from the southern bank were being answered by irregular spurts from the opposite side. These thickened and increased as fresh Union troopers came up to support their advance party. Bullets splashed in the water, throwing up sudden jets of spray; others cut white gouges in the bark of the trees. A horse screamed somewhere in the woods, and a man yelled and cursed. The firing from the north bank deepened in volume as the Union line was strengthened, and soon every battle-wise veteran in ragged butternut knew that under cover of the musketry the Yankees were forming and braced himself for yet another of the annihilating blue charges that could still be met but no longer stopped. Not that it mattered much anyway. The jig was up. Marse Robert, cornered at last, was trying without hope to draw his limping, starving columns from the jaws of a trap already nearly closed, and the world that had been the Old South was shattering about their ears. Then from the road sounded the blast of a whistle blowing "All clear!" and a swarm of men leaping from cover ran to their mounts and scurried off through the bullet-whipped woods.

The last to leave, as is entirely proper on such occasions, was the officer in command of the detachment. When his rearmost man had mounted and was away amid a shower of slugs, this one came gallantly out of the woods at a gallop, pistol in hand, and set his horse at the ditch bank. What was left of a grand bay hunter made a brave effort at a barrier that would have been no barrier at all three years before, a mere ridge of old earth not three feet high it was, but the poor brute failed at it and in its stumbling plunge threw the rider headlong and helpless into the trail in full view of his enemies a scant forty paces distant across the ford. Two or three of these ran out from cover and raised their carbines for the shot—after all war is war, and a good combat captain is worth fifty good fighting men any day—but an officer yelled suddenly:

"Don't shoot that man!"

Then he added somewhat inadequately and lamely and as if he felt it to be necessary to excuse his saving action, "I know that Johnny! He's a hell of a good bird shot!"

Across the creek the Confederate heard the order and the explanation of it.

He gathered himself, his reins and his mount and went into the saddle like an eel over a wet stone. With his long pistol at high present and his face splitting into a quick familiar grin of recognition, he called:

"Thank you, Cap'n! And so are you, suh!"

Then he wheeled his poor old crowbait—the same that once romped away from the best of 'em in the Blue Grass—and rode away after his men.

The Dean stirred in his chair. It was nearly dark outside, and "Hooter" Gordon's guitar had been silent for a long time. The Dean thought maybe he had better go along home. Miss Annie would be waiting for him.

AN
OCTOBER
INCIDENT

It is a rare occasion when the sportsman can do more than grin a very wry grin at the devastating evidences of industrial progress. Too often, in return for the doubtful blessings of more noise, smoke and speed, he finds that a good trout stream has been ruined, an ancient woodland cut away, a duck marsh converted into something that is neither mud, water or good dry land, or perhaps a favorite woodcock cover split wide open by a splendid cement highway.

Our friend, the plump and genial Judge, was quite of this opinion, and he lost some of his normal geniality whenever he contemplated the ravages wrought throughout our fair land.

He and the Captain were discussing these matters one evening as they cleaned their guns and repaired shooting gear that had seen use that day.

"What the devil can we plant, build or keep on the Kankakee Marshes, for example, half as beautiful and useful as the millions of waterfowl that were there until some damned fool drained the water out from under 'em?" the Judge protested. "And what do we get for
having Shepherd's Brook, right here in Tranquillity, turned into a trickle of pink mush so foul that a grubby dace can't live in it, let alone an honest brook trout?"

He gave a muffled, menacing snort.

"Pass the cider, please; 'tain't worked none, I hope," said the Captain, as he put his twenty-bore carefully into its case. "You're right, of course, but once in a while these industrial developments do us some good."

The Court promptly challenged the witness.

"Name one such for me," he demanded.

"Well, I was just thinking about the power company that put the dam in at the outlet of Bentick's Pond. It only raised the level about six feet, but it's flooded clear back up the brook, so now there's a whole wood lot of oak and pig walnut trees standing in about a foot of water."

"Well, and what of it?" the Judge wanted to know, settling his spectacles and regarding his companion expectantly.

"Black ducks and teal like that sort of stuff," was the response, "and Uncle Sereno Macomber says there's 'slews on 'em' up there."

"Then I'd better get out a couple of boxes of 6's for the old Scott," said the legal gentlemen, and rising went to a corner closet and began hauling out cartridges and boots. His recent quarrel with mechanical advancement seemed to have been entirely forgotten. But the other, sipping the golden cider, made from apples gathered only a week before from the farm orchard, took up the subject again.

"At least, we don't see so much of that sort of thing up here," he reflected. "Other than a few power reservoirs and an occasional quarry hole, this part of the earth is much as it was fifty years ago. Better, even, for these deserted hill farms offer the best cover in the world for upland game. Think of the woodcock shooting we've had! And the grouse! To say nothing of deer, squirrels and woodchucks! I'll bet there are twenty abandoned farms within five miles of this house."

The Judge returned to the fire to fill and light a last pipe, and then the two friends prepared for bed. The Captain's dog, a wise old setter, came in from the kitchen licking his chops with every appearance of satisfaction and, sighing, stretched himself along the hearth. Beyond the windows, the white radiance of the Hunter's Moon filled the valley; curls of drifting vapor rose from the brook where it slipped quietly through the sleeping meadows, and the walls of the old house that had sheltered so many generations of outdoorsmen creaked comfortably in the frosty air as if it, too, were settling its ancient joints and sinews for a night of sound slumber under the maples. Presently all was quiet in the house save for the soft fall of ash on the hearth and the eager, suppressed whimpering of Sport in hot pursuit of a dreamland rabbit with, for once, no chiding whistle to halt the chase. From the room under the shadowed eaves sounded the gentle, muted trumpetings whereby the Judge was wont to announce his nightly period of recuperation from the trials, pleasures, successes and failures of another day.

The two were awake early on the following morning. Long before the stars had paled over the rugged crest of the Munger Hill, they were dressed and, boots in hand, had repaired to the kitchen, where they shivered dismally until the mounting glow from the freshly kindled fire drove off the sharp chill and enabled them to lace their boots in more comfort and then seek out in the fragrant pantry the components of a simple meal. While they ate their bacon and eggs and drank scalding coffee, Sport wolfed down a working dog's breakfast of corn bread. A sizable slab of this sustaining provender went down his throat without making any visible impression on the animal's lean circumference, a phenomenon rather enviously noted by the rotund Judge.

The two gunners consumed their rations in more leisurely fashion, but with the time-saving method perfected by long experience with such early meals, and soon all three were in the car bowling down the narrow dirt road. The ghostly blooms of the clematis along the old walls had an added pale luster from the frost crystals, and the gray rails of the fences gleamed in the dissolving darkness with the same pearly coating. The delegates of a witches' conference of screech owls in the woods by the brook were retiring from their convention with a chorus of weird, falsetto resolutions apparently addressed to the approaching day, and the great owls from swamp and hill whooped their infinite disdain of such inconsequential proceedings on the part of their diminutive kinsfolk.

While the Captain drove as quietly as he might, so as not to disturb the prevailing stillness about them, his friend sniffed the air and responded gradually to the hunter's challenge.

"By George, sir! As Uncle Bill says—'I wouldn't trade places with the King of Europe at this minute,'—or the Queen, either, for that matter!" he added hastily as he remembered the hour. "I mean that while it's sharp punishment to turn out of the quilts at three o'clock to dress on a frosty floor, it's well worth the misery to be out in this air with a gun case under the seat and reasonable expectations of sport. I look back on every season with sorrow for the mornings I lay abed."

"You ought to, you fat old duffer! What with ten o'clock openings, recesses for this and for that, and adjournments for the day at three in the afternoon, and vacations and more recesses, I doubt if you jurists put in two weeks of honest work in a year. Leggo my collar now! This is my car we're riding in!"

In some dim age, a mighty subterranean force had created Bentick's Pond by thrusting a thick rampart of rock across the bed of a mountain stream. The clear water slowly rising and recoiling from the great barrier filled the deep valley and spread around the lower folds of the adjacent hills. The shores, for the greater part, were rocky, steep and wooded, with stony promontories that jutted boldly out into the depths; but there was at one end a broad marsh lying between forested slopes, where the silt deposited through ages of slow erosion now supported a tangled mass of cranberry and buttonbrush and moist meadows of wild oats and flags. The gray, weather-beaten stumps of trees uprooted by flood and freshet stood singly from the ooze or were gathered into snarls and tangles so intricate as to defy any force to separate them, save that of slow decay. Other partially submerged relics of the original forest gleamed spectrally beneath the amber, peaty waters of channel or pool, and the drift of feathers and root cuttings at the waterline indicated how favorite were these resting-places to both the wildfowl and the muskrats.

Bordering the older marsh was a wide belt of timber, now flooded to a vary-
ing depth by the action of a small dam constructed at the main outlet of the
Pond.

The two friends left the car in Uncle Sereno's dooryard, borrowed a boat
from his landing and set off. At the edge of the marsh, they brought the skiff
to shore to disembark the Captain and his dog. The Judge, for truly weighty
reasons, preferred to confine his expedition into the marsh to such channels
and ditches as would float the light skiff. The Captain, an accomplished bog-
trotter, would follow the edge of the marsh, trusting to come upon his game
breaking among the stumps or feeding upon the mast dropped from the oaks
and hickories into the quiet pools below.

"You've got the best of it," acknowledged the Judge without envy, "for
there's nothing to compare with jumping ducks on foot in overflowed woodland, but it's no game for me. If I were as light as you are, and had feet as big
as you have, it would be different. You don't weigh any more than a king
rail—and sometimes I think you resemble the bird in other ways!"

He freed the skiff by a push with his paddle, and with his gun carefully disposed, with its Damascus muzzles slanted safely above the gunwale to prevent foundering in case of an accidental discharge, he sent his craft silently
along the edge of the winding channel. For some minutes his old slouch hat
was visible to the pair on the shore moving evenly above the level of the
sedge, and then it vanished behind the bank of wildrice.

When his master had loaded the long-barreled twenty-bore Sport started
for the nearest thicket, only to be recalled.

"Not today, old boy! Come in here!"

With the dog at heel, the Captain set out to follow the irregular shoreline
where it wandered in and out among the flooded tree trunks. The brown water lay motionless, save for the swift wake of a pickerel scouting for minnows
or a tardy frog. An occasional acorn or hickory nut dislodged by the attack of
a pair of squealing jays fell with a sharp plop to rest in a watery bed until the
broad bill of some black duck should discover it. Streamers of mist drifted
wraithlike among the trees. But excepting for such sound and movement, the
overflow seemed deserted.

"Don't believe there's a duck in the place," concluded the gunner in an un-
dertone addressed partly to himself and partly to the dog, after a searching
study of the nearer marsh failed to disclose anything of significance. He
glanced curiously toward the screened channel, where his friend made
stealthy progress. He could detect at first no sign of the Judge, but as he
looked, a flock of a dozen black ducks appeared above the rise as abruptly as
if each bird had been tossed aloft by a powerful spring. Two ducks collapsed
and plunged down from the flaring, panic-stricken flock, and after an interval
the sharp double report of the gun came over the marsh. A moment later, the

Judge's head became visible over the sedge as he reloaded his gun, retrieved the tethered paddle that he had dropped overboard when the ducks rose, and moved forward to pick up his birds.

"He gets excited about the destruction of an Illinois duck marsh that he's never seen, but he's as cool as a frog when . . ."

The Captain went no further in his analysis of his friend's inconsistencies, for with a roar of beating wings and a tumult of threshed water, a great flock of mixed fowl rose within twenty paces and from a spot that only a moment before he had examined carefully and found empty apparently of all save brown water and tree trunks. It seemed to the startled wildfowler that the foreground was a solid, but illusively shifting, mass of ducks, with more streaming into the air every moment and adding to the pandemonium. Furthermore, glimpses he had here and there of white and brownish feathers and crested heads told him that there was a disconcerting representation of forbidden wood ducks in this mixed congregation and that he must be careful. Twice he was within a finger's weight of firing when he identified the target as legally taboo, but he finally managed to select a towering black duck for his first barrel, and the heavy bird plunged to hit the water with a mighty spatter. His eye then caught a glimpse of a small tan-colored duck darting like a swallow among the trunks, and though his subconscious self was urging that there were plenty of easier shots available, he risked a quick snap just as the bird swept behind a huge oak. Bark flew from the side of the tree, and simultaneously the plump little greenwing keeled head over heels from behind it and lay with his paddles feebly beating the air. The disturbed colony wheeled and planed among the treetops until each leader had rallied his panic-stricken company and swept away across the marsh. One squadron of teal, in their retreat from the skirmish, flushed too closely to the alert Judge crouching behind a clump of shivering flags, and three fell out as his redoubtable fowling piece twice took the measure of their brilliant speed.

Quiet was gradually restored. Sport waded gingerly to the fallen and sniffed curiously at this strange game. He wrinkled an expressive nose and looked at his master with eyes that said: "What in the world do you want of those things?"

Receiving no explanation, he fell in dutifully behind the Captain's sloshing heels to await with patience the time when this god of his should be restored to sanity.

They proceeded, and the wildfowler having learned again the lesson that any number of ducks can hide successfully behind tree trunks and half-submerged logs, indulged in no further surveillance of matters afar off but began to watch closely for telltale ripples and vague, indefinable movements nearer at hand. By following such tactics, he soon jumped a single black duck, a straggler perhaps from the flock, and cut him down with a load of 7's. While all this was taking place, Sport roused himself from his infinite boredom and approached a hummock of moist earth standing a few inches above the water, on which grew a sparse tangle of buttonbrush. In a foot of water, he made as perfect a stand as ever he did on dry land. When the Captain sloshed past him to investigate, a woodcock sprang twittering aloft and headed for the mainland. The first load smacked full into the gray trunk of a drowned ash, printing a pattern in the smooth wood that would have satisfied the craftsman who had bored the gun barrels, but the second, better aimed, brought the royal bird down.

"Well, boy, the Judge won't have any of these when he comes in!" The gunner shook the water from the handsome plumage and paused, as every man must do, to admire the 'cock before putting him carefully away in a pocket of his jacket.

Missing often enough to convince himself that he would never need to dread the monotony of shooting perfection, the sportsman followed his quest along the marsh. At times, he waded where shallow water and firm footing permitted, and again, he advanced cautiously along the shore. A suspicious disturbance among the rushes on the farther side of a deep slough gave him sudden pause, and he was ready when a pair of ducks took wing from the spot. Fairly centered at forty yards, the birds tumbled back into the rushes, and now the gunner realized that a goodly space of icy water, too deep for wading, separated him from his game. In vain he ordered, urged and coaxed the setter to retrieve. Sport sat on the bank and tried to explain that he was a dry-land retriever only, that rules of the Bird Dogs' Union would not permit him to substitute for Patches, the big Chesapeake, that the whole silly performance bored him to death and that anyhow a duck smelled like a handful of oily cotton waste. When his master insisted, Sport adopted a stupid look of absolute incomprehension.

"You old cuss, you!" scolded the Captain, who, for all his bitter revilings, would have shot his own hand off sooner than lift it against this old friend. "You're not so dumb and simple as you look! I ought to have you in there neck and heels! You're a great help, you confounded old quack!"

It was clear that the dog had no intention of gathering the ducks, so the gunner, who never lost a down bird if reasonable effort would save it, and whose idea as to what constituted "reasonable effort" meant any amount of toil and even sometimes the risk of life and limb, kicked off his boots and in a very few seconds stood forth on the ooze stripped to the buff and prepared to swim the slough. The water made him gasp, and his skin felt as if suddenly it had shrunk until it was much too small for him and would presently crack open. But he kept on, gritting his teeth to keep from howling at the exquisitely painful sensations. He crossed in a dozen strokes, and found his ducks in a patch of saw grass that scratched his cold skin excruciatingly. Without a pause, he plunged in again, holding his birds between his locked teeth, and hastened back to shore. Now, Sport was accustomed to the sight of his deity fully clad, and this strange aspect bewildered him and suggested to his doggish mind that some dreadful metamorphosis was taking place before his eyes. He watched these disturbing manifestations until he could endure it no longer and set up a lugubrious banshee moaning that carried far in the quiet air.

"What the devil ails you?" demanded the naked and shivering man, as he climbed out on the shore. "Sorry for me, I suppose! Just breaks your loving heart, doesn't it?"

In order to encourage a circulation that seemed about to collapse, he began a wild, fantastic dance, and in the security and privacy of the spot lashed and flung and leaped like a Hottentot.

"Been in swimmin', hev ye?" inquired a voice amusedly.

The Captain turned to find an ancient, wizened man seated on a root with an old gun across his knees, observing him with lively curiosity and a humor evidently barely restrained. Despite the Venus-at-the-Bath pose, the newcomer promptly recognized him and, without waiting for a reply to the first useless inquiry, offered another.

"Ain't you from over Tranquillity way? Some relation to the McCombers, ain't ye? Thought so. Went to war, didn't ye, or suthin'? Yis, yis! I've heard about ye. Didn't affect your mind, did it? I declare, if you don't look ridiculous enough! He! He!"

The old fellow giggled like a boy, enjoying the other's discomfiture.

"I swam out to get some ducks!" the embarrassed gunner explained, lamely.

"Hey?" with the cupped hand of deafness behind an ear.

"*I swam out to get some ducks!*" bellowed the Captain.

"Oh!" A pause ensued while the old man digested this information. "I've heard o' Chinamen catchin' ducks that way, but not no Christian. Whyn't ye shoot 'em?" he finished with a glance at the other's gun.

"*I did!*" roared the witness.

"Wal," inquired the other reasonably, "if ye shot 'em, what'd ye hev to swim out to git 'em for? That's what ye said, wan't it?"

"Oh, damn such nonsense!" ejaculated the Captain under his breath, beginning to haul on clothes over his wet skin.

"Naow, don't you git profane," his interlocutor chided sternly. "Ye prob'ly larnt that to the war, too, didn't ye? I've heard them Frenchmen air an ungodly, dancin', drinkin', profane set o' folks."

He continued his righteous homily until the other finished dressing by buckling his belt and stamping on his boots and, gathering up gun and ducks, prepared to leave the spot.

Then, observing the old man's empty game bag, he felt suddenly sorry for this poor and feeble old fellow whose withered sinews and dimming eyes denied him successful participation in the sport. Impulsively the younger man picked up the pair of ducks just retrieved at the cost of so much dignity and decorum and handed them to the old man.

"Wal, naow! That's nice o' ye, boy! I heard a dog ahowlin', an' thinkin' somebody was abusin' a pore dumb animal, I tuk my gun an' come daown— an' there you wuz a-leapin' an' a-caperin' like a frog in love! Wal, sir, I'm glad I come!"

With that somewhat ambiguous benediction, he slung his long gun over his shoulder and shuffled away.

Sport presently slipped away for a moment to stand a second woodcock in a clump of alders, and the ensuing successful shot so cheered his master that he promptly forgave his four-footed friend for his recent dereliction.

"That's enough, I reckon. Come on, boy, we'll go back and find his Honor and see if we can't do something about lunch."

But the incident was not closed yet.

"Jest a minute," a voice, by now well known, hailed him, and here, sure enough, was his ancient acquaintance hastening toward him with the air of one who has forgotten something of importance. Premonitions of further inquisition swept the Captain as the old man approached.

"Say," he began as soon as he arrived at conversational distance, "I ain't quite clear in my head *yit* why you swum that air slough to git them ducks."

"Oh Lord!" groaned the other, "have I got to go over that again?" And, aloud, he bellowed, "Well, I couldn't fly across, could I?"

"Nobody said ye could," was the tart response, "but you c'n walk, can't ye? Ain't crippled, be ye? 'Cause five rod further up—jist around the bend yonder—there's a plank bridge built on purpose so folks can git over there to fish an' pick cranberries!"

THE
ADOPTION

Written on Christmas Eve in the year 1937 to commemorate an incident, and dedicated and presented to my friend, C.M.P., Jr.

After turning past Enos' Corner it was a rough and winding road that the Captain's friend found himself following on that October afternoon when he first came to Tranquillity Township. Two centuries before it had been a mere trail hewn from the living wilderness. In that day the creaking ox cart had been used to haul the simple commodities of rural commerce, salts of lye distilled from wood ash, and bundles of wool. The French and Indian War had been brought to a close, but the countryside was not yet safe. The drivers of these ponderous vehicles, if fortunate enough to own one of the amazingly straight-shooting rifles which were then finding their way into frontier communities to replace the time-honored smooth bores, got the prized weapon up from the wagon bed and looked to its priming before approaching the Big Rock. According to tradition, that spot had been the scene of more than one roadside ambush. Lacking a rifle, the old smooth bore with its load of slugs or ball, or both, had to serve, and, lacking the smooth bore, an axe in the hands of an intrepid frontiersman had often settled the hash of a marauding Indian come skulking down the shores of the Lake in search of scalps and pelf.

But on this afternoon in the year 1936 as the traveler passed there was no painted savage with crested topknot crouching tense and wary among the scarlet sumachs that grew around the Big Rock. A red squirrel there was perched all taut and trig upon the old boulder. The little creature dropped a nut it had been gnawing, flipped a saucy tail and derisively cursed the intruder as he passed. But even that trifling demonstration was forgotten when the next bend in the old road disclosed the traveler's destination.

He recognized the old house at once from his host's description of it. There was the brook hushing its voice as it disappeared under the roadway bridge to emerge again beneath the giant elm at the other end of the dank subterranean passageway, whereupon it resumed its liquid drowsy song where it had left it off. There were the maples, six of them, arranged about the white

161

painted simple structure that had been home for so many generations of the
Captain's family. There were the lifting gracious slopes of Mount Hamilton;
its majestic pine-clad crest interposed between the mellow homestead and the
bitter winds that winter sends sweeping down the Lake from the north. There
to the east was "The Ledge," with the rocky cavern still stained with the
smoke of ancient Indian fires. There was "Wood's Hill" to the west where the
Adirondacks lay; on this autumn day its long parapet was ablaze with the
motionless, heatless flame that the frost had kindled in the maples, birches
and hickories growing upon its flanks. And there in the dooryard, surrounded
by sons and grandsons, was the living embodiment of the gentle spirit of the
place. A tiny white-haired creature, she was, fragile and lovely as the bloom
of clematis upon an old wall, yet so imbued with the indomitable essence of
life that it fairly sparkled in her eyes. Because of it no one who knew her ever
thought of her years, except as the evidence of them was reflected in her wisdom, humor, charity and tolerance.

"Now then," thought the traveler to himself as he climbed down from his
laden car, "this is Mother S. and if I can't pass muster with her I'm a goner,
for sure. The Captain, bless him, is in many respects and after all a damned
fool in so far as the choosing of his friends is concerned. He must be, for
otherwise he'd have seen long ago the fundamental, profound wickedness and
deceits of my nature. He never questioned my qualifications when he asked
me up here to shoot grouse and share his holiday. But this will be different. I
feel it in my bones that this lady is the sort of lady who really knows!"

Perhaps it was his own awareness of his miserably deceitful character that
helped him out in the end, for, as the Captain happened to know, the
warmth of the lady's understanding had often blessed an erring and repen-
tant soul. Why, there was that day when he fell into the watering trough just
before time to start for church, and he with the new linen suit fresh on his
back; then there were those long-ago spring days when bullhead fishin' had
drawn him irresistibly away from District No. 3 schoolhouse. She had understood those affairs, all right.

Well, somehow or other, the visitor survived the brief, kindly quizzical or-
deal, and then the small lady put her work-worn hand into the visitor's big
one.

"Now, listen, my lad," said the Captain at this point, "you've been long
enough getting here, what with your loafing and dillydallying and philander-
ing along the road. I don't believe you realize that although a week in Tranquillity during the grouse season seems a long time in prospect it's actually as
brief as a politician's promise and gone before you know it. There's still an
hour of good daylight left and I know of a 'run' up alongside the Marsh
where we can find some grouse and mebbe a couple of woodcock if you can
get out of your store clothes and into a shooting kit."

There was a little matter that for some time had been lying too heavily on the visitor's conscience. A small thing indeed that would have troubled no one a whit less honest and forthright than was this man, but he couldn't quite put it out of his mind, and its presence there took just the smallest part away from the full enjoyment of the occasion. He thought of it now while in his small room under the eaves of the old house he got hurriedly out of his tweeds and into a soft flannel shirt and canvas trousers.

"Damn it anyway!" he muttered, "why did I ever let the Captain think— why don't I tell him now and get it off my conscience and let him know that I ain't any business coming up here this way and meeting his mother and all the rest of 'em, God bless 'em, again and again, and accepting their hospitality, with a black falsehood on my conscience!"

Just what decision might have emerged as the result of this bitter travail will never be known, for at that point the Captain called out to him to "hustle his cakes."

"Ready, feller? Got any 8's? Good! They'll do for grouse and woodcock, too. Shake a leg, now! Sun's gettin' down close to the top of Old Defiance. It'll be dark in an hour!"

Thus adjured, the visitor hastened his preparations. The sixteen-bore Parker was drawn from its case and tenderly assembled, a carton of shot shells torn open and the contents, neat in brass and green paper, dumped into the worn pockets of the shooting jacket.

By this time, so perturbed was the guest's state of mind that it is doubtful if he appreciated the still beauty of the Marsh when his friend, the Captain, showed it to him. Long shafts of golden light streamed down the flanks of Mount Hamilton and flooded the fen. Small irregular islands of cranberry bog studded the calm surface of the water, and a swamp maple on the opposite shore glowed like a living ember against the dark background of evergreens and the pale bronze of the birches. A flight of migrating crows drew its silent ragged pattern across the sky, twisting, dipping and veering as it struggled against a wind unfelt and unheard below.

The old road beneath their feet gave way presently to a mere cart track, and that was grass-grown. Then the track merged into something even more indefinite and inconclusive that followed casually the base of a wooded hill where it seemed to be of less importance as a trail than as a dim dividing line separating the wooded slopes from the rough thickets and stony ground that bordered the Marsh.

The Captain paused to issue final instructions.

"You follow this old wood road and I'll go down into that stuff by the shore. I'm almost sure that there are birds in there feeding on thorn apples and wild grapes. When I flush 'em they'll cross this road heading for the hill. That will be your chance. If you lose me, keep on until you come to an old log cabin on a beaver meadow. When you get there stop and wait for me to join you. Good luck!"

He disappeared among the thickets. His friend set out along the shadowy trail with his gun at the ready, managing his pace to keep always abreast of his companion whose whereabouts was occasionally revealed by the sound of a boot against a stone or the momentary agitation of a clump of black alders, and once, it is to be regretted, by an unmistakable good round curse when the Captain attempted to straddle a thorn-apple bush.

The illumination faded toward twilight. Even the blue jays were impressed by the spell of the hour and flitted silently from tree to tree. High on the hillside, a gray squirrel squalled discordantly before disappearing into his hole in the huge gray trunk of a basswood tree.

From time to time there was a vague sound of muffled thunder coming from beyond the Captain. It was strangely stirring, but there were no shots nor any other sign to indicate the origin of these disturbances of the twilight calm. They seemed very faint and far away. After a time these irregular vibrations ceased entirely.

Then, so near at hand as to startle him, the tall sportsman heard the harsh scrape of a twig against a canvas sleeve and realized that his companion had closed the interval between them and was now moving only a few yards away just beyond a thicket of chokeberry bushes that bordered the path.

Mort whistled interrogatively, and the thin note was answered by an astounding commotion. There was a swift rushing rocketlike roar. The Captain's warning shout coming from the thicket, "Mark! Mark!" was unnecessary as something gray and russet swept toward him with shadowy speed. The slender barrels of the gun came up level and true as the bird crossed the trail.

The pungent smell of burned gunpowder was still in the air when the Captain came up, patiently releasing as he did so the thorns and briars that grasped at him. He discovered his guest seated with his gun beside him. Spread out on the leaves between his feet lay a grouse, the wings and broad fan outstretched to show the vivid delicate penciling of every feather. The jet ruff was still erect, and the wild bright yellow eye was as yet undimmed by the death that had struck so quick a blow. Here indeed was the lying-in-state of one of royal lineage. The Captain's guest glanced up briefly as his friend approached and then returned to the rapt contemplation of the wild dead thing before him.

"Nice shot, boy!" said the Captain, and then he sat down and lighted a cigarette and waited.

Presently his guest drew in a deep breath and raised his eyes.

"Listen," said he, "I've got to tell you something. I'm up here under false pretenses. I've no business to be here at all! I love your country, and I'd like to feel that I belong to it. I want nothing more than to be an honest Yankee sportsman. You've heard me talk about grouse shooting, but—"

"Whoa!" interrupted his companion, "Whoa! I know what it is you want to tell me. That this bird here is the first grouse you ever shot."

"Yes, but how in the devil did you know?"

"Just the look on your face, Mort Palmer, just the incredulous, astounded, delighted and remorseful look of a man who has killed his first grouse and is just a little bit sorry now that he did it."

After that the pair of them sat in silence for a little time. Then the Captain got a small flask from his jacket and poured out two thimblefuls of the smoky generous liquor, and when that was done he rose and spoke again in solemn pontifical tones.

"Drink it!" he commanded. "Know ye that inasmuch as we have abundant evidence to attest the qualities of his heart and hand, and being assured that he will never for so long as he may live, do any act, or contrive any thought or device unworthy of the rights and privileges now to be conferred upon him, I do of my own will and purpose announce and declare him, dight Mortimer Palmer, to be now and henceforth and forever a true son of Tranquillity, free and welcome to mingle with us as he may please, to sit with us at our firesides, to wander among our hills and valleys, to take as he may please a fair share of the living wild wealth of these woods and of these lakes and streams after the manner befitting an honest Yankee sportsman. Which high title and order I do now bestow upon him."

The twilight deepened over the old Marsh while the two men sat there in perfect understanding, the rarest gift of all.

A great blue heron came sailing in on motionless wings against the afterglow and settled in the shallows where the evening mists were rising. A strangely solitary bird, wild and aloof, but he, too, had his part in the ceremonial exercises now being concluded. His broad blue vanes lifted once like the banners of a herald, and his trumpet sounded the acclaim.

"Youck!" said the heron, "Youck! Yankee! Yankee!" Or so at least it sounded in the ears of the two who heard.

DUCKS
AT
STONE
BRIDGE

The sun was well down behind the darkling mass of Dresden Mountain and the long lower valley of Champlain was filling with soft autumnal twilight, when our friend, the Judge, thrust his thick, tough person through the band of little birches that fringed the Grapevine Cover. He unloaded his famous old woodcock gun and placed it carefully on the short sward of the upland pasture, pulled out his pipe and then, having seated himself on the trunk of an ancient fallen apple tree, relic of some early settler's scragged orchard, dwelt for a while in appreciative contemplation of the scene before him. His companions, the Captain and John Armistead Bristol, the latter a sportsman guest from the Deep South, were still somewhere back in the Cover threading the thickets, weary but alert, being inspired by that conviction, common to all the tribe of gunners and anglers, that the last cast of foot or of fly-rod has more of the magic of good fortune in it than all the others.

With three fat grouse and as many woodcock tucked in the spacious pockets of his weathered shooting jacket, the Judge was content to relinquish the possibility of further honors.

From his feet the ground swept downward a mile or more in a succession of slow, sweeping curves and levels to the narrow, rush-bordered channel of the lower lake, whence it rose again more abruptly with the wooded slopes of the Adirondacks. At this hour of the day, humble things—stone fences and farm buildings, the old schoolhouse on the Turnpike—gathered illumination from the fading sky and seemed to glow with a soft radiance of their own. Far below, between dark fringes of wildrice, the waters of the channel at Fiddler's Elbow burned with a passing glory of crimson.

"It must have looked like that to Benedict Arnold," the Judge reflected, "that time he hustled his little fleet toward the Tory village of Skenesboro trying to get away from old Burgoyne."

166

The ear of his imagination heard for a moment the sullen double roar of cannon, the savage whoop of the Indians and the steady throb of the British marching drums as one commander pressed onward to eventual disgrace and the other to immediate defeat. These reflections, concerned as they were with vanished shapes and heroes once so imbued with ambitious life, and influenced by the transient spirit of the hour and season, engendered a mild and not entirely disagreeable melancholy. Particularly he thought of the Captain and the perfect companionship of long, pleasant years.

"Some evening in October I suppose one or the other of us will come out of the 'Cover' with a few birds in his pocket and sit on this very log and smoke and wait. It'll look just as it does now. After a time and one by one the little yellow lights in the farmhouse kitchens along the Valley will twinkle, and then, whichever one of us it is who's sitting here, he'll come to realize that there's no use waiting any longer for a friend to come, and he'll pick up his gun and his birds and get along home." He shook off the mood. "But, Great Scott! It won't be this year or next!"

This latter encouraging conclusion was wonderfully strengthened by the crackle of brush and the homely reassuring sounds of boots and voices behind him. Presently he discerned his friends approaching, the afterglow glimmering faintly on the barrels of their guns.

"I knew we'd find him here," remarked the Captain. Being a true Yankee, he often hid profound affection under the light chaff of raillery. "Gazing at the scenery and thinking about Heaven-knows-what, and blinking like an old barn owl. This place is worse than drink to him."

"It's right pretty," the Southerner agreed warmly as he gazed at the dimming vista of lake, mountain and field.

At that moment there sounded the sibilant rush of wings overhead, and all three glanced up to see a small flock of black ducks vanishing into the gathering murk toward the lake.

"Coming in from High Pond," opined the Judge. "There should be a good many of 'em down here by now."

Even as he spoke another flock swept over and was gone almost before the eye could locate the swift, dark forms of the birds.

"Let's try 'em a whack tomorrow, Judge," the Captain proposed. "We promised Johnny we'd take him duck shooting. We'll have some fun, anyway, and something a little less vigorous than climbing hills and fighting brush would be welcome for a change."

"I really ought to go home, I s'pose," sighed Johnny. He had come to Vermont for a few days' shooting, but under the spell of good companionship, perfect weather and grand sport had already lingered long past the date he had set for his departure. It was his first visit to the New England country, his first experience with the ruffed grouse and woodcock.

"Can't get over how sweet and interestin' you darned Yankees are," he drawled. "I s'pose my old Daddy would rise up from his tomb if he saw me sittin' up here on a log hobnobbin' with a pair of abolitionists and shootin' with 'em instead of at 'em. But I reckon I'll stay. Had a letter from my partner sayin' that I might as well stay for as long as I can manage to get my hog meat and grits for nothin'. Looks to him like the millennium has surely come. Folks ain't a-lawin' no more down there. No way for a member of the bar to turn an honest penny—not even if he knew where there was one and how to turn it!"

The Judge rose and picked up his gun.

"That's settled then. We'll hunt ducks tomorrow. And now let's get down to the car and see if the Captain's lady is willing to feed our rebel prisoner."

The first hint of returning daylight found the trio rolling along the highway that skirted the eastern shore of a long, narrow lake. Great clouds of mist drifted in from the water through the hemlocks and maples and condensed in tiny beads on the windshield of the Judge's faithful chariot. The occasional glimpses that they had of the lake showed the surface still and unbroken under the blanket of vapor, save where it was briefly shattered by the sullen rise of a great pike preceded by the desperate eruption and flurry of a school of minnows frantically seeking escape in the air from the monstrous, savage peril that haunted the weed patches of their proper element. Not a breath of air came to stir the billowing fog masses. To Johnny Reb the weather signs did not appear propitious for their purpose.

"Doesn't look like fowling weather," he remarked finally to the Judge.

" 'Tisn't either—not for ordinary duck shooting. But for this particular sort of shooting we don't need wind and sleet and shivering weather. The upper end of this lake runs out into a long marsh; there's an old bridge that crosses at the point where the open water leaves off and the marsh begins. Regardless of the weather some ducks are always trading back and forth over the bridge. It's pass-shooting. The big flocks go over high, but now and then a small bunch or a single or a pair will come over in range—long range. We'll get a few of 'em. If you get tired of it, there's always plenty of grouse cover handy by, as well as a few jacksnipe in the marsh."

He turned the car into a narrow side road and after a brief journey along this narrow thoroughfare brought it to a halt behind a clump of bushes near the bridge head.

Dismounting with the others, he hauled forth a ponderous double-barreled weapon of ten-bore. Beside it Johnny's Purdey looked like a toy.

"Got it years ago to shoot geese with out in Nebraska, but it's just the thing for pass-shooting. I laid it up for some years when you couldn't buy a decent ten-bore cartridge, but they're loading 'em now. Three-inch cases—and two ounces of 3's." He showed Johnny a great magnum cartridge.

"The old arbiter of human destiny can hit the high ones, too," quoth the Captain. "My own notion is that it's not decent or sportsmanlike to shoot a duck when he's already more than halfway to Heaven. All I shoot ducks for anyway is just to keep 'em from the suffering and privations of a hard winter season."

"All you have to do," the Judge explained to Johnny as he led the way to the ancient, sagging span of stone and plank, "is to lean a chunk of broken planking up against the rail and sit down behind it. If you keep still the ducks won't pay much attention to you. We'll leave this ardent humanitarian right here with his mean thoughts and his sixteen-gauge. You'll have the center span, and I'll go on to the other end."

"Which way do they come?" Johnny asked when he had arranged a piece of planking and opened his cartridge bag.

"Both ways. You need to keep your eyes open. You wouldn't suppose that a duck could get within a mile of us unseen—but they do. Some of 'em will get by us today."

Shouldering his twelve-pound weapon, he went on some fifty or sixty yards, his footsteps sounding resonantly on the frosty planking.

Johnny settled himself and surveyed the environs. To the north, and vanishing at last where its undecisive channel turned behind a wooded headland, stretched the marsh, more clearly seen now that the mists were lifting in formless convolutions toward the upper sky. High tree-clad slopes came down steeply to the shore on either side. The expanse between was a waste of shallow, brown water, thickly snagged with weathering stumps, patches of flag and rice and dotted with the rough domes of countless muskrat houses still being increased nightly in height and thickness by the provident little builders. Below the bridge a wide channel of open water led the eye to the shimmering reaches of the lake itself.

Two dark spots materialized just at the edge of the misty mirage a half mile away. For a time they seemed to hang motionless above the water, and then in swift, concerted action shifted sidewise and swung over the center of the channel.

"Mark south!" said Johnny.

"Whistlers!" announced the Judge, as his ear caught the faint, sweet tinkle of sound that the goldeneye showers down from its barred wings.

"They're coming to the Judge," said the Captain as the nearing birds shifted and lifted a trifle. "Watch him! He's good at this!"

Higher and higher swept the pair as they approached the bridge, until they attained to what they seemed to regard as a safe level of around fifty or sixty yards.

The old sportsman had been gathering himself cautiously for the test, and now he rose in one smooth, complete motion that culminated in the "Whoom!" of the goose gun. One bird collapsed. "Whoom!" the big gun roared again, and the second of the pair pitched in a long slant to hit the water like a shell and float breast upward in the ripples, its silvery chimes forever stilled.

The double thunder of the goose gun rolled interminably between the hills and stirred a host of fowl from the marsh. Flocks of black ducks winnowed indecisively to and fro, turning always just outside of long gunshot from either shore, finally to settle again or, as some did, after mounting higher and higher, to disappear at last above the woods toward some secluded wilderness pond hole. Squadrons of teal swerved and dipped in arrowy flight, while disturbed wood ducks uttered their plaintive whistles. A bunch of bluewings flashed out from the milling, uneasy flocks and drove straight for the bridge, flying low to the water. They crossed between the Captain and the shore, only clearing the rail of the ancient structure by a few feet. That gunner, quite unready for so swift an opportunity, barely managed to fire one barrel into them as they buzzed past, but three of the tiny, plump fellows went end over end, somewhat to the amazement and much to the gratification of the gunner.

A lone merganser came out next, and the Judge, though he swung his gun muzzles out ahead of the bird, nevertheless allowed him to pass unmolested.

"Go 'long, you old sardine can," said he, "but don't you let me catch you eating trout."

Another single came over the center span, and at the proper moment Johnny cut him down.

"Redhead," announced Johnny, who knew the species well from long days at Currituck. He did not realize how rare was this consort of the lordly canvasback in these waters, until one of his companions told him that this specimen was the first they had ever encountered on the lake.

A pair of black ducks tried the gauntlet, crossing high between Johnny and the Judge, and headed, no doubt, for the shallows of Hubbardton Bay. But they went their wary way unharmed, because no one happened to notice them until it was too late to shoot.

Ducks came and went, many so high as to be far out of range even of the Judge's exceptional artillery, but now and then someone had a fair chance, and now and then a bird splashed into the channel and was tallied with a notch cut by the Captain on the edge of a plank.

"Fourteen," he announced presently, "and that's pretty good these days. I used to come up here when I was a youngster. I've often seen half a dozen gunners on the bridge at the same time and the planking covered with empty shells. There was one chap—a schoolteacher—he taught that little school up the road—who'd come down mornings and shoot until the second bell rang; and then grab his ducks and dust for his classes. He had the Judge outgunned, too. Used an eight-bore muzzle loader, an English gun that must have weighed fifteen pounds. I've watched him load it a hundred times. He'd just pour out a handful of powder and another of BB's for each barrel. It was a terrible gun for flock-shooting. One morning the old girl let go both barrels at once and knocked him flat and broke his collarbone. We brought him around, got the doctor for him, dismissed his classes and then spent half the morning fishing his gun out of the channel there with a fish pole with a nail in the butt."

Toward midmorning Johnny went to the car for a forgotten package of cigarettes.

"There were a couple of sorry-lookin' fellers hangin' around the car," he remarked when he returned.

"What'd they look like?" asked the Captain.

"They walked away when they saw me. One of 'em was middle-sized and mean-lookin'—the other one was younger and twice as big. Both dirty."

"That'll be that outlaw who has that shanty at the upper end of the marsh; he and that hulking boy of his. Shiftless critters. Make a living fishing and trapping and, so I've heard, gathering up a few chickens and pigs on moonlight nights—sort of redistributing the wealth of the community."

Noon came and the Captain went to bring the lunch basket.

"Fetch me that extra box of cartridges, will you?" the Judge called after him. "I put 'em back of the seat, I believe."

His friend returned presently with the basket and reported that an extensive search of the car had failed to disclose any more of the Judge's cannon fodder.

"Why, sho' now," complained the owner of the big gun, "I'd have swore I put in an extra box!" Then he added resignedly, "but probably I didn't. Getting absent-minded. Doesn't matter, though. Guess I've all I'll need anyway."

After lunch the Captain proposed to adventure along the wooded border of the marsh by way of finding diversion, his companions declining his invitation to join the expedition. So he went off along with a clearer conscience for having asked them. For, dearly as a sportsman may love his chosen companions, there still are times when he feels impelled to commune with the goddess of the woods and waters in solitude.

Through an ancient barway from a pasture he entered a leaf-strewn path that closely followed the meandering shore of the marsh. Great gray beeches towered above him. A pair of belated blue jays wrestled with the bristling fruit but broke off the struggle to squall discordantly as they sighted the intruder below. Two gray squirrels, made fat and frolicsome with easily gathered fare, chased one another around the wide trunk of a great basswood. The Captain paused to watch them and while following their antics with indolent eyes wished for his rifle in place of his fowlingpiece. Farther on an industrious muskrat broke the quiet surface of the water, swimming toward his home with a mouthful of building material in the form of moss and weed.

"You little unreconstructed cuss, you," the man told him softly, "how do you expect to end the depression if you work overtime? But maybe," he added, "you didn't know there was one."

His quiet progress was interrupted by a sudden tremendous roar of wings as half a dozen grouse burst out from a fringe of nannyberry bushes hung thick with clusters of smoky purple berries on which the flock had been feeding. One bird hurtling for safety was cut down in a burst of penciled feathers by a swift snap shot.

Some time later, coming cautiously around a bend of the path, the Captain surprised a flock of black ducks dozing and basking in the sunshine. As they leaped upward in a flurry of alarm, the little gun spat twice and two ducks fell back into the brown water. The shots raised a rout of waterfowl, and after the Captain had retrieved his birds with the aid of an alder sapling he sat down in the shelter of the bushes to watch the milling flocks spinning and wheeling over quiet channel and dun reed bed.

Presently he heard the sound of voices, mingled with the dull thump of boots in collision with root or stone. Two men came in sight along the path. One, the elder, was short and squat and dark of eye and jowl. He was glaring belligerently along the shore, the while in loud, blustering tones he called down curses on some unfortunate's shoulders. In one hand, the Captain saw, he carried an ancient single-barreled gun of 10-bore, and in the other a couple of dusky mudhens. His companion, whom he addressed as "Pud," was unarmed save for a hatchet and a few rusty steel traps. Twice the size of his parent, he had the vacant face, the dull eye, and the stolid, bovine look of one in whom the lamp of intelligence burned, if at all, with only a feeble, flickering flame. He dangled three drowned, bedraggled muskrats by their scaly tails and from time to time held the poor sodden creatures aloft to gaze at them gloatingly.

To his parent's menacing declamations he responded with a vacant "Heh?" without interrupting his consideration of the dead water rats.

"Dum 'em! Whoever they be, I'll larn 'em!" promised the elder.

At that instant his warlike gaze encountered that of the Captain. Noticeably startled and confused, he hesitated momentarily and then resumed his bluster.

"So thar ye be, be ye? Killin' our ducks, be ye? Yis, sir! Two of 'em, an' don't ye try to d'ny it for I kin see 'em! Don't ye now! Dum ye! Comin' up here an' killin' ducks 'at don't b'long to ye!"

Accompanying this condemnatory introduction, the speaker advanced upon the Captain threateningly, but halted when that gentleman rose from his log to disclose some six feet of lean, easy-muscled competence.

"Now, Mister," he spoke in quiet tones, "if these are your ducks—and you can prove it—you can have 'em. If they're not your ducks, you can still have 'em—if you can get 'em."

"They be too our ducks! Why they been roostin' in the ma'sh in front o' our place all Summer. Ain't they, Pud?"

"Heh?" said Pud absently, regarding his muskrats with fascinated gaze, obviously indifferent to the legal aspects of his father's contention.

The Captain said nothing, but there was that in his attitude that persuaded the other that conciliation might be preferable to threats of violence in dealing with this quiet sportsman.

"Tell ye what," offered the man with the air of one making a most generous concession, "you just gi' me a dollar for the two on 'em an' we'll call it square an' say no more about it."

"Pay you a dollar for two wild ducks I shot myself? I hardly think so, Mister!"

The Captain made a swift gesture of indignation and impatience from the menace of which the squat man recoiled in some alarm.

"Now," he continued, "get along out of here, you cussed, old two-legged mink, an' tend to your business an' I'll tend to mine!—And if you wouldn't talk so loud and so much you'd get more game!"

The other, sullenly gathering his mudhens and as sullenly directing his son to attend him, turned back along the path muttering imprecations to which his companion responded with his accustomed absent-minded monosyllable.

The Captain watched the queer pair out of sight and chuckled in exasperation.

"His ducks! Well, by the Lord Harry! The damned old thief! How is it, I wonder, that out in the woods and wild places where there's nothing to degrade a man or set him a bad example, you'll every so often run across somebody who's meaner than a wet dogskin coat! I ought to've cut a switch for him!"

Further regrets were interrupted by a sudden high-pitched rushing sound as a flock of ducks returning to the marsh dove recklessly from the upper air, cleared the treetops by a few feet, banked and turned on humming pinions and, after circling warily a few times, dropped with a long splash into the cove barely beyond the observer's line of vision.

"Right into old Sourface's lap," he guessed, as he marked the place as being about at the point reached by his unsavory acquantances.

He could even imagine the avid gleam in the man's dull eyes at the unexpected opportunity for a raking shot into the sitting fowl, his gesture imposing silence on his uncommunicative offspring with the muskrats, the cautious poking of the gun barrel through the fringe of alders, the slow, deadly aim "into the thick on 'em" and the resulting destruction. The accuracy of his estimate was confirmed by the sound of a shot, but the report came flat and curiously muffled to his ears.

The ducks rose in a spatter of wing against water, plainly audible, and this uproar was pierced by a high-pitched distressful squalling.

The Captain's long running stride brought him quickly to where Pud, still clinging to his dead muskrats, gazed in some astonishment at his parent, who writhed on the ground and squalled and moaned and clutched at a dappled forearm from which a thin, fierce jet of scarlet spurted rhythmically. A cracked and splintered gun stock lay beside the wounded man. The barrel was nowhere to be seen.

"I'm shot!" moaned the victim, "an' I'm goin' to die!"

"No great loss if you do," said the Captain unsympathetically.

Nevertheless he laid down his gun, knelt beside the victim and, slipping back the torn jacket sleeve, surveyed the damage. There was a clean, deep incision across the arm just above the wrist where a humming splinter of iron had scored.

He worked swiftly, aided by an experience grimly gained on other fields, folding a pad of torn handkerchief against the severed artery and pressing it down with a wrap of the same material twisted tight with a stick.

"Now, Pud," he ordered, "you hustle down to Johnson's and get someone to 'phone for the doctor. I'll bring your old man out. Run now! And, for Pete's sake, leggo of those muskrats! Git!"

Galvanized, Pud dropped his game and departed on his mission, followed more slowly by the Captain and the moaning, thoroughly scared parent.

A half hour later, sterilized, sutured, bandaged and safe from the threat of the glories of immediate immortality, the patient was ready to depart for home leaning heavily on Pud's arm. That individual had, of course, employed the surgical interlude to retrieve his muskrats.

Now that he had recovered from his fright, the older man was moved by some faint, vagrant sentiment of gratitude toward the Captain. In this unwonted emotional excess, he exclaimed generously.

"Mister, you kin keep them two ducks o' mine. Keep 'em, an' welcome."

"Thanks," replied the good Samaritan blandly, and since some other matters had become clear to him, he added, "and I'll just take the rest of that box of shells you hooked out of our car this morning. As a matter of policy hereafter, don't steal any more three-inch magnum cartridges to shoot in a short-chambered, pot-metal gun—not even at your own ducks!"

A
TROUT BROOK
CONVERSION

The Great Flood did many strange and terrible things in the villages and homesteads in Vermont valleys. One November afternoon after three days of rainfall, the mountains, always before so friendly, let loose such a fearful spate of dark, swirling water as none of the inhabitants had ever seen or ever wished to see again. The gentle, musical trout streams purling over the stones and chuckling underneath the alders became in the space of an hour, savage, thunderous torrents moving with an irresistible, tigerish power that nothing could withstand.

Then it was that our friend the Judge found himself, with his housekeeper, old Ellen, and his handy man, Jason, confined to the upper rooms of the fine old house on Main Street, where with a flashlight to penetrate the inky darkness they watched the dark water creep slowly up the white stairway and listened to the tumult of crashing timbers and bellowing waters outside. That his precious library and much of the beautiful old furniture were submerged in the rooms below was the least cause of the Judge's anxiety, for piercing the snarl and mutter of the torrent they heard screams and distressed shoutings. These sounds of dire human terror had been more than the courageous Judge could endure without making an attempt to rescue these old friends and neighbors. So without much of a plan to follow, and knowing no more than that he must do whatever he could do, he found a plank and with it under one arm slipped off the edge of the porch roof into the black current. It was a forlorn attempt, and nearly a fatal one. The water instantly tore the plank from him, and although the Judge was a strong swimmer he found himself as helpless in that raging force as a chip. He was submerged, smothered, tossed and buffeted, and only the fortunate circumstance that the current swept in a swirling motion between his house and the next on the street saved his life. Two violent minutes after he had let go of his own porch roof, the Judge found himself whirling past it again. He caught desperately at the overhang, clutched it, and then the strong hands of Jason and Ellen had hold of him. Gasping, bruised and half frozen, he was hauled back to safety.

Thereafter he sat wrapped in blankets and watched the water rise until at midnight it lapped at the edge of the topmost stair. Then it began a slow and sullen recession, leaving a waste of foul mud and sodden debris in its wake.

The flood, at times, displayed a sort of grim whimsicality. In the Dickinson home farther down the street, the supper was on the table when the onrush of waters drove the family to the upper rooms. When next they saw the familiar board the supper was gone, dishes and all, and a huge drowned horse lay sprawled atop the table in place of the veal potpie, the flaky cover of which the good man of the house had been about to attack with carving knife and fork when the floods came down from the hills.

There was one thing that the flood did that contributed to the annals of sport in Tranquillity. It hauled an old Stewart kitchen stove from a collapsed cabin the whole length of Wyman Valley, some four or five miles, and left it at the bottom of the big pool just above the confluence where Wyman Brook joins Hubbard's Creek. And there it lay for years deep beneath the amber water and became the principal defense of a sizable brown trout who took up her abode in a neighboring upstream pool, where she grew and waxed strong on the nourishing things the stream was always busy bringing to her.

The fish gradually attained to gigantic size and was well known to the Judge and his friend, the Captain, as well as to every angler in the community of whatever age and degree of experience. Nearly all of these devotees of the tight line and the quivering rod had had, at one time or another, a hook or two in the lip of that mighty maw, but it was well known that as long as she was "fished fair" Josephine was untakable. The trout had a simple strategy that invariably worked so well that she grew contemptuous of flies and lures. When in the course of her feeding she took one of these cunning cheats she had only to drive herself with a single sweep of her broad tail into the current at the foot of her home pool. Once there and aided by the rush of the stream, it was no trick to win to the pool below, dart through the open doors of the firebox of the old stove and emerge on the opposite side free once more of all malicious restraints.

The local fishing crowd were rather inclined to a feeling of admiration and affection for Josephine. She was thought to be a prolific lady, for one thing, annually contributing generously to increase the piscine population of the stream and the creek. The anglers liked to watch her on clear days when she wasn't feeding, lying just at the edge of a submerged reef with her great gill flaps opening and closing and the broad tail moving just enough to keep the dark body in the same spot. When visiting anlgers came to Tranquillity to try the fishing they were always taken to the willow-fringed pool and permitted to "discover" the massive Josephine. If she were in a playful mood and accepted the stranger's fly, it was worth many a fish to see the blanched face and excited gesticulations of the victim. The victim in such cases was never the big brown trout. And when after the one terrific rush she left the cast on the edge of the firebox—! Uncle Bill Paraday claimed that he learned more "emergency language" from the frenzied losers than he had in all of his four years in the Union Army.

So matters rested pleasantly, amusingly and harmlessly until the Great Blight fell upon the sporting fraternity of the village. He, the Blight, was a person loud of speech and habiliment, swarthy of countenance, with the sort of paunch that a smallish man might acquire by sitting too long and devotedly in the place of the money changers. The name he signed to the check that paid for the old Galton place was "Green," but it was generally believed that half a dozen more letters might be found on the naturalization papers if anyone bothered to look.

"I don't give a durn how many letters he's lost out of his name since his Ma gave him his first onion to cut his teeth on—he cert'nly ain't lost any money since. No, nor he ain't improved his manners much, neither!" It was Uncle Bill speaking to the Judge about their alien neighbor. "I hear he complains that the 'common people' hereabouts don't tech their hats proper when they meet him! Hell!" concluded Uncle Bill, who once was a sergeant in Stannard's Brigade.

After purchasing the Galton place Mr. Green did all things to establish himself to lead the life of a country squire, a member of the landed gentry, as he understood it. One of these was to post his land against trespass.

It bothered Mr. Green that the local workmen, carpenters, masons and masters of similar crafts whom he hired to remodel the beautiful old house couldn't seem to get into their heads the fact that they belonged to a lower social order than their employer. It was disconcerting. If he expected Dan Jones, the carpenter, to address him as "Mister Green" he found that he himself would have to address Dan as "Mister Jones." If he called the old fellow by his first name, or simply "Jones," the carpenter responded in kind and addressed his employer as "Will" or "Green." It was the same with the others. At first he wanted to discharge the whole lot and get workmen from the city who would know their places, but he was shrewd enough to see that these Yankee craftsmen gave him a dollar's worth of honest work for every dollar he paid them, and that they did it without needing to be watched. Will Lampson, for example, spent half of one Sunday re-laying a stone in a foundation wall. "Wa'n't quite satisfied with it," he explained and supplied still another surprise for his employer by refusing to accept pay for the extra hours of labor.

The men listened to his suggestions on details of construction calmly, nodding their heads if they approved and as calmly ignoring the matter if they didn't like it.

It did no good to insist.

"Mister Green," Dan Jones told him once, "we calculate to fix your haouse jest as it should be, an' it has to be done in jest sech a way. Naow, if I should do as ye say an' take that j'ist aout o' the rafters 'twouldn't be no time scarcely until the floor 'ud settle an' sag an' folks would be sayin' that Dan Jones skimped the work. So I shan't do it."

Green was curious.

"How long is it when the floor sags like you say?" he inquired.

"Wal, I dunno, exactly—fifty years, mebbe; mebbe, a hundred," said Dan, who was sixty-five years old but would risk no criticism of his craftsmanship even though he would most certainly not be where he could hear it.

Gradually the little fat fellow began to feel a grudging respect for these people who wouldn't boss or be bossed and who clung to the quaint belief that a man should do as he said he would whether the contract was in writing or in the spoken word or without any word at all, but just because a man thought he knew what was expected of him.

Dan Jones, Will Lampson and some of the rest began to say around the village that the new owner of the Galton place wasn't such a disagreeable feller as you might think, a charitable view that was not shared by Uncle Bill Paraday and others who saw the man only in his more assured and patronizing poses.

"Jest a damned, rich, pot-gutted, leetle swab!" the old veteran declared with his customary candor. "Seen him come bargin' into the Post Office t'other night 'spectin' everybody an' Old Man Hawkins to step aside an' let him up to the winder to git his mail fust. Hell!" said Uncle Bill. "An' fetchin' in horses that he can't ride ner drive, dogs that he don't now how to handle, an' guns an' fishin' tackle enough to stock a store. He can't shoot fer sour apples an' from what Jimmy Durkee tells me he can't git a trout fly the length o' the rod away from him!"

"Wal, naow, I dunno as I fully agree with ye, Uncle Bill," Will Lampson protested mildly. "I've known him to do one er two nice things, now an' then. It jest seems to me that he ain't eddicated as we be. Seems likely he come from some place where a man dassent take his shirt off fer fear o' losin' it. No daoubt he's been overbored upon an' bossed in his time, an' it's kinda natural fer him to want to do the same naow he's got a chance to."

Jimmy Durkee, the freckled, upstanding son of a war-widowed mother, agreed with Uncle Bill's opinion. So far, he was the only inhabitant of the township who would go fishing with the newcomer, and he did so only because his mother badly needed the three dollars paid him for every day spent escorting his patron along the streams of the region.

It was money earned in bitter agony, for of all things on earth Jimmy loved fine trout tackle. It was a sight to see the boy handle a rod, too, with the sure and effortless grace of a master. The Judge had come upon him one day equipped with a one-piece bamboo "pole" and a can of worms fishing the North Branch, but from the manner in which the lad watched while the older sportsman handled his four-ounce rod and the eagerness he displayed when the Judge talked to him of trout fishing, it was obvious that he had the heart of a true angler. So the Judge, from the goodness of his own great heart, fixed the boy out with an old rod of his own and some tackle and gave him a few instructions on its use. No more was needed. By the end of that season Jimmy was as proficient as his instructor, and when a second season had come and gone he was a better angler than the Judge in all except those finer details that are gained only from years of experience and that can seldom be imparted to another.

Whoever the salesman was who sold Green his fishing tackle he had known his wares and had done no worse by his unsophisticated customer than to sell him dozens of beautiful rods he would never need, flys and leaders by the gross, fine English lines and reels enough to supply twenty anglers—active ones, at that. Jimmy would have given any two fingers from his right hand to possess the four-ounce rod that his patron used so cruelly. There were moments when he would have given as many as three fingers for the privilege of cracking his arrogant employer on the head with a rock.

Those were the times when Green whipped and whaled and jerked and twisted the delicate bamboo in a manner to make a real angler weep and curse.

In time Jimmy took his man down the Wyman Brook and showed Josephine to him. He had to point her out or the paunchy gentleman never would have seen her. The old girl was in gay spirits that day and waited patiently until the angler, after a dozen wretched attempts, got a fly on the water. Then she came grandly up like a queen ascending a throne and took the bedraggled Professor in the gristle of her upper lip. Two seconds later she had hung it with her collection of trophies in the firebox of the stove, and Jimmy on the bank was looking at a small pouchy man who was closer than he ever saw anyone come to bursting with excitement, disappointment and rage. Green threshed, and he squalled, and he cursed, and he finally flung his rod on the ground with such violence that the boy winced.

In time, of course, the Master of Galton found out about Josephine's trick. His desire to possess the big brown mounted each time that he saw her. He wanted that fish, and he felt that by taking her he would show these sly Yankees something of the superior metal of the sportsman he knew himself to be. He fell to evil imaginings.

"Boy," said he to Jimmy one day, "if you can figger out how I go about it to ketch dot damned fish I would give you the fish pole, line and winder complete. Ninety-five dollars and eighty cents I paid it for the lot, too!"

"Oh, it could be done—if a man was mean enough," said Jimmy.

"How? How you do it?"

"I ain't goin' to tell you," declared Jimmy, suddenly uneasy that he had said so much.

"Huh!" ejaculated his employer, who had learned the utter futility of trying to make one of these people answer a question that he didn't want to answer. "When you want a fine fish pole you come and tell me, see?"

Jimmy felt more and more uncomfortable as the days went by. The thought of owning the splendid rod fascinated him. He could have it if he would. Easy. If he didn't do it, he'd never be able to earn enough money to buy such a rod and to think so was as foolish as to think he was the one kid in his generation who'd grow up to be President. Only more so, for two Vermont youngsters had won to the White House, and there was at least one chance in a million or so that he might get there, but things like rods and guns came a darned sight harder to a poor boy in the Vermont hills.

The subtle virus was working—and one evening a gruff and scowling Jimmy presented himself at the front door of the Old Galton House and was permitted to see the master.

"Git ready to start at six o'clock tomorrow mornin'," the boy ordered shortly. "You'll git the big trout—if you c'n hang onto her," he added.

His employer was not pleased with Jimmy's brusque tones and lack of servility, but since he scarcely knew what to do about it, he ended by agreeing to be prepared and on time for the expedition.

"That damn boy!" he muttered as he returned to his dinner. "He don't know no manners with his betters! But I should care if I ketch the fish! I teach him something afterwards, maybe."

Ordinarily even the presence of the unappreciative Mr. Green couldn't take away all of the boy's enjoyment of such a morning as greeted them when they set out for the Lower Pool. Light filaments of cool, moist vapor rose lazily from the brook when the two approached it, and the pleasant sound of water came to their ears long before they reached the spot. A mother grouse charged furiously at their feet and Green, disagreeably startled, slashed at her with his rod case.

He missed, of course, but the incident increased Jimmy's contempt for the man and for his own part in this shady adventure. It was in an unsociable silence that he set up the rod, clamped on the reel, strung the line and tied the cast.

"She's lyin' right in that slick below that stone," he advised as he handed the rod over. "Git your fly over across an' let it come down easy. When she takes it let her run."

Green followed instructions and after making a botchy job of it finally had the fly drifting toward the submerged boulder where a bulky shadow lay at the edge of the line of beaded foam. There was an instant of suspense and then the shadow moved and seemed to change color. The water swirled, the fly disappeared, the slender rod bent and sang. Josephine was on.

"Oh, gosh!" moaned Jimmy as the big fish cut into the swift current and surged downstream. Evidently she was well hooked. And this time even the clumsy action of the angler failed miraculously either to free the hook or splinter the rod.

"I've done it now," the boy thought and then for twenty minutes watched one of the worst bits of fishing he had ever seen.

The Judge and the Captain, unaware of these developments, were themselves planning to fish the Wyman Brook that morning, and as they came along to the Lower Pool they were made curious by the sound of a strident voice evidently berating someone. They emerged from the willows to see Jimmy, very wet and bedraggled and boyishly defiant, facing an apoplectic Mr. Green who was bellowing at the top of his voice.

"Yah!" he roared. "You fix it so I ketch the big fish, hey? What the hell! And now you! And I give you three dollars a day to loaf! You ain't goin' to get no more easy money! I tell you that!"

"I don't blame you fer gettin' mad," Jimmy exclaimed. "It wasn't your fault, I guess. You didn't know no better, but I did, an' I shouldn't have done what I did. I'm glad I changed my mind, an' I don't want your money, neither."

"What's up, Jimmy? What's little Brighteyes hollering about?" asked the Captain at this point. The boy looked up at these two old friends of his and he flushed.

" 'Tain't his fault. It's mine. I let myself in to do old Josephine a dirty trick. Mr. Green wanted to ketch her so bad that he offered to give me his tackle if I could fix it so he could land her. Well, I fixed it so he could, an' then when he just about had her tuckered out, I couldn't stand it an' I unfixed it again an' she got away. I guess I ain't such a hot pertater, any way you look at it," he concluded miserably.

Some trace of light dawned for the Judge, and there was a flicker of amusement in his eyes when he spoke.

"How'd you fix it, Jimmy? And then, how'd you unfix it?"

"I came down last night an' dove down an' shet the firebox door," said the boy, "an' jest now when Josephine was whangin' her nose aginst it, tryin' to get through, I couldn't stand it an' I dove in agin an' opened it for her. An' she got away!"

There was a moment's silence, and then the laughter of the two men rose over the laughter of the stream.

"Jimmy," exclaimed the Judge, "you're a cute one. You'll be President some day—sure as shootin'. Now you might, since you are wet, dive in again and take the danged doors off the hinges on that stove and hide 'em.

"And now, Mister," said he, turning to the disappointed fisherman, "we don't hold much with folks who try tricks like that. But maybe you didn't know it. Anyhow, you can quit squalling. If you've had Josephine on your tackle for twenty minutes you've had the best part of the fun, and, moreover, that's nineteen minutes and fifty-eight seconds longer than anybody else around here ever had her!"

Then something happened to demonstrate that there really are lessons in brooks—in trout brooks, anyhow—and that they are not always lost even upon the most unpromising students. With one simple, sincere gesture Mr. Green found the only open gate in the wall of the community of sportsmanship that had not yielded to his arrogant assaults. He drew a deep breath.

"I guess maybe I ain't quite got the right idee at first," he admitted. "I have learn some things! For instance I take down the posting signs tomorrow morning. Let the boys know I ain't no hog. And, by gosh, Jimmy! I tell you something else, hey? You learn me how to handle 'em right, and I give you the whole works anyhow including complete the fish pole, the line and the winder! So?"

" 'Reel,' Mr. Green, not 'winder' an' it's a 'rod' an' not a 'fish pole,' " said Jimmy by way of the first easy lesson.

GHOST
BIRDS

The impression is widespread that the inhabitants of communities in northern New England are compounded of nonvolatile substances and that their emotional nerve centers from long centuries of disuse have become vestigial. Nothing could be further from the truth. The Yankee heart is certainly as warm as anyone's and responds as readily to the touch of joy or woe; it is the Yankee's innate sense of dignity and decency that stops him from making any shallow public display of his emotions. So it is that wars, the vicissitudes of politics and other momentous events come and go according to the design of history, and though they stir the depths, they do not perceptibly ruffle the surface of the stream of existence. In case of war the young men go and the older ones try to do so. No one makes much fuss about it. When it is over the dead are bought home for burial and the wounded to be cared for, and the Selectmen put up some sort of modest memorial on the village square. Or it may be an election to determine, according to the politicians, issues of the gravest and most profound importance. Sides are chosen and stout opinions formed, but there is no pre-election red fire, and there is little bombast; victors and vanquished return from the polls without jeers or recriminations and go amicably about their daily affairs conscious of the fact that in the long run nothing of importance has been changed.

But now and then something occurs of a nature so unpredictable and unusual as to do violence to this well-tempered placidity. A few years ago the town of Tranquillity was experiencing a touch of mild hysteria over just such an unprecedented occurrence. It was occasioned by the fact that as late as the 20th day of the month of October no one had seen so much as a wing feather of the woodcock flight that comes down from Nova Scotia, Quebec and Maine. There had been an excellent crop of native birds raised in the numerous swamps and damp coverts in which the region abounds, and for a week after the season opened there had been good shooting. Then the canny, long-billed survivors had broken camp in the nighttime and gone, leaving only the dapplings of fading whitewash in the thickets and the marks of their tiny daggers in the moist earth along the edges of the alder and birch copses in the upland pastures. Since that time no gunner had so much as seen the brown and black of a rising, whistling bird—let alone taken one. Day after golden day the warm sunlight lay level across the glowing countryside. The choke-cherries growing in the corners of the roadside fences turned from wine red to black, the robins and flickers assembled their battalions in the wild grape vines in readiness for departure and the maple leaves lay spread on the sward beneath the lofty branches from which they had fallen. At evening the smoke from the chimneys of homestead and hamlet rose in the straight unwavering columns that are precursors of storm and tempest. But no wind or rain came, nor any violence of weather. Each day appeared set in the same amber chalice that had enclosed its glowing predecessors. And still the covers held none of the mysterious brown birds that work a charm upon upland gunners that in its potency is out of all proportion to the woodcock's modest size and quiet demeanor.

It is not likely that the woodcock's defection, had it continued, would have permanently altered the course of human affairs in the township, but it was a serious matter nevertheless and there was considerable domestic disturbance as a result of it.

There were gatherings of quiet, serious men at the post office and at Pingree's hardware store.

A salesman, traveling for an ammunition firm, happened upon one of these sober groups one evening just in time to hear Squint Norton gravely telling the other men that he'd "sarched an' sarched but seen nary a sign o' the leetle creeturs." The commercial man was so impressed by the gravity with which the news was received that he quite naturally supposed that someone's children had been lost in the woods. When he learned that woodcock and not children were the cause of concern he laughed aloud, and thereby lost the sale of a dozen cases of duck loads to Pingree.

The Dark-Haired Lady knew a lot more than the drummer did about such things, but even she found it difficult to understand the degree of perturbation with which the Captain viewed the situation.

"He's as restless as he was when he had the German measles," she declared to the Judge, referring to a particularly·disgraceful episode in her consort's mature career. "He watches the skies as if he expected to see Elijah's chariot coming down to take him for a ride. Every morning he's out to see how much dew has fallen on the lawn. You'd think it was all the water there is in the world."

"If it was," the Judge interjected, "it would be more than he'd need for drinking purposes, Ma'am."

The lady laughed.

"But—how can anyone complain of such lovely weather!" she continued. "What's a little woodcock anyhow? You're getting all the grouse you can use, aren't you?"

"That ain't just the point," the Judge declared respectfully, "and, come to think of it, I don't know that I can just put it into words, either, but a bird season without woodcock in it is a good deal as if you had a new fur coat and no doodads to match it. It's grand, but it ain't completely satisfactory."

"I see," said she, nodding her dark head in perfect understanding.

The very next night, after another day of quiet warm sunlight, the snow began. It came so softly that the Captain was unaware of the storm until he awoke in the morning to a dim world of seething white flakes that fell straight to earth from out of a windless, low and leaden sky.

"Darn it," he complained at breakfast. "There wasn't a sign of this last night! If we'd known of it in time we might have taken an early start and had some topnotch black duck shootin' at the Point. Too late now, and this'll all go off tomorrow."

Resigned, therefore, to a day of indoor activity, he presently retired to his big chair with pad and pencil to work on a neglected manuscript.

He was still engaged in this harmless literary endeavor when the Judge's old car came thudding into the yard about midway of the lonely, storm-bound afternoon. The older sportsman wore shooting clothes and boots and was brusque and hurried of manner.

"Come on, get your rig on," he commanded. "No time to lose!"

"There's no time at all!" exclaimed his friend. "It's an hour's drive to the Point—more'n that in this smother. We'll no more than get the decoys out than we'll have to take 'em up again."

"We ain't going to the Point," his counselor informed him. "We're going to the Williamsville Cover after woodcock. It just happens that I remember a season like this one and a day like this one back in 1901. Old Bill Ward, who shot for the market, killed fifteen pairs of woodcock that day, and I got a fair bag myself," he added modestly. "We were the only ones to go out—nobody else ever thought of woodcock in a snowstorm. They won't think of 'em to-day, either, but if the birds are coming at all they'll be here and lying in close alder cover. You'll see."

His shooting partner was openly skeptical, but he put away his pad and rose obediently. "I don't believe a word of it," said he. "In all the years I've known you I can't recall a single time when you could remember anything of any immediate or possible use. You remembered the road to Biddy's nob all right last deer season, but you couldn't remember which way to turn when we got there. In consequence dawn found us nine miles away in the streets of the ancient village of Skenesboro—and that's a hell of a place to look for a deer runway. You always remember to put the lunch in the car, too, but half the time it's the wrong car and we go hungry. I'd be a fool to trust you to remember anything worth while. I'd also be a fool to expect to shoot woodcock in a blizzard, so I don't expect it, but I'll go because anything is better than this."

Warmed by days of sunshine, the earth dissolved the first snow easily but not quite as fast as the deluge of flakes came down, so that only an inch or two of the soft wet stuff was under their boots as the two gunners crossed Briggs' pasture and entered the edge of the great stretch of black alders that filled the valley beyond.

It was a world curiously hushed, that in which they found themselves. None of the familiar sounds from highway and farmstead penetrated the shifting, sliding curtain of snow. All nature seemed in a mood to endure patiently the unseasonable discomfort without audible protest, as a philosophical wildfowler turns up his collar, bows his head and prepares to survive the miseries and inclemencies that so often attend upon his uncharitable recreation. The dank, wet stems of the alders made grotesque patterns in the opacity of the falling snow that screened the spots of color where some bright-foliaged shrub or clump of wild aster wore its gay holiday dress in defiance of the glum disapproval of the bedraggled landscape.

"There ain't a woodcock in there," declared the Captain positively. "Look at it! But it's a pretty sight, just the same, and the fire'll feel mighty comfortable when we get back to it after sloshing around in this mess for an hour or two."

The Judge had lost some of his earlier assurance, even though he wouldn't admit it. After all, it was a long way back to that day in 1901 with Old Bill Ward, and it might just be that it hadn't snowed quite so hard on that occasion as he thought it had. But he dropped a couple of 9's into his old double, raised the hammers and stepped in among the stems.

"Come on," he ordered.

The other did as he was bade. There was a ghostly atmosphere about the environment that the lean sportsman never forgot afterwards. A thin vapor rose from the earth and mingled with the flakes. In it the dark figure of the Judge, thirty paces distant, became vague, distorted and grotesque. He might have been one of Rip Van Winkle's strange Little Men of the Kaatskills finding his way back to the glen above the Hudson through the murk that enshrouded the hills.

"If he was one of 'em," thought the gunner, "I'd ask him for a draft from his 'wicked flagon.' I'm wet to the waist already and colder than a spring-house frog. This stuff is a mite too cold to be water and not quite warm enough to be called snow. And, as for woodcock—"

Something brown and spectral that whistled as it sprang rose abruptly in front of his face and went darting away through the mist and snow.

The Captain's gun came up, and its quick report sounded dull in the smothering whiteness.

The Judge called anxiously, "Get one?"

"I shot at one—or the ghost of one," was the astonished reply as the Captain went forward to find that it was no spirit bird that had drawn his fire, but a fat, brown and black hen woodcock lying in the snow beyond the alders from which she had sprung.

Examination disclosed that the bird had been resting on a spot of bare, wet ground no larger in area than a man's hand, where the outcurving root of a sapling gave protection from the snow. As the gunner shook the moisture from the vivid plumage the flat pop of the Judge's gun came to his ears, to be followed instantly by another and that in turn by his friend's calm announcement that he "believed he had a pair of them down and might need help to find them."

This help the other cheerfully gave, and while the Judge stood fast at the spot from which he had fired and pointed first in one direction and then in another, his companion found and gathered both birds.

They were following the opposite slopes of a shallow fold of the ground. A trickle of water from a hidden spring made a black, twisted ribbon among the alder roots on its way to join a more imposing stream at the foot of the pasture two hundred yards distant. Their custom, when they hunted this cover, was to follow the trickle to the main stream, then cross over a low rise and beat back along another wandering thread of moisture that so closely resembled its neighbor as to be indistinguishable except to a few bird hunters and the farmer boys who wandered through the thickets in search of game or straying cattle.

The light from the lowering sky lessened as the two friends progressed, but the pallid glow of the new-fallen snow gave a flat and toneless illumination to the eerie scene. In it the muzzles of the Judge's gun thrust out an orange tongue of flame as he fired at another twittering apparition that fluttered away into the obscurity. The birds were everywhere about them, springing from alder root and from beneath the snow-covered castles of the chimney top bush. Many there were that went away unseen in the dusk of the snow, their immediate presence and instant departure indicated only by the quick whistle and the rustle of brown, bent wings.

The brook, when they reached it, was a black, leaden stream; its dull surface took the falling flakes and quenched them like sparks. The sluggish roll of a spawning trout added no life to the scene, but only served to draw attention to the metamorphosis of a brook that only yesterday was gay in the amber sunlight and now, beneath the sinister spell of the weather, lay dark and gloomy as if it were a tributary of the Styx.

The friends stood for a long minute, during which the stream sounded never a gurgle and the only voice they heard was the sibilant hiss of the falling snow.

"We might be the last two people alive," remarked the Judge who had a fine strain of poetical imagination in him that often astonished people who knew him less well than did the Captain. "This scene makes me think of that part in the Death of King Arthur—the last great battle in the fog by the sea,

when only he and Sir Belvidere remain alive and the mist and the frost come
down upon the field."

"I know," said his friend.

Then he shivered and turned his thoughts to more practical matters.

"How many birds have you got?"

"Three," said the Judge.

"Well, I've got three, too, and I move that we start back and pick up one
more apiece and clear out for home, fire and supper. When I shivered just
then it was for three reasons: One, I'm scared of the hobgoblins you conjured
up; two, I'm wet and damnably cold; and three, I've never seen so many timberdoodles in one piece of cover in my whole life. Whoever heard of shooting
woodcock in a snowstorm?"

The Judge had moved away, and already the outlines of his solid, familiar
figure were wreathed and outlandishly distorted by the fog and snow so that
he resembled nothing that ever walked on earth, but his voice came back
warm and strong and friendly, with just a trace of kindly malice in it.

"I did," said he, "and I remembered it."

THE
TRIBULATIONS
OF
BILL JOHN

In Tranquillity Township there exists a sort of royal order. It has no charter, no signs, no grips; its members never assemble in regular meeting and would rebel violently if they were required to do so. In fact, of the two qualifications demanded of an aspirant to full companionship, one is that of being reluctant to appear at any specified place at any specified time—unless it is a bird-shooting rendezvous, a skeet match or a field-trial meeting; the other is that the candidate must be a bird shooter—and not lukewarm about it, either.

Our old friend, the Judge, is the acknowledged head of the order, with his friend, the Captain, aiding him as lord of the marches. The Dark-Haired Lady, who sometimes wonders whether she or the woodcock are first in the Captain's affections, asserts that every man in the order is anti-social, but that is an exaggeration resulting from feminine pique. For these bird shooters love their fellow man, even though they won't play bridge with him if they can think of anything better to do—and that is generally not difficult. Not one of them will put on a dinner jacket until his women-folk have brought in the rack and the red-hot pincers and displayed them as the alternative but scarcely less preferable punishment. Classified according to avocation, these good gray brothers include jurists, doctors, farmers, mechanics, day laborers, editors, accountants and so on; by vocation they are all bird hunters.

The method used by the wild African tribesmen to transmit news from one remote village to another is no more mysterious, rapid and efficacious than that employed by the members of the order to project information pertinent to its affairs. Someone loses a bird dog, and without resort to telephone or visual signaling Henry Butterfield, who lives way over in Sciota, knows about it as soon as does George Becker, who has his office on Main Street. A brother acquires a new gun, and all the rest are aware of its arrival before it is out of the express office. Within a week they will be around, one or two at a time, to inspect the new weapon. If a flight of woodcock comes in to populate the alder and birch covers of the township, word of the occurrence goes out over the grapevine, and all are apprised of it immediately and simultaneously.

The system failed once, however, and the reason for the failure was not discovered until a good while after the episode had occurred. It had to do with the activities and career of a big springer spaniel owned by one Bill John Ferguson. He had the dog and bragged about him, and then the dog disappeared and Bill John was silent. No one knew what had happened until the night when Bill John came over to look at a new double twenty-eight-bore gun that the Captain had recently received. The Judge was present, and as chief of the order determined that he was entitled to request a statement of facts from Bill John, and in the presence of the Captain he did so.

The talk began, as usual, with the expression of opinions as to the prospects for a good grouse and woodcock season. Then the Judge, who had replenished Bill John's cider glass, fixed the guest with a firm glance that could not be parried.

"Bill John," said he, "I'd like to hear what ever became of that big spaniel you bragged so much about last year."

Bill John winced and gave signs of considerable embarrassment.

"I was just going to tell you about that," said he. "I s'pose I may as well begin at the beginning."

Holding the Captain's new bird gun in one hand and his glass in the other, he mused for a moment.

"Do you know that old song, 'It's the Same the Whole World Over'?" he asked. "Well, I suffered more betrayals than that poor girl did, at the hands of that blue-blooded springer spaniel.

"He came to me as a winsome, clumsy puppy straight from a first-rate kennel that bred champion field dogs. The price I gave for him was enough to pay my year's shot-shell bill, with a half dozen bottles of 'crathur' to boot to keep off attacks of the flu and rheumatism on those cold, wet days when you have to be out because the woodcock are in.

"Having little leisure for dog training at the time and not wanting to make any mistakes with an animal that I felt was a potential champion, I picked out the one man who was admittedly the top ranker as a spaniel trainer and sent the pup along to him. You know who he is. His name is Enoch Hardin, and his training kennel is located in some of the best woodcock and grouse cover in New England, where Ace would be worked on wild birds every day. I told the dog good-by with only the brighest expectations for the future.

"With the monthly tuition bills came letters from the trainer. They were sort of funny. I thought they were just quaint. Ha!" He gave a snort that seemed to express his contempt of his own innocence. "They informed me that Ace was doing well; Enoch 'thought' Ace would make a hell of a shootin' dog; he 'thought' Ace was mebbe a hair on the slow side, but that was a good fault in a dog working on 'techy, nervous birds like pa'tridges and timberdoodles.' All his letters read about like that.

"I'm a Yankee myself, and I s'pose I should have realized that one of that breed can 'think' whatever he damned well pleases about anything on earth without involving or committing his conscience to any degree or course whatsoever. But one day I had a letter that worried me a lot.

" 'Dear Sir,' it said, 'Your spannel Ace has got the distemper bad. I hev employed a veteranary, feeling sure you would wish him to hev the best of care. I will send his bill upon receipt of same.

> Yrs trly
>
> Enoch H.' "

Bill John sipped from his glass, put it down.

"Another dog," said he, "would surely have died of the distemper and the serums administered—but not Ace. I ought to have guessed the truth from that, too, for I'd never known a really good dog to survive both the illness and its cure, but I paid the bills and was glad to learn of his convalescence and final recovery. And after that he had chorea, or, as Enoch described it, 'a kind of a twitchin' in his right hind laig but 'twa'n't nothin' to worry about.' Enoch 'thought' it would eventually disappear.

"The months slipped by at twenty-five dollars each, and finally it was September. You know how that is!"

His listeners did know, and such is the magic of that month to upland gunners that they saw what Bill John saw—the color coming in the maples; shotguns, shells and shooting coats beginning to appear in the window of Pingrees' hardware store; the meadow brooks in front of the old farmhouses smoking in the morning crispness, and again at evening when the last light from the sun had vanished above the Adirondacks. At night, if one cocked an ear toward the star-studded zenith, he could gather the slight gossip of hosts of small birds migrating southward. By such signs as these everyone in Tranquillity knows that again the shooting season is at hand.

"Two days before it opened," Bill John continued, "Ace came home. The 'some kind of a twitchin' of the right hind laig' was rather pronounced. His diploma, I realize now, was lacking in that forthrightness which is supposed to characterize these affidavits of excellence—lacking, that is, except in one or two sentences, and neither of them seemed significant to me at the time.

" 'Ace is a damned smart dog' was one of them, I remember. 'He knows how to retrieve.' Then it went on. 'Judging from yr several letters, you travel purty fast in the bresh birdin', and Ace may have some trouble keepin' up with you when you air out a-huntin', but that air a good fault in a spannel, and I think he will larn soon to keep ahead of you.

> Yrs trly
>
> Enoch H.' "

Opening day was clear and windless, Bill John told them. On such a day you can see across Lake Champlain the ramparts of old Fort Ticonderoga, standing gray and stately in ancient but invincible dignity against the flaming slopes of the mountains. The slow sound of a detached maple leaf falling and gently touching its summer companions on its journey earthward can be heard fifty paces away, while the scrambling rush of a gray squirrel up the trunk of a shagbark is startling in that clear silence.

"The ground," Bill John continued, "was moist beneath our feet; it would hold bird scent like butter. We had brought my little cocker, Pepper, along— best little cocker in the world, too—but his nose was somewhat out of joint by the presence of the big stranger with the jerky hind leg who seemed to be getting all the attention. Squint Norton was with me, carrying that old hammer gun that's bagged, I'll bet, more grouse and 'cock than any four guns in town. Squint always *thinks* he's got the best bird dog in the country, and I was aiming to take him down a peg by showing him some real bird work.

"We decided to try first the Old School House Cover. You know the place—three-quarters of a crooked mile of tiny stream flowing along the gully bottom. The soft banks are just right for the woodcock's bill—moist and full of earthworms and larvae—and there are thickets of alder, and thorn-apples and clumps of wild grapevines for the grouse. When the birds are in, it's one of the sweetest shooting runs in all New England.

"We loaded our guns and took stations, one of us on either bank, and I sent the dogs in. Ace was a bit slow at first, just as the trainer predicted he would be. He stopped to fool for a while with a mole he found in a tuft of grass, and I let him—it's bad business to hustle a young dog. Then he spent some time gazing off into the blue distances in rapt approval of the scenery and seemed none too well pleased to have his reverie interrupted.

"He didn't seem to take much interest in his work until after a while a big grouse got up under his nose in a thicket of snowberry bushes. Squint dropped it—one of those roaring, rising, right-quartering birds. It was the only bird we were to bag in that cover that morning, but we didn't know that then. The excitement seemed to galvanize Ace. Without stopping to retrieve Squint's bird, he tore out of that thicket and into another, flushing a woodcock out of range and paying no attention to my whistle.

"That was just the beginning. There ensued in that beautiful sunny gully a scene of such hellish, shameful disorder and wild confusion that I even now recall it with a shudder. Pepper, the cocker, caught the infection, or perhaps he thought that Ace's method was regarded as superior to his own close-working style and therefore was determined to show us that he was equally capable of applying these new bird-finding ideas. At any rate, after one puzzled look at me he, too, leaped into full stride, and away the pair of them went, yelping at the birds they flushed and scattering everything before them."

Bill John paused again.

"I don't need to tell you that I'm a patient man. Haven't I let Squint Norton brag to me by the hour about that mongrel of his without even telling him what I think of the egg-sucking, woodchuck-digging, rabbit-chasing hound that he claims is a bird dog? Why, I've seen that dog of his following an old Plymouth Rock hen around the yard all day long, and when she'd cluck he'd point. Kind of seemed to me that the dog lacked imagination or something. Kind of seemed to me—"

The Judge stopped him.

"Never mind Squint's dog and the hen, Bill John. We want to know what became of Ace."

"I was just coming to that," Bill John explained. "I was telling you that I'm a patient man, wasn't I? Well, I am. Don't I give up a whole day every year to go trout fishing with old George Walton and put up with his nonsense about dry flies when everyone knows wet ones are better? And don't I—well, I could go on like this all night, telling you of incidents to show that I'm a calm and reasonable sort of a man.

"I proved it that day, too. I used my whistle to call those two dogs in. I used my voice, too—low, moderate, friendly and firm, just as the dog trainers tell you to do. But they wouldn't heed. Anybody who knows bird dogs knows that the foolishest thing a man can do is to chase one of 'em that runs and won't come in to the gun when he's told to; so I didn't do it. After a while I did hurry along a trifle, thinking I might be able to get a shot at some of the grouse and timberdoodles that were boiling out way down the gully, but it didn't do any good. I did heave a few stones at Ace after a while, but, of course, I didn't hit him, damn him!

"I finally climbed the bank and set down on the grass. I was hot and tired and feeling pretty bad about the affair. My morning shooting was spoiled, of course, but what hurt me worse was Squint Norton's low humor.

"He came up and sat down beside me, and after a while he said: 'Well, Enoch was right at that. That dog did learn quick to keep ahead of you, didn't he?' Then he snickered.

"About then the dogs, having cleared out the cover to their satisfaction, came up and sat down and looked at us, the way dogs do. Ace was panting and grinning, and his hind leg was twitching like a mule's ear in fly time.

"I said, 'Squint, he knows how to retrieve, anyway.'

"To prove it, I took a loaded shotgun shell and threw it out into the grass and told Ace to fetch. He went out as pretty as any dog I ever saw at Fisher's Island. He found the cartridge, and then do you know what he did? He laid down right there and chewed it up and ate it—shot, wads, brass, paper, primer, powder and all! I'll be damned if he didn't! I sort of hoped it would kill him, but, of course, it didn't!"

Bill John put the new gun down and thoughtfully wiped his forehead. "Do you mind if I pour myself another?" he asked, and while he refreshed himself he brooded.

"I kept that dog for a whole year, and it aged me and kind of embittered me a little bit and made a cynic of me, too," he reflected sadly. "More than once during that time I'd have blown his confounded brains out if I hadn't so much money sunk in him. Once in a while, just to show me, he'd work perfectly for an hour or so, staying close to the gun, covering his ground well, dropping to shot and retrieving with style and precision that would have got us a cup if I could have depended on him to do it at a field trial."

"Help yourself to another snort," said the Judge, "and tell me what became of him."

"Well," said Bill John, "I was coming to that. I tried to sell him, and of course every man who showed any interest wanted to know about Ace's field manners. If I took him out to show, he'd behave like an untrained fumbling puppy and make me look like a fool.

"One day Henry Peabody came up from Albany to shoot with me. He didn't know anything about Ace and sort of liked his looks in spite of that leg. I took him up to the cover around Williamstown. You know the country, old orchards and abandoned farms—the best grouse cover in the world. Henry killed a bird right off, and Ace brought it to him as if he were bringing a boar's head into Westminster Abbey, or wherever it is that they eat those danged things. Then I dropped one, and I'll be darned if Ace didn't do the honors for me, too! His head was up, he stepped out high and stylish and when we took our birds from him there wasn't a ruffled feather on 'em. He knew how to retrieve, all right, just as Enoch said—when he wanted to do it.

" 'Bill John,' says Henry, 'that's a devil of a good dog you've got there. I don't even mind the game leg. He acts just like he might be the kind of a dog I've been looking for. Would you—ahem—would you consider naming me a price on him?'

" 'Well, Henry,' I told him, 'I hadn't thought of it. He's a young dog, and I've been sort of looking forward to many happy days afield with him finding grouse and woodcock for me. And then you know there's the thrill of watching a dog that knows how to retrieve. I sort of hate to give that up. Still, I suppose—I've got better than two hundred berries in him, but I presume if someone gave me three hundred I could get another spaniel, not so stylish, maybe, but one that would do me well enough.'

"Henry opened his mouth to speak. I knew then, and I know now what he was going to say. He was going to say, 'I'll give you three hundred for him.'

"But he didn't say it, and the reason he didn't say it was because just at that moment he made the best shot of his whole life. Henry's not so hot, you know, as a rule, but right then he rose for an instant from mediocrity to the heights of shooting genius, as someone has said, and made a shot that would have been a real credit to Captain Bogardus or that Britisher, Lord Gray, I think his name was, or to Abe Kleinman or Fred Gilbert—or even to me or you. It was a honey!

"To my notion, a grouse diving out of a treetop and curving off on a tangent is the hardest shot you ever get. In the first place, by the time you see him he's going so fast that you can't see him; and even if you can, he's changing his elevation so that you can't figure a lead on him.

"That's what this one did, and Henry, who never hit one like it before and never will again, tried a snap and centered that bird at a good thirty-five paces! Dead in the air it was, too, with a cloud of feathers floating above the spot where it hit the ground. It was as pretty a thing as ever I saw.

" 'Go fetch,' I told Ace, and out he went, high-headed and sure of himself, the very spit and image of perfection. He gathered the bird the way a mother lifts her first-born out of its crib and started back toward us. I tell you I felt grand right then. Halfway back he stopped on a little hummock and posed. It was beautiful.

"I let him stand there for a minute so Henry would get the effect, and then I motioned Ace to come on in. He didn't come. I spoke to him, and he didn't come. I whistled to him, and he didn't come. So, to avoid emphasizing the incident and thinking of what Henry had been about to say just before the bird flushed, I went out as casually as I could to meet Ace and take the bird. He let me get up to within ten feet of him, and then, by the Lord Harry, he gave me a devilish sort of look and away he went out of sight over the hill, and with him went Henry's bird. And with that bird went my three hundred.

"You know yourself how it is when you've made a cracking good shot—you want that particular bird more than any of the others that came more easily. It was so with Henry, and I didn't blame him much. He probably wanted to have that bird mounted. Here he'd just made the best shot of his life, and there was his bird being carried off by a mischievous dog.

"It was awful. Every now and then throughout the afternoon Ace would show up, poised on some crest maybe five hundred yards away, beautiful in a statuesque pose against the fading sky—the splendid picture of a shooting dog, with Henry's prize pa'tridge still in his mouth and his right hind leg twitching. Then he'd vanish again.

"Henry said, just before he left, and he was almost crying he was so mad: 'If I had a rifle, I'd shoot that dog and get my bird, and then I'd take his carcass and drag it and fling it through your bedroom window! And you fixin' t' sell him to me! You viper!'

"I don't know what Ace did with that grouse. He ate it probably. He didn't have it with him when he came yelling and scratching at the back door at midnight to be let in. Certainly I never saw it again."

The Judge persisted in the tone of a parent insisting that a sick child swallow the last drop of the loathsome stuff that will heal it.

"Well, what did become of Ace?"

Bill John's face brightened up a trifle.

"I'm coming to that," he said. "A month or two later a man from over in the valley came to see me. He wanted a pedigreed male springer to head his kennel. He was raising puppies for sale. I named a hundred dollars. He didn't say a word. Then I said seventy-five. Then I said fifty. Then he said, 'Twenty-five,' and I said 'Sold.'

"But when I went to get the danged rascal to put him in the man's crate, Ace dodged out of his kennel between my legs and ran into the orchard. It took me an hour of hard work to catch him and bring him back. I fell down once and tore my pants. But I got him.

" 'How is he on birds?' the old fellow wanted to know as we were loading Ace into his car.

" 'He's hell on 'em,' I told him.

" 'Well, I don't care nothin' pertickler about that in a stud dog,' said he. 'Don't care nothin' pertickler 'bout that hind laig of his'n, neither; tain't hereditary. But—'

"Just then Ace got loose again—he was as hard to hold as a young rhino—and headed for the orchard. I yelled and whistled, but he kept on going like he had something on his mind. He made a couple of casts and then went right to the place where I fell down. He stopped there and picked something up and started back with it in his mouth.

"His head was up, and he came in as prideful as a game rooster. He kept right on—right up to me, pretty as could be, and gave me what he had in his mouth. Well, sir, Judge, you'd never guess what it was. My wallet, with thirty-eight smackers in it, by jingo! Thirteen dollars of my own money and the twenty-five the old feller had just paid me for the dog. Must have lost it when I fell down."

"Bill John, I hate to press you, but where is Ace now?"

"At home, of course," said Bill John in tones of astonishment. "You didn't think I'd sell a good dog like that, did you? No, sir! I tell you what, gentlemen, when you get hold of a dog as smart as Ace, you'll do well to hang onto him."

THE JUDGE'S PROBLEM

It was an evening late in November. A raw and bitter wind buffeted the Captain when he emerged from his own comfortable domicile and made his way along the deserted street to the brick house where the Judge resided in bachelor luxury, attended by old Jason and his good wife, Ellen.

Jason now opened the door for the visitor, greeted him in friendly fashion and relieved him of his old battered trench coat.

"You'll find him in the big room," said he, "listenin' to the radio feller talkin' about what that Mooselini an' that German are up to. Madder'n a wet tomcat, too. Glad ye come. If ye hadn't he'd set an' listen an' then set an' cuss the whole endurin' evenin'."

The caller found the Judge hunched forward on the edge of his easy chair, clenched fists on his knees and hot sparks of rage blazing in his normally gentle eyes. He was manifesting his opinion of current European affairs with grunts, snortings and an occasional open-throated bellow of rage.

"The damned rascals!" he exclaimed. "Somebody ought to—"

"Hush! Hush!" his friend adjured him as one would talk to a petulant child. "Don't excite yourself! Cussing and swearing like that! Hard words won't skin Mr. Mussolini's nose."

"Look here!" snorted the exasperated jurist above the pessimistic clipped chatter of the radio, "if you ain't anything better to do than preach you can go back where you came from!"

"All right," was the reply, "I'll go, and I'll take my little piece of news back with me."

"What news? Will you quit acting like a fool and sit down somewhere?"

"Shooting news," said the other. "I thought since you did no work at all in October you might consider depriving the State of your invaluable services for another week. You won't be missed. Had another letter from Johnny Reb about that shooting ground he's located on Albemarle Sound. Wants us to come down. We could take my car. He talks of jacksnipe, ducks, geese, quail and turkeys."

The Judge moaned dolefully and shook his grizzled head. He had entirely forgotten all dictators and their sins.

"Absolutely out of the question," he declared. "Can't possibly do it. Too much work."

His friend continued as if he had not heard.

"Johnny tells about jump shooting ducks from a skiff on a wooded creek he's got down there. Mallards, bluebills and pintails, he says."

"Jump shooting, huh? Well, well! Hum! Now there's a bare possibility that I might put that Crandall matter over for a week. Been hanging fire for six years so I guess it can wait six or seven more days. When did you have it in mind to start?"

The Captain smiled. "Friday morning," he said.

Winter was riding on the mountaintops that morning as the two friends swept along the beautiful valley of the Battenkill and picked up the proud spire of the Bennington Battle Monument against the low hills in the background. Snow lay thick upon the crests and higher slopes and the air was keen and sharp. It dusted with white the nearer fields where, on a July day, men of their own blood and bone had charged the blazing lines of the best regiments of Europe to capture the four brass cannon still to be seen on the wide portico of the State House. But there was now none of the roar of battle and thrashing of drums. A few hardy mergansers swam quietly in the dark waters of the famous trout brook, slanting their slender heads below the surface as they fed.

The Judge shivered, "Gosh! It makes me squirm just to watch 'em!"

"It'll be warmer after we cross the Berkshires, and warmer still when we drop down the slope beyond the Hudson into Pennsylvania," remarked his companion. "We're heading back into warm weather at the rate of a week every three-hundred miles."

That proved to be an accurate estimate, and when after two days on the road the pair drove across a plank bridge over a narrow salt-water estuary to find themselves on the quiet main street of Tarford, in the State of North Carolina, the water was reminiscent of early October in their own home. It was twilight when they arrived and the windows of the big house sent out welcoming beams to the travelers. These glowing invitations to enter and be at home were vociferously endorsed by their tall, black-haired host as he came striding out to greet them.

"Get out o' there and come inside," said he, seizing the Judge and dragging him from his seat.

"Let go of me, you reptile," roared the jurist, delighted to see this good friend again. Then he paused to sniff the breeze like an old bird dog in strange cover. "Hum! Smells o' pine tar, bourbon, tobacco, salt water and something good in an oven somewhere."

Johnny laughed.

"What a nose! There are six fat peanut-fed greenheads in the oven waiting for you. Got 'em on the creek yesterday. Lots more where they came from, and more dropping in every night. We ought to have fine shooting."

Later in the evening Johnny asked the question common to all gun lovers on such occasions.

"What guns did you bring?"

The Judge was strictly a one-gun man. His double hammer twelve-bore had seen at least fifty years of honest service but had lost none of the velvety smoothness of locks and action. He took the weapon from its case, the lamplight striking deep gleams from the dark wood and satiny steel as the old sportsman handled it. But the Captain, with a cabinet full of weapons, was always contriving for yet one more, and obvious circumstance that he couldn't possibly use them all detracted nothing from his enjoyment. Now he displayed a long slender twenty-bore double. Its graceful lines would have caught the eye of any connoisseur even without the other evidences of fine workmanship.

"It doesn't look it," said he, "but this is a duck gun—a real Magnum twenty. The barrels are overbored a hair to get the most out of a full ounce of shot. I drove two hundred miles and spent the best part of a day at the shop watching 'em pattern these barrels. I'm a fool, I suppose," he added, handing the weapon to Johnny.

"Not this time, I'd say," their host drawled. "A man could shoot the head off a pin with this. I'd like to have the mate to it. We'll see how she does tomorrow."

Then he explained the reason why all manner of game found the region so much to its liking.

"It's the peanuts. This place is plumb in the middle of the greatest peanut-growing country on earth. You'll see field after field of 'em tomorrow. They're shipped out by the boatload, but tons and tons of them are left in the fields and the hogs turned out on 'em. The ducks come in off the Sound and the turkeys and squirrels come out of the timber to get their share. It's a very satisfactory arrangement," he concluded.

"I can well believe it after devouring that mallard Mrs. Johnny set before me," said the Judge.

"We're going to have trouble keeping the old cuss out in the field away from the fleshpots," remarked the Captain.

"Don't worry," was the rejoinder, "You'll never need call me twice to go jumping ducks. What size shot do we need, Johnny?"

"I like 7's," replied the tall sportsman, "they're big enough for a turkey if you hold for his head and neck, and they're small enough for pa'tridges and just right for 40-yard ducks. Let's go to bed."

"I declare," remarked the mountain-bred Judge somewhat grudgingly the next morning, "this is a pretty country. It's restful in a way to let your eye kind of run along over these fields and woods without always slamming up against the side of a hill somewhere."

The mist from the Sound was lifting, and as the trio drove slowly down a rutted dirt road, they looked out upon flat fields on either hand. Some of these were covered with the gray rubbish of peanut vines, while in others stood broken ranks of cornstalks, ragged and sere. Beyond the nearer fields lay great belts of dark pine woods and noble reaches of hickory, birch, persimmon and gum, glowing with autumnal colors more subdued in tone than those that a month earlier had mantled the hills in faraway Vermont.

"It looks like a good game country, all right," remarked the Captain. "Anybody can see that. Look how the plantings are broken up with the timber and those little brushy runs and thickets."

As proof of his judgment a flock of mallards rose from among the vines ahead and went slanting away over the treetops.

"They're going into the creek," said Johnny, halting the car. He pointed to a dim track that led away across the field toward a belt of trees.

"The creek's just yonder. It widens out into a little pond right there, and I've a blind at this end of it. You can't miss it. There's half a dozen blocks in the blind. If you'll take the blind," addressing the Captain, "you'll find work for that twenty-bore while I'll go on with His Honor to the head of the creek. I've a skiff there, and I'll paddle him down and let him do some of that jump shooting he's so crazy about."

They drove away as the Captain shouldered the long-barreled double and strode off across the fields. The path led him through a band of heavy timber, where squirrels scampered into the treetops, and came out upon the bank of a narrow stretch of open water from which half a hundred ducks rose as he appeared. He found the blind, a well-brushed affair built upon the great trunks of two gum trees that had succumbed to the winds of another year and now lay prostrate in the shallow water.

"Looks mighty good," he thought as he tossed out the wooden decoys, loaded the long gun and found a seat on an empty pine box. The timber crowded close on all sides but the one where the waters of the creek entered the great bay. Except for the squall of the squirrels and the whistling of the jays ransacking the lofty storehouses of the beeches, the place rested in utter silence. There was no sound of distant train or car, no stroke of axe or shout of teamster to disturb this southern wilderness. The gunner lighted a cigarette and prepared himself to enjoy every moment in this solitude of woods and water. From somewhere behind the screen of the buttonbrush a mallard gave a throaty quack and followed it with its characteristic chuckle, and presently three gorgeous green-headed drakes swam silently out from among the tangled stems behind the blind. With provoking slowness they moved nearer the blind, stopping to preen their bright plumage or to dally interminably over a morsel of mast fallen from the branches overhead. At last they were within long range, and then while the gunner waited tensely they drew slowly nearer still. At thirty paces the Captain slipped the safety and rose. The ounce of shot, hard-driven from the first barrel, caught one of the drakes at the top of his leap, and that from the second centered fairly on another as it swung away. The survivor disappeared over the woods, loosing an occasional discomfited protest at such disastrous goings on, while the gunner retrieved his birds, shook the water from their glossy jackets and laid them in the blind. They were fat enough to burst, with crops stuffed tight with raw peanut kernels.

The sound of a distant shot apprised the Captain that his companions were afloat somewhere along the creek. A pair of pintails appeared flying low to the treetops, They spied the stool and after several graceful swift casts came over the decoys flying so close together that the first barrel dropped both birds like stones.

"This looks like one of those days when we really understand each other," the fowler addressed his gun as he reloaded. "If we keep this up, we'll have to quit soon, which I don't want to do. I like it here, even if I never kill a duck."

And so, presently, he let a small flock of bluebills alight among the decoys unmolested.

"Can't compare with a mallard or a pintail for eating purposes," thought the sportsman, "and besides, I've already had my share o' your family up on Lake Champlain. So you fellows just set around and make yourselves comfortable and see if you can't toll another greenhead in for me."

Precisely that event occurred, when a lone drake appeared after a double shot back in the creek and sat himself down companionably among the unsuspecting bluebills.

He rose, however, when the man did, and with such velocity that the first charge, too confidently delivered, went a foot beneath him and the second as far above his startled head. The bluebills joined the rout, which the gunner watched until the birds were out of sight. Then he sighed.

"It always happens that way," he philosophized. "I could have hit him with a rock. Well, it just goes to show that I ain't quite perfect."

Meanwhile the Judge with his old gun across his knees was in such agreeable circumstances that he found himself wishing the creek were four times its actual length. Almost currentless, it wound in and out under the trees. At times as they pursued their silent way the channel widened to fifty paces, then closed again until the branches of the trees on opposite banks interlaced overhead.

Three fat mallards lay in the bow of the skiff that the willing host sent along with slow strokes of a paddle, surprising the fowl dozing in the secluded spots so that they leaped up in spattering alarm as the nose of the skiff, with the pudgy figure of the Judge riding it, drifted past.

Occasionally the two friends conversed in low tones, and the topic was the wild turkey. The Judge had never slain one of these majestic birds and was convinced that he never would do so.

"I could get you a shot, I think, if you're willing to give a day to it."
Johnny said. "There's a flock using right in this bottom."

The Judge sighed. "That's always the trouble. Whenever I've been in turkey country the quail or the ducks have been so good that I hated to lose a
whole day for a doubtful chance at a turkey. I guess I haven't much will
power. I know I wouldn't want to trade this kind of shooting for any other
kind, no matter what."

At intervals they heard the sharp reports of their friend's long twenty and
knew that he was having his share of sport.

Then, as they quietly rounded a bend of the stream a pair of mallards
leaped from the right-hand shore under a great pine that overshadowed the
water. The Judge fired twice, dropping both birds neatly in midstream.

"Well done," said Johnny, as he paddled to retrieve the game.

"Think so myself," remarked the jurist complacently as he reloaded.

He was about to extend his self-congratulatory remarks when a terrific explosion shook the top of the pine over their heads. Bark, twigs and needles
showered down as a great dark form fought clear of the boughs and launched
itself into the air.

"Turkey! Turkey!" yelled Johnny.

The old sportsman would have felt no greater panic and dismay if the bird
had been a hostile pursuit plane with its guns spitting, but he recovered control and brought his muzzles smoothly past the gigantic body, past the ser-
pentine neck and head. The turkey collapsed, plunging into the water with a
mighty smack and so close to the skiff that a fountain of spray drenched the
pair.

"And there's your turkey, Judge! A gobbler, and a big one, too. He'll go
twenty pounds or more, I'll gamble. What a chance that was! I reckon it's
proper for me to repeat 'Turkeys are where you find 'em.' "

The old sportsman hauled the great bird from the water with hands that
shook.

"Now," said he, "you take the gun and I'll paddle. I'm through shooting
for the day. Don't want to spoil it. Besides," he added, "if I sit in the bow I
won't be able to feast my eyes on my gobbler."

Then such a look of painful anxiety and dismay came over the old sportsman's face that Johnny exclaimed:

"What's the matter, Judge?"

"Johnny, my boy, I perceive that when with faultless aim I busted this bird
I projected myself into a dismal quandary, indeed. I must now decide
whether to have this noble fowl mounted and preserved, so that people can
come and look at him and reflect upon my incomparable skill, or to have him
cooked and eat most of him myself." He sighed heavily as he picked up the
paddle.

THE
LAST
DAY

◆━━◆

CAPTAIN MICHAEL U. GANNON, F.A., U.S.A.
SEPTEMBER 15, 1895—NOVEMBER 20, 1939

In his time Old Joe Junius was regarded as being by long odds the most soiled and slovenly inhabitant of Tranquillity Township. Happily, the highly unsanitary old pauper, now gone these many years to reap his dubious reward, has no part in this narrative other than this mention of the curious circumstance that one of the clearest, cleanest and coldest of the thousands of springs of the region bears the ancient reprobate's name. The "Old Joe Junius Spring" bubbles out from the base of a limestone ridge beside the turnpike a hundred paces from the point where the road crosses Hessian Bowl Hill into the valley below.

The hilltop is a favorite spot with the Captain and those friends who come to visit him. Deer are frequently seen there crossing to and fro between the woods and the old fields and tangled, abandoned orchards along Mud Brook. It is a fox runway, too, and well known to Bill Paraday and his companions of the Order of the Solitary Hound. Once at this spot the Captain had a glimpse of a bay lynx glaring with baleful yellow eyes from underneath a clump of pines in the pasture. The animal's brief surveillance was so charged with wild malevolence and hatred that the man felt a prickling at the back of his neck that persisted for some minutes after the grinning, tufted-eared apparition had vanished. Here it was that the Captain had brought down his first grouse, stopped dead in full flight by a charge of shot from a single-barreled Remington. In the seasons that had come and gone since that memorable event the adjacent covers had yielded many scores of 'cock and grouse into the pockets of his shooting jacket. Thus it is that the place always reminds him of great days past, even while it gives assurance of others yet to come. Down there where the narrow brush-grown gully comes down to the brook is the scene of a rare "double" on grouse—done, as he remembers well, with a favorite twenty-bore Greener—and just beyond, where an old log lies in a clump of snowball bushes, four woodcock had, on another occasion, sprung all together. Yonder, by the brook, Mort had clipped down a high-flying cock pheasant a year ago, a beautiful shot and a beautiful bird seen for that single instant, high up over the vine-covered elms in the October sunshine. There are recollections of these episodes and many more besides to persuade our friend to pause on the hilltop whenever he passes that way, especially if the hour is that of twilight and he feels, as one may feel at such times, some cast of melancholy occasioned by the splendor of the day just dying behind the far ramparts of the Adirondacks.

It is Mort's contention, well tested and proved, that the icy water from Old Joe Junius' Spring blends more agreeably with a dram of good Scotch than any drawn from other fountains. That was one reason, at least, why on an October evening in the year 1938, after a long day beside the Marsh and in the Grapevine Cover, the four of them, the Dark-Haired Lady herself, Mike, Mort and the Captain, stopped briefly at the Spring to dip up water in a tin bucket. Having done so they drove on the short distance to the crest of the hill.

There they stopped, and all got slowly out of the car. No word was spoken while Mort found the cups, into each of which the Captain then measured a noble charge of the smoky fluid of the Hebrides. To that Mike added modest measures of spring water and all sat down side by side and cup in hand on the running board facing the west where the dome of Black Mountain stood dark against a wide curtain of luminous emerald atmosphere. They were comfortably weary, for the Grapevine is three miles long and half as wide. They had covered it yard by yard that day with something to spare. A neat row of woodcock and grouse rested on the luggage shelf of the car, together with a single black duck shot that morning along the shore of the marsh. But for all these evidences of a day well spent the friends were sharing a mood of melancholy quite at variance with their normal habit.

Throughout the day, and especially at lunchtime when they had broiled sausages and made coffee over an open fire, there had been no lack of sprightly conversation, but as the afternoon wore on, it had fallen away to occasional desultory comment and finally ceased. They sat now in silence, watching the afterglow flush and fade and listening to the peaceful evening sounds of the countryside. The reason for their subdued and sober spirits lay in the knowledge that in the morning Mort and Mike would pack their shooting gear and say good-by to their friends at Tranquillity.

Finally the Captain repeated a futile remark that he had uttered a dozen times already.

"Wish you boys weren't leaving so early. The better part of the season is still ahead of us. There'll be four woodcock for every one we've flushed today, and with the leaves off you'll see twice as many grouse."

The others sighed, muttered disconsolately and shook their heads. There would be no use in going over that again. Their leaves were up and could not be extended.

Then Mike turned slightly so that he could look straight into their faces.

"I'll never be able to tell you what this has meant to me—you having me up here to share your greatest holiday. But for you, I'd never have known that there was a spot on earth so beautiful as this, and I've never known people so kind and generous." He paused. "I want you to know that," he added.

"Well, anyhow," the Dark-Haired Lady remarked, forcing a note of cheerfulness, "it's not as bad as it might be. This isn't your last visit, Mike, my lad. It's only the end of your first, and we'll have you back next season to do it all over again."

Mike shook his head.

"Not next year," he reminded them, "I'm detailed for 'Command and Staff' at Leavenworth next September—but the year after that, in 1940, on October the eighth, at six o'clock in the evening, if you wish it, I'll meet the three of you right at this very spot and we'll drink a cup to auld lang syne and another to the days ahead that we'll spend together in the Grapevine and the Long Covers and on the Marsh and the Slough."

"We'll be here," agreed the others, and one added—"And see to it that you don't fail us. It's a rendezvous, brother."

"And I'll be here then, and waiting for you surely," said Mike, using the quaint old Irish way of speech as he sometimes did when much moved. "If—" He paused and did not continue the thought, whatever it was. Perhaps it seemed to him not worth the sound of the spoken words, or perhaps he stopped because his ear had caught just then a faint foreboding message, a somber, ghostly counsel bidding him to look well upon this scene and beware of promises. He dropped his hand on the Captain's knee and let his gaze follow the faint sheen of the Turnpike where it crossed the Hessian Bowl Brook underneath the elms and ascended the low hill opposite. At that point he lost the trace, and though he strained his eyes to pierce the gloom he could not recover it, for the shades of the coming night were now so thickly gathered that the traveler could no longer see whither the old road led—nor how far.

TRANQUILLITY
REGAINED

A
YANKEE
WELCOME

A considerable number of their old friends have recently expressed a flattering curiosity concerning the whereabouts and activities of Uncle Bill Paraday, the Judge, the Dark-Haired Lady, the Captain and other more-or-less worthy persons residing in Tranquillity Township. That hamlet, with its appurtenances, grants and accretions lies, as the reader may recall, on the southeastern side of Lake Champlain, in the State of Vermont. General Lord John Burgoyne wrote home to England, following two or three smoky encounters with the inhabitants of the region, to tell the ministers of Britain that "these people are the most stubborn and rebellious in the land."

And so they are, indeed, if one comes against them with bayonets, or with the more subtle and dangerous devices of politics.

But General Lord Johnny came not as the Captain came, when, after long years spent in alien places, he was finally convinced that come weal or woe it was high time for him to return to the hills and fields of his ancestors and to re-establish himself and his dark-haired consort among their old friends and neighbors. In the years past he had been able to ameliorate his discontentment by seasonal migrations, but there came a time when these no longer sufficed.

Had the reader, on a bright afternoon of a June day, not so long ago, been one of those who occupied the battered, but comfortable armchairs which adorn the porch of Tranquillity Tavern, he might have observed our lean and graying friend in the act of dismounting, bag and baggage, gun cases and rod cases being in a noticeable majority over other items, from a public conveyance. This vehicle, with occasional lapses, fetches its passengers from the old village of Skenesboro, just over the border in York State, to release them among the hamlets in the hills. Here they may breathe the air of freedom and mingle agreeably with the descendants of those stubborn and rebellious people who gave General Johnny and his mercenaries a fiery welcome away back in the long ago.

The onlooker probably would have noticed Uncle Bill Paraday, veteran of Stannard's Brigade and Gettysburg, rising from his chair with enviable alacrity considering the number of his years, to greet the traveler, and unless he had been stone deaf he would certainly have heard the greeting, for it was given with the full-throated clarion voice that the old soldier had once employed in battle and now reserved for notable occasions, either of great wrath or great joy.

Everyone along Main Street heard the bellow and grinned or smiled according to the listener's sex and idea of decorum. The small boys started to run.

Cam Vaughn down at the foot of the hill, engaged in welding a few hundred additional miles of service into Tim Sheldrick's old truck, heard it. He was unable to catch the words.

"That was Uncle Bill," Tim announced judiciously, as if inviting attention to a violent but familiar manifestation of nature. "He's mad er glad, an' I don't know which, but I'll bet ye he's run onto one o' them New Dealers, er else somebody who ain't one an' is a friend o' his'n."

Cam listened a moment.

"Friend, I guess," said he. "Uncle Bill only fired one volley."

Cam was right. The explosion was benign.

"Garret-all-Connecticut! Ef you ain't him, you're so uncommonly favored like him that there couldn't nobody tell the di'ffunce! Haow be ye, an' haow's your womern folks? Hain't deevorced her, hev ye? Don't s'pose ye hev, fer ye hev *some* sense, leastways you uster hev some. Haow long ye goin' to stay this time?"

His knotty old paw was firmly in the Captain's grip, and his keen blue eyes looked straight into the gray ones above him.

"No, I haven't divorced her, Uncle Bill. Moreover, I don't believe I shall. She'll be along in a week or two. How's Aunt Candace?"

"Jest ez spry ez a chickadee. That womern hain't aged a mite in forty years." The old gentleman released a dry chuckle.

"I swow," he continued, "after your toilsome journey, ye must be ez dry ez a cork laig! An' so be I. Mister Perkins, here, hez some rum that don't need no further waterin' to make it swallerable. Come along an' I'll git ye some on it."

The pair thereupon retired to the cool gloom of the taproom. Presently, refreshment was set before them and Uncle Bill repeated his inquiry.

"Haow long c'n ye stay this time?" he asked.

The Captain looked at his friend, and there was a gleam of exaltation in his eye.

"Forever, Uncle Bill," said he, "Forever."

"Well," said Uncle Bill mildly, after a thoughtful pause. "Suits me, an' I rather guess won't nobody 'round here object to it, neither."

In all outward, visible characteristics, the village showed little change from its normal peacetime appearance. On the green, opposite the Bank, stood the Honor Roll, and the Captain remarked to Uncle Bill that it was a long one, indeed, for a community so small.

"Don't know where in tunket they all come from," the old soldier agreed, "but there hain't sca'cely a haouse in the hull taown that hain't got any-where's from one to six stars on its winder. Some on 'em air gold stars," he added, thoughtfully, remembering the days of his youth when he and his friends had "formed fours" on that same green and marched away to war.

He sighed, but there was a glint of battle in his eyes. "Cap'n, it don't seem right to send the youngsters off to fight, an' leave us old, useless cusses here to hum. First thing, the younguns don't know haow, an' we do. 'Spose'n we be a mite along in years an' mebbe showin' a tech o' rheumatics naow an' agin. We c'n shoot, can't we? An' if we c'n *shoot* an' can't *run* ain't we better for soldiers than fellers than c'n run, but can't shoot?

"By Judast Priest! It wan't the old V'mont Brigade that done the runnin' at Cedar Crik, if I recollect the way things wuz that day."

Uncle Bill's memories of martial glory were interrupted at this point by the entrance of the Judge, who instantly raised his voice to express his disapproval of such goings on even while he shook his friend by the shoulders until the Captain's teeth rattled.

"Heard you'd come," he bawled, "and I knew I'd find you here in the grog shop carousing with sottish companions. How long can you stay? Got your trout tackle, I hope. I took four beauties on a Evening Dun in the Sawmill Pool, and——"

"Sit down," ordered the Captain, "and do a little carousing yourself, and," he added glancing at other patrons who were observing the reunion with interest and approval, "don't give away any more military secrets."

"I didn't," said the Judge, lowering his voice and his stocky form simultaneously, "I *said* Evening Dun but I *used* a Ginger Quill."

"I might have known it, you deceitful old reprobate," remarked his grinning friend. "Darned if you ain't a sight for sore eyes, even though you speak with a forked tongue and the truth is not often in you. Here comes the grog."

" 'Tain't sca'cely wuth foolin' with," Uncle Bill interjected in tones loud enough to reach the proprietor's ears.

" 'Tain't got no more buzz to it than Aunt Sukey's razbarry shrub."

"Why, Uncle Bill! Haow c'n you say sech a thing?" exclaimed the badg-ered host. "It's the best Jamaicy, says so right on the bottle!"

"Then I pity the poor savages that lives in Jamaicy," growled Uncle Bill, well pleased with himself.

The Captain laughed aloud, savoring the old familiar homely badinage which, with all its simplicity, had for him, at least, values not always to be found in more sophisticated gatherings.

He addressed the Judge.

"Your Honor, behold, I bring you tidings of great joy. I am a free man. I have escaped the thralls of official responsibility. I have eschewed greed, ambition and the lust for power and preference. I have come home to stay until removed by force, craft or the hand of Providence. I am going to write a book—maybe two books—but I have no intention of allowing my labors on these masterpieces to interfere with a reasonable amount of outdoor recreation. That will include bullhead fishing, frog hunting, the slaughter of wildfowl, timberdoodles, pa'tridges, 'coons, squirrels, bear and deer. I own two cases of prewar twenty-bore shotshells, 7½'s and 10's, and one of sixteens charged with an ounce of Number 6 shot. I also intend to spend considerable time late in the evenings sitting on a log with you and the Doctor listening to your discourse and gazing upon the glory that is Champlain."

"Glory be," remarked the Judge fervently. His mind went running wistfully back to the days before their comradeship had suffered interruption.

"But you're going to be disappointed in the Doctor," he added.

"What about him?" his friend inquired with some alarm.

"The Doctor," said the Judge gravely, "is practicing medicine and surgery with a devotion that's nothing short of being heroic. I mean it. You see, both of the young M.D.'s went into the Army and Doc, who isn't quite as young as he was when he finished his interne stint, took over. He does a terrible lot of cussing, damning and scolding, but he does it, night and day. No one has died who could be saved, and every newborn infant for twenty miles round about, no matter where it arrived, or when, no matter, either, whether it rained, snowed, flooded or blazed, has been properly received into the world and launched upon its career with a sound, professional slap on its glowing bottom.

"If you can imagine an Angel of Mercy who would rather hunt 'coons than do anything else, and who smokes cigarettes and swears like a mule-skinner, one who has no visible wings, but who will, nevertheless, sit up all night long to be on hand for a crisis, or to make sure that some poor soul has no painful difficulty at the turnstile when the time comes—that, my boy, is our friend, the Doctor. I say, God bless him."

The old sportsman's eyes were a trifle moist as he finished.

"Me, too," said Uncle Bill. "An' do ye know, Jedge, the folks appreciate him, I do believe. They don't call him 'less they're reelly sick. Mebbe they dassent, but it kind o' looks 's if they're lookin' aout fer Doc jest ez he's lookin' aout fer them."

Meanwhile, word had gone around of the wanderer's return and one by one other old friends and cronies came in to give him greeting and to replace at Mister Perkins' limpid fount the moisture previously distilled from their carnal clay by labor and the sunshine. As the number of these well-wishers mounted it was accompanied by a rising tempo of coins rattling into the till, and the host's habitual cast of melancholy changed to one indicative of a happier mood.

Mister Perkins' metamorphosis and the cause of it were not lost on Uncle Bill.

"Look at the old cuss!" he muttered. "By the Lord Harry, he's tryin' to laugh, ain't he, an' it must be a consid'able effort, seein' he hain't had no practice at it to speak of since that Yorker from Troy give him a counterfeit twenty-dollar bill to pay for his room and board forty years ago. That quenched, ye might say, a j'yful an' a dauntless sperit."

He rose and picked up his hat.

"I must be a-kitin'," he announced, observing the leveled lances of sunlight striking though the maples outside.

His friends rose with him and, having paid the modest score and made their farewells to the assemblage, followed Uncle Bill to the door. They were followed in turn by the reproachful gaze of Mister Perkins, who immediately upon their departure fell again into his habitual atmosphere of gloom and disillusionment.

An hour later, having in the meantime hunted down the busy Doctor and received his heartfelt blessing, the two cronies were perched on a favorite log on the historic crest of Hessian Bowl Hill. The sun had vanished, as Earth spun in majesty on her eternal round. In the west long slashes of gold and crimson swept upward to the zenith but presently, while the two men watched, these last gallant guidons of the passing day lost their separate vigor and brillance and were peacefully dissolved into fading panels of green and azure above the mountains.

Finally all light was gone save that from the blossoming stars.

The Judge stirred from his reverie.

"My boy," said he, "welcome home. Things are to be with us as once they were."

And that wistful prophecy turned out to be almost true.

THE MORNING OF THE FIRST DAY

On the morning of the day following that of his return, the Captain awakened at an early hour, but he lay quietly for some minutes while gazing out the open windows toward the South Orchard and the well-remembered hump of Rock Pasture beyond. There, on one unforgettable occasion, armed with a beautiful double-barreled shotgun newly come from England, he had gone straight on a limit bag of grouse and woodcock among the pines and birches. Though highly improbable, a thing like that *could* happen again, he thought. Something moved in the light ground mist that enveloped the orchard and he saw that four graceful deer which had breakfasted there were now enjoying an exuberant frolic before retiring for the day to the wooded hill.

The Captain thought it a happy omen. A great sense of peace and well being flooded him as he realized all over again that he was free at last of the strictures, the noise and the all-pervading rush and shock of city life; free to awaken each morning to look out upon these old hills and fields clothed in the green of summer, the glory of autumn, or wearing the gleaming mantle of winter; free to wander whither he would and to revisit the scenes of old triumphs accomplished with rod, gun or rifle, and of defeats no less thrilling, at least in retrospect. He acknowledged a profound sense of gratitude to the Providence that had permitted this return to the place of his youth. More than ever, it was an island of peace in a tumultuous sea, a spot to be made forever secure from the shoutings and desperate strivings of a warring world. From this very room young men had gone forth to make this peace inviolable. The Captain thought of these boys one by one, and name by name, and thanked them in his heart.

Sympathetic persons in high places had earlier assured our friend of their conviction that he was precisely as tough and as capable of enduring hardship as he had been twenty-odd years ago, but there was, they said, the troublesome matter of regulations very difficult to get around. In due time the Captain came to the reluctant conclusion that he was in the way of becoming a pest and a nuisance to the War Department, and thereupon he withdrew with all the dignity at his disposal to assume responsibilities less exciting than those which fall to the lot of youth in wartime.

Having now concluded what were, for him, his morning devotionals, he rose and extracted a well-faded khaki shirt and a pair of trousers from his baggage, donned them, and then drew on an old pair of field shoes. His sense of well being increased as he put the more formal attire of city life away in a closet.

"Stay there, damn you," said he, "and if I never have to wear you again it will be too soon!"

Then he marched down to breakfast.

Someone inquired pleasantly concerning his plans for the day.

"Ma'am, I have a full schedule. I've got to get up on the hill to see how the young pa'tridges are coming along and then down to the marsh to investigate the young ducks. If I can find the skiff I might get you a mess of frog's legs for supper in exchange for the lunch you're going to put up for me. Anybody want to come along?"

A favorite nephew showed signs of being deeply interested in the project and presently the two of them set forth, armed and victualed.

Soon beneath their climbing feet the fields and orchards fell away below. From the crest of the great hill, when they had reached it and paused to look back, the widest field appeared no larger than a pocket handkerchief, acres were reduced to inches, and they who toiled there under the clear June skies were shrunken to the stature of midgets. In the orchard small explosions of vapor showed where the powerful spray pump carried on its endless warfare against the hordes of hostile insects, but to the watchers on the hill came only faintly the sound of the clatter of the engine and the voices of its masters.

"That's what I ought to be doing," remarked the Nephew with the half-guilty satisfaction of the idler observing the industry of his more diligent fellows, "but Dad told me to come along with you, an' I guess one day won't make much difference, will it?"

The older man smiled.

"It'll make a difference to me, my lad, having you with me," his glance resting in affectionate approval on the sturdy figure of the boy. "If I get tired you can carry my rifle and the bullfrogs. And that reminds me of a time when you were a kid and I took you perch fishing.

"You wanted to carry the string of perch home, to show your mother what a buster you were, but after a mile or so you sort of petered out, and I offered to carry the fish.

" 'Nope,' says you, 'I kin carry the fish all right if you kin carry me!' And that was the way we did it."

They crossed the hill and were descending the farther slope when their soft-footed silence was rewarded by one of the sights usually denied by Mother Nature to noisier travelers.

In a small clearing, green with clover, an old she-woodchuck and her four youngsters were enjoying the sunshine. The old woodchuck was busily feeding while the little ones wrestled and rolled like kittens, all unsuspecting of the nearness of danger. The two watchers let the play go on for some minutes and then the Captain raised his rifle.

At the shot the boy saw a puff of rock dust spurt from a stone a yard or two away from the playfellows. The tiny bullet whined away into the distance while the frantic mother hustled her young into the burrow beneath a stump, where she turned and set herself defiantly to fight a rear guard action, clashing her tusks and whistling savagely until her family was safe inside the fortress, when she, too, disappeared.

"That'll teach the old girl a lesson, I hope," said the rifleman. "Living way back in here has made her careless. Someone mean enough, or dumb enough, might come along and massacre the whole kit an' caboodle of 'em, which would be foolish, seeing that they're in their own garden and not ours, and that a dead woodchuck isn't half as interesting to watch as a live one."

"Heck, Uncle!" exclaimed the Nephew. "You pretty nearly fooled me as much as you did the woodchuck! I thought you were goin' to plug her. She still thinks so, too! Listen to her cussing you down in there—an' you the only human being, prob'ly, that's ever done her a good turn!"

After performing this thankless service, the pair went on and came soon to a region well known to both of them as Sam's Swamp. The swamp itself was small, a shallow depression scooped from the lower hillside in the dim ages by the tail of a wandering glacier. Throughout the centuries Nature had labored diligently and precisely with particles of soil brought from here and there, with seeds and sunshine, with growth and decay and with growth again to make Sam's Swamp a fit place for pa'tridges, woodcock, deer and 'coons. A clear stream meandered silently through the thickets of alders and birches.

Beyond the damp margin to the west stood an army of noble beeches, their roots and foliage mingling with those of the neighboring hickories and the maples in a common quest for the two indispensables, moisture and sunlight.

On the opposite side the irregular terrain was covered with thickets of birch, pine, hazel and wild apple trees, and threaded by worn cattle paths.

Late in April if one went quietly and found a moss-covered seat in this wild amphitheater he would not need to wait long before the throb of the drums of the grouse came to his ear, and, if he were expert, he might catch a glimpse of Sir Ruffs himself striding to and fro on his drumming log, a ruffling gallant, sans sword, but wearing a cloak far handsomer than Romeo's. Still earlier in the season, while scarves of snow yet shone with ghostly radiance in sheltered places, the observer could have seen in the twilight the curious mating flight of the woodcock and he might have listened to the 'cock's croaking serenade, which is not as tuneful to the human ear as apparently it is to that of his shy sweetheart.

In other years the Captain had often come to spy upon these innocent woodland ardors, but the time of ecstasy had by now changed to that of domestic anxiety and care. Today he and his companion hoped to find evidence that these earlier romances had been abundantly blessed.

Suddenly there was a muffled, menacing sound at the side of the path. It was a sound as full of deadly warning as the buzz of a rattlesnake, and both men recoiled involuntarily from the savage charge of a creature the size of a bantam hen.

Just at the moment when it seemed certain that the intruders would be annihilated the little hen checked her charge and changed her tactics. Well she knew that in that first instant, her brood had vanished, and that each chick of them was now frozen immobile in a spot where the color of its downy coat blended perfectly with that of the dead leaves and grasses.

Now the brave little hen became a pitiful thing indeed. Her plight should have gentled the most lustful heart, for her right wing appeared to have been broken and she was obviously suffering from serious internal injuries. Merely the putting forth of an enemy hand or a paw while she groveled there helplessly and her capture would be sure, or so it seemed.

"See if you can grab her, feller," instructed the Captain. "I'll stay here until you come back."

The Nephew laid down his rifle and made a lightning-like snatch, but the bird, convulsed by the agony of her grievous wounds, was still an inch or two beyond his fingers. He tried again and with a similar result. The little hen actually seemed to want to be caught and to have her misery ended once and for all, but the very throes of distress defeated her by always twitching her bruised body from beneath the closing hand.

As the Nephew and the crippled bird continued their crab-like progress along the path, the distance between the hand and the spreading tailfeathers subtly increased. Soon it was a foot, then two, then a full yard, and then, miraculously, the owner of the tailfeathers experienced a complete recovery, which she signaled by remarking, "Pr-r-r-t!" as she sailed away and was lost to sight in the undergrowth.

The Captain and the boy were laughing.

"Did you hear what she said when she took off?"

"Yes, sir. She said 'Pr-r-r-rt!' "

His uncle chuckled.

"That's what it sounded like. What it meant was, 'Stick tight, kids! I fooled the bloody-minded scoundrels!'

"Now let's see if we can find any of 'em. Shuffle your feet so you won't step on one. They're right about us."

Beneath his searching eye a sere brown leaf moved spasmodically in response to the pulsations of the tiny timorous breast beneath it, and the man's gentle hand closed softly upon a small dab of down, which, still obedient to the mother's injunction, lay quietly in his palm, confident that even in this extremity, her wild love still covered her helpless offspring with the saving cloak of invisibility.

The tall sportsman set the tiny pa'tridge again upon the ground and carefully replaced the betraying leaf.

Then the companions went their way, treading softly, and saying naught.

Twice again before they left the place, they recoiled before similar charges delivered by irate womenfolk of the pa'tridge clan, but these, after the first involuntary defensive start, they sheepishly ignored and so came at noontime to the "Old Stun Bridge."

THE
FROG
HUNTERS
◆—◆

In its youth the Old Stun Bridge had been well able to support the heaviest vehicular traffic of its time. The sturdy stone abutments reaching out from either wooded shore still stand firmly, though grass and smartweed sprout and flourish rankly in the dank crevices. Only the center span, built of hardwood planks, shows signs of yielding to the decay incident to disuse and neglect. The sagging stringers are now partly submerged in the clear brown water which once they cleared in a single leap. With the weariness of years, they warn the wayfarer to step lightly and quickly over their sodden decrepitude or risk a ducking. Long ago and one by one, the little cluster of log cabins on the farther shore collapsed into their stone-lined cellar holes. The rough acres, which never yielded more than the bare means of a precarious livelihood for those who dwelt there, have long since been recovered by Nature as the original grantee. Here and there in the open spaces the visitor can see the ridged contours of what was once a field of potatoes, or spy the orange flame of an alien patch of lilies planted by some vanished hand. These, and a scraggly but defiant lilac bush or an apple tree guarding its acid fruit with crooked spiny branches, are the only visible evidences of man's brief, unprofitable dominion.

The two kinsmen, munching their sandwiches in the cool shadow of a pine on the shore, found no flaws in the scene even though they acknowledged a feeling of sympathy for the settlers who had fought hereabouts their grim and losing struggle against the wilderness.

"I wonder why folks ever picked out such a place when they had the whole country to choose from," the Nephew pondered.

"Probably they didn't," said the Captain. "Probably Wentworth Benning, the old shyster, sold someone a grant of land, and that feller divided it up and sold the pitches to poor folks who didn't know what they were buying. They'd been told of the rich and fertile soil of the 'Grants,' but I don't suppose the speculators told 'em that there were rocks up here, too. They'd come up over the wilderness trails from the older settlements, bringing their families and what little furniture they had. Maybe they had a cow and a pig. If they found that by chance their pitch lay in a valley, they were lucky, but wherever it was, valley or mountain, they had to dig in or starve, for they couldn't move again. Some of them probably did starve, and a good many were killed by the Indians, but those who survived were tough specimens, I can tell you.

"When I was a boy," he continued, "some of the descendants of the original settlers still lived in those old log cabins. I used to hunt and fish with 'em, and while they had their faults, they were far and away the best woodsmen I've ever seen. They lived mostly on salt pork, flour, potatoes, lard, vinegar, and fish and game. The first woodchuck meat I ever ate was in Jim Hooper's cabin, which stood right yonder. Wasn't bad, either."

He rose to his feet, gazing out across the shining watery waste of the marsh, whence came now and again the resonant voices of the bullfrogs, uttering deep and solemn advice to an all but heedless world.

"If you didn't know that a frog is a feeble-witted critter you might think that they're saying something worth listening to," observed the Nephew.

"Like politicians," agreed the other, who cherished a lively disrespect for that noisy, inglorious breed.

They found the skiff, battered and scarred by more than one generation of bullhead fishermen, but still reasonably seaworthy, tied to the bank. Its owner was an amiable fellow who gathered most of his living from the bullheads and muskrats which inhabited the marsh in great abundance. In all probability he had never seen or heard of a boat that didn't leak a bit here and there, and he would doubtless have been suspicious of such startling integrity had he encountered it.

He now came down the path from his shack to give his greetings.

"Goin' frawg-huntin' be ye? Yis, yis. Well, sir, you'll find plenty on 'em. By Jeeswax, I hev been on the p'int o' fetchin' a mess o' frawgs' laigs daown to your folks, but I been turrible busy huntin' gingshang so s't I c'n dig it come fall.

"Sartinly, you c'n take the boat! She's an almighty good one, ef I do say so."

His eye ran lovingly over the dingy craft and as he gazed upon the, to him, sleek and graceful lines, his mind went, as any yachtsman's would, to visions of longer voyages and greater adventures than any he had known.

"Yis, sir, she's a good one, an' next summer I'm a-goin' to h'ist her aout o' here an' haul her over to Champlain an' put her in. I shall hev one o' them little enjines hitched onto her, an', by Jeeswax, I'll run her clear'n to Canerdy an' back."

He was still engrossed with the breath-taking possibilities of this cruise when the two frog hunters stepped into the argosy of her owner's hopes to proceed upon one of their own which seemed much more likely of achievement than the grandiose dreams of the "gingshang" digger.

As the Captain picked up the paddle and prepared to shove off, James roused from his contemplation of a peaceful invasion of Canada and spoke again.

"Hol' on, Capting! By Jeeswax! I got a good mind to paddle fer ye. I ortn't to take the time, right naow, when I'm so all-fired busy gingshangin', but, dang it all, a feller hez to hev some fun, oncet in a while. I love to see ye shoot a rifle an' I know jest where to find the frawgs. You git up forards there towards the baow eend an' I'll hev ye aout there in the shake o' a lamb's tail."

Obediently, the Captain picked up his rifle and moved forward while amiable James, recklessly bent upon an afternoon of sport at whatever later cost in ginseng, took the paddle and deftly headed the skiff toward the cranberry bogs that lined the winding channel of the marsh.

From this watery jungle, lush with the resurgent growth of summer, came a measured booming chorus of such volume as to indicate the presence of a considerable number of musicians.

"Hark to 'em!" exclaimed James, whose speech was frequently embellished by quaint Elizabethan phrases long in disuse save by scholars and Shakespeareans. The mystery of the survival, here on the quiet, nearly deserted shores of a Vermont marsh and issuing from the tobacco-stained lips of a shiftless illiterate, of the speech of Kit Marlowe and his friends of the Mermaid Tavern, was one that had often intrigued the Captain, but he never found the explanation for it. James knew no more concerning his ancestry than the rumor that there was "Injun" blood in his veins. The earliest records of the Township gave no clue. Apparently when the first Town Clerk of Tranquillity had sharpened his quill and arranged his ink horn and sand-box conveniently, preparatory to the listing of the resident taxpayers and paupers, the progenitors of James, the "gingshang" digger, had already been long established in a log cabin on the "Beaver Meadowes."

"Hark to 'em!" said James, again, while the bright drops fell from his poised paddle, "ef there's ez many on 'em ez there seems to be, an' ef they're ez big ez they saound, we'll hev us a mess o' frawgs' laigs in no time. Yis, yis."

He took a stroke or two and paused again to inquire if the Captain had an extra cigarette or two.

"I busted my pipe," he explained, "an' I run aout o' long-cut chewin' terbaccer. I been too all-fired busy huntin' gingshang to git daown to Fenimore Shepard's store. Speermint an' wintergreen leaves don't seem to satisfy, somehaow."

The tobacco was passed and the voyage resumed.

An old black duck, rusty in her summer plumage, spied the approaching skiff and vanished silently into the tangled stems of the cranberry bushes together with her numerous brood.

"Naow, look at thet! Ef the young'uns hed been able to fly," quoth James, "she'd hev quacked to 'em, an' they'd hev took wing, the hull kit an' caboodle on 'em, an' scairt the livin' hell aouten us wi' their racket. But they can't fly, an' she knows it, so she does the next best thing, which is to scatter 'em aout and hev the leetle critters make so many small winklin' waves that ye can't see nothin'. They haint' none o' 'em more'n tew rod from us right naow, but I'll bet ye a jug o' cider, ye can't spy a one. No, sir."

Their leisurely course was marked by the skittering leaps of countless frogs too small to draw the fire of the hunters. Bitterns clanked in the rushes, or rose to awkward flight as the bow of the skiff invaded their precincts.

"Thar, Capting, is in all-fired big frawg a-settin' yander on that ol' root. Naow le's see ef you're ez sharp ez you useter be."

The Captain spied the squat shape of a huge frog and an instant later the thin crack of the rifle rang out.

James moved to retrieve the game. He noted with approval the location of the tiny bullet hole.

"Yis, yis. That's the way to do it. I guess ye still know haow to handle a rifle."

He surveyed the bulky victim.

"I'll bet ye, thet ol' cuss hez et more'n one leetle duck in his time, too. Naow a frawg haz a pooty good life of it, when ye stop to think. Come winter an' faoul weather an' he jest digs daown inter the mud an' goes to sleep. He don't hev to wear himself aout a-haulin' firewood an' feedin' it into the stove the way us poor unfort'nit humerns must do. Come spring agin an' up he comes all rested up an' ready fer high jinks. He hunts up an ol' stub or suthin' to sit on an' Nature fetches him his meals."

He sighed enviously as he considered the many luxurious advantages enjoyed by frogs.

"But, then agin, thar he be, wi' a bullet hole in his head an' the skillet a-comin'. I p'sume to say that he's awishin' right naow 'at he wuz me er I wuz him."

The Nephew took the next shot and acquitted himself well.

The hunt went on while James guided the skiff through the labyrinthine ways, meanwhile drawing his passengers' attention now and then to some curious manifestation of the obscure activities of the shy denizens of the marsh.

Once as they journeyed they were startled by a violent threshing in the water ahead of the craft where some creature struggled desperately.

"It's a pick'rel a-ketchin' a duck, I do believe, er mebbe a sea sarpint. Damned ef it don't look like one!" exclaimed the boatman. "Yis—no tain't nuther! What in tunket is it?" He urged his craft close and suddenly they were able to see, not the predatory jaws of a fish, or the scaly crest of a prehistoric monster, but the evil head and thick body of a great water snake engaged in an attempt to swallow a lively muskrat. The little muskrat was squalling frantically for help, but its screams assuredly would have been in vain had the Captain not been on hand with his ready rifle to champion the poor victim. With a single shot he broke the snake's back and the muskrat, without pausing to acknowledge its gratitude, vanished beneath the surface.

" 'Hain't he a miza'ble lookin' cuss?" James inquired, as they watched the writhing, dying snake. "Damn 'em! I wisht all the cussed reptiles in this ma'sh had only one head an' I hed my deer rifle. They ketch ducks, an' frawgs, an' fish, too—'ceptin' bullheads, which air hard to swaller whole—an' there's baound to be one o' the stinkin' ornery critters quiled on the haft o' a feller's paddle to pop ye one when ye reach for it."

"Are they poisonous?" the Nephew asked.

"Some say they be an' some say they 'hain't. I ruther guess they 'hain't fer I been bit by 'em, two, three times, an' I sartinly didn't die, although my hand swole up consid'able an' was turrible sore fer a spell."

The sun was by now well down toward the western hills. It was determined that of frog legs they had what James described as a "harndsome mess," so the skiff was returned to its home landing, where with the deftness gained from much practice, the ginseng hunter prepared the game for the skillet, and then having accepted a generous gift of tobacco from his visitors, bade them farewell with a hearty invitation for them to go "bullheadin' " with him some night soon.

Elsewhere in the world there was sound and fury; here, only the slow musical clank of cowbells from the upland pastures, the croak of a night heron, and the soft mystery of the June twilight.

BULLHEAD
FISHING

On an evening, not long after the frog hunt, the Captain and his young kinsman came along a crooked path through the birches that brought them to the door of a dilapidated shack beneath a pine tree. This was the earthly home of James, the ginseng hunter. The builder and present occupant of the edifice had small regard for plumblines and levels. His specifications called for nothing more than four standing walls and a reasonably weatherproof roof.

After a brief attempt to maintain the dignity of a residential structure, the cabin had relaxed gradually to a more comfortable posture. As the months joined and became seasons, and the seasons became years, it had made small compromises with the law of gravity, easing a strain here and there on the insistent complaint of a joust, beam or snow-burdened rafter. In time, these trifling easements had changed the outward aspect of the cabin considerably, and greatly for the better. First it had lost the raw appearance of green unpainted pine boarding and with it had gone the grim respectability of its bearing for one better suited to its surroundings. At last it had abandoned all pretense of decorum and yielded itself to the same drowsiness which so frequently overcame the easy-going architect of its being.

A bent elbow of stovepipe protruding from one ramshackle wall emitted a diminishing spiral of woodsmoke which drifted away and dissolved in the languid air. A twin spiral, less fragrant, rose from the bowl of the ginseng hunter's pipe where he sat at ease on his doorstep. It had no noticeable effect on the great cloud of mosquitoes which whined hungrily about the smoker's head.

The sun had set long since, but all the details of the marsh and its environs were still distinguishable in an unearthly radiance shed from the fading sky. Or it might have been that the water and the woodlands were now releasing the mellow shafts of sunlight which they had absorbed during the day.

A lingering aroma drifted from the cabin's single door to inform even a distant wayfarer that James had supped on a skilletful of fried fish and onions.

"Don't the 'skeeters bother you, Jim?" the Nephew asked, when greetings had been exchanged.

"No, sir, not naow they don't. When they fust come aout in airly spring they pester me a mite, but I soon git use't to 'em."

One, at least, of his callers thought that it might indeed be easier for James to get used to the mosquitoes than for the insects to become accustomed to their host's weatherbeaten, smoke-stained epidermis, but he kept the opinion to himself, and spoke instead of their hopes for the night, to which James responded with his customary amiability.

"Yis, yis. 'Course ye c'n go bullheadin'. Thar's the skiff, an' thar's the lantern, an' jedgin' from the looks o' the chimbley, a feller'd most hev to hev him another lantern to find this un."

He produced a piece of rag and cleaned the soot away and then, with a thoroughness not characteristic of his housekeeping methods, he trimmed the wick and lighted it. The lantern was to illuminate their activities.

"A bullhead ain't a bad feller ef ye c'n see him an' know haow to ketch 'holt on him," said he, as he gathered the rest of his simple gear and untied the skiff, "but they're miza'ble cusses when you reach aout fer 'em in the dark. Hev ye ever sot daown on one o' 'em? No? Well, by Jeeswax, I hev, an' I want to tell ye thet I riz up aout o' thar with great alacrity an' vi'lence. I don' want no more on it, I c'n tell ye."

He ceased paddling long enough to give the scar of his old wound a tenderly reminiscent rub.

"It hurts yit, whenever I think 'baout it," he explained.

By now all light had drained from the sky. Only the crest of the great hill to the west was discernible. The marsh and its environs were covered by a thick blanket of sultry darkness which shut out all objects beyond the reach of the feeble rays of the lantern on the bow, yet James unfailingly kept the skiff on a true though tortuous course along the winding channel, and finally brought her battered nose squarely against the fishing stake that marked the established center of the bullhead population.

The Nephew made her fast with a bit of line and all hands rigged their tackle.

The two guests set up their short bait-casting rods. James placed his confidence in a peeled sapling as crooked as the course he had steered.

"I swow!" he exclaimed, as he tossed out a writhing mass of nightcrawlers upon the opaque water, "I do b'lieve that my fishpole hez warped a mite, but the end seems to be squar' wi' the butt. Hev ye ever obsarved haow straight an' pooty a saplint looks until ye cut it an' trim it?"

They were silent for a time while they listened to the wild voices of the woods and waters and waited for the gentle but stubborn tug of a hungry bullhead in the dark depths of the channel. Moths fluttered with foolish persistence against the lantern in vain attempts to destroy themselves. Owls hooted portentously in the pines, and a night heron high in the darkness sent down its weird and doleful cry. The frog's orchestra boomed and twanged on all sides, its volume apparently undiminished by the recent activities of the riflemen.

The three companions were well settled in that hypnotic reverie common to all still-fishermen when the peace of the midsummer night was shattered in startling fashion by a violent explosion occurring not ten feet away. A great burst of spray came over the low gunwale, extinguishing the lantern and drenching the crew.

"What in hell—" began the Captain in profane dismay, and knew the answer before James gave it.

"Beavers! The danged leetle cusses! Don't know ef you know'd they come back, two-three year ago. Ef ye didn't, ye sartinly do naow. I don' know haow many times they'v scairt me mos' to death wi' their consarned tricks. Fust time they did it, I wuz settin' here all by myself mindin' my business an' thinkin' haow it would be ef one o' them German underwater boats got into the ma'sh an' went to whangin' 'round, when all to oncet, 'Bang! Cup Plung!' she went an' dum near draownded me."

He re-lighted the lantern and order was restored aboard ship.

"Dang him!" grumbled James, his nerves still vibrating unpleasantly. "I'd love to give that leetle joker a rap on the snout with the paddle to teach him manners. 'Tain't a good thing fer a man o' my years to be subj'cted to sech sudden discumbloberations. No, sir."

"I'm glad they're back," acknowledged the Captain, "but I'd just as soon they'd toss their depth bombs somewhere else."

The mischievous beaver withdrew to engage in more profitable exercises and tranquillity reigned again for a time.

The next interruption was a welcome one. The Nephew's rod tip began to twitch and then went downward under a strong steady pull to which the boy responded in kind. If it cannot be said of the bullpout that he fights with the dash and brilliancy of a Lee, it must be admitted that he shows the stubborn strength and deadly persistence of Lee's great opponent.

This one lived up to the highest traditions of his clan, fighting a narrow, rugged, uninspired battle in the depths and continuing it even after it had been landed in the boat where it flourished its javelins viciously and growled out imprecations against its captors.

"He's a nice un," remarked James. "He'll weigh half a paound er more, an' he's a he. See them scars where he's bin a-fightin'? Naow, it's a curious thing an' I've watched it many a time. When a pair o' bullheads set up haousekeepin' they dig a hole inter a mud bank some'ere an' whilst Miz Bullhead lays her aigs an' takes care of the younguns, ol' Mister Bullhead stays aout i' the front yard an' fights ever'body that comes a-nigh. He don' care haow big they be, neither, he'll tackle any of 'em, ketch ez ketch kin."

There were indications that the supper bell had rung in the bullhead community, for James immediately wrenched a second grunting captive from the water and deftly extracted the hook from its wide, bewhiskered maw.

For an hour while the night drew on into deeper and ever deeper mysteries, there was scarcely a moment of inactivity. The banqueting bullheads seemed never to notice that those of their company who engulfed a writhing lump of nightcrawlers immediately vanished into the upper darkness and never returned to the place of their abode. The fish bucket, half filled with water, was black with a mass of squirming indignant bullpout.

"I b'lieve we've got a harndsome mess on 'em," said James, inspecting the catch. " 'Nuff's 'nuff, ez the man says, an' I hain't one to play hawg, an' I know you fellers hain't neither. But ef ye hain't in no hurry to go hum, I jest want to show ye some fun naow that we've completed the princ'pal bus'ness. Le' me hev your line, sonny."

He poked a cautious paw among the unreconciled captives in the bucket and withdrew a dace, a soft and tasteless fish, worthless for any purpose except that which James now contemplated.

He cleaned the boy's hook and neatly affixed the dace, which seemed not to resent the indignity.

"Naow, ef ye'll heave it aout nigh to the aidge o' the bank an' kinder jiggle it a leetle naow an' agin suthin' might happen."

The Nephew followed instructions, but for some time nothing of note occurred and James saw fit to beguile time with an anecdote.

"Once upon a time the Devil an' St. Peter hed words. Seems thet thar wuz a line fence separatin' their prop'ties an' the agreement betwixt 'em wuz thet St. Peter'd keep one half up an' Ol' Beelzeebub'd keep up t'other half.

"Well, sir, the Devil kinder let his share go daown, posts rotted an' busted an' the wires got rusty an' tangled up, an' fin'lly St. Peter got tired o' sech doin's an' he spoke to the Devil abaout it.

"Sezzee, 'You hain't 'tendin' your half o' thet fence ez ye orter, an' ez ye promised to do,' sezzee.

" 'Well, naow,' sez the Devil, 'I guess mebbe I hev been a mite careless, Saint,' sezzee, 'but the's some sort o' a carruckus goin' on on airth,' sezzee, 'fightin' ' sezzee, 'an' sech like, 'an' I've more'n hed my hands full wi' new folks comin' in,' sezzee.

" 'Likely you hed a hand in startin' the trouble,' sez St. Peter quite severe, 'but whether ye hev er not, I hain't a-goin' to put up wi' it no longer,' sezzee. 'You'n me hev drawed an' signed a 'greement coverin' this situation,' sezzee, 'an' it's been duly witnessed an' the Taown Clark hez it in his box,' sezzee, 'an' by Judast Priest,' sezzee, 'ef ye don't do ez ye agreed, I shall sue ye completely aout o' Hell,' sezzee.

"Well, sir, at that Ol' Scratch slapped his sides an' switched his tail an' laughed an' laughed.

"Fin'lly he quieted daown to jest an ord'nary snigger an' sez, sezzee—"

The narrator got no further for at that moment the surface of the dark water was ripped asunder, the boy's short rod was nearly torn from his hand.
They had a brief and indistinct glimpse of a great fish in the air before it fell
back with a heartshaking splash and the reel began to whine.

"Gee-ho-so-phat!" exclaimed one awe-stricken observer, "that air fish is ez
long ez my laig! Hang onto him, Bub, but not too tight least he bust yer pole!
Look at thet! Gosh *a'mighty!* Thar he goes agin! Oh, my Lord, ain't he a ol'
solacker!"

James continued his exhortations at the top of his voice, silencing the bullfrogs and the owls, but no one protested for the sight of that raging leviathan
and the sounds of its furious struggles up and down the channel were sufficient warrant for the shoutings.

The boy and his rod were bent in a battle that would have been awe-in-
spiring enough in full daylight, but now in the darkness, relieved only by the
one yellow light, the fight took on a significance which did not escape the
Captain. It was as if a primordial terror had risen from the depths of time to
challenge one of his own kin and blood. He felt that here as elsewhere in the
world raged a struggle between two forces, one of which represented sanity
and courage, while the other could well stand for all that is savage, cruel and
brutal in beasts and men.

He gave his few instructions in a low voice which the boy heard beneath
the excited vociferations of James.

After ten minutes of raging, lunging and leaping combat the great pike began to acknowledge the flexible mastery of the rod. The violence and speed of
its lunge diminished and while it still managed to raise its savage head above
the water to show the menace of its great maw, it could do no more. Its surrender was unconditional when it was finally brought alongside the skiff, and
James, during a tense but silent moment, shoved a thumb and forefinger
firmly beneath the gill covers and dragged the monster inboard.

"Thet fish," said he in a voice that sounded soft, low and velvety in con-
strast to its previous stentorian outbursts, "thet fish will weigh—" he paused a
moment to re-survey the length and thickness of the creature. "Thet fish will
weigh danged close to twenty-fi' paounds, er else I'm a hoodang."

And so it did when it was brought to the scales.

The Nephew gazed upon his prize, and it was noted that there was slight
tremor running through him, only a portion of which could be laid to the
strain of holding the rod against the surge of a quarter of a hundredweight of
northern pike, but the Captain was proud to discover that the youngster was
otherwise in full command of himself.

"Jim," said the Nephew a few minutes later above the murmur of water at
the bow, "what was it that the Devil said to St. Peter?"

"Har!" exclaimed the "gingshang" hunter in some surprise. "Well, sir, the
Devil sez, sezzee, an' he laughed agin when he said it, '*Sue* me out o' Hell, will
ye? Well, Saint, le' me ask ye suthin'. Whar air ye a-goin' to fin' yer
lawyers!'"

KEEPING
THE
SABBATH
—•◆•—

One afternoon at the time of the year when the wild plums are in bloom along the old stonewalls and Belden's Brook is rid of the last of the snow water, the Judge and the Captain, homeward bound from an excursion, stopped to call upon a well-loved friend. Their immediate destination was the garage at the foot of the hill close by the little river which divides the village. An old truck was being operated upon as they entered the shop and one of the operator's oil-stained shoes was visible under the vehicle's sagging running gear. A shower of brilliant sparks came forth mingled with a stream of mild objurgation as the workman wrestled with his tools.

When the Captain kicked the exposed shoe the torch shut off with a loud pop. The shoe was withdrawn and a head appeared.

"Just wanted to ask if you're makin' any money," the Captain explained.

"No, I ain't makin' a cent," said the voice from the floor, "but I'm havin' an awful lot of fun!"

"Well, come out o' that then," the Judge ordered, "and we can tell you how to have more fun."

He opened his creel to display half a dozen sleek trout glowing like the jewels they were, laid upon a green bed of moss.

"That's what Belden will do for you if you have a Ginger Quill tied on a number 14 hook. Tomorrow is Sunday. Yes or no?"

Not the least valued of those residents of the Township is Cameron Vaughn, who operates the garage at the foot of the hill. Here he strives cheerfully and expertly to restore to health and service the invalid vehicles of his neighbors, even as the Doctor labors with their owners. Often late at night the passerby may see the greenish glare of the blow torch as Cam works to repair someone's mower, or to revive a wheezing, haggard relic of the days of the Glidden Tours, so that communication can be reestablished between the village and some ancient farmhouse remote among the hills.

Tranquillity can claim no better citizen nor one more industrious than he, yet the woods and waters have laid Cam in allegiance, and with irresistible power. At certain times and seasons he is drawn away from his shop by the same mysterious voice that moves the trout in the streams, and the wildfowl in the fens and marshes. It has been noted by several observant housewives that Cam's are not the only ears to hear the beguiling summons.

"Naow look at thet!" exclaimed a lady to her neighbor. "There they go agin, the hull kit an' caboodle on 'em, laughin' an' kerryin' on! There's the Jedge, an' Cap'n Macomber jest come home, an' thet Cam Vaughn, a-fishin', I'll bet ye." There was a trace of envy in her tones as she watched the Judge's old car disappear. "I don' know what it is gits into 'em, but I've seen it happen, time an' ag'in. One day they're all 'tending to bus'ness good an' faithful ez c'n be. Come tomorrow, aye, yis, or no, they're fryin' aigs at three o'clock in the morning an' disturbin' the neighbors. Then, whisht! away they go, jes' ez if they'd all been yanked by the same string!"

"Well, I guess mebbe they *be*," her friend replied charitably, "but I never knew harm to come of it, after all. They seem to enj'y it an' I say that if you've got ye a man thet c'n find a way to enj'y himself wi'aout bustin' the Ten Commandments an' gittin' hung er jailed, fer massy's sake, let the critter do it. Fryin' an aig at three o'clock in the mornin' ain't the Unpardonable Sin, an' a mess o' traout er a couple o' pa'tridges air welcome fare. Wouldn't want to live on sech rations all year 'raound, least ways I don't b'lieve I should, though to be sure I hain't never tried it. My man jest don't seem to take to huntin' an' fishin'."

Deacon Guidance Witherbee, the hen-pecked zealot who for the sum of three dollars would place in the hands of any suffering sinner a means of access to the "subtile emernations o' individual paower in accordance to the laws o' the Speckrum," took a more disparaging view of these lapses. Never having done an honest day's labor in his life the old scalawag yet held the sternest convictions as to the nobility of labor. He managed to gain a living for himself and his sharp-tongued spouse chiefly from the sale of specific remedies, which were reasonably and profitably popular throughout the neighborhood in spite of the Doctor's outspoken condemnation of them. It was strange indeed that anyone within range of the Deacon's healing founts suffered from any indisposition, for Guidance could produce, for three dollars, cash, a sovereign cure for every ill. The "Rheumatics" bottle gave off an aroma distinct from that rendered by the "Bladder Stone" specific, but the alcoholic content of each of the items in the Deacon's pharmacopoeia never varied from the original standard of 96 per cent proof. This fact may have accounted for the remarkable cures reported and the grateful testimonials printed in the leaflet which accompanied each bottle.

Occasionally, although less frequently in recent years, Guidance was called to conduct revival services by a group of tough-minded religionists who clung to the hell and damnation theory. On such occasions and when well braced by a tumblerful of "Goiter Cure" the Deacon held forth with a vindictive fury equal to that of Cotton Mather. Not infrequently an apprehensive sinner saw, or thought that he saw, the flames of Perdition blazing waist-high around the fervent Deacon, but like Abednego, Meshach and Shadrach, they never consumed him.

From his kitchen window he also had observed the passage of the Judge and his friends on this Sabbath morning.

"Naow," said he to his wife, "thar they go agin. Flaoutin' the Lord's Day an' a-headin' fer Belden's Brook, I hain't a daoubt, to ketch traout, the consarned heathen!" He swallowed and was compelled to pause for a moment while he considered the carnal appeal of a platterful of crisp brooktrout. His thoughts went speculatively to dynamite and nets.

Then, in the unctuous tones of one who feels himself to be so securely wrapped in the mantle of eternal salvation that he can afford to take a doleful pleasure in considering the grim sulphurous prospects of the unrighteous, he resumed his sour commentary.

"Naow, wife, I've labored mightily wi' 'em, man an' boy, an' my rewards, praise the Lord, hev been meager. Two, three year ago, 'memberin' haow aour Lord 'n' Saviour mingled wi' the sinners an' the harlots, I went so fur ez to jine 'em a-cuttin' daown a bee tree. I figgered in thet way I might soften their wicked hearts, dum 'em, to the emernations, an' git 'em to humble their sperits afore Jehovah. Wal, I wuz jest a-heavin' pearls to hawgs ez it turned aout, fer one er more on 'em sicked them d——, sicked them bees onto me an' dang near stang me to death."

"Well, they *moved* ye, didn't they," Minnie remarked unsympathetically, "an' that's sartainly suthin'. An' they fetched me a pail o' honey, which is consi'da'ble more'n you ever brung into this haouse. I declare, ef they'd ast me, I'd go 'long wi' 'em."

For a moment a wistful expression rested on her harsh and cheerless features.

"I uset to go fishin' wi' Pa when I wuz a young un," said Minnie, and then she slammed the skillet into the sink with such extraordinary violence that her husband leaped as if he had been shot.

Perhaps some of the Deacon's "emernations" reached Cam, who was at the moment setting up his rod beside a sparkling pool and sniffing the fragrance of a June morning, or perhaps it was the voice of the water singing its cheerful hymn to its Creator, or it might have been that out of the corner of his eye he had seen just then the quiet rolling rise of a fish at the foot of the pool; but, whatever the reason, Cam felt moved to say Grace, and he did so in his own way.

"I presume that some folks consider Sunday fishin' to be wicked, but I swear I don't b'lieve it. It don't seem to me that the Lord would want folks to stay indoors, a-swelterin' and a-prayin', on a day like this, after He'd gone to all the trouble o' makin' it on purpose for 'em to look at, an' listen to, an' smell. There's even times when I kind of like to go to church myself. But," he added candidly, "I notice that they generally come on days when the weather is unfavorable—'ceptin' for duck season, o' course."

"Amen to that," said one of his companions, "and now how shall we divide the stream? Suppose you start in here, Cam, and I'll take on up ahead. Cap'n can drive along in the car and take the next stretch and we'll all meet at the old bridge for lunch."

Cam put a leader under a pebble to soak in the shallows of the pool and while he waited for it to become supple he sat on the green bank and considered the state of his emotions, which, we may assume, did not differ greatly from those of other honest anglers who at the beginning of a perfect June day find themselves in similar situations. There was the living stream, untried as yet, cool and enticing, inviting the fisherman to test his skill at reading the riddle of its pools and riffles and to demonstrate his knowledge of the habits of its wary denizens.

"It's like Christmas when I was a youngster," thought Cam, "or like stepping into the alders on opening day of bird season."

He might have continued his soliloquy upon the peculiar joys of the sportsman, but at that moment the fish which he had observed earlier rose again and engulfed some tiny voyager without, as Cam put it, spilling a drop of water.

"You'll weigh a pound or better, brother, an' I wish I knew what you like best for breakfast."

He searched his fly box and selected a minute creation as delicate and as precisely fashioned as the living insect itself. The tiny wings were of sober gray and so were the hackles and the diminutive tail. It was a perfect imitation of some one of the myriads of small beings condemned to exist for years in cold and darkness that they may know for a few hours the buoyancy of flight in the sunlight and warm air overlaying the dungeons beneath the stream bed.

The angler affixed the fly to its tippet and made a short experimental cast which satisfied him.

On the next cast the line went out gracefully. The fly hovered for a moment and fluttered down upon the water. But the big trout let it pass, and the angler tried again with no more success. Then as the tiny craft came gliding down on its third voyage there was a shadowy movement beneath it, and the fly vanished.

Five minutes later, Cam led his fish to the net.

"Mister," said a pleasant voice behind him, "that's a pretty fish and, if I may say so, you handle a fly rod as well as anyone I've ever seen."

The speaker, garbed and equipped for angling, had been standing well back from the stream observing every detail of the duel with approval.

Cam replied with genuine modesty, "Do you really think so? All I know about fly fishin' I've learned myself and I've never been sure if I've been on the right track."

The stranger smiled and lifted the fish. "You'll do all right in any company," he added.

He produced cigarettes and they chatted amicably for a few minutes when Cam, whose heart had warmed to the man, offered him his own place in the stream and gave him a description of the water above them.

The other declined.

"No, thank you. It's mighty kind of you, but I shan't disturb you. Do you happen to know Captain Macomber? My name is Coykendall, and I'm a friend of his. He wasn't expecting me for I hadn't notified him, but his wife thought I might find him on this stream."

Cam beamed upon him.

"My name is Vaughn, and the Cap'n's a darned good friend o' mine, too. Heard him speak of you a thousand times. Matter o' fact, I'm fishin' with him today. He and the Judge are just above me. You can't miss 'em. Certainly glad to make your acquaintance. Live somewhere's down in Connecticut, don't you?"

"That's right," said the other. "I've heard a lot about you, too, and I'll see you later."

He set off along the green bank, and Cam noticed that his new friend kept away from the stream to avoid disturbing any of his own prospective victims.

The countryside glowed like a great emerald save where the stream pierced it with gleams of gold and silver. Birds sang with the ardor of spring, and all these sights and sounds were pleasant to the visitor, who presently spied the stout figure of the Judge knee deep in a riffle. That worthy came ashore to give him heartfelt greeting and to show him a gleaming pair of eight-inch squaretails.

Now, as he proceeded, the rising voice of the stream told of faster water ahead, and when he came to it he found his friend there and in deep trouble.

The high brush-covered banks at this point forced the stream into a narrow chute and there, standing nearly waist deep and braced against the powerful current, was the Captain. Evidently, he had a good fish on. He was trying to bring it to him against the current, since the nature of the bottom made it impossible for him to follow his trout downstream to a less turbulent battleground. The rod was responding nobly to the strain, and slowly, a foot or two at a time, the fish lost ground, while the watcher, himself unobserved, held his breath and prayed for the welfare of the leader.

At last the Captain had his fish beside him and reached for the landing net. But the landing net was not there.

"Damned if he ain't forgotten it again!' 'exclaimed his friend. "Now what's he goin' to do?"

The angler glanced at the stream banks seeking a shallow spot where he might run his fish aground. There was none. His only alternative was to grab it. Now there's a manner of seizing a trout over the gill covers that paralyzes the creature, and one may hold him safe and secure, but due to the force of the water and the instability of his footing, the Captain missed the mark. He had the fish, however, and raised it from the water to the level of his own eyes. In that statuesque pose, it looked to the visitor as though the Captain and the trout were carrying on an earnest conversation, as perhaps they were beneath the sound of the stream.

Then the noble tableau of man and fish began to deteriorate, slowly, at first, with a persistent wriggling on the part of the trout and desperate counter moves made by the angler to enforce the arrest. Ralf had time to note that the fish was as long as the Captain's forearm, when it slipped free of the clutching fingers and vanished, leaving the angler off balance so that he struggled desperately and futilely for several seconds with a great waving of arms and rod. Then, he, too, vanished beneath the rushing torrent in a mighty explosion of foam and flying drops.

The Captain came to the surface some yards downstream, and the first sounds to enter his ears after he had emptied them of water were those of human hysteria or lunatic laughter.

Seeking the cause, he saw his friend rolling over on the greensward, twisting and gasping in the throes of agonizing mirth.

Like a good angler the Captain had clung to his rod, and with it in hand he waded grimly ashore and approached the sufferer.

"Hell and damnation!" said he, bitterly, addressing the contorted humorist on the grass. "This is indeed the last straw! Can't I lose a fish and get damn near drowned without you coming all the way from Connecticut just to look on? By Judas Priest! My body would have been halfway to the Big Falls by now for all the help you gave me, you damn sadist! I s'pose it would be funnier yet if I broke a leg—or my rod." He added the last as it came to his mind that a broken leg will heal, but that a four-ounce Chubb trout rod will not.

Then he sat wetly down and joined the hilarity.

After a little time they recovered themselves, except that Ralf occasionally interrupted his condolences with a single uncontrollable high-pitched whoop.

"Gimme that flask, confound you. I know you've got one, and the water in the brook is cold enough to freeze a weaker man."

It was thus that the Judge found them when he came along fetching the Captain's hat, which the brook had delivered to him as a final prankish gesture.

He listened to the tale, took a nip from the flask to help the Captain dry out, and was continent of his mirth, for as the reader of these memoirs has learned by now, it is less entertaining to be told of a fellow creature's ludicrous disaster than it is to observe it at first hand.

And Cam, when he came along, took also a dram in sympathy for his wet friend. He laughed not at all, but there was a lively twinkle in his brown eyes as he remarked that it was just too damn bad Deacon Witherbee hadn't been there to see how the Cap'n kept the Sabbath.

THE
DREAMING
CAT

◆

The distressful cries of a pair of robins brought the Captain to the window with a rifle in his hands, but, though he had been quick, indeed, he was too late to prevent a kidnaping and a murder, and too late, also, to avenge these crimes. He had only a brief glimpse of the criminal, a big yellow housecat, sneaking off through the shrubbery with a young robin in its teeth.

"Damn him!" he exclaimed bitterly.

"What's the matter, my lad?" asked the Dark-Haired Lady. "Why the naughty, naughty word?"

Her husband used the word again.

"Somebody's damned tomcat just killed one of our young robins. It happens every year; just when the young birds are learning to fly, all the cussed purring pets in town are after 'em. I claim the damned critters ought to be killed off, or, at least, people ought to have to pay license fees to keep 'em. I wish I could've got a shot at that yellow so-and-so."

"My! My! More bad language," said his helpmeet. "Tsk, tsk! Cats catch rats and mice, you know, my boy. And *some* people like 'em."

The Captain was unappeased.

"Cats *don't* catch rats, Ma'am. At least, I've never had proof of it. They dassent, for a rat'll fight. And they don't work very hard at their mousing, either. You needn't tell me about Dick Whittington. It's a pretty poem, but it's my notion that Dick should have been put in the stocks for bringing cats to a place where there had been no cats previously. I know that the Egyptians worshipped cats; but they also married their own sisters, which goes to show you what a fine lot they were."

Still clutching his rifle and watching for any sign of the enemy, he continued his lecture on *Felis domesticus.* The Dark-Haired Lady had heard it before, of course.

"C-a-t, cat. Something is damnably wrong with an educational system that requires our young to learn to spell 'cat' before they can go on and learn how to spell 'dog,' by Judas! 'A domesticated carnivorous animal, kept to kill mice and rats, and as a pet,' says the dictionary. Hah! A 'pet,' says Noah. Well, a pet is supposed to display evidences of loyalty an' affection, isn't he? Have you ever heard of a cat pulling a drowning child out of a creek? Ever hear of a cat awakening the family when the house caught fire? No. The cat sits on the bank yawning and licking its paws and lets the young-un drown, or it sneaks down off the back porch, leaving the family to burn to death, for all it cares. If it so happens that they don't burn to death and can still buy milk and fish and liver, the cat'll come back. If they *do* burn, or *can't* buy liver, your cat'll find someone who didn't and can, and it'll purr and rub against your leg and sleep in your easy chair an' go on producing more cats to kill robins—mice, too, if it isn't too much work an' if the mouse isn't too sassy. Damn 'em!"

He stopped suddenly, much to the surprise of the mother of his children, who had expected to hear a great deal more about cats, especially that part about the white man's foolishness in bringing the rats and mice to America and then bringing the cats over to kill the rats and mice. It wound up with an oratorical question, "Wasn't *that* a hell of a fine idea?"

Her husband stood the rifle in a convenient corner and picked up his hat.

"Goin' over to Cam's house," he explained, cryptically, leaving the Dark-Haired Lady to shake her bewildered head, as she so frequently had reason to do, over the unpredictableness of her favorite specimen of the genus *Homo*.

The Captain had seen a vision. The glimpse he had had of the yellow marauder kindled a tiny spark far back in the train of his memory. It burned and sparkled like the fuse of a firecracker, now reduced to a mere smoulder, now leaping in brilliance across an inch of psychic space until it finally reached the charge and exploded into a noble idea.

Nancy answered his knock at the Vaughn door.

"You'll find him sitting under the appletree," she said. "He's out there with a gun watching for the cats that are after our birds," she added with a noncommittal smile. It was the exact duplicate of the one the Dark-Haired Lady had given him five minutes earlier.

Cam was seated in a lawn chair. He had a bottle of ale at his elbow and a .22-caliber rifle rested across his knees. He was watching the grape trellis with the deadly concentration of the stillhunter and the sniper when the Captain hailed him.

"Sit down," said Cam in cordial tones of welcome. "I'll fetch another bottle."

When he returned from the kitchen he explained his armed vigilance.

"There's a damned big yellow tomcat hangin' 'round here an' catching my young robins."

"I know," replied his visitor, "he's just grabbed one out of our lilac bush, an' that's what I want to talk to you about. I just thought of something.

"Have you got any o' those box traps you used to catch rabbits with?"

Cam nodded.

"Good! Now then, about six years ago, I was down in Dorchester County, Maryland, shooting quail and woodcock along the Black River Marshes. One morning I was working along the edge of a bay, which we'd call a slough up here, when I heard a hell of a crow fight going on up ahead of me. I thought they'd found an owl, but I was wrong.

"What they had was a tomcat, a big yellow cuss. He was lying on a stub of a dead limb about thirty feet up—I s'pose my dogs had been chasing him—and he wasn't very happy, either. The crows were raising hell with him."

Cam's eyes brightened, as he began to discern a pattern in his friend's discourse.

"I stood behind a little bush," the Captain continued, "and I shot crows until I had to quit because of an ammunition shortage. Then I shot the tomcat.

"Those crows, Cam, paid no attention to me whatever. They didn't seem to see me, or hear the gun. They couldn't see or hear anything but that damned yellow, thieving tomcat. Do you follow my notion?"

"That I do," said Cam, "and I b'lieve you ought to have a prize o' some sort for thinkin' this business out. I do indeed. I've got a sackful of odds an' ends an' leavin's of shotgun ca'tridges I've been saving for crows. I'll fetch a box trap over to your house an' I'll set one myself. A fish head'll fetch him, don't you think?"

He paused. "But how c'n we get the damned cuss up a tree when we catch him?" he asked.

"Poodle harness," replied the Captain with the modest air of a man who has anticipated every possible contingency.

"I've got one that we used to put on our little Scottie when we walked him out to let him desecrate our neighbor's shrubbery twice a day. It'll fit that damned cat to a T. Then all we have to do is to run a long cord through the ring, tie a rock to one end, peg it over the limb and haul Grimalkin up to his perch and let him survey his kingdom.

"We'll squawk on a crow call just enough to get one of 'em to come in. Then, brother, all we'll have to do is shoot."

Under the cloak of darkness the two box traps were set, one in the grape trellis and another under the Macomber lilac bush.

In the morning the fish head had disappeared from the Captain's trap, but the trigger had failed to trip. Cam had had better luck.

He phoned his friend and announced cryptically that Cousin Felix was at his house and wanted to go crow shooting.

"O.K." said the Captain. "I'll pick up the Judge and we'll be right over."

The Judge had not been told of the plot and he expressed some doubt as to the sanity of his two companions when he learned the nature of the contents of the writhing sack than Cam loaded into the car.

"That's Cousin Felix," they told him gleefully. "He's going to have the time of his life."

"I ain't a bit sure that this is humane, or even legal," remarked the Judge when matters were explained, "but it sounds interesting."

"You must look at it from the point of view of Cousin Felix. After all, he's our guest, ain't he?" the Captain reminded him. "He loves birds 'most to death and he's going to see lots of 'em today.

"What we need now," he added, "is to find a place where a big tree with a dead limb on it stands at the edge of a patch of woods on a little hill, and not *too* close to human habitations."

They were familiar with every aspect of the terrain for miles around and in no time at all they had selected a battle site that promised to meet every requirement. Cam was even able to describe the old butternut tree with a dead limb suitable for Cousin Felix's role. He remembered it well, for he had shot many a fat squirrel out of it.

Cousin Felix appeared to be in a mood less than serene as they drove along the quiet country roads in the warm June sunshine; his cursings, whenever a bump in the road reminded him of the indignities he suffered, were almost melodious.

"Sounds like he's singin' to himself," said Cam.

"Sounds like the Horst Wessel to me," said the Captain, who had brought along a pair of heavy gloves in case Cousin Felix should fail to cooperate in the matter of the poodle harness.

It was fortunate that he had made this provision, for Cousin Felix demonstrated a marked antipathy for the poodle harness when the party arrived at the butternut tree and he was being prepared for the ascension. He fought and he squalled, and he managed to draw a little blood from his persecutors before the straps were snug. He was hoisted aloft willy nilly to his perch on the dead stub and there he crouched, his yellow eyes glaring with hate and his brindle tail a-bristle with rage.

The conspirators formed their ambuscade in a growth of young hemlock and prepared for the fray.

The Captain got out his crow call and produced a series of low malicious notes that were intended to inform every crow within hearing that one of his fellows had located an enemy in an exposed and vulnerable position.

There was no audible reply, but almost immediately a single black scout came over on silent wings and immediately saw the bundle of yellow fury on the limb of the butternut.

His shout of rage, summoning all hands to battle stations, carried more conviction than the Captain could produce, so that worthy person put aside his wooden crow call and set himself for action.

Within the space of a few seconds the air above the butternut tree was filled with a swooping, swarming, yelling mass of crows. The original assault squadron was constantly being reinforced by fresh flights arriving in haste and anger from more distant crow garrisons which had been inflamed by the horrid sounds of battle.

The state of Cousin Felix's temper did not improve under dive bombing, to which he was instantly subjected. With his tattered ears flattened against his ugly head he was the picture of rage incarnate. His lightning-fast strokes, delivered as his attackers swooped past him with snapping beaks and yells of fury, never touched a feather.

In this pandemonium the guns began to speak, but the hysterical crows gave no heed. No doubt they attributed their casualties to Cousin Felix. The uproar mounted until it was all but deafening.

The gunners shot until their guns were hot. The Captain was the first to run out of ammunition. With his last cartridge he knocked a hatful of feathers out of a crow as the bird pulled out of a power dive. Presently the Judge, and then Cam, had to stop for the same reason.

The battle had lasted twenty minutes and the carnage had been considerable. Dead crows lay all about the place, but it was not until the gunners stepped out of concealment that the survivors reluctanty withdrew to an adjacent hill where they perched in a big maple tree and continued to shout and argue. Occasionally, a bold fellow would come back to make one more pass at the hated enemy.

The dead were counted and the cripples dispatched.

Cousin Felix, a thoroughly demoralized animal by this time, was as loath to come down from the tree as he had been to go up, but he was finally pulled from his perch and lowered into his sack.

"He appears to be a mite overstrung," Cam observed, "but otherwise he seems to be all right. I couldn't see that the crows were actually peckin' him—they just popped their beaks as they went by."

"I'll bet Cousin Felix has had a change of heart about birds. If we can find enough ammunition we could train lots of cats this summer," said the Captain, who was greatly pleased with the manner in which his scheme had worked out.

The Judge, too, was enthusiastic.

"What a shoot that was! I don't want to hear anything more about horned owls and decoys after this. Give me a brindle tomcat every time."

Returning, the party stopped a half mile outside the village and released Cousin Felix from his thralldom. He seemed to know of a short cut leading to his home, for he wafted himself over a four-foot hedge and departed with the speed of an arrow.

"Could be he don't like us," mused Cam.

"Could be," agreed the Captain.

That evening in the Spooner home on West Street, Mrs. Spooner triumphantly called her husband's attention to a very peculiar thing.

Their cat, a brindle tom, was asleep in a corner of the room farthest from the door. His pads twitched spasmodically, his ears flattend and his tail bristled. A low moaning sound came from his throat.

Mr. Spooner suffered cats, but did not love them. He was always sitting down on one and losing a year of his life.

"George! Look at Tabby!" exclaimed Mrs. Spooner, who believed that Tabby's kittenless state indicated a moral achievement on the part of her pet. "Just look at her!"

"Ma'am, your danged cat, as I've told you before, ain't a her, he's a he."

"Well, anyway, George, you've always held it up that cats have no souls because they don't dream like dogs do. Well, you look at Tabby! If she isn't dreaming and talking in her sleep, I want to know."

ONE
TO GET
READY

The narrow southern extremity of the Lake which leads from Fort Ticonderoga to the village that was called Skenesboro on the old colonial maps
is a region of singular beauty and charm. From the rugged cliffs of gray limestone which rise abruptly from the eastern shore it is no more than a long rifle
shot to the foothills of the Adirondacks on the opposite bank. Between these
massive barriers lie great marshes, the haunt of wildfowl and muskrat and
also, in due and proper season, of the fraternity of gunners, fishermen and
trappers who go there seeking sport or profit.

It was nearly sunset of a quiet September day when two men descended a
steep wooded bluff on the eastern shore and after briefly surveying their surroundings found seats for themselves on the exposed roots of a great butternut tree which grew at the water's edge.

They were dressed in worn and faded shooting clothes, and their long boots
were splashed with mud, but, other than a pair of hatchets, they bore no
weapons.

One of them, a lean and grizzled individual, fished out a package of cigarettes and offered it to his companion.

"No, thank you, my boy," said the Judge, "I believe I'll fill my pipe."
Which he proceeded to do, and when the tobacco was well lighted he rested
his thick shoulders against the gray bark of the butternut and lifted his gaze
in owlish contemplation of the scene before them.

There was a curious unwonted atmosphere of complacency and virtue
about the pair. They grinned at each other and the Judge between puffs
emitted a low and happy sound. Had it issued from any throat other than
that of a dignified Justice of the Supreme Court it could only have been described as a purr.

"When it comes to the business of duck shooting," he remarked senten-
tiously, "there's nothing like being forehanded, my boy. I'm good an' tired of
leaving things to the last minute an' having to flounder around in the dark

241

trying to locate a place to shoot from and building blinds in places where no ducks come, and, like as not, if they *do* come, the dawn's early light discloses that the dang blind is wrong side to or something. A blind ain't worth much, you see, if you can't see the ducks and the ducks can see you. That ought to be apparent even to a person of your questionable intelligence."

The Captain snorted.

"I've heard that song before, you old, fat, slothful devil. But who's responsible for our present very favorable prospects? Who was it that found you drowsing at your desk and forced you to come out here and engage in a little unwonted activity? I'll tell you who it was; it was—"

The Judge interrupted. "*I know* who it was! I wasn't asleep, I was just momentarily relaxing from my labors," he declared, "but let it pass. The main thing is that the day after tomorrow we can arise at a reasonable hour, partake of a satisfactory breakfast, pick up Cam at his house and proceed without heat, discomfiture, or undue haste to the Big Slough. Once here we will, or *I* will, wet my right forefinger and hold it aloft. Having by this means determined the direction of the wind we'll know which blinds to occupy and from then on it will be merely a matter of shooting ducks."

"The easiest thing in the world," agreed the Captain.

Before them spread the flat alluvial marshes covered, at this season, with rippling banks of wild oats and rushes as yet untouched by frost. A winding channel of open water divided the green morass. In times past this narrow waterway had been a link in the principal line of communication between the Province of Quebec and the settlements of the Hudson River Valley. But for a thousand years before that, these verdant shores had known the light ripple of the canoes of Iroquois and Algonquin war parties. The Jesuits, too, had passed this way on the grim path to martyrdom. Afterward, for a century and a half, the cliffs echoed again and again to the roll of drums and the squeal of pipes, the crash of musketry and the thunder of heavy ordnance as the reverberations of an Old World quarrel rose and fell and finally died away in the forests and mountains of the New.

Then, following Burgoyne's disastrous invasion, for many peaceful years, barges laden with tea, salt, soft iron billets, gunpowder and other necessities and luxuries had voyaged northward to the settlements and landings to return with cargoes made up of the rude products of the frontier.

When the coming of the railways finally ended the romantic boisterous heyday of the "canal boaters," the craft continued in diminished numbers and dingier aspect to carry burdens of lumber, coal, oil and other supplies, accepting these humble tasks without complaint.

Our friends beneath the butternut tree were made aware that they were about to witness the passage of a group of these burthen-bearers, for the valley echoed the slow rhythmical thud of an engine, and presently a tug swam into view around Maple Bend trailing three long barges under its plume of smoke. As it proceeded, the silent reaches of the marsh came to noisy life. The slow waves spreading from blunt bows raised the vegetation in long, hissing undulations which brought acute dismay to the rails and bitterns hiding in the rushes. Great pickerel darted from their ambuscades; startled black ducks and teal sprang aloft from the suddenly agitated pools where they had been basking and preening, countless frogs and turtles felt the mounting panic and plopped incontinently overboard from the mudbanks and bits of water-log-ged driftwood along the shore. A kingfisher, who had learned long since how he might reap profit from these alarms, sat quietly upon a willow stub until a school of nervous minnows darted into view and then, with a triumphant rattle and a downright plunge, snatched a silvery fish for his supper.

All these signs and activities were observed with profound interest by the two friends as the boats drew slowly past in single file. The dark-skinned men who made up the scanty crews seemed as drab and weatherworn as their barges, but they returned the salutes of the two spectators with an air of grave condescension as befitted courtesies shown mere landlubbers by those whose noble lot it is to ride the mighty deep. Their laundries of frayed shirts and overalls fluttered dejectedly from lines stretched amidships, like the sorrowful battle signals of a fight already lost.

"Canucks," said the Judge, disparagingly, as he observed the dark and sul-len visages of the men. "I can smell shag tobacco and onions."

And that may well have been partly true, for a man with a clay pipe be-tween his teeth sat on the stern of the last barge holding a trolling line with which he alternately released and retrieved the trailing spoon which spun and glittered far to the rear of the procession.

Even as they watched the line suddenly jerked taut in the fisherman's hands. That worthy instantly leaped to his feet and released a flood of shouted epithet and instructions in French. His pipe fell to the deck unno-ticed while he hauled away at his heavy tackle. A fat woman in a faded red wrapper appeared at the cabin door, adding her shrill comentary to the hub-bub as she ran to the assistance of her man, whose pipe now lay in shattered fragments beneath his prancing feet. The entire fleet came to life. Men, women and swarms of children appeared magically at every vantage point on the preceding craft to give aid and counsel to the valiant comrade.

It was evident that not all of the onlookers were in strict agreement as to the best method of dealing with a ten-pound pickerel, for there were shouts of "Doucement, doucement! Non de Dieu!" rendered in falsetto, and others at the extreme opposite, both in vocal register and counsel, bawled, "Hardi! Mon gar!" and "Pool heem een, Jacques, ma frien'!"

But Jacques, obviously a sensible angler, had a well-proved method of his own and gave no attention whatsoever to the shower of admonition raining upon him. His first powerful tug had lifted his fish halfway out of the water, and there, by rapid manipulation of the line assisted in no small way by the four-knot speed of his vessel, he kept it. The pickerel skittered helplessly along the surface completely deprived of any means to resist either in its natural element or in the fatal rarefied atmosphere above it.

So, swiftly and ignominiously, the fish was brought alongside. The fat woman retrieved it with a boat hook.

As the stern of the barge slid from the view of the two men on the shore, the heard a final tragic declamation from Jacques. It was clear and distinct in the brooding twilight.

"Marie! Marie! I gat de feesh, ho kay, but I'll was be bust mah sacre goddam peep all to Hell!"

The two men on the shore exchanged glances.

"Well, Jacques, mah frien' " said the Captain, rising to his feet, "in the words of the poet, 'there is no joy unmixed with woe'."

The Honorable Justice also rose and tapped his pipe bowl against the tree while his glance ranged again over the green watery meadows to the towering ramparts of the mountains beyond. The muted throb of the tugboat now turning the angle of the narrows above came pleasantly to his ears.

"I wish," said he, "that I'd gone in for canal boating. Let's try it a whack sometime and hire passage on one o' 'em to Montreal. We can take our guns and fishing tackle and see the sights and have fun."

"Have you ever *been* in one o' those cabins?" inquired his friend. "No? Well I have, and thought myself lucky to get out again before the bugs ate me up. Also there were certain antique fragrances in there that I knew were all of a hundred years old. The pea-soupers don't seem to mind it, bein' brought up on it. But the idea in general is a good one and maybe someday we could charter a cleaner craft of some sort and make a trip of it. We'll get Cam and the Doctor to come along. Ralf, too, if he can get away, and we'll load up with supplies and go where we please." Still dwelling upon the engaging prospects of such a voyage, he set out along a dim grass-grown path that led to the top of the bluff. The other followed.

The Big Slough, where they had built their blinds and where they proposed to establish themselves on the opening day of the wildfowl season, was one of a score of shallow irregular bays which are characteristic of the area. At some prehistoric period these sloughs had been deep fissures battered into the great limestone barrier to the east. The tempest-tossed waves of an inland ocean had dashed in thunder against the castellated cliffs, and monstrous creatures had fought and bellowed where today the gentle wood duck rear their broods and one will hear no sound more terrifying than the drums of the grouse, the chatter of the squirrel and the gasping bark of the red fox.

As the great waters receded they brought down as tribute deposits of rich silt from the hills and this as it settled in the depressions of the emergent shore formed the typical slough, which is in fact a tributary of the Lake rather than an integral part of it. The marshes are moistened by spring-fed brooks, which spread their waters over the flat expanses of silt and drain away at last into Champlain through a maze of winding creeks and channels moving imperceptibly beneath a canopy of oaks, elms and buttonwood trees.

The ducks against whose safety and well being our friends conspired were almost without exception natives of the locality, born and reared in these pleasant backwaters and grown fat and succulent upon a rich and varied diet. There were black duck, bluewing and greenwing teal, with an occasional rare cinnamon. There have also been noted in recent years increasing numbers of widgeon, pintail and the gray mallard. Inasmuch as these latter species had been almost entirely absent for many years, their return is hailed by the local gunners as a significant and happy sign. And then there are the wood duck, hordes of them, to delight the eye and ear of the wildfowler even while they exasperate him by continually offering fair shots that can only be taken at the risk of inviting legal vengeance administered at the hands of a rural Justice of the Peace.

None of the great flocks of migrants which in October and November sweep southward along the Lake ever visits or tarries in the sloughs. These environs remain forever secured to the uses and enjoyments of the puddle ducks, the rails, bitterns and the statuesque herons, and to the frogs and the frog-hunting raccoons, the muskrat and the mink, the partridge that feeds upon the wild grapes and the beechnut mast, and the woodcock that loves the moist banks.

Twice each twelve months the somnolent tranquillity of the sloughs is disturbed. The first of these noisy invasions is that of the wildfowlers who, on opening day, and intermittently thereafter until the marshes freeze, occupy every pot-hole and point. They do a prodigious amount of shooting and bag an amazingly disproportionate number of ducks. Again in the spring, for a week or two, the light skiffs of the muskrat trappers plow their dim trails through the sodden waste and floating debris that was midsummer's lovely mantle. Woe betide the muskrat who thinks at this season to enjoy his nocturnal supper at his accustomed dining-place on a half-submerged log, for there will be set a snare for his undoing. Woe to him also if, on his way to visit his lady love, he crosses open water, for his journey is more likely to end with a tiny bullet from the trapper's rifle in his brain than in the delights of amorous dalliance.

As far as the Judge, the Captain, Cam, and a dozen other male residents of Tranquillity were concerned, the last day of the closed season was one of intense industry, but not one of profit.

The Judge gazed upon a lengthy petition of sorts bound in blue paper covers and came to no conclusion whatsoever except that the profession of Law is a dull and wordy business at best. At eleven o'clock in the forenoon he gave it up and phoned the Captain, to ask him to lunch at the Tavern.

The Captain accepted with alacrity, for all morning long he had been interrupted by discouraged voices inquiring if he knew of *any* place where a man could lay hands on a box of twelve-gauge 6's or 2's or 4's or even 8's. It was a source of great satisfaction to him that he could do so and that he did. Thanks to the recent and timely benevolence of a nameless Christian, a whole case of twelve-gauge 6's reposed in the basement. It was enough to get him elected to the United States Senate if he ever wanted to run for that office, but what with trips to and from the basement his manuscript suffered. Immediately after the Judge called he pushed his pages aside and made a final descent to the basement. He returned with five boxes of twelve-gauge 6's, and addressed the Dark-Haired Lady.

"One box for Bill Reed's boy. One box for Jim Gamble. One box for Frank Sheville. One box for the Superintendent of Schools, and one box for the little Parson who lives down the lane. They will call for 'em, and they will ask 'how much.' Tell 'em to go to Hell, particularly the Parson. The Lord giveth and the Lord taketh away."

He was gone and the Dark-Haired Lady realized that nothing could be done about it even if she had wished to do anything. She picked up a dust mop and listened for the doorbell.

Cam, meanwhile, was in no better case. Nancy, who was his wife, and far above his desserts, had come down to the office to straighten out the scratches and scrawls that recorded her husband's business transactions. She brought to order such items as "P. Douglas, welding seat, $2.50." "Jake Goodrich, removing carbon, grinding valves, $6.80." "Starting motor for B. Daniels, $.25. Damn fool didn't have ignition on."

She was dutifully entering cogent information in the ledger and chuckling occasionally at her husband's whimsies, while Cam and his helper assembled their tools and advanced upon a mud-spattered Ford truck. But before a blow could be struck, Al Wilson stuck his red head in at the door to inquire whereabouts did Cam intend to go tomorrow, and did he know by any chance where a man could lay hands on a box of twelve-gauge 6's? These and such as these are questions that can't be answered in one or two sentences, and considerable time passed while Cam elaborated and Al agreed.

"But, don't, for Pete's sake, tell the Cap'n I sent ye," he admonished, as Al set forth with a gleam of hope in his eyes.

He had scarcely vanished when Rick Davis came in on identical business. Following Rick came the little Jones boy, the one with the twisted leg. He'd gotten hold of a twenty-bore single-barrel and kind-hearted Cam found a box of shells which he gave to the eager-eyed lad along with some top secret advice as to where to go and what to do.

Then the phone rang, and he heard Nancy say, "I'll tell him. He'll be along right away."

She spoke to her husband.

"That was the Judge, Cameron. He wants you to come up for lunch at the

Tavern." There was a twinkle in her gray eyes. "I told him you'd come right along. You might as well. All you've done this whole enduring morning has been to pick up that hammer and put it down again. Run along now, little man, and have a good time."

"By Crimus, Ma'am. I b'lieve you're right! Duck huntin' generally takes three days if a man's lucky—one to get ready, two to go, and three to pick ducks. There ain't any use tryin' to go against Nature."

He laid the hammer gently down on the bench.

"You'll be there," said he to the hammer, "when I get back."

At the Tavern the host welcomed the Judge and led him furtively away to the big kitchen, where, with a reverent gesture, he lifted the cover from a battered hamper.

It was filled with oysters, fresh and cold and bedded in seaweed. The old sportsman reached for a knife. The opening shell released a breath of brine, fog and the winds of the sea, and then the oyster, a creature of humble aspirations, which only yesterday had believed that it was firmly and permanently cemented to a rock some three fathoms down in the Atlantic Ocean, entered the legal profession.

The host beamed upon his guest.

"Now, sir, ain't they prime eyesters? I declare, I'm as praoud o' 'em almost as if I'd raised 'em myself. 'Git 'em fresh,' sez I, 'or leave 'em be.' Dang these poor washed aout things thet hev been shucked an' froze an' thawed out an' froze agin. I won't tech 'em. They ain't bigger'n a shotgun wad, an' they taste much the same. 'Course these here prime eyesters cost ye a leetle extra, but who wants to feed his purse an' starve his stomach?"

"You never spoke a truer word," said the Judge solemnly. He could eat hardtack and singed bacon when necessary, and relish the fare; but he was a sensible man with a taste for chops, steaks, venison, bullheads, brook trout, game and seafood.

"Now then, Cameron and the Captain will have lunch with me and I believe we can handle three or four dozen of these fellows among us, and somewhere near a gallon of ale. Yes, and a modicum of horse radish and vinegar and a good store of those butter rolls your Missus makes."

The host flipped a pad from his pocket and made some entries with a pencil.

"Yes, sir, Jedge. You shall hev it right on the dot." Then, the business secured, he put the pad away. "Goin' duck huntin' tomorrow, I s'pose? Well, sir, I'd dearly love to go myself. Would too, if I had any ca'tridges for my gun. Prob'ly you wouldn't know where a man could lay his hands on a box o' twelve-gauge 6's?"

AND
TWO
TO GO

During the night the Lake had drawn over it a thick blanket of white wool as a protection against the threat of frost in the upper air. Every familiar aspect and landmark had been swallowed up in the silent opacity which concealed from the occupants of the car first, the presence, and then the identity of all objects up to the very moment of imminent collision. The fact that Cam and the Captain were anxiously endeavoring to penetrate the deceptive curtain gave the Judge, who was driving, little comfort and no help whatever, for when something monstrous and menacing swam down upon them in the ocean of mist he saw it as quickly as did his passengers, and if it had not been so, their warning cries would have been too late to stop him from plunging the chariot into the creek, or folding it up accordion-fashion against the base of a sturdy elm. Nothing was what it seemed to be in the swirling phantasmagoria. The creek resembled the road and the road resembled the creek. A late wandering 'coon, when suddenly confronted by the glaring headlights, looked like a grizzly bear for an instant before the animal reassumed its proper proportions and vanished in the murk. A plot of cropped alfalfa into which the Judge turned in order to get away from the dangerous proximity of the creek turned out to be a field of standing corn, and the Judge drove strongly across a dozen rows before the thump of roasting ears against the windshield and the yelps of his companions made him aware of his error.

Thereupon he stopped the car and the engine and addressed the fog-bound universe.

"A back-seat driver is a damned fool to begin with," he announced, giving expression to an idea that he had been entertaining for some time. "I believe that I can see as far into this soup as either of you fellers—a mite farther, perhaps, to judge from your reactions. If I'd waited for you to holler we'd have been halfway up that 'coon tree back there. But let that pass. The point is that if I hear another yip out of you we'll leave the car where she sits and walk the rest of the way. It ain't much more than four miles farther. What do you say to that?"

"Nothin', Your Honor, and we're both sorry that you misunderstood us. We weren't finding fault with your driving. We like the way you do it, don't we, Cam?"

"Why certainly," agreed Cam with much heartiness. "I ain't had such a nice time since the pigs ate my little brother."

The Judge appeared to be mollified, and in the absence of further suggestions from his passengers he steered a precarious course onward to their destination.

The jurist's wet forefinger, when he exposed it upon arrival, gave no indication of a breeze from any direction. In the pre-dawn darkness the world about them lay hushed and breathless. Far away a farm dog chivvying his cows yapped like a sergeant major, and near at hand there was the slow drip of water from the saturated foliage, the plop of a feeding fish or a diving muskrat and then, and best of all, the throaty reveille of a black duck, "Quaaa-quaa-qua," as he summoned his dusky company to salute the dawn, never dreaming that it would usher in a day of fright and death-from-ambush for the Clan of the Webbed Foot.

They were three merciful men, but the voice of the wildfowl sounding through the mist roused in them wild echoes from the dim ages, long before men had learned to till the soil or practice law for their daily bread.

"Hear that old fellow," muttered Cam, and there was a predatory gleam in the Judge's normally kindly eyes as he drew his famous old hammer gun from its case and assembled it.

Unlike his two friends, the old sportsman never had to undergo the pleasant agony of choosing from an arsenal of weapons a special gun to suit the occasion. Not he. Let others spend small fortunes on duck guns, goose guns, partridge guns, and woodcock guns. He scorned such nonsense. Except for a pair of beautiful muzzle-loaders inherited from a sporting ancestor who had died on the field of battle, our friend had only one shotgun to his name, and for two score years he had used it with great and equal success upon all manner of flying game from woodcock and snipe to the lordly turkey and the Canada goose. It was a nobly proportioned piece of twelve bore, and the Captain, who as a connoisseur admired it greatly, had once determined that the left barrel had been bored half choke while the right was no more than a strong improved cylinder. According to the highest authorities on the ballistics of the shotgun, the Judge therefore had a weapon that was nearly ideal for the shooting of light-feathered upland game birds, but which would be practically worthless for anything else. Yet its owner, who knew little and cared less about the intricacies and exactitudes of the science of ballistics, could with an ounce of 9's and the same gun, tip a woodcock into the birches at fifteen paces without ruffling a feather, or stop a goose dead with an ounce and an eighth of 2's at four times that distance.

Nor would the Judge have anything to do with the heavily charged modern cartridges, after having tried a couple of them. In his light gun they jarred him painfully.

"By the Lord Harry," he remarked, rubbing his jaw, "if I've got to stand up to that sort of thing every time I shoot a duck, I'll quit shooting ducks. I don't give a darn if they'll shoot a mile, which they feel as if they would. The fact remains that I can't hit a duck that far, and anyway, you don't need to eviscerate the poor critters if all you want to do is to kill 'em."

So, forswearing the doubtful benefits of progress, he continued to use his favorite brand of shell loaded with three drams of good Dupont powder, and to use them with such consummate skill that his companions were confounded and often made to wonder if they knew as much as they thought they did about these vital matters.

Cam was armed, surprisingly enough, with a fine new double-barrel of twelve bore, which, until recently, had been dedicated by the War Department to the savage business of shooting Nazi paratroopers and spies. When none of these unsavory scoundrels appeared to violate the peace of the neighborhood, a remote authority allowed Cam to purchase from the Ordnance Department for the sum of fifteen dollars and fifty cents a notable fowling piece. In those strange days when the clouds never discharged upon the earth and its inhabitants anything but lightning, rain, hail and snow, it would have cost him five times that amount at Pingree's Hardware Store.

"The feller that had this gun in the State Guard told me that it shot slugs fine an' that with buckshot he thought a man might maybe hit a mule once in ten shots at four rod," said the proud owner, "but it did all right with number 6's when I tried her on crows."

By the time the three had assembled their gear the fog had lifted somewhat, and a wan light was about them.

"I believe," said one, "that daylight'll bring a breeze from the south. In that case, a couple of us should be on the Point and t'other one in the little blind near the muskrat house."

"I'll take the muskrat blind since I know where it is, and you and Cam go to the Point," the Captain volunteered, "and let us pray that the far-shooters and spoilsports all overslept and stayed at home."

"I ain't hoping too much," remarked Cam, "for there is generally at least one of the danged fools to every marsh on opening day tryin' hard to kill ducks so far away that if he did kill one, it would spoil long 'fore he could get it."

The Captain's blind was nothing more than a low clump of tangled buttonwood brush which thrust its crooked arms and twisted fingers from the ooze, grasping for its humble share of air and sunshine from a footing too unstable to support the weight of its loftier neighbors on the shore. He had added a few sprigs and cuttings here and there in an attempt to heighten the illusory quality of the pattern created by the confusion of broken lines and deceptive shadows. Neither he nor his companions just across on the Point had decoys, for they needed none this early in the season. The wildfowl, bewildered by the shooting on the neighboring sloughs, could be expected to seek refuge from the unwonted tumult in these hitherto peaceful fens without further inducement in the way of wooden effigies.

The gunner hung his leather cartridge bag on a convenient sapling, and opened its flap. Then, with his gun loaded and all preparations made, he seated himself on a root and gave himself up to the contemplation of his surroundings. It still lacked a few minutes of the zero hour, but he did not need to consult his watch, for a salvo from a dozen guns would inform him promptly when the time came.

The light strengthened and the mist, warned of the near approach of the Lord of the Day, began to loosen its clammy hold upon the woods and waters. It formed its silent legions into diaphanous columns which rolled and twisted slowly above the trees. Now the shore line beyond the narrow waterway was visible, enabling the watcher to see his companions making their final preparations. Even as he looked, their heads and shoulders disappeared from view and the slight sounds of their furtive activities ceased.

More even than the sharp excitement and action which was soon to come, the Captain relished these last moments of anticipation. It is at this time that Man, the Hunter, is able to free himself from the irksome swaddling-clothes of conventional society. For a little space he finds himself repossessed of an ancient heritage. In some degree, he experiences a physical regeneration, also. The rank fragrance of the marsh strikes more sharply in his nostrils; his vision is magically cleared; the dull scales of habit fall from his eyes, so that he no longer looks without also seeing; the slightest sounds from fen, and forest suddenly become as distinct and significant to him as they had been in the ears of hairy Esau and of all other mighty hunters of the ages past.

These were the thoughts that occupied the Captain's mind that morning, as he sat with his ready gun in his hands and realized that two score years of wildfowling had not taught him how to suppress the convulsive shivers that ran through him.

The Doctor had once explained that the whole business was the result of a glandular activity, "more adrenalin pumped into the blood stream," said he, and the Captain received this scientific information with a respect that approached reverence. He also observed on more than one occasion, that despite his knowledge of the cause, the gruff old healer evidently had no cure for it, since he himself shook like a wet spaniel whenever a flock of black ducks set their wings to his decoys. Moreover, the Doctor hadn't been able to name the thing that started the adrenalin pump.

"Just as well, too," thought the Captain, "for if we ever manage to find out everything about everything it will be an exceedingly dull existence. If I ever get to the point that I don't quiver in a duck blind at zero minus five, I shall sell the best fowling piece in the world and devote the proceeds to the advancement of the cause of temperance, for the delights and amenities of good drinking, eating, and of more or less ribald talk will also have been lopped off by the same cruel stroke, and we shall find ourselves in a pallid world indeed."

These philosophical reflections were interrupted by the sound of a shot somewhere to the south, and then came an uneven fusillade as other skirmishers opened fire. A double report near at hand roused the marsh before him, and in an instant the place was noisy with the quackings and spatterings as, flock after flock, the startled host of wildfowl took wing.

A gaunt blue heron stumbled aloft, discharging a copious ballast as it rose, together with a stream of hoarse-voiced curses upon the ill-mannered folk who had spoiled his fishing. The panic spread throughout the marsh as alarum followed alarum. A partridge making a breakfast upon the wild blue grapes in a vine-draped tree nearby added to the mounting tumult by taking off with a thunder of wings louder by far than the sounds made by the flock of teal which at that moment swept over the Captain's blind like a flight of arrows. Now, in all directions, ducks were moving restlessly. Several small flocks passed within a few yards of the hidden gunners, who were hard put to it to hold their fire.

"If we shoot at 'em while they're going out," Cam whispered with his eyes following a pair of black ducks, "they won't want to come back, but if we let the big bunches go they'll come back later in singles and pairs, just the way we like 'em."

The sound of firing increased on all sides. It seemed possible to trace the passage of a single flock of birds as it swung to and fro above the neighboring marshes from the volleying that greeted it from a score of ambuscades near and far.

"Now you know there's a devil of a lot more ammunition around here than I've been led to suppose," the Judge remarked.

"And most of it's being wasted," the other observed. "See that flock flare over yonder! Somebody shot at 'em away up there. Didn't want 'em to get too close prob'ly. If that's what he's scared of he could save money by bringing along a dishpan an' whangin' on it with a rock. But he's turned 'em, an' if they're left alone I b'live they'll come in."

The small flock of black ducks swept overhead. They were out of range but the thrilling sound of their flight came clearly to the ears. It died away as the birds passed from view behind a distant wooded hill.

Cam and the Judge crouched motionless with heads bowed as in prayer. One spoke in low tones: "They're makin' a turn. They're makin' a turn."

There was a long minute of tense immobility in both blinds, for the Captain was also alert and from his vantage point had been better able to observe the aerial maneuverings which would have seemed vague and without purpose to eyes untrained in plotting the shifting, evasive tactics of a leader drake whose squadron has heard the whistle of shot. He had seen the turn and the deceptive spiral dip that the old drake executed a half mile beyond the slough, which meant that he had decided to bring his family into this peaceful-seeming cove. The Captain slipped the safety button on his gun to the "off" position.

"That old feller is going to bring 'em in past the point, turn 'em downwind, bring 'em back over Cam and the Judge, turn 'em again and land the whole lot right in front of me. Only he won't land 'em and there won't be so many of 'em, either, if the boys are awake and do their duty."

There is no wildfowler worthy of the title who is not convinced of his ability to predict what a flock of ducks will do once it has taken wing. It is a harmless foible. The fact that the prophet is nearly always completely wrong causes him no dismay, nor does it lessen his confidence in his perspicuousness.

The Captain shared this delusion, and was greatly encouraged when the flock reappeared beyond the point flying some thirty yards above the water. It turned into the wind in precise accordance with his prediction and swung back. As it passed, the hidden guns spoke and three of the birds pitched down to float lifelessly among the wild oat stalks. The survivors flared toward the Captain, who felt that the day had begun auspiciously when a single well-aimed shot brought a lofty straggler crashing into the buttonwood almost within reach of his hand.

He had scarcely reloaded when a plump little teal coming from nowhere popped over the blind. The first hasty shot was a clean miss at fifteen yards, but the second charge tumbled the saucy little duck into the willows.

Presently the Judge won the unqualified admiration of his friends by executing a perfectly timed double on a pair of gray ducks that came over so high that the Captain thought them to be out of range until his sharpshooting friend proved otherwise.

And now the ducks driven off the neighboring marshes began dropping in, and the gunners were busy. For an hour the shooting reminded the Judge of red-letter days he had enjoyed on the great waterfowl marshes of the Gulf Coast and in Arkansas.

So far they had not been annoyed by overeager gunners, but they were not to escape one disagreeable experience. It came when a pot hunter sneaking along the wooded shore fired a load of shot into the blind where Cam and the Judge were crouching. Cam was badly stung and also thoroughly aroused.

He shouted a warning and rose to his feet.

The offender bore a striking resemblance to the late Italian dictator, and his response was in keeping with his appearance.

"Why de Hell you fellas no git where somebody see you! Huh?" adding a ferocious curse and a menacing gesture.

Cam took a single cartridge from a pocket of his jacket and held it up to view.

"Listen, Mister Mussolini, this one is loaded with buckshot, an' if you shoot into us again you're goin' to get it!"

He spoke with the calm authority of a man who intends to execute his promises.

"To Hell wit' you!" said the careless one bitterly, but it was only a token of defiance for he turned and stumbled off in the direction whence he came.

"Just as well *that* brother wasn't using buckshot," Cam remarked, "he'd have killed the pair of us deader'n a hammer."

"I believe, Cameron, that you *would* have shot him."

Cam grinned, and rubbed his sore spots.

"Maybe I would," said he.

A lone mallard drake now appeared high above the trees on a scouting mission apparently, for he showed no sign of making a landing. The green-head is rare in the locality, and therefore it is highly prized. The Captain was sorely tempted. Though high, the big bird was coming straight over him at the best angle for a long shot. The gunner yielded and had the intense satisfaction of seeing the drake crumple at the shot. It hit far back on the slope with a solid thud.

"Gosh!" exclaimed Cam. "Did you see that one! And he's shooting that little sixteen-gauge gun, too."

The Judge explained. "That little sixteen ain't just an ordinary sixteen. One of the best gunmakers in the world made three of 'em before he satisfied our long-legged friend over yonder. When the brother is in the groove, as he was just then, that gun'll kill ducks even higher than that."

He continued.

"We were shooting down on Mattamuskeet, let me see, two, no, three years ago. The old boy was in good trim. He was reveling in one of those 'can't-miss-'em-if-you-want-to', 'shoot-the-head-off-a-pin' spells which come to us occasionally and make us realize that we're but a little lower than the angels. All the guides on the Lake came up to our room the first evening to look at 'the big ten-gauge magnum' we'd had in our blind that day. They couldn't believe it when he handed 'em a little six-and-a-half-pound double-barrel.

"The second day there went even better, and he pulled off a double on a pair of geese that I'll swear weren't less than seventy yards up. Both of 'em stone dead, too. It was one of the prettiest shots I ever saw. Everybody on the Lake saw it, too, and *that* night we had more beverages proffered us than we could manage. It's quite a gun and he knows it, for he's kept it for twenty years or more."

The sound of footsteps announced a second visitor.

"Maybe Mussolini's coming back to see if I meant it," remarked the younger sportsman. Then his eye caught a glimpse of a uniform. "No, it ain't Mussy. It's the Game Warden making his rounds."

The Warden was an old and highly respected friend, and he paused to give them news of how the day had gone on the other marshes.

Cam seized an opportunity.

"Tom," said he, "there was a fat, dirty-lookin' cuss came along here an hour or so ago pot hunting. He stung me good with a load of shot. It just came to me that he might not have a license even to shoot ducks."

Tom grinned. "He didn't, and he did have three wood ducks. Bill Pickett got him, and he's on his way right now to tell the Justice how come."

The Warden stopped to chat with the Captain, and then went his way satisfied that no high crimes or misdemeanors had been committed here.

Save for an occasional shot, there was nothing now to disturb the customary quietude of the marshes, for the greater part of the wildfowl had discovered that enemies noisier and more dangerous and terrifying than the duck hawk and the mink had invaded their summer homes. Their flocks were now resting safely on the open waters of the Lake and, it may be, counting their casualties of the morning.

The mudhens were comforted by the pervading silence and timorously emerged from seclusion to swim jerkily here and there while with increasing boldness they snatched their breakfasts from the brown water. The heron, too, came sailing in on set and silent wings and made an awkward landing on his long stilts. Thereafter for some minutes he stood tense and erect while he examined the familiar scenes for any sign of danger. Finding none, he relaxed his vigilance and resumed the unending effort to satisfy an appetite as sharp as his gaunt form suggested.

"The trouble with Old Beak and Legs," said Cam in low tones to his companion as they watched the big bird impale and swallow a six-inch dace without visibly increasing its meagre bulk, "is that he don't hang on to his rations long enough to take any nourishment from 'em. If he had three, four loops in his insides to slow down his digestion, that feller would be fat as butter an' wouldn't have to work so steady at his fishin'."

This critical analysis of the heron's internal deficiencies apparently had the effect of reminding the speaker of his own, for he offered a suggestion that was received favorably by his companion and which was promptly endorsed by the Captain when they mentioned it to him.

So they withdrew to the vicinity of the car and while one built an "Indian fire" to broil a rack of the spicy little sausages for which Tranquillity was famous, another laid out the bread and cheese and the Judge pried the caps off the ale bottles which he had thoughtfully provided.

The ale was cool and sweet and mildly bitter on their tongues.

Cam lowered his mug.

"Better than swamp water," said he.

" 'Much has been said in praise of ale,' " remarked the Captain. "That's a quotation, and here's another. My good friend Pitkin called it to my attention and it pleased me so much that I memorized it. It's by George Borrow, who wrote a book some ninety-odd years ago. The speaker has just given a pitcher of ale to some poor disconsolate people at an English tavern.

" 'They could have found water in the road,' says George, 'but they wanted not water. Meat and bread? Go to, they were not hungry. Money? What right had I to insult them by offering them money? Advice? Words, words, words. Friends, there is a time for everything: There is a time for a cup of cold water: There is a time for strong meat and bread: There is a time for advice, and there is a time for ale—and I have generally found that the time for advice is after a cup of ale.' "

His audience expressed their unlimited approval of the Borrow sentiment and the Judge added:

"Very good, indeed, my boy, but I don't seem to require your advice, as maybe I shall after another mug of ale."

While he was finishing it, the chef pronounced the sausages at the proper state of crisp, fat-spurting succulency, the lid of the battered coffee pot was clicking gently and the three friends began their leisurely meal.

As they ruminated, their glances roamed over the fields and hills and marshes. They spoke or were silent in their companionship. One noted the tell-tale crimson thread of an ivy vine woven through the untouched greenery of the elms and reflected that the ivy and the water maple are the first of the forest sentinels to tell of the coming glory and splendors of autumn. Cam, a fox hunter, traced a wooded notch above a distant sheep pasture, and concluded it would be a fox-crossing when his old hound took up his patient musical profession in bleak November. Another's thoughts were of a lonelier character, for he was recalling days like this when they had shared the wild-fowl and the beauty of this scene with an eager smiling boy who was at the moment somewhere on the high seas bound for old battlefields that were still fresh in his own memory despite the passage of the years.

The Judge must have read these thoughts, for he gave his friend the gentle compassionate smile that had power to make the heart glow.

Cam broke the silence.

"Wasn't something said around here about 'far-shooters' an' what should be done with 'em?" he asked the Judge.

"B'lieve I did hear our friend here declaiming somewhat about the wicked practice," agreed that worthy. "Why do you ask?"

"Oh, I suppose the cuss is talking about my mallard drake," said the Captain. "I've been expecting it from one or the other of you. But I earned that bird, my friends, for I bet a life-long reputation on that shot. If I'd missed him, you'd be reminding me of it from now on. But I didn't miss him, as you can very well see if you examine the corpus delicti. And note that there's at least six shot in it."

He picked the mallard out of a row of dead ducks and passed it to Cam.

Cam grinned and handed it back.

They lacked not many birds for their limit bag, and since no one cared greatly if it happened that the bag might be a few short at the end of the day, they decided to utilize only the last hour of the legal shooting day, that time when the skeins of returning wildfowl could be viewed against the sunset skies, and the Slough and its surroundings would gather a swiftly changing beauty from the glowing firmament.

Cam went off to confirm his suspicion of the fox crossing; the Judge dozed, and the Captain, taking his gun along, in case he should jump a flock of ducks in the course of his wanderings, set out to explore the upper reaches of the little creek that fed the Slough and to make a census of the local partridge population.

The sun was well down when he returned. He had added a single black duck to his bag and had found encouragement to hope for other holidays to come in the presence of two goodly flocks of full-grown grouse. Cam had proved his knowledge of the habits of the resident foxes, and the Judge, between naps, had thought of something that he wanted to communicate to the Governor.

They returned to their blinds and if, now and again, ducks swung past without receiving the salute to which their rank entitled them, it might have been because a gunner had been absorbed at the moment in watching a flight of ten thousand blackbirds passing to their roosts in the cattails and rushes below Fiddler's Elbow. Another might have been too much engrossed in observing how the light of the passing day wrought its magic upon the ancient ramparts that enclosed the valley.

With the last shot of the day, Cam dispatched a crippled bird and was glad that he had been able to administer a merciful end to the unfortunate creature.

Then they gathered their ducks and in the twilight crossed the field to the car, but having arrived there, they did not immediately enter the chariot, but instead they sat for half an hour watching the scene while night came striding down the distant flank of Bald Mountain.

The Judge produced a flagon, the contents of which, when the stopper had been removed, gave off the fragrance of burning heather, and the three friends in great contentment proceeded to fortify themselves against the chills and vapors.

Cam regarded his share of the game with a satisfaction somewhat tempered by the realization of grievous labor yet to come.

"Dang it!" said he, finally, "I love to shoot 'em an' I hate to pick 'em. I'll be up half the night wrastling with those birds. I've tried to make Nancy understand that pickin' ducks, skinnin' squirrels an' cleanin' fish are her proper responsibilities, but she can't seem to get it through her head. Yet she's a smart girl, too, in some ways."

"Smart in *all* ways," remarked the Captain by way of amendment.

THE
WOODCOCKERS

Ralf Coykendall, the Captain's good friend from Connecticut, had come up to help the Vermonters open their woodcock and "pa'tridge" season. It was now ten o'clock of a crisp October night and the little owls were giving their eerie calls and responses in the maples surrounding the Captain's house. If anyone had glanced in at the lighted window his spying would have been rewarded by the spectacle of three—for the Judge was also present—worthy gentlemen taking their ease before the fire. It was a goodly sight to see, for, as has often been noted by various artists, there is a benign atmosphere which envelops gunners and anglers at rest that is rarely to be found in groups gathered from other motives. The firelight gleamed upon the racked weapons which shared the walls with books and etchings and paintings of sporting scenes, and struck amber reflections from the tall glasses with which all were provided. If the non-existent Peeping Tom had been psychic he might have sensed a light tension underneath the calm relaxation of the trio, but this came from no discord among our friends; it was in fact no more than the anticipatory tremor that even the boldest veteran may feel at the prospect of action on the morrow.

They had been discussing old times and adventures and how each had been initiated into the kindred arts of venery and angling.

Ralf was speaking.

"Occasionally Uncle George Townsend would say, 'Some days start off different than others and I'll be damned if I don't think this is one of 'em.'

"I was never quite sure what the old gentleman meant by that remark, nor just what conditions, climatic or otherwise, led him to the suspicion. I generally hung around pretty close to see if he got some mysterious confirmation.

"Uncle George, who lived next door to us, was not my uncle—rather, he was everybody's uncle.

"If, half an hour or so after his first speculation, I saw him begin to make journeys between his house and the barn, I'd be encouraged and I'd keep well within range. Sometimes he would state his conclusions, but more often he would call from the barn door.

" 'Hey, Bub, we'd better get started. You get your coat an' tell your Ma we won't be back 'til after supper. I've got lunch packed for both of us.'

"In his old four-cylinder coupe we'd head off for some destination undisclosed, until I could guess it from the direction in which we were going. It might be down Seneca Castle way to fish certain small trout streams, or to Sodus Bay for a day's boat fishing for perch and rock bass. Sometimes we'd go to Geneva and hire a boat and fish deep with copper lines for the great Seneca Lake trout. In cold weather we'd often fetch up at Fred MacMillan's boatyard in Sodus Point and sit all day around the big pot-bellied stove, yarning in an aromatic atmosphere of pine shavings and spar varnish, while Fred slowly and skillfully fitted and fastened the planking on one of the double-ended rowboats for which he was famous.

"In gunning time these convictions about the nature of the day would reach Uncle George at an earlier hour. Often it would be only a little after midnight when gravel persistently thrown against my window would fetch me out of bed to find him on the lawn below.

" 'There's goin' to be duck in the marsh up at the head o' East Bay,' he'd inform me in hoarse conspiratorial tones. 'You git dressed an' bring your gun. I got shells 'nough for both of us, and breakfast is cookin'. Leave a note for your Ma.' "

Ralf paused and shifted his position slightly to get a better light on a Schaldach watercolor showing a woodcock dropping in to a landing in a cluster of white birch saplings.

"That was long ago, but as I approach what then seemed to me to be Uncle George's ancient age, I'm nearer to an understanding of the source of those whisperings that, for him, marked a day as likely to be 'different.' In fact, I'm hearing such a message right now, and presently I shall quit swinging my legs, get down off Fred MacMillan's tar barrel, and snatch a few hours of restless slumber. You must be tired of my gabbling."

"Not I," the Judge assured him, with the Captain's full approval. "I consider it a mighty interesting discourse, and before taking my reluctant departure I shall propose a health to all the 'Uncle Georges' in the world. Matter of fact, I had one, myself."

"And so did I," said the Captain, "and it's a great pity that there are no Uncle Georges in Germany and Japan. But then, those cusses don't deserve to have 'em."

So the toast was drunk, the good nights were said, the fire was banked. The little owls had also finished their discourse, and silence descended upon the old house.

The household was early a-stir, however, with the Dark-Haired Lady busy in the kitchen getting breakfast while the Captain fixed the lunch box. He cut thick pink slabs from a cold round of roast beef. These were fixed between slices of bread and well plastered with a special cement made from dairy butter, peanut butter and sharp mustard forcibly united in a bowl according to a recipe that the mason had picked up somewhere in his travels. He wrapped half a dozen of the great sandwiches, tucked the package into an empty wooden shell box along with a smoke-blackened coffee pot, and added such oddments as doughnuts, cheese and apples.

Ralf had come into the kitchen dressed in shooting clothes. He watched the sandwich making with interest and approval.

"Couple of those will be darned handy 'long about noon," he opined.

"If we have good fortune today," said his host, "I'll broil some birds for lunch tomorrow. I know a good way to do it. You take some butter, some sour cream if you have any, currant jelly, mustard and a spot of burgundy. Melt 'em all together and then keep sozzlin' your birds in it while you're broilin' 'em. It's good."

"Sounds like it, but where in h——, where in heck did you find the recipe?"

"Figgered it out myself," the Captain admitted complacently, "though I got the sour cream and mustard part from a little restaurant that used to be on the Rue Charbonne in Paris. I hate to think that right now the bloody Boche may be stuffing Joseph's chicken into their muzzles. They even use a fork as if they were ramming a cannon, damn 'em."

"Stop swearing and eat your breakfast," the Dark-Haired Lady ordered. "You oughtn't to be so intolerant. They can't *all* be bad."

"Sieg Heil," her husband growled good naturedly. "They're *all* good when *you're* holding the club, Ma'am, as I have reason to know, having been present at a previous demonstration of their virtue and loving kindness. And furthermore, if one of 'em in a gesture of friendship should take a nick out of our favorite and only son, you'd be over there laying about with a broad axe, if you could."

The Dark-Haired Lady smiled and handed him a plate of scrambled eggs and sausages.

"I was only hoping to head off Lecture Number Two," she explained to Ralf. " 'What to do with Germany' is the title. Number One is 'What to do with Japan.' It calls for earthquakes and inundations. Lecture Number Three is 'What to do with the Greasy Politicians,' and it takes him about an hour to deliver it. Number Four Lecture concerns house cats. Beyond the house cats, politicians, Nazis and Japanese nationals, he has no animosities and many friends, although some of them are in jail for minor offenses. Things like burglary in the night time," she added. "He's always getting letters written on State Penitentiary stationery asking him to please see the Governor about a rank miscarriage of justice. He's loyal to the point of loaning a spade to a grave-robbing friend," she concluded sweetly, and with a deadly accuracy that silenced the Captain's guns for the time being.

The Judge's entrance served to turn the conversation into channels that had nothing to do with intolerance or grave-robbing.

He accepted a cup of coffee poured from the red pot.

"I suppose it's to be the Mud Brook Cover, ain't it?" he inquired.

As may be assumed our friend knew well the rules of English grammar and observed them, too, but on light-hearted occasions and in intimate company he found it pleasant and appropriate to indulge now and then in one or another of the colloquialisms which are so remarkably comfortable and come so readily to the tongue.

There was something analogous about the Judge's "ain'ts" and his shooting jacket which sported more holes than canvas. Aunt Ellen who "looked after" the Judge's domestic affairs had condemned the tattered garment several seasons back as being beyond repair even by her expert and thrifty hands, but the old sportsman refused to surrender it.

"Shucks!" he protested, "I've just got it sort of broken in." And by dint of a complicated arrangement of safety pins and fish line the coat was able to contain upland game birds, a pipe and tobacco pouch, even though it dropped an occasional cartridge and could no longer give to its wearer protection against a light fog, much less a rain shower.

Mud Brook has its source in the Marsh. It is misnamed, for the complexion of its current is not due to the presence of mud, but rather to the brown seepage from the root masses of the dense thickets of alder, birch and willow which flank its slow and tortuous course.

Ralf, who was of that advanced school of thought which upholds the theory that water from any source is potable if it blends well with bourbon or Scotch, had long ago pronounced his opinion on the wholesome character of the stream, and certainly no woodcocker had ever died from the drinking of it when so blended.

The soil was a clay loam. Without sufficient rain, it became harsh and impenetrable. At such times, woodcock were not to be found in the thickets, but the case was different when the heavens opened in late September. Then every cattle-path and small depression became a shallow pool and its margins were likely to be marked with the neat patterns made by the bird's poignards and splattered with the white dapplings which to the gunner indicate the probability of a russet and black package of treasure lying close by.

The ground was in this ideal condition when our friends deployed on the eastern edge where thickets of birch and poplar saplings came up to the pasture fence. The foliage had not yet fallen and that meant quick work for eye, hand an gun.

Ralf, being less familiar with the cover than the others, was placed a few yards from the fence so that he could maintain his bearings and at the same time take on any smart woodcock trying to turn the line of gunners by flying back over the open pasture.

The Judge was next in line at a twenty-yard interval and the Captain covered the right flank with his favorite twenty-bore double. By great good fortune the long-legged sportsman had a plentiful supply of his favorite wood-cock loads. Only a month or two before that fatal December day, a big sporting goods store had overhauled its ammunition vault to dispose of odds and ends, remnants and relics at a bargain counter. To his great delight the Captain found there a full case of twenty-gauge shells loaded with two drams of Dupont powder and three-quarters of an ounce of number 10 shot. Age had not impaired the cartridges in the least. He slipped a couple into the breech and gave the starting signal to the skirmishers who now moved forward. Each man covered his assigned strip carefully by quartering back and forth like a well-trained springer. As a substitute for the nose of the absent springer the trio employed diligence and leg work so that no yard of promising ground escaped investigation. It could be argued that it is quite as thrilling to have a bird spring from invisibility to breath-taking flight right under one's nose without the slightest warning, as it is to observe the merry wriggle of a springer's rump as the dog makes game.

The first bird to flush was neither woodcock nor pa'tridge but a great cock pheasant. The bird had run across the front of the line to hide in a clump of grass where Ralf all but stepped on his gaudy back. In spite of the shock resulting from having this ornithological bazooka fired in his face, Ralf mounted his little Francotte and dropped the big fellow stone dead some twenty-five paces out in the pasture.

The Captain spied fresh white splashes at the edge of a damp thicket and his careful reconnaisance produced the signpainter, a big hen woodcock, which rose with a great bustling of wings and the famous whistle which can be duplicated by drawing a wet forefinger along the side of an empty bottle. The gunner allowed the bird some fifteen yards of "law" and fired not an instant too soon. The old cartridge went off with the flat unconvincing pop of a "squib" load, but the woodcock turned over in the air and came back to earth with an audible thump. Not a feather was awry when the gunner picked up his bird. The light charge of fine shot had done the trick neatly and as expeditiously as an ounce and a half of goose shot could have done.

The Red God who presided over the destinies of the inhabitants of the Mud Brook Cover had special orders for Ralf that day. It seemed that the gentleman from Connecticut wasn't to be shown a woodcock until he had proved himself on other game. That the woodcock were "in" was made clear by the warning shouts and occasional shots on the right, but so far he had seen but one bird, curving down over the thickets and far away.

Just ahead of him was a stand of mulberry bushes heavy with clusters of dark fruit, which in size and shape so resembles the dung of a domestic animal that some earthy Yankee farmer had re-christened the parent shrub, with the result that if you ask a resident to be shown a mulberry, you will be told that "they don't grow 'raound here," but if you inquire for a "nanny-berry bush," your friend will show you plenty of these favorites of the pa'tridge and the robin.

Well, there was a pa'tridge in Ralf's nanny-berry bush and it is not to the discredit of the gentleman from the Nutmeg State that he missed his bird when it was in the clear, and then with the aid of his grouse shooter's radar killed it stone dead after it had flashed out of view behind a thicket. It fell within the Judge's forward sector and he announced presently, and to Ralf's delight, that he had it in his pocket. He hoped it would remain in that dubious container.

After that, the Red God let Ralf in on the woodcock fun.

It was getting on to lunchtime when they reached the end of the strip where a clear spring fed a tiny rivulet and there sat down to enjoy rest and to-bacco.

While thus engaged a great flight of migrating crows began passing over-head. They came streaming down from the North, squadron after ragged squadron, in a column that extended for miles.

The Captain pulled his crow call from a pocket of his jacket.

"If you fellers will take station in the edge of those alders I'll try to get 'em to come down. If I can, you'll have some fun."

Taking his own station, he loaded his weapon with heavier charges and be-gan to send exciting messages to the crows. The ragged lines waverd and pres-ently a single scout came down to look over the situation and see if sport with fox, owl or housecat was to be had.

The Captain dropped the scout neatly upon a patch of greensward in full view of his comrades. Bedlam broke loose. Flocks of crows turned back on their courses to join the melee and were in turn joined by yelling flocks hurry-ing in from the North. No crow saw his enemies until it was too late for him to report his baneful discovery, and it is doubtful if his frantic squawks of warning would have been heeded in the general hysteria that prevailed.

The Captain, although extremely busy with his crow call and his gun, saw a woodcock out of the corner of his eye. The bird had been resting nearby un-til, impatient of the turmoil, it rose from the edge of the alder thicket and flew low around the end of the cover. No one else had a glimpse of it. With-out loss of pace the gunner whirled and fired through the narrow strip at the point where he thought the bird should be.

The crow battle went on until ammunition supplies were dangerously low, and the gunners emerged to count the slain and dispatch two cripples.

Then the Captain walked to the point of the thicket and returned bearing a fine hen woodcock.

"It was flying with the crows," he explained blandly to his bewildered friends.

"I believe you're lyin' like Hell," remarked the Judge suspiciously, "but I can't prove it. I never yet heard of a timberdoodle hitch-hiking a ride with a flock of crows. *I believe you potted it on the ground.*"

And he'll never know the truth until and if he reads this simple tale.

The cover was large enough to keep three active gunners busy all day long even though they visited only the likeliest spots. These are thickets and "corners" which hold some special attraction for woodcock that is not discernible to the human eye.

The Judge remarked upon this curious characteristic while he opened bottles and they prepared for lunch.

"Over there, on a line taken from the Munger barn to that big pine is a two-acre pocket where you'll find woodcock if there's a single bird in the cover, and it differs in no way that I can see from fifty acres surrounding it where you'll *never* find a bird unless it happens to be one that you've flushed out of the pocket and missed."

"It's a woodcock restaurant, I guess," remarked the Captain. "Probably that pocket is as famous among woodcock as Antoine's is to human gourmets. It serves the snails an' slugs just to the taste of Mr. and Mrs. Woodcock and party."

The Judge persisted.

"But how do the young birds, raised in Quebec or Nova Scotia, happen to know how to find the address?" he inquired.

"Who knows anything much about woodcock?" his friend asked. "Just that they come and they go, that a timberdoodle's eyes are so placed that he can see where he's been and where he's going without turning his head. Also he's hard to hit and he's easy to hit. You can kill fifteen straight and miss the next fifteen just as easily. He belongs to the family of shorebirds for some strange ornithological reason. The hen woodcock does or does not carry her young between her thighs, and these thighs are probably the most succulent morsel known to epicures. I might add that the woodcock is the most beautiful of all upland game birds and that doubles on timberdoodles are extremely rare, indeed, and memories of these remarkable events are cherished among gunners. The woodcock, my friends, is the only bird that can promote the illusion that it is flying backward, forward and to port and starboard simultaneously, or all at once. The bill of the male woodcock is shorter than that of the hen, but not always. The bird loves moist thickets such as these, but I once shot a limit in twenty minutes' time plumb on the top of one of the highest mountains of the Blue Ridge. A woodcock has been encountered on Madison Avenue, in New York City, and I'll bet you five cents that the bird was calm and imperturbable and ever so much more dignified than the Mayor."

The lecturer paused briefly for refreshment. His companions were careful not to interrupt the discourse. In a moment he resumed.

"You can harry and plague a wild turkey or even a pa'tridge into doing something foolish, but never a woodcock. There is no place for hysteria in his brain. I am told that the British have a barbarous custom consisting of broiling the heads of woodcock over a candle flame and devouring the brain, but I can't swear to it. The bird has only one bad habit, from which no one suffers but himself. It is that when flushed he will generally, though not always, fly into the open where he is vulnerable to seven-eighths of an ounce of number

9 shot. The pa'tridge, unless you have scared him out of his wits, won't do this. I once flushed four pa'tridges while crossing a field of shocked corn. The shocks were so widely spaced that you'd have called it open shooting until four pa'tridges showed you how wrong you were. They made it look like a dense forest, and I made a pretty double on two stacks of fodder. If there'd been four woodcock in that field every bird of 'em would have given me a fair shot.

"Once upon a day, which His Honor will recall, he flushed a pa'tridge out of a hedge in the Gardner Cover. It came over me high and I killed it with my first barrel. The bird fell into a patch of poplar saplings and must have come right close to hitting a woodcock which had been sitting there meditating. As the pa'tridge struck, the woodcock bounced, and I dropped it with my left barrel. I was a happy man that day."

"You were more than that," remarked the Judge maliciously. "You were exalted. You quit the field, and ran back to the car where later I found you with a death grip on my flask, which I carry as a palliative for wet feet and briar scratches. You were gazing at your birds and your bird gun all laid out on the greensward. I recall it well. I had to pry your fingers loose, one by one."

The Captain ignored him.

"On one other occasion when I lacked witnesses, even mean, stingy and calumnious ones, I made a similar mixed double in the Sawmill Cover, but that time I hived the woodcock with my right barrel and the pa'tridge with my left. The gun," he added virtuously as if to bestow honor where honor was due, "was a Greener double twenty, Crown Grade. I wish I'd kept it. I was a fool to let the Doctor talk me out of it, by Judas."

For all his loquacity, inspired in part by the successful results of the morning's shooting and the prospect of an equally successful afternoon, the Captain had not been negligent in the process of restoring his wasted tissues. Between syllables, sentences and paragraphs two massive sandwiches had gone down his gullet, an undertow of nourishment flowing against the rising tide of speech.

The sun shone and the southerly breeze coming up after a night of frost was gentle. There was no Mud Brook Cover listed in Tranquillity's telephone directory nor any nagging sense of urgency to mar the occasion for Ralf, who had so recently been a victim of the cruel devices of urban life, with its concomitants of stomach ulcers and incipient nervous breakdowns.

He counted a brace of woodcock, a pa'tridge, and a gorgeous cock pheasant in his bag. The coffee was hot and fragrant, the doughnuts and cheese went well together, and his friend was in a discursive mood. His gaze dwelt upon the autumnal glory of the landscape wherein the blue gentians of the lowlands and the pale golden bloom of the witch hazel of the upland pastures shared the honor of being the last flowers of the season.

In a distant field a party of crows, stragglers from the great vanguard which they had challenged, was busily engaged in picking up crickets and frost-stricken grasshoppers. Their voices, as they discussed the quality of their fare, were pleasantly muted; there was no hint of the quarrelsome arrogance of midsummer when King Crow had ruled the avian world with beak and claw. A fleet of belated robins, silent and breathless with haste, paused briefly in a wild grape vine to victual its tiny ships before resuming the southern voyage.

Ralf laid fresh billets on the small fire, not because he was cold but for purely esthetic reasons, and reminded the Captain that he had been talking about the lore of the timberdoodle.

"It ain't so much what we know about the bird as it is what we *don't* know about him," his friend said. "That's what makes him interesting. The question of what Mr. Hokumpake and his lady do with their spare time has interested scientists and plain, ordinary gunners as well. Speaking for myself, I hope we never find out, for if we do, we'll lose more than we'll gain. Not that there's much danger, for the woodcock keeps his secrets well.

"There are places in this Cover where if you did a little digging you'd turn up the brass heads of shot shells that were fired at woodcock eighty years ago. I sometimes think that along toward twilight if you had a rabbit's foot in your pocket, you might come upon the shades of a pair of those old gunners sitting on a stump, smoking their pipes and counting their birds. And why not? For woodcock and woodcockers are alike in this respect, they'll come back if they can to the same cover year after year.

"I don't know how many woodcock I've shot, but it would be a considerable figure. I've never got accustomed to the business, however, and every bird I flushed this morning was as much a thing of wonder and mystery as was the first bird that fell to my gun.

"And that, my brothers, concludes the Scripture lesson, except to say that more has been written and said in praise of our strange little friend than has been done in celebration of fair women and brave men."

The meal was finished, but no one evinced any impatience to resume the sport. Finding birds without the aid of a dog requires a deal of exertion and they were pleasantly weary. Besides it was remarkably agreeable to lounge in the October sun.

Ralf spoke of dogs and the Judge explained that Cam Vaughn had owned the last great grouse and woodcock dog in Tranquillity.

"We used to think we had to have a dog," said he, "and of course a good dog is a great help, but in these times of short seasons there are few opportunities to develop a first-class animal. We've had cockers, springers, pointers and setters, and some of them were good and some were not.

"We had a springer named Ace who, first and last, cost us about three hundred dollars. He'd work fine when he felt like it, which was not often, and he was a natural born thief. He learned to open the ice box door and steal the roast of beef. In doing so the first time, he upset the milk bottles, which betrayed him. He was escorted to the scene of the crime and given a lickin'. It taught him something, too, for he learned to open the door and remove the steak without disturbing a thing, and he closed the door afterwards, by Judas!"

The Captain laughed bitterly.

"We sold the cuss for twenty-five dollars," he recalled, "and never got the money."

"Then there was Old Man Pepper, a golden cocker, and a thorough gentleman. A great hunter, too. He'd retrieve from water, but never on land. He'd got it in his head that we could do that ourselves. He died, and after several successors had been tried, we realized at last that we weren't getting any fun out of our gunning when we had to spend the whole day fuming, cursing, hollering and chasing half-trained dogs. Now we work harder but we don't have hysterics and fits of blind rage."

He rubbed out his cigarette and picked up his gun.

"Let's go over and look at the woodcock restaurant," he suggested.

As they approached the magic spot a fat hen rose at Ralf's feet and flew low around the edge of a thicket, where it went down in a drift of feathers. The shot started another bird which the Judge snapped neatly as it lifted above the golden crowns of the birches.

It was clear to everyone that this was a hot corner, for the ground was splashed with markings indicating that a flight of birds had come in. The glade echoed to shouts of "Mark! Mark!" usually followed instantly by report of a shotgun and occasionally by two reports, for none was immune to error and a woodcock is not always where it seems to be, and even if it is, the wavering fall of a shot-cut white birch sapling is good proof that the bird was behind the unfortunate birch when the shot was fired. At least two woodcock escaped being brought under fire because their pensive uncertain flight courses made it impossible for the Judge to shoot without filling Ralf full of shot, and Ralf couldn't fire without doing damage to His Honor or to the Dark-Haired Lady's gentleman. The Captain had and lost a chance for a double when he had to use his second barrel on his first bird while from the corner of his eye he saw the second prize fly straight away down a cattle path.

There was a roar and a bellow from the direction of the Judge and Ralf looked up to see a pa'tridge driving straight over him above the birches at a height of not more than twenty-five feet.

He snapped at it and the bird went down with a noble thump, somewhat to the gunner's dismay, for at such close range the game would surely be in shreds. It wasn't, however, for due to a fortunate combination of good shooting and a touch of luck the close-flying shot charge had neatly decapitated the bird. Not a single pellet had touched the plump body. The game was unspoiled for the broiler, and the tale of its killing unmarred for the gunner's later recollections.

Perhaps Frank Forrester would never have troubled to log the day in his diary, but Time has a way of changing and, sometimes, of heightening the values of human experiences, and so it was in this case.

When the last shot had been fired and all the birds were in, the grateful gunners counted a neat total of twelve woodcock, half as many grouse and two cock pheasants whose raucous-voiced curfews would never again ring out over the swales and thickets of the Mud Brook Cover.

While the Judge fished for his flask amidst the collection of important trifles in his shooting bag, and the Captain dipped water from the brook, Ralf laid the game in an orderly row, gently smoothing each disordered feather.

It was a goodly sight and, while each of them could recall many days from the past when the bags had been far greater, no one was inclined to find fault with the tally, realizing full well that conditions today are not, for example, as they had been on the banks of the Sangamon River in the year 1880.

The Judge thought of this as he poured a generous libation into each waiting cup.

"Five dozen woodcock a day wasn't unusual back in those times," said he. "But a man couldn't possibly remember all the details of a day like that, could he? And if he can't do that he's lost the best part of his sport, ain't he?"

The last rays of the descending sun illuminated the glowing mantles of the wooded hills and mountains and, sitting there, they felt the sudden chill that presages a night of white frost, but there was no chill in the hearts of our three friends as their eyes met in all loyalty and affection above the rims of the tin cups.

They toasted the woodcock and raised another to the pa'tridge.

"Hell," exclaimed His Honor, magnanimously, "let's not be mean about the matter. Let's h'ist a small one to the doggoned ringnecks. At least, they're 4F game birds and very good on the table."

AT
THE
TAVERN

Mister Perkins' Tavern is a popular gathering place on winter evenings, for it is both warm and cozy. It is equally popular on summer evenings when the moths form a sacrificial nimbus around the lamp above the door and the whippoorwills are calling, for then it is cool and cozy. The quality of Mister Perkins' ale is invariably good in any weather, but Deacon Guidance Witherbee is slanderous when he refers to the little room as a "grogshop," and he is wrong, too, in his conviction that ale alone constitutes the attraction that persuades the fishermen, hunters and trappers of Tranquillity to rally there occasionally. The truth of the matter is that, wittingly or not, the host profits from an essential and insatiable need common to all right-minded brethren of the rod, gun and rifle. These folk yearn for a quiet place and a reasonable opportunity to describe their exploits to an appreciative and interested audience. It was to serve the same purpose that in other times the Waubanakis lighted their council fires on the shores of Petowbowk and dismissed the squaws. No matter how many scalps a man has taken or how many and heavy the trout he has creeled, he finds it impossible to produce an adequate description of his prowess when his womenfolk are present and listening.

Around the Indians' council fire a warrior was permitted to embellish his tale. If, as was true of Rip van Winkle, a brave found it necessary to review, amend and repeat the story of his exploits several times before he himself was satisfied with it, he could always do so in complete confidence that none of his friends would notice, much less question, apparent discrepancies between the first telling and the last. The red men understood very well that a man requires time for meditation, study and analysis following an event or an adventurous exploit in order to appreciate his own greatness, the skill that he demonstrated and the courage he displayed. Submitting themselves to this kind of impartial scrutiny, most men find that they were actually nobler and more skillful than they had noticed at the time.

Ale and toleration were to be found at Mister Perkins' Tavern, and both of these godsends were being provided for the small company present when, on a night in January, Cam and the Captain came in. They removed their overcoats, shook the snow from these garments, and having exchanged greetings with the other guests, sat down and beckoned for the services of the host.

The current narrator promptly resumed his story, which had been interrupted by their entrance. He was a man of homely agreeable countenance and clad in work-worn denims. He had been discussing the purchase of a new rifle.

"Well, sir, by Judast, my womern gi' me a consid'able goin' over when I fetched that rifle hum.

" 'There ye go,' sez she, 'spendin' money thet ye can't afford on another gun!'

"Well, I guess most o' ye know haow womern folks'll hang on to a grievance. Ef ye keep silent it makes her mad, an' ef ye try to pacify her she'll git madder yit."

The speaker's observations received unanimous but cautious approval, for this indeed was dangerous ground.

" 'I'll bet thet gun cost ye ez much ez fifteen dollars,' sez she.

" 'Yis marm,' sez I, 'but I shall git 'nough mushrats to pay for it, an' more,' sez I."

" 'Oh, fudge!' sez she."

The storyteller refreshed himself with a deep draught from his mug.

"Well, sir, the very next mornin' one o' the young uns come a-runnin' into the caowbarn where I was milkin' an' he sez, sezzee, 'Pa, there's a mushrat a-settin' on the bank o' the crik jest daown by the big butt'nut tree,' sezzee.

" 'Git me my rifle,' sez I, an' he hypered an' fetched it.

"Well, sir. I took an' I sneaked up to the aidge o' the bluff an' thar sot Mister Mushrat. I drawed a bead on him an' teched her off, an' jest ez I did so, I seen another critter move in the willers 'tother side o' the crik, an' I looked an', by Judast, it wuz a fox. He wuz kinder dark an' shiny, an' he stood thar wi' one paw raised off the graound jest like a bird dog does, lookin' at me.

" 'You're one o' them damn wuthless Sampson foxes,' sez I to myself, 'but you're miz'able hide'll fetch one, two dollars,' sez I to myself.

"Well, sir, I drawed a bead on him an' daown he went, deader, by Judast, than Julia's Ceaser. So I got into my skift an' poled 'cross the crik an' got him, an' I took him an' the mushrat up to the haouse an' skinned 'em.

"My womern come aout an' watched me.

" 'I s'pose, Joseph,' sez she, 'thet you think thet leetle mushrat an' thet ol' fox'll pay fer your gun an' my radio,' sez she.

" 'No, marm, I don't,' sez I, 'but Rawl Hassett'll give me a dollar an' a half fer the mushrat an' mebbe two dollars fer my cross fox,' sez I, 'an' while thet ain't riches, I call it dang good pay fer ten-fifteen minutes o' labor.' "

" 'Fudge,' sez she. 'You don't know what labor is!' sez she."

He paused again for refreshment, receiving meanwhile the supreme tribute of silence. There was no one present who had not heard the tale over and over again. No one was bored, however. In the first place, the story proved again how wise and sensible it was for men to expend odd sums of money upon rifles, shotguns, and fishing tackle; how divinely guided they were when, rather than listen to a lecture on "The World to Come," they went bullhead fishing and caught "a harndsome mess' for breakfast. Furthermore, and strangely, it was a true story of a thumping victory won by one of themselves in the war between the sexes.

During the interim, Cam fished a pickled egg from the pellucid depths of Mister Perkins' jar.

"Well, sir. Thet very night I took them two pelts up to Rawl's. First I give him the mushrat. 'Prime fur,' sez Rawl. 'Two dollars on thet one,' sezzee. Then I throwed daown the Sampson fox onto the caounter an' Rawl took a good look at it.

" 'Joe,' sezzee, 'I du b'lieve thet we hev naow p'jected aourselves into the aree o' high finance,' sezzee. 'Shan't take no advantage,' sezzee. 'Hain't seen but two-three of 'em in my lifetime,' sezzee, 'but by Judast,' sezzee, 'it's my idee thet thet there pelt's wuth 'raound six-seven hundred dollars. Yis, sir!' sezzee.

" 'Tell ye what,' sezzee, 'I'll handle it fer ye at ten cents on the dollar,' sezzee, 'an' git the best price I c'n git,' sezzee.

"Well, sir, I went hum, an' I give the mushrat money to Judy.

" 'Oh, fudge,' sez she, 'an' I p'sume thet cross fox didn't fetch nothin'. Well, Joseph, you'll have thet gun paid for in ten-twelve years an' I'll still be wantin' a radio.' "

"Two-three days Rawl come daown, an' he come to the barn where I wuz milkin'.

" 'Joe,' sezzee, 'I wuz right. Thet fox wuz a silver gray fox, jest ez I suspicioned, an' here's a check from the New Yorkers fer seven hundred an' sixty-five dollars to prove it!'

" 'Judast Priest! *No!*' sez I.

" '*Yis*, by Judast,' sezzee.

" 'Well, sir, by *Judast,*' sez I."

There was a great shaking and nodding of heads among the listeners, and if any were envious of Joseph's good fortune, it was not apparent.

A little man who had been perched on his chair like a chipmunk, holding his head cocked to catch every word of the narrative, now wanted to know if Joe's 'womern wuz satisfied when she seen the New York feller's check.'

"Well, sir," said Joe, weighing his words, "I wouldn't say that she was fully satisfied exactly. Ef she wuz she didn't show it, but I c'ld see that she wuz most almightily stubbed."

The extraordinary event was still being discussed and various opinions were being expressed upon the nature, origin, character and habits of foxes when a vigorous stamping of boots at the door announced the belated arrival of Uncle Bill Paraday.

His cheeks were as red as an Astrakan apple from the frost, and his eyebrows and whiskers sparkled with its crystals. He was in his customary imperious mood. With no more greeting than that conveyed by a quizzical glance from his blue eyes, he joined Cam and the Captain. His roar blasted the ear drums.

"Perkins! Fetch me a mug o' hot buttered rum, an' stir yer stumps! See to it thet ye don't fergit the rum part of it."

"Why, Uncle Bill, you allers git an honest, bony fidy, legil meajure when ye come here, an' ye can't deny it," protested the host.

Uncle Bill ignored him.

"Did I hear su'thin' said 'baout foxes?" he demanded accusingly, and as if he had smelled a conspiracy.

"Garrett all Conne'ticut! You fellers don't know nuthin' 'baout foxes!" He turned to Cam. "Vaughn, you got some small idee 'baout fox nature an' what the critters'll do an' won't do, but the Cap'n hain't, fer he won't go a-huntin 'em, the lazy cuss. Joe, there, ever since he kilt thet silver gray two-three year ago, by a stroke o' pure fool's luck, hez been settin' himself up ez a born foxer." His clear blue gaze swept over the cowed culprits. "Bet ye a dime agin a doughnut thet he's jest been tellin' ye jest exactly haow he done it. Hain't he?"

His bright glare was fixed upon the now unfortunate Joseph, who squirmed, and almost wished that he hadn't shot the fox.

"Well, sir, Uncle Bill, I wuz jest a-tellin' 'em a leetle mite 'baout haow it happened, an'—"

"Knew it!" roared Uncle Bill in triumphant tones.

The Captain interrupted the massacre.

"Perkins, for Heaven's sake, hurry up with Uncle Bill's grog!"

"Sartinly, sartinly, an' here you be, jest the way you ordered it, Uncle Bill. Three aounces o' good Jamaiky, hot water, a ha' spoonful o' sugar, a spoonful o' lemon juice, hunk o' butter 'baout ez big ez a walnut, an a mojicum o' the spices o' Araby."

He placed a steaming mug before the old fox hunter, who sniffed the aroma and then sipped the heart-warming beverage with modified approval.

"Wouldn't s'prise me none ef I faound a cussed Ayrab in it somewhere's er other," said he, "but never mind. When I come to him, I shall know haow to deal with the camel-ridin' cuss."

He sipped again and there was a noticeable relaxation of tension in the room as the benevolent spirits pervaded Uncle Bill's chilled members.

When he spoke again all, or nearly all, traces of his former bright-eyed belligerence had vanished, dissolved apparently by the pungent vapors trailing upward about the old man's eagle beak.

"Naow, then, " he volunteered, "I'll tell you fellers su'thin' 'baout foxes, ef ye care to hear it, an' it's su'thin' I'll bet ye none o' ye ever heard of. Mebbe Vaughn hez, but I daoubt it. Did any o' ye ever hear o' sech a thing ez a fox turnin' on a haound an' givin' him a hell o' a lickin'?"

Cam shook his head.

"Thought not," said Uncle Bill with evident satisfaction. "It jest goes to show ye su'thin' thet the cussed Injuns always knew, namely, an' to wit, thet ye c'n never tell jest haow a wil' critter will behave.

"Guess most on ye know my blue tick haound, an' ef ye do, ye must know't he's a peaceable ol' cuss an' not a provoker o' vi'lence, ez Deacon With-erbee'd say. Neverth'less, he'll fight fer his rights when he hez to do so. Jest like when Billy Knipes busted free from the domernation o' his womern.

"Billy wa'n't no saint, ez ye may recall, but he wuz a fairly reliable feller, all said an' done. His worst fault, if it could be called sech, wuz thet he loved to go bullhead fishin' over to the Paowder Mill Pond nights in the spring an' summer wi' a pint o' Old Crow fer comp'ny. His woman, Ollie, her name wuz, 'ould set up for him an' when he'd come hum, 'long 'baout midnight, wi' his lantern an' a pail o' bullheads, listenin' to the bull frogs an' the squinch aowls an' ez happy an' j'yous ez a mortal man c'n be, Ollie, who wuz a big womern, consarn her, 'ould snatch Billy right aout from betwixt his bullheads an' his lantern an' give him a flaxin'. Garret all Conne'ticut! On nights when the wind wa'n't blowin' I c'ld hear the poor cuss squalling fer quarter clean to my place.

"Candace would hear it, too, an' she'd fin'lly sigh an' say, 'Oh, the poor soul!' I wa'nt never sure which one o' 'em she meant."

Uncle Billy interrupted himself to demand another of those 'mis'able leetle potions' from Mister Perkins.

"Le's see, where wuz I? Oh, yis, tellin' you fellers su'thin' 'baout foxes.

"Well, sir, come a night when Billy come hum empty-handed. He hedn't ketched no fish an, worse yit, he'd stubbed his toe comin' up Bigelow's Hill an' fell daown an' busted his lantern.

"Ollie never said a cussed word, but her eyes wuz blazin', an' she hauled off an' cuffed Billy into a corner o' the kitchen. But *thet* time she went too fur. Billy wuz properly scairt, an' came aout o' the corner a-sluggin', ez the radio fellers say. I should dearly hev loved to see the doin's," said Uncle Bill wist-fully, "but a married couple's entitled to a meajure o' privacy. But it was Ol-lie, consarn her, who did the squallin' *thet* night.

" 'Tain't too much to say thet it made a new man aout o' Billy, an' when I up an' asked him one day haow he'd managed it, he sez, sezzee, 'Well, sir, Uncle Billy, I'm a peaceable cuss, ez ye well know, but thet wuz a time when

I re'lized thet I hed to fight er die. An' do ye know?' sezzee, 'it's made all the diff'unce in the world?' sezzee. 'Why, Ollie's even took to goin' bullheadin' wi' me,' sezzee, 'friendly an' biddable ez c'n be.' "

"How about the fox that licked hell out o' your hound?" the Captain inquired.

"I'm tellin' ye 'baout it fast ez I c'n, ain't I?" said the old gentleman, indignantly.

"Le'see, naow, it was jest 'baout a month ago. There wuz a fresh fall o' snow, an' Will Belden got a notion he'd enj'y a fox hunt. He come up to the haouse an' talked me into it. So I got my gun an' called Sport an' we sot aout. There'd been an old dog fox hangin' 'raound the big ridge back o' Bunker's place. We'd raouted him aout a couple o' times before, an' it wan't long 'til Sport hed him goin'. The fox took off daown towards the ol' quarry dump, jest ez he allers hed, an' I sent Will up to Bunker's sugar orchard an' told him to take his stand by the sugar haouse. I clumb the hill to where there's a big rock. From there ye c'n see the hull length an' bre'th o' the ridge.

"I could hear Sport a-calling the figgers off to the saouth, but it wuz a dummed slow dance fer the snow was deep an' it hampered 'em some.

"By'n'by the fox turned an' pooty soon I seen 'em comin' back. They wa'n't neither on 'em runnin'. They wuz walkin', an' Sport wa'n't ten rod behind the fox, an' gainin', fer every naow an' agin the ol' fox 'ould stop an' look back at the dog, an' whenever he did so every hair on him 'ould stand on eend an' he'd look to be ez big ez a yearlin' b'ar."

"He was gettin' mad, wa'n't he?" asked Cam.

"Madder'n the devil," the old hunter agreed. "I could see thet he wuz 'baout sick an' tired o' bein' druv from his bed an' made to walk ten, fifteen miles in deep snow. Futhermore, he'd 'baout decided to do su'thin' 'baout it.

"I sez to myself, 'Thet ol' cuss is primin' his courage an' when he gits it good an' primed he's goin' to tackle thet dog an' I shall see su'thin' I've heard of but never obsarved before,' sez I.

"Well, they come along fer 'baout a half a mile in thet fashion, wi' the dog gittin' closter an' closter, an' the fox gittin' madder'n madder. Sport hed his nose daown into the snow an' I know he didn't see the fox, ner did he hev any idee haow close the critter wuz.

"Fin'lly the fox walked aout onto a ledge, an' thar he stopped an' set his coat a-bristle. I knew thet he'd made up his mind to go to war.

"Sport come pokin' along singin' like hell an' enj'yin himself no eend. The ol' fox let him git up to 'baout the length o' this room, an' then, sir, he jumped him."

Uncle Billy loosed a crackle of mirth as he contemplated Sport's surprise and discomfiture.

"By Judast Priest, I'd hev give su'thin' to hev seen the expression on thet dog's face. He must've figgered thet somehow er other he'd made a *grievous* mistake an' hed run full chisel into the Sugar Hill catamaount. Oh, dear me suz!

"The fox act'lly knocked him eend over eend, but Sport riz up in what ye might call a noble rage at bein' so cruelly put upon when he wa'n't doin' nothin' in the worl' but mindin' his own business wi' malice toward none.

"You fellers hev heard cat fights, an' ye've heard dog fights. Some of ye hev witnessed dog an' coon fights, but ye ain't never heard ner seen a dog an' fox fight. Sech a yippin', an' a-yaowlin' an' a-cussin' in fox language an' dog language! Daown they went clean over the aidge o' the ledge all rolled up together in a ball an' the snow flyin'. They rolled clear aout into the medder, an' there the both on 'em unanimously 'greed thet they'd hed 'baout enough of it. The fox walked aout into the middle o' the medder an' laid daown. He wa'n't feelin' any too good, an' neither wuz Sport, who'd been bit clean through both ears. He come up to me wi' the blood drippin' off his ears an' he sez, sezzee, plain ez words, 'Where wuz ye, an' your goldarned weapin, whilst I wuz a-fightin' the hull German Army bare handed an' single handed?' sezzee.

"Brother Perkins, I b'lieve I'll hev another one o' them Ayrab beverages an' then I'll be gittin' hum," said Uncle Bill.

"Hol' on," exclaimed the little man who looked like a chipmunk. "What in tarnation happened then? Did ye quit an' go hum, or did ye git the fox?"

"Neither one, by Judast. Ol' Sport fin'lly agreed thet ef I'd go 'long wi' him an' keep clost by wi' my gun cocked, he'd continer to foller the aowdacious critter who hed used him so aoutrageously.

"So we went daown to the medder where the fox wuz an' he, seein' thet all the forces o' Hell wuz naow arrayed agin him, got up an' started walkin'.

"We walked him up past the sugar haouse at jest abaout twelve rod distance, an' Will Belden come aout wi' his danged automatic an' shot at him four times wi' number 4 shot, which air too light fer foxes, anyway, an' once wi' a load o' number 2's, which wuz the last ca'tridge in his magazine.

"Undaoubtedly, fer I wuz clost enough to see the snow fly, William Belden would ha' kilt thet fox deader'n a wedge ef he'd started aout wi' the number two ca'tridge 'stid o' storin' it clean daown in the toe o' the damned weapin. It follers thet thet damned ol' dog fox ez still racin' an' chasin' on Bunker's Ledge, ketchin' Bunker's chickens, sassin' Sport, an' obstructin' Jestice, Life, Liberty, an' the Pursuit o' Happiness."

A
WARM DAY
IN MARCH

On a balmy windless afternoon in the latter days of the unpredictable month of March, the Captain became convinced that there was nothing of greater or more immediate importance to himself, his heirs and assigns, than the performance of that operation which in Tranquillity, and doubtless in other communities blessed with an abundance of groundhogs, is known as "Sightin' in the Woodchuck Rifle." This annual procedure is midway between being a chore and a ritual, for the sighter-in must submit to the drudgery of getting his equipment together, tacking up his target and filling and placing a sandbag to serve as a rest for his rifle; but when these things have been done, the labor is more than paid for by the sound of the razor-edged voice of the rifle. To the ears of the initiate, that quick and brittle note is music, and if it is also accompanied by the appearance of a tiny round hole in the exact center of the bullseye the devotee experiences an exaltation that is nearly religious in the degree of its intensity.

The Captain's woodchuck rifle was famed for its remarkable accuracy. It was, in fact, a remarkable weapon. In a way it resembled the Constitution of the United States of North America, for it was the product of the minds and hands of many men who sought perfection.

Descendants of old Eliphalet Remington had drilled, grooved and polished the long heavy barrel; George Hyde, the king-pin gunsmith, had fitted the barrel to a strong, delicately precise single-shot action invented by one whose name is as well known to the sportsmen of today as it was to the American riflemen of seventy-five years ago, when the "Sharps" was the pride of buffalo hunters and Indian fighters. John Hutton then carved the stock and fore end from tough dark walnut wood. He fastened swivels and slings and finally, with no more delay than is to be expected of a gunsmith, placed the completed weapon in the reverent hands of the Captain, who lost no time in discovering that, with it, it was possible to drive a tack at one hundred yards on a windless day.

276

The Dark-Haired Lady had just finished a letter to one of her young, and had somehow managed to compress a world of devotion into a V-mail cover.

"Think I'll walk up to Uncle Bill's and do a little target shootin'. Like to come along? It's a rare day outdoors, Ma'am."

"I would indeed," replied the lady. "That is, if you'll be willing to put up with warmed-up baked beans for supper."

The Captain was fumbling about in a closet for his corduroys and a pair of field boots, and his voice was muffled.

"What's wrong with warmed-up baked beans?" he asked. "'I shall eat what is set before me and ask no questions for Conscience's sake.'"

And so, after trifling delays and returns for forgotten items, the pair set forth.

The sun gave an unmistakable hint of its midsummer ardor. In the small depressions and on the northern slopes of the hills the last stubborn drifts of the long winter were to be seen, the soiled, untidy rearguard of the retiring Arctic enemy. The travelers felt the dank expiring breath of these doomed stragglers upon their faces as they passed, but their hearts were gladdened by the sight of swelling buds and of new grass. A pair of friendly bluebirds bore them company for a distance, flying from fence post to fence post while they piped the march with music that spoke only of peace, beauty and good will.

The ground was pleasant to feet that had been so long shackled by the treachery and discomfort of ice and snow. The walkers lengthened their stride gratefully and struck off across fields which only a fortnight since had been so cumbered by a heavy blanket of snow as to be all but impassable to man or beast.

It was not long until they spied the neat white house standing beneath the maples.

"I'll go in and visit with Aunt Candace," the Dark-haired Lady announced.

Her escort had no need to inquire as to his old friend's whereabouts and occupation, for the measured sound of axe strokes came from behind the woodshed. There he found Uncle Bill splitting away at a small mountain of chunk wood.

His approach had been silent and unobserved, and the visitor watched for some minutes while the old man labored contentedly in the sunshine. His coat hung from a peg and his blue shirt contributed a touch of warm homely color to the scene.

The old veteran swung his axe with the effortless grace of the seasoned chopper. Under strokes that seemed almost gentle in spite of the explosive "hah" with which the workman emphasized each downward sweep of his blade, the stubborn blocks of beech and maple fell apart as if by their own volition into triangular segments of dimensions suitable for the fire-box of Aunt Candace's kitchen stove. There was no chunk however hard, knotty and tough, that could withstand the synchronic magic of Uncle Bill's "hah" and his axe. Occasionally the old gentleman would attack a particularly stubborn, twisted specimen in order to prove his supremacy, but his usual practice was to roll these recalcitrant members aside to season throughout the hot summer months and so become prime fuel for the big fireplace, wherein the very obduracy of a rock maple chunk was transformed into a genial shin-warming virtue quite fit for frosty nights in mid-winter.

The air was redolent with the fragrance of newly riven wood. A number of bees which had awakened early from the coma that still bound their fellow workers had found their unerring way to the only available source of sweetness in the neighborhood, and were busily filling their tiny pouches from the sap that exuded from the blocks of maple in Uncle Bill's woodpile.

"Git off o' there, ye leetle cuss," said Uncle Bill addressing an eager bee, "I hain't nothing' agin ye an' I don't want to hurt ye, but ye're right spang an' astraddle o' the split, an' I can't be responsible fer yer safety."

Then, as he watched the worker bee gather the beads of sweet sap, he relented and put down his poised axe.

"Well, then, go ahead wi' yer business, an' I'll hev a smoke."

As he turned to his coat for his pipe and pouch, he came face to face with his guest.

"Garret all Conne'ticut! Whar'd ye come from?" he exclaimed in gruff tones that did nothing to conceal his joy in the meeting. "Ye might's well kill a feller ez scare him to death. Well, sir, naow thet ye're here ye might ez well set daown an' pay fer yer keep wi' the news o' what's goin' on in the war."

This the Captain did while Uncle Bill nodded his gray poll, or shook it sadly accordingly as the news was good or sorrowful.

"Wars don't change," opined the old veteran, " 'cept in the way they're fit. All these new-fangled weapins don't reelly change 'em insofar ez it consarns the feller thet's fightin', and' marchin', an' bein' took sick, an' freezin', an' sweatin', an' layin' in the mud an' gettin' humsick fer his folks an' bein' waounded er kilt. Only there's a lot more on 'em in this un than in aour times, but they don't feel a mite better er worse'n we did, don't b'lieve they do. A feller thet ain't hed him no vi'tuals fer three-four days in this war is jest ez hungry, but no hungrier, I 'spose, than his grandpa wuz a-follerin' Gineral Grant. A feller thet's humsick is humsick, an' a bullit is a bullit, an' miz'ry is miz'ry naow jest ez it wus in George Washington's time."

He sighed deeply, and changed the subject.

"Goin' to practice up a leetle, be ye? Well, ye'd better, fer the woodchucks air commencin' to come aout, an' I shall want ye to be on hand to pertect my prop'ty."

He rose and after poking about in a corner of the woodshed hauled forth last year's sandbag.

"Kept it fer ye. 'Twill save ye the labor o' makin' a new one," said the old gentleman.

"Indeed, it will. Won't you come along and try my rifle?"

Uncle Bill's eye brightened.

"Mebbe I'll do so, by'n'by, fer I've always loved to shoot a rifle. There wuz a time when I cu'd fetch home my share o' the turkeys, too, ef I do say so." In his voice there was a hint of wistfulness for the vanished days of his youth and the prowess that had been his, for the tireless muscles and the hawk-like vision that never blurred.

"Yis, an' pa'tridges an' squirrels, too, when I went a-huntin'. Shucks, boy! I hain't sca'ly no more'n a animated Eegyptian mummy, ye might say. Got so's't I can't read fine print in the 'Ery' wi'aout puttin' on specs," he added, mournfully contemplating this latest evidence of disintegration.

At that moment the buxom form of Aunt Candace appeared at the corner of the woodshed. She was followed by the Dark-Haired Lady. They had evidently been eavesdropping on their menfolk, but neither of the ladies showed any sign of penitence. Aunt Candace, with a shawl across her shoulders, was in a mood both tender and indignant. Her companion seemed to be amused.

"William Washington Paraday, you stop talking that way! I never yet heard of an Eegyptian mummy who was able to devour two griddlesful of buckwheat cakes and a skilletful of sausages, not to mention coffee and doughnuts, an' then foller an old haound dog all the way to Moscow Medders an' back. Fiddlesticks! Anybody would think you're an old man, if they hadn't lived wi' you for more years than I c'n count. Land sake's alive!"

Aunt Candace, who had been a school teacher until Uncle Bill had campaigned a successful wooing, closed the subject and found a seat beside her spouse.

"Yis, Ma'rm," said Uncle Bill.

The eyes of the Dark-Haired Lady and the Captain met for a moment and they smiled.

Then Uncle Bill picked up his axe; the Captain took up his rifle, and presently the little valley echoed again to the sounds of the axe now punctuated at intervals by the crack of the rifle, while the two housewives enjoyed the sunshine and womanly conversation.

After a time, at his friend's bidding, the old man desisted from his labors to try a few shots with the rifle, with results that made up for any disappointment he had suffered from a difficulty in deciphering the small blurred type of the weekly paper.

"Thet's a danged good shootin' weapon," he remarked admiringly. "Did ye ever hear o' Berdan's Sharpshooters? Well, sir, they hed rifles su'thin' on the same style ez your'n."

The Captain saw a chance to draw Uncle Bill into an anecdotal mood.

"Did you ever see the Sharpshooters in battle?" he inquired.

"Yis, sir, an' I'll tell ye su'thin' about it ef ye care to hear, but 'fore doin' thet I should like to put a motion 'fore this s'lect committee, namely, an' to wit, an' to whom it may consarn. Splittin' wood is a thirsty occupation an' so, I b'lieve, is rifle shootin'. Naow, therefore, Mister Mawderator, I move ye thet the party o' the first part, known near an' far by the name o' Paraday, be, an' hereby is, instructed an' ordered to proceed wi'aout delay to said Paraday's suller an' fetch us aout a pitcher o' prime cider. Do I hear any objection?"

"No, sir."

"The ayes hev it," said Uncle Bill as he departed, to return in a few minutes with a beaded pitcher and two glasses.

Tobacco was lighted, and at that point Aunt Candace declared that, aye, yes or no, the Macombers were going to stay to supper.

At the Dark-Haired Lady's feeble polite protest, the old lady asserted that it wan't going to make anyone any trouble. She had two cold boiled chickens and it wouldn't take her five minutes to roll out a crust, cut up the faowl and make a chicken pie. Besides, she said, she hadn't scarcely had a chance all dwinter long to talk to anyone except an animated Eegyptian mummy.

The Captain had what was either a certain negative honesty or complete shamelessness about him, for he offered no protest at all, and boldly announced that the Macombers would be darned glad to stay for supper. The Dark-Haired Lady's wavering motion thus was lost, and she and Aunt Candace retired kitchenward, leaving the cronies to their cider and their tales.

"Now tell me about Berdan's Sharpshooters, Uncle Bill."

The old veteran sipped his cider and his blue gaze seemed to focus upon scenes that were far away from the peaceful New England farmstead. He gazed again upon the hills, fields and orchards surrounding a little village in Pennsylvania, a village whose somnolence had been suddenly shattered by the incredible violence of a battle. He himself was one of a mere handful of living witnesses, one of the few fragile graybeards whose eyes had seen the billowing smoke of volleys and roaring batteries.

"You asked ef I'd seen the Sharpshooters in action, didn't ye?

"Yis, sir, I did, an' on several occasions, an' one o' 'em wuz at Gettysburg.

"It wuz the third day o' the fightin' an' we wuz a-layin' behind a stunwall on the Ridge. The Sharpshooters wuz daown in front o' us, whar there wuz a turnpike an' a couple o' farm haouses an' barns an' sech, crackin' away every chance they got an' duckin' back to load up agin. There wuz a couple o' batteries daown there wi' 'em, an' I tell ye it wuz an almighty noisy place to be in.

"Then, all to once, we see the artillery fellers fetchin' up their horses an' retirin' the guns at full gallop in claouds o' dust an' paowder smoke. The Sharpshooters begun to stream back, too, stoppin' naow an' agin to load an' fire.

"Oh, I tell ye, it wuz su'thin' to see."

Uncle Bill took a long pull at his cider but his gaze never left that faraway place.

"An' then all to once aour own guns heshed up an' I sez to myself, sez I, 'this is a hell o' a time to run aout o' ammernition,' sez I, an' from what I've heard since, Gineral Lee thought so, too, an' ordered Gineral Longstreet to charge, but Gineral Longstreet, he hemmed an' hawed, an' then Gineral Pickett hed all the bugles blow 'Charge' an' aout they come, rank on rank, wi' their flags a-flyin' an' their bay'nets shinin.'

"Well, sir, I don't know haow it wu'd hev turned aout ef our guns hed actu'lly been aout o' ammernition, which they wan't. Seems they'd jest took time to swab aout the gun berrils an' cool 'em a leetle an' when the Rebels wuz jest abaout up to the turnpike, dressin' their lines to the right, stiddy an' calm, aour artillery opened up agin, a-rippin' an' a-ragin'.

" 'Baout then we got aour orders, an' we riz up an' went double quick daown the hill a piece into a leetle gully where Cap'n Goodchild tol' us to lay daown. He wuz a smart feller.

" 'Naow, boys,' sezzee, 'lay flat ez ye c'n. The Johnnies air a-comin', but they won't be able to see ye until they're on top o' that leetle hill. Let 'em fire first, fer they'll be s'prised an' they'll shoot high. Then each of ye pick yer man an' let him hev it.'

"Well, sir, that's the way it wuz. The Rebels come a-stormin' along an' they never did know we wuz there ontil they wuz within ten rod er less. They halted an' let sliver, but they wuz s'prised an' they wuz shootin' daown hill. The only feller to git hit on aour side wuz a boy named Stafford from Poultney Town. He must hev riz up er su'thin', fer he took a ball square betwixt the eyes.

"Then it wuz aour turn, an' we didn't miss, but it took consid'able hammerin' 'fore we convinced the Johnnies thet the hill wan't no place fer 'em."

"They were brave men," said the Captain by the way of tribute to those who had died for a lost cause.

There was a flash of pride in the old soldier's eyes.

"Course they wuz!" he said. "They wuz Americans, wan't they?"

They sat in silence for some time, absorbed in the grim picture that the words of the old warrior had painted. To the east the sunlight climbed the mountains. The rugged buttresses of these great hills already stood in the purple shadows of twilight and the air was chill with a forewarning of the nightly frost.

"Well, I must git at my chores," said Uncle Bill at last, "an' then we'll go in an' find aout fer aourselves whether two cooks air better'n one, er vicey vercey."

THE
WOODCHUCKERS

The Dark-Haired Lady was expecting company.

The threat of a long evening of conversation conducted in a proportion of three parts female to one part male, with that single part receiving, if it was not entirely ignored, the vacant-eyed inattention of distaff individuals who obviously wished that the prattler would cease and desist and permit the trio to resume a discussion of Betty Bingsley's approaching marriage, drove the Captain from the comfort of his own modest living room into the outer darkness. Lest the reader take too great concern at our long-legged friend's eviction and subsequent sufferings-in-exile, it should be explained that the darkness was not that of the Pit, but only the bewitching half-darkness of a clear summer night; a night when it seemed possible that a man with a long-handled landing-net might sweep the firmament and creel a limit of planets, satellites and the small fry of the constellations swimming in the clear pool of the sky.

In his bitter loneliness and hopeless destitution, the poor outcast strode rapidly along Washington Street whistling "Madelon" as he went. His heels rapped sharply upon the slate pavement. Without his consent or approval, the course taken by his toes and faithfully followed by his heels brought the night wanderer to the hospitable door of Mister Perkins' Tavern.

A small but very select group of Tranquillity's nonconformists gave him greeting.

Uncle Bill Paraday was the first.

Time, the leveler of all things, had made small progress in the reduction of the tough old fox hunter. He complained of rheumatics, but the twinges were not enough to interrupt his expeditions. He complained of his failing vision, which was in such dreadful condition that he could no longer read the Probate Court announcements in "The Era" without putting on his spectacles. This did not constitute a reasonable physical disqualification, for no one who could read the notices wanted to do so. Sergeant Paraday's poll was white, but arrayed against that fact was the circumstance that at the moment of his least age Uncle Bill had had no poll of any shade or color whatsoever.

And now in further proof of his victory over Time, he greeted the Captain with a roar that would have drowned out a broadside from the "Kearsarge."

"Been chased aout o' haouse an' hum by a passel o' womern folks, hain't ye?" he challenged.

The Captain cheerfully admitted the charge, and added that the three women were still there in case Uncle Bill wanted to face 'em.

" 'Not I! Not I!' ez the dog said when he got a lickin' fer killin' a hen. One on 'em is twicet ez many ez I c'n deal with," the old man admitted.

"An' thet reminds me," he went on, with a gesture that included Cam and the Judge, "I've been lookin' fer some o' you fellers to come up an' clean aout some o' my woodchucks. Got more on 'em than I actually need. I cu'd do it myself wi' some o' them damned pizen gas bombs, but I don't like the idee o' pizen. I hain't mad at the leetle cusses an' I don't begretch 'em a bellyful o' clover naow an' agin ef there hain't too many on 'em. My idee is thet one woodchuck to a medder is abaout right, by Judas."

During the discourse the Village Liar had entered the Taproom and was now nursing a mug of ale and listening intently to the conversation. He was a gangling, loose-jointed man with a moustache that Wild Bill Hickok could have been proud of. Uncle Bill insisted that all of Joe's "growing strength" had gone into his moustache. His eyes were brown, sad, and earnest. There was very little that could be said in his hearing upon any subject whatever that would not serve to remind him of a deed of valor or skill which he had performed in the past. By trade he was a paperhanger, but unlike another of that calling his prevarications harmed no one and were considered by some to be entertaining.

"Look at the old cuss!" muttered Uncle Bill in a gusty aside to his companions. "He's primin' his pump fer a good un."

The Liar wiped a patch of foam from his moustache, fixed the Captain with a candid gaze and spoke.

"Speakin' o' woodchuck shootin'," said he, "I want to tell ye' 'baout a shot I made one time. I wuz workin' fer Charley Brown up to Hubbardton.

"Naow Charley wuz a gret hand wi' a gun an' one evening arter we'd et supper, Charley sez to me, sezzee, 'Joe, le's go daown to the Saouth Pastur. I'd like to see ye shoot a woodchuck.' I see him wink at the hired man an' I figgered Charley wuz up to su'thin'. 'Hain't got no rifle,' sez I. 'Take mine,' sezzee, 'I've heard a lot o' fellers talk abaout yer shooting,' sezzee, 'an' I'd love to see a sample of it.'

"I didn't make no objection, an' Charley went an' fetched aout the rifle."

"What kind of a rifle wuz it?" asked a little old man who, from the extreme brightness of his eyes and the alert cock of his head, always reminded the Captain of a chipmunk perched on a stump.

"Well, naow, le' me see. I b'lieve it wuz a Winchester repeater. Yis, thet's what it wuz, a Winchester forty-four. Danged good weapin, too.

"Well, sir, we sot aout an' went until we come to a leetle knoll an' stopped to look.

"Charley sez, 'Joe, hain't thet a woodchuck daown there next to the stun-wall? Yis, 'tis,' sezzee, 'fer I seen him move.'

"Well, sir, thet woodchuck didn't look no bigger'n a fly speck, he wuz so fur off.

" 'Haow abaout the sights on this gun?' sez I.

" 'Jest exactly right,' sezzee. 'Go ahead an' shoot.' "

The narrator now went through the motions of a man cocking and aiming a rifle.

"So I ups an' drawred daown an' teched her off—Kerblam!

" 'Joe, ye missed him,' sez Charley, grinnin' like a Chesher cat.

" 'No, sir,' sez I,' an' ef it won't tire ye to walk thet fur, come along an' I'll prove it,' sez I. 'An' more'n thet,' sez I, 'Ye'll find thet I put the ball plumb through thet critter's head.' "

"Off hand?" asked the Chipmunk Man, incredulously.

"Yis, *sir*," replied the other with complete candor.

He drank deeply from his mug. He had come to the end of his tale apparently.

"Hol' on! Did ye kill the woodchuck?"

"Sartinly," replied the paperhanger with an air of faint surprise at being asked such a foolish question. "Deader'n a wedge, by Jeeswax. An' when Charley see the bullit-hole right plumb at the butt o' the ear, he sez, 'Joe, thet wuz the gol darndest shot I ever see,' sezzee, 'I'm a-goin' to pace if off,' sezzee. An' he did."

Again he seemed to have lost interest in the tale and it needed another query from the Chipmunk Man to overcome Joe's innate modesty sufficiently to enable him to satisfy the curiosity of his listeners.

"Haow fur wuz it?"

The Village Liar seemed to be bored and his reply was given reluctantly and with a sigh.

"Well, sir, Charley made it jest egxactly nine hundred an' eighty-four paces."

Uncle Bill roused himself and shook off the enchantment of the outrageous tale.

"Hah!" he barked. "Thet must o' been quite a shot. Yis, yis. Pluggin' a woodchuck in the butt o' the ear, offhand, wi' a forty-four—I b'lieve ye said 'forty-four,' didn't ye, Joseph—at better'n a half a mile is fairly good shootin', I sh'uld say."

Joe turned his mournful, deprecatory gaze upon the old man.

"Why, Uncle Bill! Ye don't misdaoubt me, do ye? Ef ye do, ye c'n ask Charley Brown ef it hain't so, every word o' it."

Uncle Bill cackled.

"I shall sartinly do so ef I come acrost him," he promised, "which I hain't in no way sartin thet I shall, not havin' hed any firsthand reports on life beyond the tomb. An' since it hain't likely thet we c'n soopeeny a witness who's been dead fer ten years I, fer one, am willin' to b'lieve thet ye kilt thet woodchuck deader'n a hammer at a lineal distance o' nine hundred an' eighty-four paces jest ez ye said ye did, wi' reasonable allowances fer Charley's stubbin' his toe naow an' agin, an' havin' to cut 'raound a bog an' a hill whilst he wuz a-meajurin'."

Cam and the Captain were the riflemen. The Judge rarely used the weapon except for an annual sortie into the North Woods during the deer season, in the course of which he seldom failed to get his buck with a rifle that was generally considered by his friends to be obsolete. Its cartridges were loaded with what the Captain once described as "half a pint of black powder." The great leaden slug would have inflicted serious damage upon a modern battleship. One box of twenty cartridges had been sufficient to carry the owner through nearly two score years of game shooting. One reason for this was that the Judge was an excellent stalker and, Indian fashion, always got himself into a favorable position and at such close range that a miss would be all but impossible. Then the heavy bullet, moving at bumblebee velocity, did the gory business quite as effectively as the high-speed projectiles which his friends used. When threatened by an ammunition shortage the Judge got out a can of black powder and a bullet mould, melted a dab of tallow and another of beeswax with which to lubricate his missiles, and reloaded the veteran cases.

Despite his casual interest in rifle shooting, the Judge was present and beaming when the woodchuck hunters got together on the following afternoon. To the amusement of his two friends, he carried his heavy ordnance which, when borne in his left hand, almost balanced the weight of a dozen blue-nosed cartridges in the right hand pocket of his jacket.

"You're still listin' a point to starboard," Cam observed, "but I guess it won't do any harm. On a ten-mile course the heft of the bullets will fetch you right back to where you started from." But the jurist's good nature was proof against the quips and gibes of his companions.

"I feel that I ought to take an active part in this bloody business and share the reward."

"What reward, for Pete's sake?" one inquired.

"It is obvious that you fellers don't pay enough attention to things," said the Judge patiently. "You ain't observant. I am. Today is Saturday and every Saturday throughout the years has seen a large brown pot of beans placed in Aunt Candace's oven. There'll be brown bread and, I imagine, some cowslip greens, and we'll be asked to eat after our labors. I am not one to—ahem— ignore the Lord's will when it is made known to me."

"You're a confounded pot-lickin' hypocrite. I've a good mind to shove you out of the car," his friend told him.

The Paraday homestead was a place of beauty and orderly serenity at any

season and in any kind of weather, but on this May afternoon it would have
been especially difficult for any passerby not to feel a twinge of envy for the
gentle souls who had earned by faithful loving service the right to live there.
The sheltering maples were putting forth their new green-gold foliage and
delicate bloom. Uncle Bill's orchard gave the impression to one visitor that a
patch of roseate sunset cloud was bivouacked there. The soft air was laden
with a spicy fragrance that no *parfumier* could ever hope to capture and confine in a crystal flask, and it was vibrant with the hum of bees driven to frantic endeavor by the sweet abundant loot of honeydew cupped and chaliced in
millions of blossoms in hedgerow and orchard. The swallows were busy, too,
building their mud-and-wattle summer homes under the eaves of the barn,
but each bird after depositing its tiny trowelful of cement, took the long way
back to the mudpuddle in order to demonstrate the exquisite art of flight to
all beholders. Even Aunt Candace's red poultry knew the magic of the day,
and the dull and foolish chatterings of the harem acquired a lilt that was as
nearly musical as any fair-minded critic could expect to issue from the lips of
a matronly Rhode Island Red hen.

Our friends debouched into this green and fragrant paradise and went
around to the kitchen door to announce to Aunt Candace the arrival of an
armed force. She welcomed them with a smile and an invitation to enter and
to have a glass of cider and a doughnut.

The invitation was accepted. While the old lady was in the cellar drawing
the beverage, the Judge shamelessly and stealthily opened the oven door and
revealed a brown earthen pot, which simmered gently and filled the room
with a mouth-watering fragrance.

The sound of Aunt Candace's foot on the cellar stair was heard, and the
Judge closed the oven door quietly and resumed his seat by the woodbox
with an "I told you so" expression on his broad and placid countenance.

Their hostess informed them that her husband was fixing fence in the
North Pasture. He was expected to come home in plenty of time for his
evening meal.

"An', of course, you boys must stay for supper. That is if you c'n get along
on baked beans and brown bread and new cowslip greens," she added.

"Ah, hah!" exclaimed His Honor mendaciously, "I *thought* I smelled baked
beans. There's nothing better, ma'am."

The Captain was outraged.

"Aunt Candace," said he, "that man is a deceitful scoundrel. He *knew*
you'd have baked beans for Saturday supper. He told us so. And that's why
he's here. If I were you I'd send him packing. Furthermore, he was snoopin'
in your oven while you were out of the room."

The little old lady received this information with a laugh that was as clear
and delightful as a girl's, and gave the culprit prompt forgiveness for his mis-
deeds.

One of the amenities of woodchuck shooting is that the rifleman can get as much or as little exercise from the sport as he wishes. He can range far over the hills and valleys, spying out his game from a distance, or he can seat himself on a sunshiny knoll commanding a wide field of view and smoke his pipe in tranquil comfort while waiting for the resident woodchucks to emerge from their burrows.

This latter method appealed to the Judge, and his friends left him with his rifle across his knees and his plump shoulders relaxed against the trunk of an apple tree, in a state of great contentment.

The birds which had departed at his arrival now returned and the watcher had an opportunity to mark the affinity between orchards and the bluebirds, robins and kinglets. A pair of flickers became convinced that the Judge was no enemy and returned to the task of chiseling a home in the dead stub of an old tree, yelling joyously at one another during their brief rest periods. A cock partridge down among the thickets of the South Pasture added his sonorous thunder to the jubilee chorus, reminding the Judge of great days he had enjoyed with the ancestors and kinfolk of the gallant drummer.

"Success to your courtin'," remarked the listener.

Twice from the direction taken by his friends, he heard the vicious crack of a high-powered small caliber rifle and mentally crossed off two of Uncle Bill's woodchucks, for his companions were old hands at the trade, and with their telescopic sights and heavy single shot rifles, they rarely missed. So expert were they that they would not shoot at a woodchuck at less than a hundred paces, regarding such short-range shooting as being extremely unscientific and akin to murder. A grizzled head exposed above a boulder at two hundred yards was the sort of target that drew the interest and fire of these experts. The Judge could picture them now bending over their prey comparing notes on "minutes of angle" and "holding into the wind."

Heretofore, the Judge had given little heed to this quasi-scientific jabber, for none of it seemed to apply either to his weapon or his method. A woodchuck at one hundred yards was as safe from the old rifle as it would be if it were in the innermost chamber of its subterranean citadel. His rifle, as he had been told more than once, "didn't shoot bullets; it pitched them."

He interrupted his cogitations and his observations of the flickers to survey the foreground. At the base of an apple tree a short distance away, where a patch of fresh earth indicated a burrow, the grizzled great grandfather of all the woodchucks on earth was regarding him with a beady eye. A "prepare for action" signal rang out in the battle stations of the Judge's pudgy body, he who had been scornful of such ignoble game. Slowly, very slowly, under the suspicious eye of the woodchuck he got himself into position and brought the front sight into the notch of the rear sight and then both to bear on the spot where the victim's bow tie would have been had the gentleman been properly dressed for dinner.

Then the valley was filled by a deep rumbling roar as of an earthquake, and that part of it in the vicinity of the apple tree was blotted out under a pall of dense white smoke.

Peace was no more.

The horrified flickers departed, yelping distressfully, preceded or followed by the robins and bluebirds. Everyone in the neighborhood who had wings flew, and those who had holes or burrows dove into them and lay shivering in fright, while the monstrous echoes rebounded between the Ledge and Mount Hamilton.

Cam and the Captain felt the tremor and heard the boom of the Judge's weapon. The pair of experts looked at one another and sat down on a stone wall to laugh it out before resuming their own highly specialized operations.

When they had finished, the luminous twilight of early summer lay across the land and the whippoorwills and frogs had relieved the daytime choristers. The woodchuck population had been scientifically reduced to "one to a medder."

The Judge, when they came up to him, exhibited a raveled sleeve that might once have been a hoary-headed marmot.

He wanted to know if either one of 'em knew where he could obtain a real woodchuck rifle, and he also wanted to know, in the same breath, if they thought it polite to make Aunt Candace and Uncle Bill wait for their suppers.